RESPONSIBLE GOVERNMENT AND THE AUSTRALIAN CONSTITUTION

This book looks at responsible government under the Australian Constitution. It undertakes a detailed examination of the history leading to the incorporation of responsible government into the Constitution, examining the political history and constitutional ideas which informed the framers' views. It draws on this history to develop a theory of responsible government and explore its implications for the interpretation of the Constitution and the structure of modern government in Australia.

The book fills a major gap in our knowledge of the intellectual background of the Australian Constitution by explaining the constitutional ideas that have shaped the text and structure of the Australian Constitution. It contributes to worldwide debates about constitutional interpretation by showing how rigorous use of history can lead to novel interpretations of constitutions without being tied to the 'dead hands of the founders'.

Volume 28 in the series Hart Studies in Comparative Public Law

Hart Studies in Comparative Public Law

Recent titles in this series:

The Scope and Intensity of Substantive Review
Traversing Taggart's Rainbow
Edited by Hanna Wilberg and Mark Elliott

Entick v Carrington
250 Years of the Rule of Law
Edited by Adam Tomkins and Paul Scott

Administrative Law and Judicial Deference
Matthew Lewans

Soft Law and Public Authorities
Remedies and Reform
Greg Weeks

Legitimate Expectations in the Common Law World
Edited by Matthew Groves and Greg Weeks

The Dynamics of Exclusionary Constitutionalism
Mazen Masri

Constitutional Courts, Gay Rights and Sexual Orientation Equality
Angioletta Sperti

Australian Constitutional Values
Edited by Rosalind Dixon

Human Rights in the UK and the Influence of Foreign Jurisprudence
Hélène Tyrrell

The Nordic Constitutions
Edited by Helle Krunke and Björg Thorarensen

Regulation in India
Design, Capacity, Performance
Edited by Devesh Kapur and Madhav Khosla

New Media and Freedom of Expression
Rethinking the Constitutional Foundations of the Public Sphere
András Koltay

Why Religious Freedom Matters for Democracy
Comparative Reflections from Britain and France
for a Democratic 'Vivre Ensemble'
Myriam Hunter-Henin

The Role of Monarchy in the Modern Democracy:
European Monarchies Compared
Edited by Robert Hazell and Bob Morris

Responsible Government and the Australian Constitution

A Government for a Sovereign People

Benjamin B Saunders

·HART·
OXFORD · LONDON · NEW YORK · NEW DELHI · SYDNEY

HART PUBLISHING

Bloomsbury Publishing Plc

Kemp House, Chawley Park, Cumnor Hill, Oxford, OX2 9PH, UK

1385 Broadway, New York, NY 10018, USA

29 Earlsfort Terrace, Dublin 2, Ireland

HART PUBLISHING, the Hart/Stag logo, BLOOMSBURY and the Diana logo are trademarks of Bloomsbury Publishing Plc

First published in Great Britain 2023

A catalogue record for this book is available from the British Library.

A catalogue record for this book is available from the Library of Congress.

Library of Congress Control Number: 2023936469

ISBN: HB: 978-1-50995-579-4
ePDF: 978-1-50995-581-7
ePub: 978-1-50995-580-0

Typeset by Compuscript Ltd, Shannon

Foreword

This is a book about the system of national government established by the first three chapters of the Australian Constitution. They are headed 'The Parliament', 'The Executive Government' and 'The Judicature'. Specifically, this is a book about the nature of and relationship between the institutions of national government established by the first two of those chapters viewed from the perspective of the institutions of national government established by the third. Fundamentally, it is a book about the relationship between all three of those sets of institutions of national government and those to whom the Constitution refers as 'the people'.

The Constitution refers to 'the people' in two quite distinct manifestations. The first is 'the people' acting as nation-builders in rare and important moments of constitutional time. The people in that manifestation are those who are described in the preamble to the Constitution as having 'agreed to unite in one indissoluble Federal Commonwealth' under the Constitution and who, since becoming so united, have on rare occasions agreed in referenda to make alterations to the constitutional text. The people in that manifestation are constitutive. They are the creators of the Constitution and are the ongoing source of its authority as higher law. That is so even though very few of the people might be described as 'the framers'.

The second of the distinct manifestations of 'the people' is the people whose government is regulated and sustained by the Constitution. They are the people who remain the ongoing source of the authority of the Constitution as higher law now acting intra-constitutionally in ordinary time. The people in that routine manifestation are those by whom the membership of the Senate and the House of Representatives, as constituent elements of the Parliament, is required by the constitutional text to be directly chosen in periodic elections and to whom the Senate and the House of Representatives are by those means directly accountable. And it is the people in that manifestation to whom Ministers of the Executive Government are indirectly accountable by reason of being required by the constitutional text to be drawn from the membership of the Senate or the House of Representatives.

The constitutional structure established by the people acting in moments of constitutional time to facilitate government by and for the people acting in ordinary time has been recognised to instantiate two great constitutional principles. Each of those principles is assumed in the constitutional structure rather than prescribed in the constitutional text. Each is the product of history. Neither exists, nor has it ever existed, nor could it ever exist, in an abstract form disembodied from observed institutional practices. Neither therefore is, nor has it ever been, nor could it ever be, the subject of definition as distinct from description.

An appreciation of those principles and their interrelationship is essential to an appreciation of the design and practical operation of the Constitution. It is essential to understanding the constitutionally authorised functioning of the institutions of national government which the Constitution establishes and sustains. It is essential also to discerning the limitations which the Constitution expressly and impliedly imposes on the powers of a range of institutions of government within the 'indissoluble Federal Commonwealth'.

One of the two great constitutional principles instantiated in the Constitution is 'the rule of law', which has been recognised to be assumed in the separation of the Judicature from other institutions of national government and in the nature of the Constitution as higher law. First coined in the second half of the nineteenth century as a label for a principle already by then centuries in the making, 'the rule of law' has long captured the attention of constitutional scholars. That is no doubt because the principle has been seen to be at once enduring, intrinsically legal and intrinsically theoretically contestable.

The other of the two great constitutional principles instantiated in the Constitution is 'responsible government', which has been recognised to be assumed in the constitutionally prescribed relationship between the Executive Government and the Parliament and in the constitutionally prescribed relationship of each to the electoral processes by means of which the Executive Government and the Parliament is each ultimately electorally answerable to the people acting in ordinary time. First coined around the middle of the nineteenth century as a label for a principle then newly emergent in the United Kingdom and then an object of colonial aspiration, 'responsible government' has attracted comparatively less attention in constitutional scholarship. Perhaps that has been in part because it has been seen to be an intrinsically political principle, dependent largely on conventional practices rather than on formal legal constraints and in part because of the difficulty of pinning it down. Its contours have been seen to be inherently elastic and its features have been seen to be in a process of perpetual development. By the second half of the nineteenth century, it had become a subject of colonial experimentation. With the advent of the Constitution, it continued to change.

Recognising the essentiality of 'responsible government' to the design and practical operation of the Constitution, the High Court relied on that principle at critical junctures throughout the twentieth century. It did so early in the twentieth century both in orientating its general approach to interpreting the constitutional text and in expounding the nature of the power exercised by the Executive Government. It did so later that century in discerning express and implied limitations on the power of the Parliament to restrict the capacity of the people to engage in informed electoral choice. Along with references to 'the rule of law', references to 'responsible government' have continued with greater frequency in this century.

There is tension involved in reconciling the essentiality of such an evolving and intrinsically political principle with the fixed text and structure of the Constitution. For the High Court at the apex of the Judicature, resolving that tension in conformity with the rule of law has presented and will continue to present challenges.

The question of the extent to which the text and structure of the Constitution ought to be seen to foster the development of responsible government has now long been addressed by means of the adoption of an expansive interpretation of the constitutional text insofar as that text is expressed to confer power on the Parliament and the Executive Government and through the adoption of a minimalist approach to the drawing from the constitutional structure of implications which would restrict the power so conferred. By and large, the open texture of the constitutional text has been taken to indicate the making of constitutional room for outcomes that are the product of legislative and executive choices constrained principally by political accountability.

The more difficult questions are and will continue to be those as to the extent to which fidelity to the notion of the essentiality of responsible government to the constitutionally authorised functioning of institutions of government require the Constitution to be understood as mandating some measure of judicial protection for some features of responsible government. Risk one way lies in the potential for backsliding by the Parliament or the Executive Government were those who command a current political majority permitted by an exercise of legislative or executive power to stifle or impede one or more of the political processes by which they are assumed within the constitutional design to be politically constrained. Risk the other way lies in the potential for judicial mollycoddling to be counterproductive: to end up undermining the robustness of the political processes upon which the vitality and adaptability of the constitutional principle of political constraint depends.

This book does much to augment constitutional scholarship on responsible government within Australia. In so doing, it will do much to assist in future judicial consideration of issues of that kind. This contribution is important.

Drawing impressively on colonial history, and on the history of the development of political thought, Dr Saunders portrays responsible government within Australia as a 'political model of constitutionalism' embodied in a written constitution framework. The framing of the Constitution, he cogently argues, was deliberately non-prescriptive: the form of responsible government which the Constitution was conceived by its framers to facilitate was understood by its framers to be a form of popular sovereignty which would be dynamic and which would evolve in ways which they sought neither to predict nor constrain.

He presents a strong argument in favour of judicial restraint, not only in considering constitutional limitations on political outcomes, but also in considering whether, and if so when, the need might be thought to arise to save responsible government from itself.

Justice Stephen Gageler
High Court
Canberra
May 2023

Acknowledgements

THIS BOOK INCORPORATES some material that was previously published in Benjamin B Saunders, 'Responsible Government, Statutory Authorities and the Australian Constitution' (2020) 48(1) *Federal Law Review* 4 doi.org/10.1177/0067205X19890445 which is reprinted with kind permission of SAGE Publications.

For providing comments on various chapters in one form or another I thank Ros Dixon, Matthew Groves, Simon Kennedy, Dan Meagher, Graeme Orr, Sandra Pyke, David Tan, Greg Taylor and John Waugh, who have all helped improve the book, but to whom no remaining errors should be attributed.

I particularly wish to thank Nick Aroney for his significant input and guidance throughout the writing of this book.

I am grateful to Deakin Law School and my colleagues there for a wonderful environment in which to undertake research.

I thank my parents, Reg and Angela, for their support and encouragement over the years and I thank my parents in law, Wes and Loretta, for their continual kindness.

I thank my children, Amelia, Theodora, Rupert, Audrey and Augustin, for daily joy and welcome distractions.

Above all I thank my dearest, loveliest Elizabeth, who has been unfailingly supportive.

S. D. G.

Contents

Abbreviations

1891 Bill	*Draft of a Bill to Constitute the Commonwealth of Australia*, as adopted by the National Australasian Convention, 9 April 1891.
1898 Bill	*Draft of a Bill to Constitute the Commonwealth of Australia*, as adopted by the Australasian Federal Convention, 16 March 1898.
Convention Debates (1891)	*Official Report of the National Australasian Convention Debates, Sydney, 2 March to 9 April 1891* (Legal Books, 1986 [1891]).
Convention Debates, Adelaide (1897)	*Official Report of the National Australasian Convention Debates, Adelaide, 22 March to 5 May 1897* (Legal Books, 1986 [1897]).
Convention Debates, Sydney (1897)	*Official Record of the Debates of the Australasian Federal Convention, Second Session: Sydney, 2 to 24 September 1897* (Legal Books, 1986 [1897]).
Convention Debates (1898)	*Official Record of the Debates of the Australasian Federal Convention, Third Session: Melbourne, 20 January to 17 March, 1898*, 2 vols (Legal Books, 1986 [1898]).

Table of Cases

1

Introduction

> We must not, however, attempt to fix the present pattern of responsible government as a thing to be clung to for all time; we must allow scope for its development – for its being moulded to fit the political ideas of each generation. Responsible government, as we know it, is a new thing, and a changing thing, it depends largely upon unwritten rules which are constantly varying, growing, developing, and the precise direction of whose development it is impossible to forecast. To try to crystallize this fluid system into a hard and fast code of written law would spoil its chief merit; we must be careful to lay down only the principles of popular government, leaving the details of form as elastic as possible.[1]
>
> Robert Randolph Garran (1897)

I. INTRODUCTION

The High Court has described responsible government as 'the central feature of the Australian constitutional system'.[2] As it touches the formation of government and the manner in which the Prime Minister and the ministry are appointed, the meaning and nature of responsible government are of crucial importance to the political system established by the Constitution. However, the Constitution is not especially enlightening as to the nature of responsible government.[3] It is nowhere defined, and the Constitution does not indicate any awareness of its key features such as the cabinet,

[1] Robert Randolph Garran, *The Coming Commonwealth: An Australian Handbook of Federal Government* (Angus & Robertson, 1897) 149.

[2] *R v Kirby; Ex parte Boilermakers' Society* (1956) 94 CLR 254, 275 (Dixon CJ, McTiernan, Fullagar and Kitto JJ). See also *Amalgamated Society of Engineers v Adelaide Steamship Co Ltd* (1920) 28 CLR 129, 146–7 (Knox CJ, Isaacs, Rich and Starke JJ); *Commonwealth v Colonial Combing, Spinning and Weaving Co Ltd* (1922) 31 CLR 421, 438–9, 446 (Isaacs J); *Victorian Stevedoring & General Contracting Co Pty Ltd v Dignan* (1931) 46 CLR 73, 114 (Evatt J); *Marks v Commonwealth* (1964) 111 CLR 549, 557–558 (Kitto J); *New South Wales v Commonwealth* (1975) 135 CLR 337, 364–365 (Barwick CJ); *Lange v Australian Broadcasting Corporation* (1997) 189 CLR 520, 557–558 (Brennan CJ, Dawson, Toohey, Gaudron, McHugh, Gummow and Kirby JJ); *McCloy v New South Wales* (2015) 257 CLR 178, 224 [106] (Gageler J), 279 [301] (Gordon J); *Murphy v Electoral Commissioner* (2016) 261 CLR 28, 112 [260] (Gordon J); *Comcare v Banerji* (2019) 267 CLR 373, 437 [149] (Gordon J).

[3] BR Wise, *The Commonwealth of Australia* (Pitman, 1909) 193.

Prime Minister, the opposition or political parties, let alone attempt to set out their roles and powers.[4]

A precise and comprehensive definition of responsible government is elusive, and although it is a familiar concept, it remains controversial in key respects. As put by George Winterton, 'while the core of the British principle of responsible government is clear, the edges are fuzzy and ill-defined'.[5] Gordon Reid described responsible government and ministerial responsibility as 'notoriously confusing concepts in modern government'.[6] Unsurprisingly, there has been debate over how best to define responsible government,[7] what the conventions of responsible government are,[8] whether current political arrangements are consistent with responsible government,[9] and what weight to give responsible government when interpreting the Constitution.[10]

Responsible government derives from several maxims of the British Constitution including the convention that the head of state acts on the advice of the ministry and the convention that the ministry of the day must possess the confidence of Parliament in order to hold office and must resign when it ceases to command that confidence.[11] In essence, therefore, responsible government is the principle that the government is a creature of, and accountable to, Parliament, which is supposed to play a key role in scrutinising the actions of the executive and holding it to account.[12] These conventions condition the exercise

[4] W Harrison Moore, *The Constitution of the Commonwealth of Australia*, 2nd edn (Melbourne, Charles F Maxwell, 1910) 168. Note that s 15 of the Constitution, which was inserted in its current form in 1977, contains some recognition of the existence of political parties.

[5] George Winterton, *Parliament, the Executive and the Governor-General: A Constitutional Analysis* (Melbourne, Melbourne University Press, 1983) 2.

[6] GS Reid, 'Responsible Government and Ministerial Responsibility' (1980) 39 *Australian Journal of Public Administration* 301, 301.

[7] RS Parker, 'The Meaning of Responsible Government' (1976) 11 *Politics* 178; RS Parker, 'Responsible Government in Australia' (1980) 15 *Politics* 11; JR Archer, 'The Theory of Responsible Government in Britain and Australia' (1980) 15 *Politics* 23; HN Collins, 'What Shall we do with the Westminster Model?' in RFI Smith and Patrick Weller (eds), *Public Service Inquiries in Australia* (St Lucia, University of Queensland Press, 1978).

[8] Geoffrey Marshall, 'What are Constitutional Conventions?' (1985) 38 *Parliamentary Affairs* 33; Geoffrey Lindell, 'The Role of a State Governor in Relation to Illegality' (2012) 23 *Public Law Review* 268; Richard Mulgan, 'Assessing Ministerial Responsibility in Australia' in Keith Dowling and Chris Lewis (eds), *Ministerial Careers and Accountability in the Australian Commonwealth Government* (Acton, ANU E Press, 2012); Judy Maddigan, 'Ministerial Responsibility: Reality or Myth?' (2011) 26 *Australasian Parliamentary Review* 158; IDF Callinan, 'Responsible Government – in Dilution' (2008) 52:4 *Quadrant* 16; Luke Raffin, 'Individual Ministerial Responsibility During the Howard Years: 1996–2007' (2008) 54 *Australian Journal of Politics and History* 225.

[9] David Hamer, *Can Responsible Government Survive in Australia?* (Canberra, Department of the Senate, 2004) 344, 355–6.

[10] Geoffrey Lindell, 'Responsible Government' in PD Finn (ed), *Essays on Law and Government* (North Ryde, Law Book Co, 1995) vol 1, 80–93; see further ch 7.

[11] Samuel Walker Griffith, *Notes on Australian Federation: Its Nature and Probable Effects* (Brisbane, Government Printer, 1896) 17–18; John Quick and Robert Randolph Garran, *The Annotated Constitution of the Australian Commonwealth* (Sydney, Angus and Robertson, 1901) 704.

[12] Section 83 of the Constitution, in requiring funds drawn from the Commonwealth Treasury to be appropriated by law, underscores this accountability.

of legal power but are nowhere written or codified in a constitutional document and are not judicially enforceable.[13]

This book examines the constitutional principle of responsible government in the Australian constitutional system. It does so by means of a detailed historical analysis of how responsible government became incorporated into or assumed by the Australian Constitution and draws from that account to develop a theory of responsible government under the Australian Constitution. It then considers the implications for the interpretation of the Constitution and the structure of government today.

This book argues that two interlinked themes are central to the Australian constitutional principle of responsible government, namely constitutional evolution and popular self-government. The Constitution establishes a government for a sovereign people, and embodies a deliberately flexible form of executive so that the sovereign people of Australia may shape their institutions to govern themselves as they see best.

II. RESPONSIBLE GOVERNMENT AND THE CONSTITUTION

There are three principal trends relating to the incorporation of responsible government into the Australian Constitution and its relevance today.

A. Responsible Government and the Senate

The compatibility of responsible government with the Senate was one of the crucial and most divisive issues to be debated by the framers of the Australian Constitution at the Federation Conventions. Given its importance, discussions of the framers' views regarding responsible government in the constitutional and political science literature often focus narrowly on this question.[14] Focusing on this issue, however, perpetuates a narrow and inaccurate conception of responsible government. Seen through the lens of this controversy, responsible government requires an executive selected by and accountable solely to the lower, more representative house of Parliament. By contrast, federalism, as conceived by the framers, incorporated into the constitutional structure an upper house with co-ordinate or nearly co-ordinate powers to those of the

[13] Geoffrey Marshall, *Constitutional Conventions: The Rules and Forms of Political Accountability* (Oxford, Clarendon Press, 1984) ch 1; Nicholas Aroney, 'On the Distinction Between Law and Convention' in Brian Galligan and Scott Brenton (eds), *Constitutional Conventions in Westminster Systems* (Cambridge, Cambridge University Press, 2015).

[14] Eg, Brian Galligan, 'The Founders' Design and Intentions Regarding Responsible Government' (1980) 15 *Politics* 1.

lower house, including the power to reject taxation and appropriation Bills.[15] Notwithstanding reservations about their compatibility, the framers attempted to adopt both into the Constitution.[16] The High Court has described the successful combination of both responsible government and federalism in the Constitution as the framers' most 'striking achievement'.[17] Others have argued that, by doing so, the framers incorporated contradictory principles into the Constitution.[18] This view was expressed in the federal Conventions, most famously by Winthrop Hackett, who argued that if the framers adopted the 'extreme step' of grafting responsible government upon the Federation, then 'either responsible government will kill Federation, or Federation ... will kill responsible government'.[19]

Typically, the tension between responsible government and the Senate is resolved in favour of responsible government, or, more accurately, a particular conception of responsible government. Several scholars have noted that the standard paradigm in Australian political science is to view responsible party government as the dominant characteristic of Australian political institutions, according to which the Senate is seen as an anachronism.[20] One of the most prominent advocates of this approach was LF Crisp, who, in his influential text *Australian National Government*, attacked the Senate as undemocratic and a threat to responsible government:

> It is impossible to reconcile sound democratic principles with the power of a Second Chamber constituted as is the Australian Senate to hold to ransom a Government with a clear House of Representatives majority and mandate to govern from the latest House general election.[21]

Crisp saw responsible cabinet government as the core feature of the Australian system of government and considered a strong Senate to be incompatible with responsible government because it has the potential to interfere with

[15] Sampford criticised the equation of 'federalism' with '[a] senate constituted on the basis of equal representation for each State': CJG Sampford, 'Reconciling Responsible Government and Federalism' in MP Ellinghaus, AJ Bradbrook and AJ Duggan (eds), *The Emergence of Australian Law* (Sydney, Butterworths, 1989) 357–8.

[16] Elaine Thompson, 'The 'Washminster' Mutation' (1980) 15 *Politics* 32.

[17] *R v Kirby; Ex parte Boilermakers' Society of Australia* (1956) 94 CLR 254, 275 (Dixon CJ, McTiernan, Fullagar and Kitto JJ); Cheryl Saunders, 'Future Prospects of the Australian Constitution' in Robert French, Geoffrey Lindell and Cheryl Saunders (eds), *Reflections on the Australian Constitution* (Annandale, Federation Press, 2003) 219. See also Gordon Greenwood, *The Future of Australian Federalism*, 2nd edn (St Lucia, University of Queensland Press, 1976) 55.

[18] Eg, Brian Galligan, *A Federal Republic: Australia's Constitutional System of Government* (Melbourne, Cambridge University Press, 1995) 47.

[19] *Convention Debates* (1891) 280.

[20] Andrew Parkin, 'Pluralism and Australian Political Science' (1980) 15 *Politics* 50; Galligan, *A Federal Republic* (n 18) 5; Stanley Bach, 'Crisp, the Senate, and the Constitution' (2008) 54 *Australian Journal of Politics and History* 545, 551. Note also JR Nethercote, 'Professor LF Crisp and the Australian Senate: A Comment on Stanley Bach's Analysis' (2009) 55 *Australian Journal of Politics and History* 557.

[21] LF Crisp, *Australian National Government*, 5th edn (Melbourne, Longman Cheshire, 1983) 349.

the working of majoritarian democracy.[22] As such, proponents of this view argue that the exercise of the Senate's powers should be subordinated to the requirements of responsible government.[23] Implicit in this view is an attack on the compromise the founders struck between responsible government and the demands of federalism; it also treats a particular conception of responsible government as the definitive meaning of that concept.

The constitutional crisis of 1975 triggered extensive debate about the adequacy of the framers' achievements and the tension between responsible government and the Senate. Colin Howard and Cheryl Saunders considered that the key conflict at the Federation debates was between the insistence on a powerful second chamber and responsible government which required that the ministry derive its authority from the confidence of the lower house of Parliament. This conflict was resolved by attempting to combine both, which ultimately proved incompatible. Howard and Saunders argued that:

> The fundamental cause of the constitutional troubles which came upon Australia in 1975 lies in the self-contradictory character of our machinery of government. The framers of the Australian Constitution wished both to create a federal structure and to preserve parliamentary government of the British kind. These two aims were, and are, incompatible. The delegates to the constitutional Conventions attempted to make them compatible by creating the Senate as an expression of the federal idea and the House of Representatives as an expression of the parliamentary idea and combining the two in one institution.[24]

In their view, the 1975 crisis was a direct result of the fundamental tension incorporated by the framers into the federal constitutional system.[25] Winterton similarly argued that there was 'a direct conflict' between the British conception of responsible government and the federal model incorporated into the Constitution, and that the framers' lack of clarity was 'a serious and dangerous mistake, which sowed the seeds for future constitutional conflict'.[26] In considering the constitutional validity of the actions of the Governor-General and others during the crisis, scholars have argued that the framers would have expected that the legal power of the Senate to refuse supply should not be exercised so

[22] Campbell Sharman, 'Australia as a Compound Republic' (1990) 25 *Politics* 1, 4.

[23] Bach (n 20) 551–2.

[24] Colin Howard and Cheryl Saunders, 'The Blocking of the Budget and Dismissal of the Government' in Gareth Evans (ed), *Labor and the Constitution, 1972–1975* (Melbourne, Heinemann, 1977) 286. See also Helen Irving, *Five Things to Know about the Australian Constitution* (Cambridge, Cambridge University Press, 2004) 93.

[25] See also Brian Galligan, 'The Kerr-Whitlam Debate and the Principles of the Australian Constitution' (1980) 18 *Journal of Commonwealth and Comparative Politics* 247; Joan Rydon, 'Some Problems of Combining the British and American Elements in the Australian Constitution' (1985) 23 *Journal of Commonwealth & Comparative Politics* 67; Geoffrey Sawer, *Federation Under Strain: Australia 1972–1975* (Carlton, Melbourne University Press, 1977) 121–3; Winterton (n 5) 5–11; Paul Kelly, *November 1975* (St Leonards, Allen & Unwin, 1995) 15–17.

[26] Winterton (n 5) 3–5, 6.

as to interfere with the operation of responsible government, especially where a government holds the confidence of the lower house.[27]

This book argues that it is simplistic and inaccurate to equate responsible government with lower house dominance. It is true that the framers expected responsible government to function in accordance with the principles of the British Constitution, which included the requirement that the ministry must hold the confidence of the lower house. It is also true that certain framers considered that lower house predominance and upper house weakness was of the essence of responsible government, and sought the adoption into the Constitution of an idealised understanding of responsible government modelled closely on the British Constitution as it functioned at the time of Federation. However, the framers overwhelmingly held to a conception of responsible government as an inherently changeable system, drawing on standard accounts of the British Constitution. For the majority of the framers, lower house dominance was not of the essence of responsible government but rather a historically contingent development in a continually changing constitutional system. Lower house predominance reflected the particular circumstances of the British Government which prevailed in the late nineteenth century, and the framers expected further evolution as it was adapted to the Australian context.

B. Party Discipline and the Defeat of the Framers' Expectations

The standard narrative is that the development of the disciplined two-party system in the early twentieth century frustrated the intentions of the framers. It has been argued that the framers intended to incorporate the nineteenth century ideal of parliamentary government into the Australian constitutional framework, and that this assumed the independence of the member of Parliament (MP), parliamentary control of the executive, and did not rely on the existence of political parties. According to this account, the framers did not anticipate key aspects of the present system such as party discipline and executive dominance of Parliament.

In their influential volume *Australia's Commonwealth Parliament 1901–1988*, Gordon Reid and Martyn Forrest argued that the framers intended to embody the 'parliamentary ideal' of representation into the Australian Constitution. They noted that the framers intended that the Senate would protect the interests of the states, but that some framers questioned the underlying premise of this view, presciently arguing that the Senate would divide on party lines rather than along state lines. However, according to Reid and Forrest, the majority of delegates believed that the primary political divisions in the Commonwealth would be along state lines. Accordingly, they argued that the framers chose to

[27] Howard and Saunders (n 24) 265–6; Winterton (n 5) 10.

ignore the issue of party and subscribed instead to the liberal theory of representation, namely that MPs would follow their own consciences, 'free of any obligation to government, patron or political party'.[28] In a separate piece Reid argued that executive control of Parliament is exactly contrary to the expectations of the founders, who anticipated that Parliament should control the executive.[29]

Jim Chalmers and Glyn Davis argued that the framers incorporated the traditional conception of responsible government into the Constitution, which, they argued, relied on independent voting by members and fluctuating coalitions of interests to form government. However, political parties have undermined the key assumptions on which the relationship between Parliament and the executive was premised, replacing responsible government with party government: '[t]he fusion of factions into disciplined political parties replaced responsible ministerial government with responsible party government'. They considered that this reversal would have profoundly disappointed the expectations and intentions of the framers. By not prescribing the form of responsible government but leaving its working to unwritten conventions, the framers allowed political parties to dictate the relationship between Parliament and the executive, so that the latter controls the former, rather than the converse. Accordingly, they argued, the framers committed a 'grave folly' in incorporating responsible government into the Constitution, while ignoring clear warnings about the impending consolidation of parties.[30]

Ian Marsh argued that the period 1901–1909 was 'the most fertile and creative in Australia's brief political history'.[31] Consistent with colonial politics, politics in the early Federation period was characterised by the existence of multiple parties, independent voting by MPs and support building by fluctuating coalitions of interests. In this period, Parliament was a 'substantial arena' where contested issues were meaningfully debated, governments were regularly defeated and leaders were required to negotiate with other parties and MPs to win support for their policies, in contrast to the ritualistic role it now plays. Marsh argued that the extra-parliamentary organisation developed by the Labor party, with its strict discipline of parliamentarians, challenged these norms and

[28] GS Reid and Martyn Forrest, *Australia's Commonwealth Parliament 1901–1988* (Carlton, Melbourne University Press, 1989) 12.

[29] GS Reid, 'Parliamentary-Executive Relations: The Suppression of Politics' in Henry Mayer (ed), *Australian Politics: A Second Reader* (Melbourne, Cheshire, 1970) 502.

[30] Jim Chalmers and Glyn Davis, 'Power: Relations Between the Parliament and the Executive' (Research Paper No 14, Parliament of Australia, 2000) 1–2, 11, 21. Davis elsewhere argued that parties and the cabinet are recent grafts onto the Westminster system: Glyn Davis, 'Executive Government: Cabinet and the Prime Minister' in John Summers, Dennis Woodward and Andrew Parkin (eds), *Government, Politics, Power and Policy in Australia*, 7th edn (Frenchs Forest, Longman, 2002) 51.

[31] Ian Marsh, *Beyond the Two Party System: Political Representation, Economic Competitiveness, and Australian Politics* (Melbourne, Cambridge University Press, 1995) 272.

prompted other parties to adopt similar structures and strategies. As a result, the Free Trade and Deakinite groupings fused to form the Liberal Party, ending the liberal concept of representation and the multi-party system.[32]

For these writers, the formation of the disciplined two-party system in 1909 radically altered the nature of Australian politics, in unintended and undesirable ways, and contrary to the framers' intentions.[33] According to Harry Evans, this system 'obscured the character of the founders and their work' and had the framers foreseen this development, they would likely have drafted the Constitution differently.[34] Brian Galligan argued that the Australian Constitution was predicated on a 'liberal consensus' based on factional politics and that it was 'not designed to cope' with the polarised bipartisan class politics that prevailed after Federation.[35]

This book challenges the standard narrative that the contemporary practice of politics is a departure from the expectations of the framers. First and foremost, the narrative is highly anachronistic and misunderstands the parliamentary ideal of responsible government, reading contemporary distrust of party politics back into the Federation era. As pointed out by Birch in 1965, the 'liberal' view of the British Constitution was an idealised picture.[36] Chapter two argues that a stable two-party system was considered necessary to the proper functioning of responsible government, and it was considered that too many independent MPs would lead to instability, executive weakness and the frustration of parliamentary business. A stable party system was a constitutional assumption for the functioning of responsible government rather than an unwanted addition to that system. A related point is that their arguments paint an idealised and unrealistic picture of colonial politics in Australia. As discussed in chapter three, contemporaries often sharply criticised colonial politics for its instability, partisanship and inability to transact business in Parliament, and many considered the cure to be a strengthening rather than the abandonment of party government. The post-1909 party system may have intensified certain problems, but it undoubtedly ameliorated others. The standard narrative understates the benefits of political parties and the extent to which a stable party system was desired by many contemporaries and framers.

[32] ibid 274, 277, 283.

[33] See also Michael Coper, *Encounters with the Australian Constitution* (North Ryde, CCH Australia, 1987) 254; Jean-François Godbout and Monika Smaz, 'Party Development in the Early Decades of the Australian Parliament: A New Perspective' (2016) 51 *Australian Journal of Political Science* 478. Labor historians also tend to emphasise the extent to which the Labor party fundamentally challenged existing norms and practices of responsible government: eg, NB Nairn, 'The Political Mastery of Sir Henry Parkes: New South Wales, 1871–1891' (1967) 53 *Journal of the Royal Australian Historical Society* 1, 5, 9–10.

[34] Harry Evans, 'Reflections on the Founders', *The House Magazine*, 1 March 1995, 8.

[35] Galligan, 'The Kerr-Whitlam Debate' (n 25) 255.

[36] AH Birch, *Representative and Responsible Government: An Essay on the British Constitution* (London, Allen & Unwin, 1964) 72–8.

More fundamentally, the framers held to a very different conception of responsible government than that attributed to them by these writers. In particular, even if it were possible for the framers to have foreseen the rise of the disciplined party system, they saw responsible government as an inherently unconstrainable form of government and did not consider they could predict or prescribe the way politics should function. The framers believed, following James Bryce, that the people would govern themselves in the way they chose regardless of well-intentioned constitutional requirements, and that the working of the Constitution would not necessarily conform to their intentions.

C. The Constitutionalisation of Responsible Government

In the Australian context, there is a tendency to argue for a greater 'constitutionalisation' of responsible government, and some judicial acceptance of such an approach. Some scholars have argued that the conventions of responsible government should have greater constitutional effect or even be judicially enforceable;[37] others have argued that responsible government has implications for the structure of government, limiting the types of executive agencies that may be created and prescribing the structures of accountability that must exist.

James Stellios recently argued that, as a result of the greater recognition of representative and responsible government by the High Court in the implied freedom and executive power cases, '[i]t would seem to follow that the rules, derived from constitutional convention, which are designed to ensure that the will of the people's representatives, and ultimately that of the people themselves, is made effective will also be seen as rules of law implied in the Constitution'.[38] Thus, many of the conventional rules relating to responsible government, such as the principle that the Governor-General must act on the advice of the ministry, are clear, binding, and fundamental to representative democracy, and ought to be treated as rules of law.[39] George Winterton argued that responsible government is clearly implied in the Constitution and that the High Court has shown a willingness to give 'constitutional status' to at least some of the elements of responsible government.[40] Further, he argued that 'the implied constitutional requirement that, except when exercising a "reserve power", the Governor-General must act only on ministerial advice ought to be judicially enforceable'.[41]

[37] See Nicholas Aroney et al, *The Constitution of the Commonwealth of Australia: History, Principle and Interpretation* (Port Melbourne, Cambridge University Press, 2015) 418–22.

[38] James Stellios, *Zines's the High Court and the Constitution*, 6th edn (Annandale, Federation Press, 2015) 369.

[39] ibid 370.

[40] Winterton (n 5) 4–5.

[41] ibid 125.

Geoffrey Lindell argued that the British system of responsible government 'does not countenance the existence of government officials for whom no one is accountable or responsible in the Parliament', and so legislation which establishes government officials or entities which are not under the control of a minister may be of questionable constitutional validity.[42] In the UK, the creation of a Parliamentary Ombudsman was initially resisted on similar grounds.[43] John Goldring also considered that there was some doubt as to whether the Commonwealth had the power to create independent statutory authorities.[44] Discussing the position of executive agencies exercising statutory functions, JE Richardson argued that section 61 of the Constitution mandates that the Governor-General must retain a residual role to ensure that Commonwealth legislation is administered consistently with the intention of Parliament, and that any act which sought to remove this residual responsibility would be constitutionally invalid.[45] Such views see ministerial responsibility as central to the accountability of public agencies.[46] These arguments will be discussed further and critiqued in chapter seven.

III. THE ARGUMENT OF THE BOOK

The arguments discussed in the previous section initially seem very different. They do, however, share something in common, namely a teleological and anachronistic reading of history, and they also posit a relatively static conception of responsible government. For Crisp, Howard and Saunders and Winterton, the dominance of the lower house, especially in relation to finance, is a key feature of responsible government. For Reid and Forrest and the other scholars discussed above, an idealised form of responsible government believed to have been practised in the mid-nineteenth century is the ideal form to which the political system today should return. A similar understanding of responsible government arguably underlies the views of those who argue for its constitutionalisation and judicial enforcement.

This book argues that the concept of responsible government embodied in the Australian Constitution is complex and multi-faceted and reflects a

[42] Geoffrey Lindell, *Responsible Government and the Australian Constitution – Conventions Transformed into Law?* (Leichhardt, Federation Press, 2004) 18 (emphasis in original removed).

[43] Terence Daintith and Alan Page, *The Executive in the Constitution: Structure, Autonomy, and Internal Control* (Oxford, Oxford University Press, 1999) 31.

[44] John Goldring, 'Accountability of Commonwealth Statutory Authorities and "Responsible Government"' (1980) 11 *Federal Law Review* 353.

[45] JE Richardson, 'The Executive Power of the Commonwealth' in Leslie Zines (ed), *Commentaries on the Australian Constitution* (Sydney, Butterworths, 1977) 84–5.

[46] On the centrality of ministerial responsibility see also *Hughes Aircraft Systems International v Airservices Australia* (1997) 76 FCR 151, 245–6 (Finn J); Meredith Edwards et al, *Public Sector Governance in Australia* (Acton, ANU E Press, 2012) 62.

strongly political conception of constitutionalism. Two themes are central to the Australasian conception of responsible government, namely evolution and popular self-government. The fundamental features of responsible government developed through a process of historical growth, which means that responsible government is inherently evolutionary: as put by JA Cockburn, the essence of the British Constitution was 'elasticity and development'.[47] In addition, a political conception of popular sovereignty is a crucial element of the Australian conception of responsible government. As noted in chapter six, there have been different conceptions of popular sovereignty throughout history, including both 'constitutive' and 'political' accounts. This book argues that the Australian Constitution gives effect to both of these conceptions, given that the Constitution was approved by popular referendums, and is intended to ensure that the mechanisms of government give effect to the will of the people.

Underlying the Constitution's deliberate lack of specificity as to the principles of responsible government is a belief that the conduct and practice of responsible government is inherently unconstrainable, and that its working cannot be prescribed by law or even predicted in advance. Responsible government is better seen as being assumed rather than prescribed by the Constitution. Reflecting one important strand in political theory regarding the functioning of political institutions, the functioning of responsible government depends on the character of the people and their representatives rather than the prescriptions of the Constitution; as put by James Bryce, the practical character of a system of government depends on the party system under which it functions, and on 'the political habits of the people'.[48]

These principles dovetail into a dynamic conception which explains why the Constitution does not attempt to entrench a particular form of responsible government, nor specify its leading features. The people should have the right to govern themselves in the manner they see fit, and the manner in which they choose to do so will vary from time to time. The Constitution thus imposes minimal contraints on the ability of the Australian people to design institutions of government and mechanisms of accountability. The Constitution establishes a government and a Parliament for a sovereign people, and provides for a deliberately flexible form of executive so that the people of Australia can shape their institutions to govern themselves as they think best.

To make this case, this book develops an account of responsible government under the Australian Constitution, drawing from the historical context relating to the incorporation of responsible government into the Constitution. It aims in particular to explore the understanding of responsible government held by the framers of the Constitution and their intentions in incorporating

[47] John A Cockburn, *Australian Federation* (London, Horace Marshall, 1901) 100.
[48] James Bryce, *The American Commonwealth*, 2nd edn (London, Macmillan, 1891) vol 1, 291.

it into the constitutional structure.[49] There have been few detailed studies of this context, or the framers' views and intentions when incorporating responsible government into the Constitution.[50] Those that do exist typically relegate the issue to a subset of the question of the relative powers of the houses of Parliament.[51] This is surprising, because an understanding of the key principles relating to responsible government as expounded in the leading texts, and parliamentary practice in the colonies prior to Federation, is crucial to a proper understanding of responsible government and the Constitution. Much of the framers' understanding was assumed rather than expressly stated; as put by Brian Galligan, '[i]t is obvious that the meaning of responsible government cannot be established from the constitutional text'.[52] The text of the Constitution does not define responsible government and is cryptic about the structure and powers of the executive,[53] and so to properly understand the nature of responsible government under the Australian Constitution it is necessary to read it in light of the historical and constitutional context.

Chapters two to five of this book examine the concept of responsible government as it was understood at the time of Federation and its incorporation into the Australian Constitution. The framers drew on leading British constitutional writing in the late nineteenth century, as well as Australian ideals of self-government to develop a distinctly Australian conception of responsible government. Accordingly, chapters two and three discuss the historical, political and constitutional context to the Federation Conventions in order to reconstruct an accurate picture of thinking at the time of Federation regarding responsible government. That context is not determinative of the framers' views, but it is necessary to properly understand them.[54]

Chapter two examines the doctrine of responsible government as expounded by key British constitutional writers. In the Australian colonies, responsible government was inherited from and modelled on the British system of government. The British Constitution had come to embody responsible government through a long period of evolution; responsible government was the form the British Constitution took for a relatively brief period in the mid to late nineteenth

[49] In this book the terms 'framer' and 'delegate' are used interchangeably to refer to a member of the 1891 or the 1897–8 National Australasian Convention. *Cf* JA La Nauze, *The Making of the Australian Constitution* (Carlton, Melbourne University Press, 1972) vii.

[50] Prior studies include Michael Crommelin, 'The Executive' in Gregory Craven (ed), *The Convention Debates 1891–1898: Commentaries, Indices and Guide* (Sydney, Legal Books, 1986); Winterton (n 5); Galligan, 'The Founders' Design' (n 14); Frank Roland McGrath, *The Intentions of the Framers of the Commonwealth of Australia Constitution* (PhD Thesis, University of Sydney, 2006).

[51] Eg, Galligan, 'The Founders' Design' (n 14); McGrath (n 50) pt 1.

[52] Galligan, 'The Founders' Design' (n 14) 1.

[53] Crommelin (n 50) 147.

[54] *Cf* Quentin Skinner, *The Foundations of Modern Political Thought* (Cambridge, Cambridge University Press, 1978) vol 1, x–xi; Quentin Skinner, 'Meaning and Understanding in the History of Ideas' (1969) 8 *History and Theory* 3, 48–9.

century. Responsible government must be understood in the context of the way the British Constitution was conceived. As it was unwritten, it was not conceived as a body of laws separate from the conventions and practices which gave life to the institutions of government, but included those conventions and practices. The Constitution therefore included the way the government was worked by the people, and was often described as 'organic' and 'living'. This meant that any modification to the laws or even the customs or political practices which related to the British Government meant a modification to the Constitution itself. Those practices and conventions were constantly changing, and so change was seen as a constitutional principle. Winthrop Hackett accurately captured this when he said that '[t]he beauty, the virtue of the English system is its plasticity, its elasticity. Generation after generation introduces some novel feature, and its working conditions again change'.[55]

Responsible government must therefore be understood both diachronically and synchronically. The long history of parliamentary government was considered to furnish authoritative precedents, which were expounded in important works on the British Constitution such as those written by Walter Bagehot, Alpheus Todd, William Hearn, Earl Grey and William Anson from the 1860s. Yet, as it was not fixed, the British Constitution could be adapted and moulded to the circumstances of the time, providing flexibility within an overall framework of continuity.

Chapter three examines the history of responsible government in the colonies prior to Federation. It notes that responsible government modelled on the British Constitution was introduced into the colonies (except Western Australia) in the 1850s. It examines key secondary literature relating to the functioning of responsible government in the colonies in the period leading up to the Federation debates. It will be noted that the emergence of parties in each colony took a distinctive route and that a key concern during the pre-Federation years was the instability of colonial politics.

Chapters two and three also discuss the critiques of cabinet and responsible government which were made prior to and during the Federation period. The Conventions in which the terms of the Australian Constitution were debated took place in 1891 and 1897–8. Around this time, there was considerable debate in Britain and the Australian colonies about responsible government. Tract writers, members of Parliament and parliamentary inquiries vigorously debated the merits and workings of responsible government. Contemporaries debated issues such as cabinet solidarity, ministerial dominance of Parliament, the corrupting demands of party loyalty, the inconsistency and hypocrisy of ministries, the diminishing role of the MP, and the inability of Parliament to properly hold the government to account. Seemingly contradictory assertions were made about the inability of Parliament to properly transact business

[55] *Convention Debates* (1891) 279 (Hackett). See also 468 (Wrixon).

and the weakness of the executive. Much of this criticism was directed at the pre-party cabinet system as it functioned in the colonies, before Labor was a significant force in Australian politics. In response to these criticisms, contemporaries argued that the system of responsible government should be abandoned and replaced with a system of 'elective ministries' modelled on the system of government which existed in Switzerland.

These debates were well known to the framers. Some of the Victorian framers participated in a royal commission established to consider the functioning of responsible government, and other framers wrote proposals for the adoption of the elective ministry system. Similar proposals were voiced during the Federation debates, but were not successful in preventing responsible government from being incorporated into the Constitution. How the framers responded to these powerful critiques sheds important light on how they conceived responsible government.

Chapters four and five examine the views of the framers and their resulting impact on the Constitution. They examine the Convention debates and significant writings and speeches of the framers around the time of Federation which discussed the question of responsible government. The Convention debates 'remain the basic source for contemporary intentions in the writing of the Constitution',[56] and contain the record of the framers' debates relating to key issues such as the proper definition and functioning of responsible government and whether to incorporate it into the Constitution. In addition to the Convention debates, many framers also gave speeches and wrote key works and articles around the time of Federation, which are also an important source of material explaining their views.

Chapters six and seven consider the implications of this historical context for understanding and interpretating the Constitution. Chapter six develops an account of responsible government under the Australian Constitution, drawing on the context, the views of the framers and subsequent High Court decisions. Chapter seven considers the implications for interpreting the Constitution and analyses several lines of cases which have employed the concept of responsible government in constitutional interpretation. One principal implication is that courts should be cautious about attempts to 'constitutionalise' responsible government and about drawing implications from the incorporation of responsible government into the Constitution which limit the ability of the people and their representatives to govern themselves.

Chapter eight concludes, noting that government has changed significantly since Federation and responsible government needs to evolve to keep pace with those developments. The Constitution has been expressly designed to accommodate such changes: changes in the structure of government since Federation are not a departure from the 'true' principles of responsible government, but rather

[56] John Waugh, 'New Federation History' (2000) 24 *Melbourne University Law Review* 1028, 1039.

a legitimate evolution in response to circumstances and societal values which the Constitution is deliberately structured to provide for. Constitutional arrangements relating to responsible government 'need to be capable of development and adaptability'.[57]

IV. HISTORY AND CONSTITUTIONAL INTERPRETATION

The place of history in constitutional interpretation is contested. The High Court has emphasised that its role in constitutional interpretation is to determine the meaning of the provision in question objectively from the language used and has often expressed a reluctance to employ extrinsic materials such as historical materials when interpreting the Constitution.[58] In particular, the Court has denied the relevance of the subjective intentions of the framers.[59] Further, within the constraints of the text, it is considered undesirable to confine the meaning of the Constitution to the historical meaning as at Federation, and it is often argued that the interpretation of the Constitution should keep pace with social and other developments.[60]

This book develops an account of responsible government by reading the Constitution in light of its historical context. The method adopted by this book is to read the Constitution first as a historical text, written in a particular context in order to achieve certain defined goals. This is a stronger claim than simply that history is one of the many factors that may be taken into account. Rather, I argue that the Constitution must be understood first as a historical text, and that it cannot be interpreted without an understanding of its historical context. The Constitution is not, and was not intended to be, a self-referential document, and it cannot be understood solely from an examination of its text. This is particularly true in relation to the provisions of the Constitution which relate to the executive, because the constitutional text, interpreted solely with reference to the language employed, presents an utterly misleading picture of the working of the Constitution. The provisions of the

[57] *Mulholland v Australian Electoral Commission* (2004) 220 CLR 181, 189–90 [9]–[10] (Gleeson CJ).

[58] *Amalgamated Society of Engineers v Adelaide Steamship Co Ltd* (1920) 28 CLR 129, 142, 149 (Knox CJ, Isaacs, Rich and Starke JJ); *A-G (Cth) ex rel McKinlay v Commonwealth* (1975) 135 CLR 1, 17 (Barwick CJ), 47 (Gibbs J); Henry Burmester, 'The Convention Debates and the Interpretation of the Constitution' in Craven (ed) (n 50) 25.

[59] Stephen Donaghue and Thomas Wood, 'The Evolving Role of History in Constitutional Interpretation' (2020) 31 *Public Law Review* 248; *Cole v Whitfield* (1988) 165 CLR 360, 385 (Mason CJ, Wilson, Brennan, Deane, Dawson, Toohey and Gaudron JJ); *Re Wakim; Ex parte McNally* (1999) 198 CLR 511, 551 [40] (McHugh J); *Eastman v R* (2000) 203 CLR 1, 46 [146] (McHugh J); *Singh v Commonwealth* (2004) 222 CLR 322, 337 [21] (Gleeson CJ), 385 [159] (Gummow, Hayne and Heydon JJ).

[60] Jeremy Kirk, 'Constitutional Interpretation and a Theory of Evolutionary Originalism' (1999) 27 *Federal Law Review* 323, 333–5; see also Jeffrey Goldsworthy, 'Originalism in Constitutional Interpretation' (1997) 25 *Federal Law Review* 1, 28–35.

Constitution which incorporate or assume responsible government are deliberately sparse and rely on unwritten understandings and conventions which must be gleaned from other sources.[61] Accordingly, those provisions cannot be understood without an understanding of the broader context, which includes the intentions of the framers in incorporating responsible government into the Constitution. The Constitution includes many specialised constitutional terms such as 'executive power' without defining those terms. In so doing, the Constitution assumes the existence of a body of specialised constitutional law which gives content to the meaning of those terms. These terms now derive their legal authority from the Constitution, but their content must be ascertained from sources outside the Constitution. That is to say, the Constitution must be interpreted in light of the common law and constitutional law which the framers assumed when drafting the Constitution.

Another necessary element of understanding the Constitution is the views and intentions of the framers. The Constitution has a particular purpose, and various provisions of the Constitution cannot be understood without knowing the intentions which resulted in their drafting. This is not to suggest that the framers' intentions have any normative significance in and of themselves. Rather, it is simply to treat the Constitution as a text written in a specific historical context by particular authors. The framers' intentions are relevant only to the extent that they can be ascertained and are relevant in explaining the text.

It may be queried whether it is possible to ascertain the intentions of the framers as to a particular issue or provision. The framers were not a homogenous group, but held differing and sometimes competing opinions as to what the Constitution should embody. It is commonly argued that it makes no sense to speak of the 'intent' of a particular statutory or constitutional provision[62] and High Court judges have described the concept of legislative intention as a 'fiction' or 'metaphor'.[63] Echoing a frequently made argument, Dawson J argued that the intention of Parliament 'is somewhat of a fiction' and that individual MPs or the government 'do not necessarily mean the same thing by voting on a Bill or, in some cases, anything at all'.[64] It is also true that the framers' intentions relating to certain provisions of the Constitution are not always apparent from the Convention debates; for example, some provisions were adopted with little or no debate or explanation as to their meaning. For reasons such as these

[61] Howard and Saunders (n 24) 265.

[62] See, eg, Max Radin, 'Statutory Interpretation' (1930) 43 *Harvard Law Review* 863, 870–1; Kenneth A Shepsle, 'Congress is a 'They', Not an 'I': Legislative Intent as Oxymoron' (1992) 12 *International Review of Law and Economics* 239.

[63] Richard Ekins and Jeffrey Goldsworthy, 'The Reality and Indispensability of Legislative Intentions' (2014) 36 *Sydney Law Review* 39, 41.

[64] *Mills v Meeking* (1990) 169 CLR 214, 234; Sir Daryl Dawson, 'Intention and the Constitution – Whose Intent?' (1990) 6 *Australian Bar Review* 93.

it is not possible to ascertain the underlying purpose of some clauses of the Constitution with any certainty.[65]

Recent works have defended the concepts of group agency and legislative intention. Different approaches have been proposed in the literature. Among others, Richard Ekins, Christian List and Philip Pettit have argued that it is coherent to speak of the intentions of groups, being (in Ekins's words) 'the coordinated pursuit of a common purpose by means of a jointly accepted plan of action'.[66] Applied to the legislature, there is nothing incoherent about the proposition that legislatures have 'specific intentions in the form of purposes or plans of action which are properly ascribable to the legislature rather than to its members'.[67] On this account, legislative intention is not merely the aggregate of the intentions of the individual legislators but is the legislature's reasoned response to a particular matter by adopting a particular course of action.[68] Others have argued that legislative intentions must be formed at least partly by the aggregated attitudes of individual legislators.[69] For the purposes of this book I accept that group intent is a coherent position, and it is not necessary to decide between these accounts.

It is therefore meaningful to speak of the intentions of the framers. Discerning the framers' intentions is not a speculative attempt to consider how the framers might have resolved present-day controversies which were 'not present to the minds of those who contributed to the debates'.[70] Rather, the intention of the framers is their jointly accepted resolution of a particular issue. The provisions of the Constitution were adopted after being debated by the Federation Conventions which occurred in 1891 and 1897–8. During those Conventions the framers followed an agreed process, adopting procedural rules modelled on the rules of parliamentary procedure (including resolution of disputed matters by majority vote) and ensured that an official record of the debates was kept.[71] The *Convention Debates* contain a detailed written record of their deliberations and the positions they reached. Thus, the intention of the framers in relation to a particular issue is the reasoned response of the Federation Conventions to that issue, as recorded in the *Convention Debates*.

[65] Alex C Castles, 'The Voyage of the "Lucinda" and the Drafting of the Australian Constitution in 1891' (1991) 65 *Australian Law Journal* 277.

[66] Richard Ekins, *The Nature of Legislative Intent* (Oxford, Oxford University Press, 2012) 53; Christian List and Philip Pettit, *Group Agency: The Possibility, Design and Status of Corporate Agents* (Oxford, Oxford University Press, 2011) 77.

[67] Neil Duxbury, *Elements of Legislation* (Cambridge, Cambridge University Press, 2013) 115.

[68] Ekins (n 66) 46, 224, 243; Justice Stephen Gageler, 'Legislative Intention' (2015) 41 *Monash University Law Review* 1, 12.

[69] David Tan, 'Uncommon Legislative Attitudes: Why a Theory of Legislative Intent Needs Nontrivial Aggregation' (2021) 34 *Ratio Juris* 139.

[70] *New South Wales v Commonwealth* (2006) 229 CLR 1, 97 [120] (Gleeson CJ, Gummow, Hayne, Heydon and Crennan JJ).

[71] See *Convention Debates* (1891) 8–10; *Convention Debates*, Adelaide (1897) 7–8, 10, 16.

For many provisions of the Constitution, it is possible to determine the framers' intentions. Many provisions were adopted after extensive debate in which competing positions were advocated, and so there exists a record of the intentions of the framers in relation to those matters which explains why a particular decision was reached. However, such a record does not exist in relation to all the provisions of the Constitution.

A coherent picture of the framers' intentions relating to responsible government can be put together based on the terms of the Constitution, read in light of the Convention debates and the historical and constitutional context of Federation.[72] There was a significant body of constitutional writing which informed the framers' understanding of parliamentary government which they frequently referred to and whose terminology they adopted. The topic of responsible government, and its relation to the powers of the Senate, was discussed at length, and leading framers such as Edmund Barton gave lucid explanations of the incorporation of responsible government into the Constitution.[73] It is therefore possible to glean an accurate understanding of the framers' views and their intentions regarding the compromise position relating to responsible government that came to be embodied in the Constitution.

I do not argue in this book that development or change in the meaning of constitutional provisions is impermissible. As noted, many terms in the Constitution are not defined. One consequence of this is that the meaning of these terms must be determined from sources outside the Constitution. A second consequence is that, by not defining these terms, the Constitution allows for continued evolution in their meaning. The incorporation of terms whose meanings are given content by constitutional law and common law also implies the incorporation of the methods of the common law and British constitutionalism, which include evolution and change.

V. POLITICAL AND LEGAL CONSTITUTIONALISM

An important theme of this book is that responsible government under the Australian Constitution reflects a tension between political and legal models of constitutionalism. The dominant model of constitutionalism today is legal constitutionalism, as evident in the widespread adoption of codified Constitutions and judicially enforceable Bills of Rights.[74] Although more elaborate definitions could be offered,[75] legal constitutionalism is essentially

[72] Greg Craven, 'The Convention Debates: Still More Sinned Against than Sinning' (1998) 1 *New Federalist* 67, 68.

[73] *Convention Debates* (1898) 2469–70.

[74] Robert Brett Taylor, 'The Contested Constitution: An Analysis of the Competing Models of British Constitutionalism' [2018] *Public Law* 500, 503.

[75] See, eg, ibid 501–11; Thomas Poole, 'Back to the Future – Unearthing the Theory of Common Law Constitutionalism' (2003) 23 *Oxford Journal of Legal Studies* 435.

the idea that legal mechanisms such as a written Constitution with the existence of judicial review, the common law or an entrenched Bill of Rights provide the most effective mechanisms of government accountability and ensure better substantive outcomes such as protecting rights. Legal constitutionalists believe that the political branches of government, being subject to the whims of majoritarian politics, are inherently liable to act arbitrarily and infringe individual rights and liberty; thus, the democratic process is in need of being checked by the courts.[76] Fundamental rights stand (or ought to stand) apart from politics and not be revocable by majority vote in Parliament; respect for rights is a condition of the legitimacy of majoritarian decision-making.[77] Legal constitutionalists also consider that judicial decision making is more suited than political decision making to determining certain types of questions such as issues of rights or justice; as put by TRS Allan, 'common law adjudication is superior to the legislative process as a means of resolving questions of justice, even where the latter is accompanied by wide consultation to ascertain public opinion and preceded by vigorous political debate'.[78]

By contrast, political constitutionalists consider that the exercise of power should be held to account primarily through political rather than legal processes and that political mechanisms are more effective in doing so.[79] Political constitutionalists accept the inevitability of disagreement and that there may be no consensus on many questions of rights or justice that exists apart from and antecedent to politics.[80] Political constitutionalists consider that it is undemocratic for judges to possess the power to invalidate legislation on the grounds that it infringes rights or liberty;[81] further, while the judicial process has an important part to play in, for example, ensuring that executive action is validly authorised by law, it is inapt for deciding certain matters, especially matters of policy or conflicts between rights.[82] In perhaps its most extreme form, Posner and Vermeule argued that neither the courts nor the legislature are able effectively to constrain the executive; instead, politics and public opinion alone provide sufficient checks on abuse of power.[83] Although political constitutionalism

[76] See, eg, TRS Allan, *Constitutional Justice: A Liberal Theory of the Rule of Law* (Oxford, Oxford University Press, 2001) 3.

[77] TRS Allan, *The Sovereignty of Law: Freedom, Constitution, and Common Law* (Oxford, Oxford University Press, 2013) 330; Sir John Laws, 'Law and Democracy' [1995] *Public Law* 72.

[78] TRS Allan, 'Common Law Constitutionalism and Freedom of Speech' in J Beatson and Y Cripps (eds), *Freedom of Expression and Freedom of Information* (Oxford, Oxford University Press, 2000) 22.

[79] Graham Gee and Grégoire CN Webber, 'What Is a Political Constitution?' (2010) 30 *Oxford Journal of Legal Studies* 273.

[80] Jeremy Waldron, *Law and Disagreement* (Oxford, Oxford University Press, 1999); Conor Gearty, *Principles of Human Rights Adjudication* (Oxford, Oxford University Press, 2004) 64.

[81] Jeremy Waldron, 'The Core of the Case Against Judicial Review' (2006) 115 *Yale Law Journal* 1346.

[82] Adam Tomkins, 'The Role of the Courts in the Political Constitution' (2010) 60 *University of Toronto Law Journal* 1.

[83] Eric A Posner and Adrian Vermeule, *The Executive Unbound: After the Madisonian Republic* (Oxford, Oxford University Press, 2011).

originated in a descriptive account of the British Constitution, it has been articulated more recently as a normative theory which draws its theoretical underpinnings from the political theory of republicanism, including the principle of freedom as non-domination.[84]

Responsible government in Australia embodies a political model of constitutionalism within a written Constitution. Responsible government is a fundamentally political model of constitutionalism given that its functioning depends on conventions which are not judicially enforceable, and that political mechanisms are the principal means of holding the government to account. Central to the Australian conception of responsible government, one of the fundamental principles underlying the Australian Constitution, is 'the centrality of the political process' whereby the Australian people acting by 'ordinary constitutional means' are 'firmly acknowledged as the principal constraint on government power'.[85] As the High Court wrote in the *Engineers* case:

> When the people of Australia, to use the words of the Constitution itself, 'united in a Federal Commonwealth', they took power to control by ordinary constitutional means any attempt on the part of the national Parliament to misuse its powers. If it be conceivable that the representatives of the people of Australia as a whole would ever proceed to use their national powers to injure the people of Australia considered sectionally, it is certainly within the power of the people themselves to resent and reverse what may be done. No protection of this Court in such a case is necessary or proper.[86]

There are also important elements of legal constitutionalism in Australia, most obviously the existence of a written Constitution which places legal limits on legislative and executive power, with an independent judiciary empowered to enforce those limits.[87] Australia has no constitutionally entrenched Bill of Rights and the Constitution contains limited protection for human rights.[88] Thus, there is an important role for judicial review, but this is limited to ensuring the consistency of legislative and executive action with the Constitution.

The Australian constitutional tradition thus contains significant elements of both political and legal constitutionalism,[89] where each have their distinct

[84] See especially Richard Bellamy, *Political Constitutionalism: A Republican Defence of the Constitutionality of Democracy* (Cambridge, Cambridge University Press, 2007); Adam Tomkins, *Our Republican Constitution* (Portland, Hart, 2005).

[85] Stephen Gageler, 'Foundations of Australian Federalism and the Role of Judicial Review' (1987) 17 *Federal Law Review* 162, 184, 197. See also Stephen Gageler, 'Beyond the Text: A Vision of the Structure and Function of the Constitution' (2009) 32 *Australian Bar Review* 138, 147.

[86] *Amalgamated Society of Engineers v Adelaide Steamship Co Ltd* (1920) 28 CLR 129, 151–2 (Knox CJ, Isaacs, Rich and Starke JJ).

[87] Kenneth Hayne, 'Rule of Law' in Cheryl Saunders and Adrienne Stone (eds), *The Oxford Handbook of the Australian Constitution* (Oxford, Oxford University Press, 2018).

[88] See generally George Williams and David Hume, *Human Rights under the Australian Constitution*, 2nd edn (South Melbourne, Oxford University Press, 2013).

[89] Lisa Burton Crawford and Jeffrey Goldsworthy, 'Constitutionalism' in Cheryl Saunders and Adrienne Stone (eds), *The Oxford Handbook of the Australian Constitution* (Oxford, Oxford University Press, 2018) 358.

role within the institutional distribution of competences among the legislative, executive and judicial arms of government. The courts have a defined role; it is considered that some types of decisions are for the executive, not the courts,[90] and that it is for the Parliament to determine matters of policy.[91] Some matters 'are not suitable for judicial determination'.[92] The traditional orthodoxy in Australia is that courts should only incrementally develop the law and should avoid an overtly politicised role.[93] However, there is not always agreement as to what, precisely, the proper scope of the court's role ought to be and it is difficult to draw a sharp boundary between 'law' and 'politics'.[94] The Constitution 'is a political instrument, and the role of judicial review necessarily involves the Court in decision-making that has political ramifications'.[95] As Dixon J wrote in *Melbourne Corporation*:

> The Constitution is a political instrument. It deals with government and governmental powers. … It is not a question whether the considerations are political, for nearly every consideration arising from the Constitution can be so described, but whether they are compelling.[96]

I argue that responsible government in Australia manifests an uneasy tension between political and legal mechanisms of accountability, which arises from the inclusion of a fundamentally political form of constitutionalism within a written Constitution. The functioning of responsible government will be affected by the specific requirements of the provisions of the Constitution, and given its centrality to the Constitution, responsible government must be taken into account to some extent when interpreting the written text.

It is undeniably the case that the political process and its products are often uninspiring. There has been a decline of public trust in political institutions and democracy, prompting reconsideration of the effectiveness of political mechanisms of accountability.[97] Australian parliaments have been described as 'wastelands of adversarial partisan politics'[98] and some believe that they

[90] Chris Finn, 'The Concept of 'Justiciability' in Administrative Law' in Matthew Groves and HP Lee (eds), *Australian Administrative Law: Fundamentals, Principles and Doctrines* (Port Melbourne, Cambridge University Press, 2007) 154.

[91] See, eg, *Commonwealth v Australian Capital Territory* (2013) 250 CLR 441, 452 [1] (French CJ, Hayne, Crennan, Kiefel, Bell and Keane JJ).

[92] Henry Burmester, 'Limitations on Federal Adjudication' in Brian Opeskin and Fiona Wheeler (eds), *The Australian Federal Judicial System* (Carlton South, Melbourne University Press, 2000) 227, 256.

[93] Jason Pierce, *Inside the Mason Court Revolution: The High Court of Australia Transformed* (Durham, Carolina Academic Press, 2006).

[94] See generally Brian Galligan, *Politics of the High Court: A Study of the Judicial Branch of Government in Australia* (St Lucia, University of Queensland Press, 1987).

[95] James Stellios, *The Federal Judicature: Chapter III of the Constitution*, 2nd edn (Sydney, LexisNexis, 2020) 211.

[96] *Melbourne Corporation v Commonwealth* (1947) 74 CLR 31, 82.

[97] Yee-Fui Ng, 'Political Constitutionalism: Individual Responsibility and Collective Restraint' (2020) 48 *Federal Law Review* 455, 457.

[98] John Uhr, 'Reforming the Parliament' in Clement Macintyre and John Williams (eds), *Peace, Order and Good Government: State Constitutional and Parliamentary Reform* (Kent Town, Wakefield Press, 2003) 228, 231.

are ineffective in checking the executive.[99] The enactment of extensive legal mechanisms of accountability testifies to the inadequacy of political mechanisms, including responsible government. As Kirby J has noted, the growth in administrative law remedies in the late twentieth century 'occurred at a time when the theory of ministerial responsibility, as an effective means of ensuring public service accountability, has been widely perceived as having serious weaknesses and limitations'.[100] Untrammelled parliamentary sovereignty means that '[i]mportant freedoms are at the mercy' of Parliament, 'generally manipulated by the executive government which cannot even claim the support of a clear majority of the electorate'.[101] Given this, some argue that only the courts can be trusted to protect rights.[102]

The tension between political and legal models of constitutionalism that relates to responsible government can be seen in the following trends, which will be discussed in detail in later chapters. First, in recent cases the High Court has discerned from the principles of representative and responsible government an implied limitation on legislative and executive power, which requires that any restrictions on the freedom to communicate regarding government and political matters must be justified according to a European-derived proportionality test. However, given that the Commonwealth Parliament is required to consider the compatibility of all legislative proposals with human rights,[103] the effective consequence is that, where legislation is challenged, the Court now engages in an examination of the compatibility of the legislation with rights, adopting a similar methodology but against a narrower canvas.

Second, there has been persistent uncertainty since Federation about the content of executive power, in particular the power to enter contracts and expend funds in the absence of prior legislative authorisation. In important recent cases the High Court has significantly limited the scope of non-statutory executive power.[104] The centrality of responsible government to the Australian constitutional system, and concerns about the functioning of responsible government in practice, played a significant role in these decisions. The result of these decisions is that the executive is required to seek statutory authorisation for its activities, thereby engaging more closely with the parliamentary process. However,

[99] Tomkins, *Our Republican Constitution* (n 84) 40.

[100] *Hot Holdings Pty Ltd v Creasy* (2002) 210 CLR 438, 467 [92].

[101] TRS Allan, 'Legislative Supremacy and the Rule of Law: Democracy and Constitutionalism' (1985) 44 *Cambridge Law Journal* 111, 116.

[102] Poole (n 75) 441, 451; in *Baker v R* (2004) 223 CLR 513, 539 [66] Kirby J argued that, subject to the Constitution, 'only the courts of this country stand as guardians of proportionality and the avoidance of serious excesses and departures from the international law of human rights to which Australia has subscribed'.

[103] Human Rights (Parliamentary Scrutiny) Act 2011 (Cth) ss 7–9. Similar requirements are contained in Human Rights Act 2004 (ACT) ss 37–38; Charter of Human Rights and Responsibilities Act 2006 (Vic) ss 28–30; Human Rights Act 2019 (Qld) ss 38–41.

[104] *Pape v Federal Commissioner of Taxation* (2009) 238 CLR 1; *Williams v Commonwealth* (2012) 248 CLR 156.

the effectiveness of the legal mechanisms mandated by the Court depends, to a significant extent, on the very political considerations which caused the perceived problems with the functioning of responsible government in the first place.

The third way in which this tension is evident is that there have been persistent proposals to constitutionalise various aspects of responsible government. These include calls to codify the conventions of responsible government and make them judicially enforceable, and suggestions that implications should be drawn from responsible government for the structure of government, limiting the types of entities that can be created consistent with the Constitution.[105] This book argues that drawing implications which limit the power of the Parliament in relation to the structure of government is inconsistent with the nature of responsible government as inherently designed to enable flexibility to create novel governance arrangements, and arguably hinders rather than promotes effective accountability.

These developments and proposals have a common thread, namely the desire to impose greater legal mechanisms of accountability for matters that traditionally were considered to be within the purview of politics. The history of the interpretation of responsible government under the Australian Constitution can therefore be viewed as a cautious trend towards imposing legal constitutionalism onto a fundamentally political system, thus eroding the political nature of accountability. However, the acceptance of this trend by the courts has been hesitant, and where legal mechanisms have been imposed, it is not clear that these have resulted in more effective accountability.

The trends noted in this section, including the widespread adoption of administrative law mechanisms and remedies, could be seen as testifying to the inadequacy of responsible government and parliamentary mechanisms of accountability. On the other hand, the principle of responsible government as incorporated into our Constitution is expressly designed to allow for such developments. They could be seen, therefore, as vindicating the wisdom of a flexible and non-prescriptive approach that allows successive generations of the Australian people to establish novel governance arrangements.

[105] Lindell, *Responsible Government and the Australian Constitution* (n 42) 18.

2

Responsible Government in the British Constitutional Tradition

> Parliamentary Government derives its whole force and power of action from the exercise of an influence which is at least very much akin to corruption. … Parliamentary Government is essentially a government by party, and one of the bonds by which all parties are kept together is that of the selfish interests of their adherents.[1]
>
> Earl Grey (1864)

I. INTRODUCTION

THIS CHAPTER EXAMINES the British concept of parliamentary government as expounded in the authoritative treatises on the British Constitution at the time of Australian Federation. As explored in later chapters, the framers incorporated responsible government modelled on the British system of government into the Australian Constitution.[2] The framers acquired their understanding of responsible government from two principal sources, namely the experience of the working of responsible government in the colonies in the latter half of the nineteenth century, and the leading works on the British Constitution. An examination of those writings provides important background for understanding the framers' views.

In legal literature, responsible government is often conceived primarily as a series of principles or conventions relating to the formation and operation of government. The two key conventions were, first, the British monarch only acted on the 'advice' of the ministry, which was responsible to Parliament for the policy and administration of government; second, the ministry was required to maintain the confidence of the House of Commons in order to hold office. Thus, at the core of the doctrine of responsible government was the linking of the government's tenure of office with the confidence of the lower house.

[1] Earl Grey, *Parliamentary Government Considered with Reference to Reform*, 2nd edn (London, John Murray, 1864) 41, 43.

[2] *Williams v Commonwealth* (2012) 248 CLR 156, 204 [58] (French CJ), 349 [508] (Crennan J); John Quick and Robert Randolph Garran, *The Annotated Constitution of the Australian Commonwealth* (Sydney, Angus and Robertson, 1901) 706–7.

It should also be noted that responsible government was not a contextless set of constitutional maxims, but was considered to rely for its proper working on certain political conditions and realities, and it was thought that responsible government would not function properly where these did not hold true.

The effectiveness and role of Parliament can be analysed from the perspective of a 'liberal' or an 'executive' model.[3] A liberal model sees parliamentary independence, deliberation, and control of the executive as fundamental to the idea of responsible government, and considers that parties have the potential to distort this ideal.[4] By contrast, an executive model prioritises stability, unity, and the ability to pass legislation efficiently, and a stable party system is often considered necessary to enable this to occur. In the Australian context some scholars have argued that the practice of responsible government after Federation has departed from the framers' expectations, based on a liberal conception of responsible government.[5] Elements of a liberal ideal were certainly an important part of the nineteenth century British and Australian conceptions of responsible government. Parliament's functions included appointing the government, holding it to account by watching over and scrutinising its activities and controlling public finance by granting or withholding supply. It was considered essential for MPs to be independent so that they might consider each matter brought before the Parliament on its merits, and for Parliament as a whole to have sufficient strength and freedom to be able to hold the executive accountable. Without independence, MPs would become mere slaves of party or constituency and Parliament would be unable to carry out its constitutional functions properly.

However, elements of an executive model were also considered important, perhaps even more so than liberal ideals. Contemporaries considered it to be necessary for governments to have stable working majorities, and that political parties provided this stability. Without moderately disciplined parties, a government could not rely on a stable majority and Parliament would be unpredictable and potentially chaotic. The leading constitutional writers considered a two-party system to be essential for the proper working of responsible

[3] This terminology is taken from David Clune and Gareth Griffith, *Decision and Deliberation: The Parliament of New South Wales, 1856–2003* (Sydney, Federation Press, 2006) 9–16.

[4] See discussion in Ron Levy, Neomal Silva and Benjamin B Saunders, 'Deliberation at the Founding: Deliberative Democracy as an Original Constitutional Value' (2017) 28 *Public Law Review* 41.

[5] GS Reid and Martyn Forrest, *Australia's Commonwealth Parliament 1901–1988: Ten Perspectives* (Carlton, Melbourne University Press, 1989) 12; Jim Chalmers and Glyn Davis, 'Power: Relations Between the Parliament and the Executive' (Research Paper No 14, Parliament of Australia, 2000); Glyn Davis, 'Executive Government: Cabinet and the Prime Minister' in John Summers, Dennis Woodward and Andrew Parkin (eds), *Government, Politics, Power and Policy in Australia*, 7th edn (Frenchs Forest, Longman, 2002) 50–1; Ian Marsh, *Beyond the Two Party System: Political Representation, Economic Competitiveness, and Australian Politics* (Melbourne, Cambridge University Press, 1995).

government and that stable government would be impossible where there were three or more parties. While it is true that parties sat uncomfortably with ideals of independence, they were considered an inevitable feature of responsible government, and were legitimate to the extent that they stood for political principle rather than the mere desire to obtain office.

Elements of both liberal and executive models were considered to be features of the British Constitution, leading to the seemingly contradictory view that Parliament should supervise and control the ministry, but also that the ministry should direct and control the proceedings of Parliament. Thus, responsible government was nuanced, complex, and not always entirely consistent. This lack of complete logical consistency was not, however, seen to be a defect. The British Constitution was unwritten and had come to embody responsible government through a long period of evolution; indeed, change had come to be seen as a constitutional principle, part of the British Constitution. It was considered that, in contrast to the 'mechanical' or 'artificial' contrivances of European constitution-makers, the British Constitution was organic and living, not artificially created, defying strict logic or codification, but reflecting the political habits and temper of the people.[6] As it was not fixed and rigid, the British Constitution could be adapted and moulded to the circumstances in which it functioned, while providing an overall framework of stability and continuity.

In an age which tended to idealise the institutions of British Government,[7] it is not surprising that writers conceived the British Constitution in normative terms, providing a standard for 'the rightful and proper conduct of government'.[8] Many writers considered that certain forms of change (especially significant enlargements of the franchise) would upset or destroy essential constitutional principles: indeed, writers such as Walter Bagehot and Earl Grey wrote important works specifically intended to warn of the dangers of enlarging the franchise. A descriptive account of the British Constitution as inherently evolutionary did not readily accommodate strongly normative prescriptions about the way the British Constitution should function; contemporaries nevertheless attempted to make such prescriptions, in effect seeking to entrench a particular stage of development of the British Constitution. Those who did so often found that the march of events was liable to render their normative prescriptions outdated as constitutional principles considered vital at one time were swept away in the next.

[6] Eg, William Edward Hearn, *The Government of England: Its Structure, and Its Development*, 2nd edn (Melbourne, George Robertson, 1886) 2.

[7] Miles Taylor, 'Introduction' in Walter Bagehot, *The English Constitution* (Oxford, Oxford University Press, 2001) ix.

[8] Michael Foley, *The Politics of the British Constitution* (Manchester, Manchester University Press, 1999) 13.

II. FROM PREROGATIVE TO PARTY GOVERNMENT

Prior to the period of responsible government, the British Constitution was seen as a 'mixed and balanced Constitution' in which the main powers were the King, the House of Lords and the Commons, and which were said to provide a mutual restraint upon each other.[9] Until well into the nineteenth century the choice of the ministry was regarded as the personal prerogative of the monarch;[10] the support of the sovereign was more important in the maintenance of a ministry than the confidence of Parliament and several notable ministries were formed, and maintained, while lacking a majority and suffering numerous defeats in the Commons.[11] There was an expectation that the Commons would give a 'fair trial' to the ministers appointed by the monarch, and only withhold confidence where the ministry proved unworthy of this trust.[12]

In 1841 Sir Robert Peel moved a motion that the Melbourne ministry did not possess the confidence of the House of Commons and that 'their continuance in office under such circumstances is at variance with the spirit of the constitution'. The carrying of this motion was considered to establish the principle that the Commons determined the composition of the ministry by granting or withholding its confidence.[13] Thus, by the mid-nineteenth century, the government was carried out by the ministers of the Crown who were responsible to Parliament.[14]

Parliamentary government is sometimes conceived exclusively in terms of a liberal model which sees deliberation, accountability and the representative character of Parliament as fundamental. On this view Parliament consisted

[9] William Paley, *The Principles of Moral and Political Philosophy* (Indianapolis, Liberty Fund, 2002) 332; Sir William Blackstone, *Commentaries on the Laws of England*, 15th edn (London, 1809) vol 1, 50–1; JL de Lolme, *The Constitution of England* (London, 1826) 38, 51, 57, 116; Homersham Cox, *The British Commonwealth* (London, Longman, 1854) 58–66; Lord Henry Brougham, *The British Constitution: Its History, Structure and Working*, 2nd edn (London, Griffin, Bohn and Co, 1861) xix, 4.

[10] AH Dodd, *The Growth of Responsible Government: From James the First to Victoria* (London, Routledge & Kegan Paul, 1956) 120; J Steven Watson, *The Reign of George III, 1760–1815* (Oxford, Clarendon Press, 1960) 79; *The Annual Register for the Year 1763* (London, 1764) vol 6, 41; *The Annual Register for the Year 1827* (London, 1828) 100–2.

[11] Alpheus Todd, *On Parliamentary Government in England: Its Origin, Development, and Practical Operation*, 2nd edn (London, Longmans, Green and Co, 1887) vol 1, 143–7, 200–3; John M Ward, 'The Responsible Government Question in Victoria, South Australia and Tasmania, 1851–1856' (1978) 63 *Journal of the Royal Australian Historical Society* 221. Note also EN Williams, *The Eighteenth Century Constitution, 1688–1815. Documents and Commentary* (Cambridge, Cambridge University Press, 1960) 60; DB Horn and Mary Ransome (eds), *English Historical Documents, 1714–1783* (London, Eyre & Spottiswoode, 1957) 122.

[12] *The Parliamentary History of England* (London, 1819) vol 35, 1115; 'Sir Robert Peel's Address to the Electors of the Borough of Tamworth' (1835) 53 *Quarterly Review* 261, 266.

[13] John Manning Ward, *Colonial Self-Government: The British Experience, 1759–1856* (London, Macmillan, 1976) ch 6.

[14] Vernon Bogdanor, *The Monarchy and the Constitution* (Oxford, Clarendon Press, 1995) 14; Ward, *Colonial Self-Government* (n 13) 201.

largely of independent MPs whose support was necessary to stay in office; government was not simply a prize awarded to the party which won the most seats in a general election, but was formed through building coalitions of like-minded MPs. Parliament acted as a watch dog, scrutinising the activities of the ministry and voting it out of office where it proved defective in administration. This view considers independence crucial to enable MPs and Parliament as a whole to exercise these functions and essential for responsible government. Parties are seen as distorting this independence, and hindering the proper working of responsible government.[15] In an influential essay Richard Crossman argued that in Bagehot's day the individual MP was able to defy the party whip and had freedom to speak and vote as he chose. It was this independence that enabled the House of Commons to function as a genuine check on the executive; with the loss of this independence parliamentary control became a fiction.[16]

While this picture is not wholly wrong, it anachronistically interprets nineteenth century history through the lens of later distrust of parties. It is certainly true that the independence of the MP was an important concept in nineteenth century constitutional thought: the ideal was that each MP would be substantially independent, that is, not enslaved to any influence which governed his vote.[17] MPs should be free to act in accordance with their own convictions and act in the national interest, determined after due deliberation in Parliament, rather than simply following the demands of party or any 'pernicious local influence' which may distort their proper judgment.[18] This presupposed that the individual MP could and should genuinely exercise his own judgment in parliamentary deliberations, and had the meaningful ability to participate in discussions and debates, propose motions and other measures and generally exercise his voice in the Parliament.[19] This concept applied to individual MPs as well as Parliament as a whole: that the House of Commons elected a ministry in which it possessed confidence assumed a genuine freedom of action by the House and a genuine control over the government.[20] The House should not be a 'mechanical majority', dutifully approving every government initiative as by rote, but should independently scrutinise everything put before it.[21]

[15] Examples include Reid and Forrest (n 5) 12; Chalmers and Davis (n 5); Davis (n 5) 50–1; Marsh (n 5). See also AH Birch, *Representative and Responsible Government: An Essay on the British Constitution* (London, Allen & Unwin, 1964) 114.

[16] RHS Crossman, 'Introduction' in Walter Bagehot, *The English Constitution* (Glasgow, Fontana, 1963) 43.

[17] As classically expressed by Edmund Burke, 'Speech to the Electors of Bristol' in *The Works of Edmund Burke* (Boston, Little & Brown, 1839) vol 2, 12.

[18] Grey (n 1) 70–1, 121.

[19] Todd, *On Parliamentary Government in England* (n 11) vol 2, 370, 375, 380; Cox, *The British Commonwealth* (n 9) 114, 134; Grey (n 1) 77, 119–21.

[20] Hearn (n 6) 555; Walter Bagehot, *The English Constitution* (London, Chapman and Hall, 1867) 176.

[21] Thomas Erskine May, *The Constitutional History of England*, 10th edn (London, Longmans, Green, 1891) vol 2, 95.

In the early nineteenth century the House of Commons was composed largely of independent gentry who were grouped in different patterns of interest.[22] Although the main features of party management existed,[23] there was little party cohesion and governments could not be sure they would get their way in the Commons.[24] However, this was to change markedly. One highly significant change during the mid-nineteenth century was that the cabinet came to dominate the proceedings of Parliament. While it has been argued that party organisation and discipline effected this dominance,[25] in fact cabinet dominance pre-dated the development of party discipline and was a contributing factor in its development. Commencing in the early 1800s a series of reforms to parliamentary procedure were made which significantly increased government control of business and which reduced the ability of private members to debate matters.[26] As a result, by the 1850s the individual MP was 'a relatively unimportant cog in the legislative machinery'.[27] The decline in stature of the individual MP and increase in power of the cabinet went hand in hand with, and indeed may have prompted, an increasingly party-oriented electorate, which came to vote for MPs on the basis of their party affiliation.

Angus Hawkins has argued that parliamentary government relied on the existence of political parties which were sufficiently cohesive to withstand the royal prerogative, yet sufficiently fluid to ensure that the Commons, and not the electorate, was sovereign, by leaving open the possibility of a ministerial defeat without a dissolution.[28] By the mid-nineteenth century, British politics was carried on by means of a two-party system, characterised by relatively high levels of party cohesion, and indeed this was considered essential for the functioning of parliamentary government. Even during the 'golden age' of English parliamentary government, therefore, few MPs were not aligned with one of the major parties, and the individual MP had much diminished in importance.

[22] Valerie Cromwell, 'The Losing of the Initiative by the House of Commons, 1780–1914' (1968) 18 *Transactions of the Royal Historical Society* 1, 10. 'Independent' here is intended to mean 'not dependent', such as men of learning or wealth.

[23] A Aspinall, 'English Party Organization in the Early Nineteenth Century' (1926) 41 *English Historical Review* 389.

[24] Asa Briggs, *The Age of Improvement, 1783–1867* (London, Longman, 1959) 187.

[25] A well-known early articulation of this view was by M Ostrogorski, *Democracy and the Organization of Political Parties* (London, Macmillan, 1902).

[26] Peter Fraser, 'The Growth of Ministerial Control in the Nineteenth-Century House of Commons' (1960) 76 *English Historical Review* 444; Josef Redlich, *The Procedure of the House of Commons: A Study of its History and Present Form* (London, 1908) vol 1, xxxii–iii, 206; Sidney Low, *The Governance of England* (London, Fisher Unwin, 1914) 68–9, 78, 85–7; H J Hanham, *The Nineteenth-Century Constitution 1815–1914: Documents and Commentary* (London, Cambridge University Press, 1969) 148–9; see also Todd, *On Parliamentary Government in England* (n 11) vol 2, 376.

[27] Gary W Cox, *The Efficient Secret: The Cabinet and the Development of Political Parties in Victorian England* (Cambridge, Cambridge University Press, 1987) 134. See also JJ Park, *The Dogmas of the Constitution: Four Lectures* (London, B Fellowes, 1832) 39–40.

[28] Angus Hawkins, *British Party Politics, 1852–1886* (New York, St Martin's Press, 1998) 2, 11.

By the mid-nineteenth century '[t]he true 'non-party' man is hard to find'.[29] There were few floating parliamentary voters, most MPs obeyed a party whip and even MPs who claimed to be independent often gave consistent support to one party.[30] Party discipline and cohesion fluctuated, being strong in certain periods and weaker in others, but increased markedly from the 1850s to the 1870s. Loyal partisan voting became the predominant pattern of mid-Victorian politics, and from the 1870s there were high levels of party cohesion.[31] As put by Cox, voting for the party rather than the man appears to have become the 'dominant feature of English electoral behaviour from 1868 onwards'.[32] Party became the essential basis of government.[33]

Historical analysis also shows that scrutiny of the government by independent MPs was largely mythical. Backbenchers who defied the party whip were typically from the extreme wings of a party rebelling against the moderate centre rather than defending the legislature against the tyranny of the executive. That is, backbench independence contributed little to parliamentary control of the executive.[34] Accordingly, the liberal account does not accurately depict either the reality of the working of nineteenth-century parliamentary government or the conception of responsible government held by constitutional writers.

The period from around 1841 to 1886 is sometimes considered to be a 'golden age' or 'classical' period of parliamentary government,[35] being replaced by a system of party government from around the 1880s.[36] Thus, although responsible government is typically considered to be one of the defining features of the British Constitution, it had a relatively short heyday, being a

[29] DED Beales, 'Parliamentary Parties and the 'Independent' Member, 1810–1860' in Robert Robson (ed), *Ideas and Institutions of Victorian Britain: Essays in Honour of George Kitson Clark* (London, Bell, 1967) 13.

[30] ibid 10, 18.

[31] Cox, *The Efficient Secret* (n 27); John D Fair, 'Party Voting Behaviour in the British House of Commons 1886–1918' (1986) 5 *Parliamentary History* 65.

[32] Cox, *The Efficient Secret* (n 27) chs 9, 10. Quote from p 136. See also Gary W Cox, 'The Development of a Party-Orientated Electorate in England, 1832–1918' (1986) 16 *British Journal of Political Science* 187.

[33] TA Jenkins, *Parliament, Party, and Politics in Victorian Britain* (Manchester, Manchester University Press, 1996) 8–9.

[34] Hugh Berrington, 'Partisanship and Dissidence in the Nineteenth-Century House of Commons' (1968) 21 *Parliamentary Affairs* 338; Frederic Harrison, 'The Crisis of Parliamentary Government' (1882) 11 *Nineteenth Century* 9, 11.

[35] Eg, Taylor (n 7) xix; William Edward Hartpole Lecky, *Democracy and Liberty*, new edn (New York, Longmans, Green and Co, 1903) vol 1, 21; David Beetham and Stuart Weir, *Political Power and Democratic Control in Britain: The Democratic Audit of the United Kingdom* (London, Routledge, 1999) 30; Sir Alastair Goodlad, 'Political Structure and Constitutional Reform in the United Kingdom' (Papers on Parliament No 38, Parliament of Australia, 2001); Malcolm Aldons, 'The 'Elective Dictatorship' – Fact or Fiction?' (2002) 17 *Australasian Political Review* 69; Phil Larkin, 'Ministerial Accountability to Parliament' in Keith Dowding and Chris Lewis (eds), *Ministerial Careers and Accountability in the Australian Commonwealth Government* (Acton, ANU E-Press, 2012).

[36] Hawkins, *British Party Politics* (n 28).

particular stage in the development of the British Constitution which prevailed during the mid to late nineteenth century.

III. THE NINETEENTH CENTURY THEORY OF RESPONSIBLE GOVERNMENT

The previous section noted that the heyday of responsible government was during the period from approximately 1841 to 1886. During that time authors such as Alpheus Todd,[37] William Hearn,[38] Earl Grey[39] and Walter Bagehot[40] wrote treatises attempting to explain the principles of the British Constitution, and these works were influential in Britain and the Australian colonies around the time of Federation.[41] This section examines the doctrine of responsible government as expounded by those writers.

The cardinal feature of the British Constitution was that it was not written, and had not been created, but had developed over a long period of evolution: it 'was never made, in the sense in which the Constitutions of many other countries have been made'.[42] As such, there was no one authoritative source from which to derive the principles of the Constitution, but its principles had 'to be collected from statutes, from legal decisions, from observation of the course and conduct of the business of politics';[43] as put by one historian, the Constitution 'was not a set of documents but a reading of history'.[44] The principles of the Constitution had to be discerned by means of a painstaking analysis of history and precedent and it was impossible to understand the British Constitution without considering the history of how it developed into its present form.[45]

[37] Todd, *On Parliamentary Government in England* (n 11).

[38] Hearn (n 6). Hearn was a widely respected scholar: see, eg, AV Dicey, *Introduction to the Study of the Law of the Constitution*, 6th edn (London, MacMillan, 1902) 19–20.

[39] Grey (n 1).

[40] Bagehot (n 20). This work was considered by contemporaries to be the first to have accurately explained the working of parliamentary government: eg, Dicey (n 38) 19; Edward Jenks, *The Government of Victoria (Australia)* (London, Macmillan, 1891) 206.

[41] Todd, for instance, was referred to by Glynn as the 'leading authority on parliamentary government in the colonies': *Convention Debates*, Adelaide (1897) 915, and was frequently cited by contemporaries: eg, *South Australian Register*, 8 February 1884, 5; *West Australian*, 24 July 1894, 6; *Sydney Morning Herald*, 22 July 1884, 7; 'Political Prospects', *The Capricornian*, 26 May 1888, 2; *The Mercury*, 17 September 1884, 3; *Evening News*, 6 July 1899, 8.

[42] Edward A Freeman, *The Growth of the English Constitution from the Earliest Times*, 3rd edn (London, Macmillan, 1890) 19–20, 56–8, 90–1, 114–7; Grey (n 1) 8; Hearn (n 6) 1–2; Lord Macaulay, *History of England: To the Death of William III* (London, Heron Books, 1967) vol 1, 20; John Millar, *An Historical View of the English Government, from the Settlement of the Saxons in Britain to the Revolution of 1688* (Indianapolis, Liberty Fund, 2006 [1803]) 11; Edward Fischel, *The English Constitution* (London, Bosworth and Harrison, 1863) 4–5.

[43] William Reynell Anson, *The Law and Custom of the Constitution*, 3rd edn (Oxford, Clarendon Press, 1897) vol 1, 37.

[44] Robert Saunders, 'Parliament and People: The British Constitution in the Long Nineteenth Century' (2008) 6 *Journal of Modern European History* 72.

[45] Anson (n 43) vol 1, 2, 13

English law recognised no clear distinction between laws which were fundamental or constitutional and laws which were not: the Constitution was simply 'the result of the ordinary law of the land'.[46] James Bryce, whose treatise *The American Commonwealth* had a significant influence on the framers,[47] wrote that:

> there is in England no such thing as a constitution apart from the rest of the law: there is merely a mass of law, consisting partly of statutes and partly of decided cases and accepted usages, in conformity with which the government of the country is carried on from day to day, but which is being constantly modified by fresh statutes and cases.[48]

That is, the British Constitution was not a written document but consisted of the mass of statutes, judicial decisions, precedents and conventions relating to the institutions of government.[49] Thus, 'the Constitution' was conceived as broader than legally enforceable rules, and the practices, usages and conventions according to which the government was conducted were considered to be as much a part of the Constitution as law. One implication of this was that change was a key constitutional principle. This stemmed from the evolutionary origin of the Constitution, but also due to its nature, as any modification to the laws or even the customs or political practices which related to the British Government meant a modification to the Constitution itself. The Constitution had seen significant changes over time, which had been brought about 'partly by legislation, but far more by slow and silent alterations of practice and of usage', typically to adapt to the changing needs of society.[50] Those practices and conventions were constantly changing, as the political views and inclinations of the people changed, and so the British Constitution was a constitution in constant flux.[51] It was not simply that the Constitution was subject to change as all Constitutions are, but that change itself was a principle of the Constitution;[52] as put by Australian framer JA Cockburn, the essence of the British Constitution was 'elasticity and development'.[53] Accordingly, the British Constitution did not

[46] Dicey (n 38) 85, 199.

[47] Stephen Gageler, 'James Bryce and the Australian Constitution' (2015) 43 *Federal Law Review* 177, 182; Matthew N C Harvey, 'James Bryce, 'The American Commonwealth', and the Australian Constitution' (2002) 76 *Australian Law Journal* 362; JA La Nauze, *The Making of the Australian Constitution* (Carlton, Melbourne University Press) 18; Harry Evans, 'Bryce's Bible: Why Did it Impress the Australian Founders?' (2001) 8 *New Federalist* 89.

[48] James Bryce, *The American Commonwealth*, 2nd edn (London, Macmillan, 1891) vol 1, 237. See also W Harrison Moore, *The Constitution of the Commonwealth of Australia*, 2nd edn (Melbourne, Charles F Maxwell, 1910) 83.

[49] For a contemporary statement to this effect, see *R (Miller) v Secretary of State for Exiting the European Union* [2018] AC 61, 137 [40].

[50] Grey (n 1) 8.

[51] ES Creasy, *The Rise and Progress of the English Constitution* (London, 1853) 6; Lord Hugh Cecil, *Conservatism* (London, Williams & Norgate,1912) 219–22; Dicey (n 38) 29.

[52] Anson (n 43) vol 1, 36.

[53] John A Cockburn, *Australian Federation* (London, Horace Marshall & Son, 1901) 100.

consist simply of the arid text of a legal document, but was conceived as flexible, organic, 'a living Constitution', a 'Constitution in being'.[54] As a fundamentally unwritten system, the British Constitution closely aligns with political accounts of constitutionalism; indeed, as noted in chapter one, political constitutionalism has its roots in a descriptive account of the British Constitution.

Many writers noted that the changes which had affected the British Constitution occurred within the context of outward continuity. As Freeman put it, the constitutional history of England was 'mainly a record of silent changes in the practical working of institutions whose outward and legal form remained untouched'.[55] Walter Bagehot famously contrasted the 'dignified' and the 'efficient' elements of the English Constitution; outward continuity in the dignified elements such as the monarchy and the House of Lords acted as a disguise which concealed considerable change in the efficient elements such as the cabinet and the House of Commons.[56] Bagehot here was merely echoing the views of earlier writers; in 1832 John Park argued that the outward forms of the Constitution ceased to accurately depict the reality of its functioning, which was carried out by the House of Commons.[57] Thus, many of the most significant changes that had taken place were changes of practice and convention rather than law.

According to Todd, three maxims of the British Constitution provided the foundation for parliamentary government: 'the personal irresponsibility of the king; the responsibility of his ministers for all acts of the Crown; and the inquisitorial power and ultimate control of Parliament'.[58] In like fashion, Bryce argued that the British parliamentary system consisted of four principles. First, the head of the executive is irresponsible; responsibility instead attached to the cabinet, that is, the body of ministers who advised her. Second, the ministry sat in Parliament, being chosen by a majority, and in effect forming a committee of the legislature. Third, the ministry was accountable to the legislature and must resign as soon as it lost its confidence. Finally, there was the principle of cabinet unity, namely that the ministers were jointly and severally liable for their acts.[59] Earl Grey summarised the nineteenth century conception of parliamentary government as follows:

> It is the distinguishing characteristic of Parliamentary Government, that it requires the powers belonging to the Crown to be exercised through Ministers, who are held responsible for the manner in which they are used, who are expected to be members of the two Houses of Parliament, the proceedings of which they must be able generally

[54] Walter Bagehot, *The English Constitution*, 2nd edn (London, Chapman and Hall, 1872) 1; Anson (n 43) vol 2, xvii–xviii; Hearn (n 6) 2.

[55] Freeman, *The Growth of the English Constitution* (n 42) 109, see also 90, 111. Todd made a similar observation: Todd, *On Parliamentary Government in England* (n 11) vol 1, 6.

[56] Bagehot (n 20) 11, 80. Dicey made a similar observation: Dicey (n 38) 405.

[57] Park (n 27) 7–9, 38–9.

[58] Todd, *Parliamentary Government in the British Colonies*, 2nd edn (London, Longmans, Green, 1894) 3; Todd, *On Parliamentary Government in England* (n 11) vol 1, 3.

[59] Bryce (n 48) vol 1, 88–9. See also 86, 215, 271.

> to guide, and who are considered entitled to hold their offices only while they possess the confidence of Parliament, and more especially of the House of Commons.[60]

The legal theory was that the Sovereign was the source of all executive power and that the acts of the government were his or her acts.[61] British law had long held that 'the king can do no wrong', which meant that no wrongdoing could be attributed personally to the monarch. As the Constitution must provide a remedy for any wrongs done by government, this principle required that responsibility for maladministration or illegal conduct be attributed elsewhere, namely the Crown's ministers and advisors.[62] The irresponsibility of the King therefore required that the ministers were responsible for every act which was done in the name of the Crown,[63] but, since the ministry could not be responsible for that which they could not control, they needed to be able to determine the policy of the government.[64] Thus, in practice the Crown acted only on the advice of his or her responsible ministers, which meant that government was carried on by the ministry: formerly 'the King or Queen governed through Ministers, now Ministers govern through the instrumentality of the Crown'.[65] In this way the forms of a monarchy were retained while the actual practice of government had been republicanised. The 'dignified' elements of the Constitution served to excite the reverence and allegiance of the population for the institutions of the British Government while enabling the 'efficient' parts to govern with vigour and strength.[66]

Thus, the exercise of the Crown's legal powers was conditioned and controlled by constitutional maxims, requiring the monarch to act through the agency and upon the advice of advisors who were responsible to Parliament.[67] The royal will was not the personal will of the monarch, but rather his or her 'official will, enlightened by the advice, and carried into effect through the agency, of councillors and ministers recognized by the law and personally responsible both for their advice and for their acts'.[68] The ministry was drawn

[60] Grey (n 1) 4. See also Charles Buller, *Responsible Government for Colonies* (London, James Ridgway, 1840) 6, 15–16.

[61] Dudley Julius Medley, *A Student's Manual of English Constitutional History*, 4th edn (London, Blackwell, 1907) 82; Anson (n 43) vol 2, 98.

[62] Blackstone (n 9) vol 1, 245; Joseph Chitty, *A Treatise on the Law of the Prerogatives of the Crown* (London, J Butterworth, 1820) 5; Todd, *Parliamentary Government in the British Colonies* (n 58) 2–3.

[63] Todd, *Parliamentary Government in the British Colonies* (n 58) 11.

[64] Todd, *On Parliamentary Government in England* (n 11) vol 1, 273–4, 384; vol 2, 134.

[65] Anson (n 43) vol 2, 41. See also Edward A Freeman, 'Presidential Government' in *Historical Essays*, first series (London, Macmillan, 1871) vol 1, 383.

[66] Bagehot (n 20) 4–12, 40. See also Angus Hawkins, *Victorian Political Culture: 'Habits of Heart and Mind'* (Oxford, Oxford University Press, 2015) 240.

[67] John Allen, *Inquiry into the Rise and Growth of the Royal Prerogative in England*, new edn (Longman, Brown, Green and Longmans, 1849) 7, 25; Anson (n 43) vol 1, 9, vol 2, 28; Todd, *On Parliamentary Government in England* (n 11) vol 1, 384; Low, *The Governance of England* (n 26) xxiv; Paley (n 9) 337.

[68] Hearn (n 6) 18; Todd, *On Parliamentary Government in England* (n 11) vol 1, 270, 305–6.

from Parliament, especially the House of Commons, which supervised the government and held it to account for the discharge of its functions.[69] Given its role in maintaining the government, the House of Commons was the centre of the English constitutional system, the arena in which the contest for power was carried on.[70]

The key feature of the system of responsible government was, in Bagehot's famous words, 'the nearly complete fusion' of the executive and legislative powers in the cabinet.[71] The cabinet was described as the 'buckle' or the 'three-fold hinge' which connected the monarch, the Commons and the Lords.[72] Under responsible government the cabinet was composed of ministers who held seats in Parliament, being drawn particularly from the lower house. The cabinet was at the same time an executive and a legislative body and came to dominate Parliament's legislative agenda, such that it was nearly impossible for legislation to be passed without its support, thus uniting the executive and legislative branches.

Underlying the doctrine of responsible government was an ethic of accountability, namely the fixing of praise or blame on the right shoulders. Indeed, responsibility was used in contemporary writings as a synonym for accountability.[73] The cabinet system concentrated responsibility for legislation and administration in the government, and so if a bad statute was passed or a good Bill rejected, the responsibility was clear, falling on the ministry in power, the party supporting the ministry and the members who voted. This accountability was provided primarily through Parliament. One of the prime functions of Parliament was to exercise scrutiny over the executive's activities; Parliament could call upon ministers to explain their conduct, censure them and also impose the ultimate sanction of withdrawing confidence, forcing the government out of office.[74] Making the ministry responsible to Parliament for the activities of government was therefore a crucial part of responsible government.[75] Accountability to the electorate and the nation as a whole was also provided through public opinion and elections.

These 'liberal' elements of parliamentary government sat uneasily with a strongly executive conception of cabinet. Although today government dominance of Parliament is sometimes bemoaned,[76] contemporary writers

[69] Grey (n 1) 22–4; Anson (n 43) vol 2, 211.

[70] Grey (n 1) 27; Bagehot (n 20) 12, 14, 24, 28, 42, 44, 164.

[71] Bagehot (n 20) 12; Grey (n 1) 4–5.

[72] Bagehot (n 20) 15; WE Gladstone, 'Kin Beyond Sea' (1878) 127 *North American Review* 179, 194; Todd, *Parliamentary Government in the British Colonies* (n 58) 19.

[73] Eg, Bryce (n 48) vol 1, 112, 147, 162, 176, 287.

[74] Bagehot (n 20) 218; Grey (n 1) 22–3. Note also John Stuart Mill, 'Representative Government' in *Utilitarianism, Liberty, and Representative Government* (London, John M Dent & Sons, 1910) 239.

[75] Anson (n 43) vol 2, 44–5, 91.

[76] Eg, Neal Blewett, 'Parliamentary Reform: Challenges for the House of Representatives (1993) 65 *Australian Quarterly* 1; Geoffrey Brennan, 'Australian Parliamentary Democracy: One Cheer for the Status Quo' (Papers on Parliament No 22, Parliament of Australia, 1994).

considered it necessary for the House of Commons to be subject to firm leadership. British parliamentary government was, after all, government by a public meeting[77] – a meeting at which every MP had the right to be heard, move motions and participate in debate. Bagehot wrote that '[c]aprice is the characteristic vice of miscellaneous assemblies',[78] and so, in order to prevent the proceedings of the House from descending into a disorderly rabble, it was argued that the House needed strong leadership.[79] Contemporaries argued that it was the role of the ministry, which represented the authority of the Crown, to direct the proceedings of Parliament and guide its deliberations.[80] Cabinet dominance allowed strong and unified action and avoided conflict between the executive and legislative branches,[81] which went hand in hand with a concern for stability.[82] Contemporary writers constantly emphasised the need for strong, stable government,[83] which required governments to possess a sufficient majority to control the legislative agenda of Parliament and pass their measures. Weak governments were generally considered to be poor governments.[84]

Parties were considered essential to maintain this stability. While contemporary writers stressed the importance of independence, noting that without it MPs could not maintain a meaningful scrutiny of the government's actions, many were also very cautious about the supposed virtues of independence.[85] A large number of independent MPs made it difficult to form a stable and reliable ministry and to conduct parliamentary business in an efficient manner.[86] Independent MPs were less likely to be responsible for their behaviour, because although they could propose amendments to legislation, they would not be responsible for implementing those measures.[87] As a result, parties were

[77] Low, *The Governance of England* (n 26) 55; Bagehot (n 20) 172: 'of all odd forms of government, the oddest really is government by a *public meeting*'.

[78] Walter Bagehot, *The English Constitution and Other Political Essays*, rev edn (New York, D Appleton, 1902) 49.

[79] Hearn (n 6) 549; Low, *The Governance of England* (n 26) 67.

[80] Todd, *On Parliamentary Government in England* (n 11) vol 2, 132–3, 288–9, 394.

[81] Bagehot (n 20) 18–20; Grey (n 1) 17–22; Hearn (n 6) 117–8.

[82] The stability of Victorian British politics has been noted by historians: eg, HCG Matthew, 'Disraeli, Gladstone, and the Politics of Mid-Victorian Budgets' (1979) 22 *Historical Journal* 615, 642.

[83] Eg, Paley (n 9) 349; May (n 21) vol 2, 97–8; Macaulay (n 42) vol 4, 45.

[84] Todd, *On Parliamentary Government in England* (n 11) vol 1, 32, vol 2, 414; Grey (n 1) 99, 136–8, 220–30.

[85] Todd, *On Parliamentary Government in England* (n 11) vol 2, 394, 413–4; Edward Hughes, 'Sir Erskine May's Views on Parliamentary Procedure in 1882' (1956) 34 *Public Administration* 419, 420–424; Hanham (n 26) 138, 162; Frederic Harrison, 'The Deadlock in the House of Commons' (1881) 10 *Nineteenth Century* 317, 336; 'Extracts from the Diary of an MP' (1833) 3 *Tait's Edinburgh Magazine* 409, 413–4.

[86] Todd, *On Parliamentary Government in England* (n 11) vol 1, 132, vol 2, 413–4; Grey (n 1) 100; Mill (n 74) 235. See also May (n 21) vol 2, 129, 202; *Federalist No 58* in Alexander Hamilton, James Madison and John Jay, *The Federalist Papers*, Clinton Rossiter (ed) (New York, Mentor, 1961); Jeremy Waldron, 'The Dignity of Legislation' (1995) 54 *Maryland Law Review* 633, 637–41.

[87] Bagehot (n 54) 38. There is an interesting description of the irresponsibility of opposition in Anthony Trollope, *Barchester Towers* (London, Dent, 1966 [1857]) 173.

considered necessary to provide the stability and efficiency which were essential for the proper functioning of Parliament.[88]

Accordingly, parliamentary government was widely considered by contemporaries to be government by party, and political parties formed one of the constitutional assumptions underlying responsible government in the mid Victorian period.[89] George Cornewall Lewis said that a parliamentary system 'can only be conducted by the combined operation of parties'.[90] Bagehot considered that party was inherent in the nature of responsible government: '[t]he House of Commons lives in a state of perpetual potential choice; at any moment it can choose a ruler and dismiss a ruler. And therefore party is inherent in it, is bone of its bone, and breath of its breath'.[91] Earl Grey wrote that parliamentary government was 'essentially a government by party', motivated by the selfish interests of party adherents[92] and considered that a certain measure of party discipline was necessary to maintain the strength of the ministry, which was necessary for stable government.[93] Bryce considered that parties were necessary both for stable leadership and in order to achieve legislative progress. Citing the US experience, he noted that members' independent judgment led to weakness and inconsistency in legislation and that without some sort of organisation and the guarantee of party support, an assembly would be a mob and there was little hope of passing measures.[94] Bryce described whips as a settled part of the British constitutional machinery and essential to the discipline of English parliamentary armies.[95] It was also considered that the existence of three or more parties had a destabilising effect on Parliament and placed the major parties at their mercy.[96] Todd wrote that coalitions were 'contrary to the very foundation principle of parliamentary government'.[97] Bryce considered that the British Constitution 'is a system whose successful working presupposes the existence of two great parties and no more'.[98]

While conceding their necessity, many writers were ambivalent towards parties.[99] Bryce argued that, while party government was necessary, it was an unfortunate necessity, distorting loyalties and often providing a cloak for

[88] Grey (n 1) 43; Lord Robert Cecil, 'Parliamentary Opposition' (1855) 101 *Edinburgh Review* 1, 3; TA Jenkins, 'The Whips in the Early-Victorian House of Commons' (2000) 19 *Parliamentary History* 259.

[89] Hawkins, *British Party Politics* (n 28) 2.

[90] United Kingdom, *Parliamentary Debates*, House of Commons, 10 June 1859, vol 154, col 356.

[91] Bagehot (n 20) 176.

[92] Grey (n 1) 43, 49.

[93] ibid 112, 230–40.

[94] Bryce (n 48) vol 1, 203, 148.

[95] ibid vol 1, 199–200.

[96] 'Party Government' (1886) 125 *Westminster Review* 429, 446–7; Bagehot (n 20) 95–6.

[97] Todd, *On Parliamentary Government in England* (n 11) vol 2, 160. For a contemporary view, see Vernon Bogdanor, *The Coalition and the Constitution* (Oxford, Hart, 2011).

[98] Bryce (n 48) vol 1, 281.

[99] Eg, Randall E McGowen and Walter L Arnstein, 'The Mid-Victorians and the Two-Party System' (1979) 11 *Albion* 242, 252.

'falsehood and knavery'; thus, 'whatever tends to diminish its mischievous influence upon the machinery of administration' was to be desired.[100] Todd noted that under a party system, the judgment of ministers was 'insensibly warped by party considerations'.[101] Edmund Burke famously defined a party as 'a body of men united for promoting by their joint endeavours the national interest upon some particular principle in which they are all agreed', which remained the litmus test for the legitimacy of parties for many years.[102] According to this conception, parties formed upon the basis of a common set of principles were beneficial to the life of the nation, while parties formed on any other basis were illegitimate: the ideal was of parties of like-minded MPs joined by 'voluntary subordination rather than unconditional obedience'.[103] By the late nineteenth century this increasingly failed to reflect the reality.[104]

It is well known that unwritten conventions and understandings were (and are) considered essential to the functioning of responsible government.[105] One key distinguishing feature of responsible government was the conventions and usages that conditioned the exercise of the legal powers of the Crown.[106] There were two important conventions attached to responsible government, namely the principles of individual and collective responsibility. These conventions have been discussed in many places and are well known, and so will not be considered in detail here.[107] Under the principle of individual responsibility, each minister was responsible for the conduct of his department, was required to answer questions in Parliament concerning the business of the department and had to resign upon any personal misconduct.[108] The principle of collective responsibility meant that the cabinet as a whole was responsible for government policy and each minister was required either to defend the government's policy or resign.[109] Collective responsibility was essential as the cabinet increased in

[100] Bryce (n 48) vol 1, 70, 118.

[101] Todd, *On Parliamentary Government in England* (n 11) vol 1, 306.

[102] Edmund Burke, 'Thoughts on the Cause of the Present Discontents' in *The Works and Correspondence of the Right Honourable Edmund Burke*, new edn (London, F & J Rivington, 1852) vol 3, 170. Similar definitions were offered by Francis Lieber, *Manual of Political Ethics* (Boston, Little and Brown, 1839) part II, 413; May (n 21) vol 2, 158; 'Party Politics' (1881) 619 *Fraser's Magazine* 132.

[103] Hawkins, *British Party Politics* (n 28) 13–15.

[104] Anson (n 43) vol 1, 139; Bryce (n 48) vol 1, 68, 150.

[105] Bryce (n 48) vol 1, 383.

[106] Allen (n 67) 5, 25; Paley (n 9) 328.

[107] See generally Ivor Jennings, *Cabinet Government*, 3rd edn (London, Cambridge University Press, 1969); Geoffrey Marshall, *Constitutional Conventions: The Rules and Forms of Political Accountability* (Oxford, Clarendon Press, 1984); Ian Killey, *Constitutional Conventions in Australia: An Introduction to the Unwritten Rules of Australia's Constitution* (Melbourne, Australian Scholarly Publishing, 2009).

[108] May (n 21) vol 2, 86; Todd, *On Parliamentary Government in England* (n 11) vol 2, 471–84.

[109] Hearn (n 6) 218.

importance and became an 'effective legislative machine', as it ensured that the cabinet would act in a united fashion.[110] The individual and collective responsibility of ministers required the cabinet to be consistent and united on all policy questions, enabling clear accountability for government policy and action.

The House of Lords occupied an inferior position under responsible government, being part of the 'dignified' rather than the 'efficient' elements of the Constitution. Although its legal powers were identical to those of the House of Commons, in practice the lower house had progressively become more dominant, because it was the more representative chamber.[111] The Commons was the house in which governments were made and unmade, and the censure or approval of the Lords had no impact on whether the government continued to hold office.[112] Accordingly, the function of the House of Lords was to act as a 'revising, regulating and retarding House',[113] but the real centre of gravity was the House of Commons. One of the key prerequisites for this function was the independence of the Lords from the government of the day and the lower house, which enabled them to freely criticise the executive with no expectation of favour or promotion from the government.[114]

Although the House of Commons was far from democratic by today's standards, it was considered that government must be responsive to public opinion.[115] By being required to maintain the confidence of Parliament, the government was placed under the scrutiny of the people's representatives, with the aim of ensuring that governments would not pass laws to which the people were opposed. There was a vigorous culture of public debate that Parliament could not ignore, despite the restricted franchise.[116] Ultimately, public opinion determined in whose hands public power was entrusted.[117] As will be discussed in later chapters, the Australian framers were to amplify this theme and make it central to their views of responsible government.

The restricted franchise was not considered a defect, for it was not thought possible or desirable to have every opinion represented in Parliament; rather, only well-informed opinions had the right to be heard and represented.[118] Bagehot infamously said that '[t]he working classes contribute almost nothing

[110] Gary Cox, 'The Development of Collective Responsibility in the United Kingdom' (1994) 13 *Parliamentary History* 32; Anson (n 43) vol 1, 106–7.

[111] Bagehot (n 20) 127, 328; Anson (n 43) vol 1, 335; Todd, *On Parliamentary Government in England* (n 11) vol 1, 8, 73, 131–2; David Lindsay Keir, *The Constitutional History of Modern Britain Since 1485*, 7th edn (Black, 1964) 477.

[112] Todd, *On Parliamentary Government in England* (n 11) vol 1, 37–40.

[113] Bagehot (n 20) 142.

[114] ibid 143, 159.

[115] Dicey (n 38) 374–9.

[116] Saunders (n 44).

[117] Grey (n 1) 5, 27.

[118] ibid 211–2; Todd, *On Parliamentary Government in England* (n 11) vol 2, 485: 'the verdict of the House of Commons itself derives its strength and efficacy from its being a true reflex of the intelligent will of the whole community'.

to our corporate public opinion' and considered that the masses were not fit for an elective government.[119] Many writers considered that the working of responsible government depended on a representative system that was not fully representative.[120]

Despite this, popular sovereignty was a key element of the nineteenth century understanding of responsible government.[121] Alpheus Todd wrote that, in a parliamentary government, 'rule and authority must receive the sanction of popular consent, though it does not necessarily emanate from the will of the people'.[122] Dicey was the clearest exponent of this. As is well known, Dicey considered that the supremacy of Parliament was 'the dominant characteristic of our political institutions', under which Parliament has 'the right to make or unmake any law whatever; and, further, that no person or body is recognised by the law of England as having a right to override or set aside the legislation of Parliament'.[123] While he was a strong proponent of the sovereignty of Parliament, Dicey also affirmed a concept of popular sovereignty. Dicey reconciled the two concepts by distinguishing between legal and political concepts of sovereignty, arguing that 'the essence of representative government is, that the legislature should represent or give effect to the will of the political sovereign'.[124] The will of the electorate was 'sure ultimately to prevail on all subjects to be determined by the British government', which meant that the electorate in Great Britain held political sovereignty.[125] Although the focus of Dicey's treatise was the law of the Constitution, the political conception of sovereignty was 'fully as important as the legal sense or more so'.[126] The conventions of the Constitution were 'intended to produce harmony between the legal and the political sovereign power'.[127]

IV. THE BRITISH CONSTITUTION UNDER SCRUTINY

The British Constitution had many admirers. Earl Grey asserted that 'Great Britain stands distinguished among the nations of the earth for the prosperity it has enjoyed, and for the social progress it has made during the time it

[119] Bagehot (n 20) 80, 203.
[120] George Harris, *The True Theory of Representation in a State* (London, Longman, Brown, Green, Longman and Roberts, 1857); Grey (n 1) 66–8, 78; Todd, *On Parliamentary Government in England* (n 11) vol 1, 19. See also Rudolph Gneist, *The History of the English Constitution* (London, W Clowes, 1891) 438; Paley (n 9) 340, 349; Bagehot (n 20) 182–4, 191–2, 276.
[121] Benjamin B Saunders and Simon Kennedy, 'Popular Sovereignty, 'the People', and the Australian Constitution: A Historical Reassessment' (2019) 30 *Public Law Review* 36.
[122] Todd, *On Parliamentary Government in England* (n 11) vol 1, 2.
[123] Dicey (n 38) 37–38.
[124] ibid 373.
[125] ibid 70.
[126] ibid 71.
[127] ibid 382.

has been under a Parliamentary Government'.[128] Hearn considered that 'while the mechanical contrivances of [European and American] political inventors have crumbled away in the hands of the projectors [sic], the goodly tree of British freedom … still increases its stately bulk, and still extends its unequalled development'.[129]

But such praise was rarely unqualified. Grey himself acknowledged that parliamentary government derived 'its whole force and power of action from the exercise of an influence which is at least very much akin to corruption'.[130] From the mid-nineteenth century, and particularly in the 1880s and 1890s, a growing number of voices expressed concerns with the working of parliamentary government. Many believed that parliamentary government was 'on its trial'; some considered that party government was 'remarkable only for its inconveniences'.[131] Writers such as Sidney Low argued that the standard accounts of the working of the Constitution no longer accurately described the British Constitution by the 1890s.[132]

The distinctive feature of parliamentary government was that the ministry of the day held office by maintaining the confidence of the lower house of Parliament. This feature, which required leaders to cultivate parliamentary majorities, underlay nearly all of the concerns with cabinet government.[133] It distorted the incentives of MPs, who could not regard measures dispassionately but were constantly forced to consider the impact on their party.[134] The energy of parliamentarians was devoted to their maintenance in office and the service of their party rather than the state.[135] Members of Parliament had a constant inducement to promote themselves in order to increase their reputation and chances of obtaining office, irrespective of whether their actions were in the national interest.

Despite this underlying agreement as to the cause, the criticisms levelled at cabinet government were not always consistent. Some considered that parliamentary government led to excessive weakness. In 1893 Frederick Fisher argued that 'to make the executive authority constantly dependent upon the temper of a popular assembly' was to invite 'vacillation and weakness'.[136] James Fitzjames

[128] Grey (n 1) 11–12.

[129] Hearn (n 6) 2.

[130] Grey (n 1) 39, 41.

[131] 'The Crisis of Parliamentary Government' (1882) 53 *Saturday Review* 4; 'Party Government' (1886) 125 *Westminster Review* 429, 433.

[132] Sidney Low, 'If the House of Commons Were Abolished?' (1894) 36 *Nineteenth Century* 846; Sidney Low, 'The Decline of the House of Commons' (1895) 37 *Nineteenth Century* 567. Bagehot acknowledged in the 1872 revised edition of his work that significant changes had taken place since the first edition: Bagehot (n 54) 1–45.

[133] See, eg, 'Party Government' (1886) 125 *Westminster Review* 429, 447–8.

[134] David Syme, *Representative Government in England: Its Faults and Failures* (London, K Paul, Trench & Co, 1881) 62.

[135] 'Party Government' (1886) 125 *Westminster Review* 429, 435, 438.

[136] Frederick V Fisher, 'Party Government' (1893) 140 *Westminster Review* 425, 426.

Stephen argued that parliamentary government led to executive weakness and made any permanence or continuity in the management of public affairs impossible, because at any moment the government could be turned out and its policies reversed.[137] The Australian colonies had seen ample evidence of this, and British observers were critical of the state of responsible government in the colonies.[138] The system of 'government by combat' also tended to weaken the institutions of government, for it had the effect that half the ablest men in the country spent their time fighting with the other half.[139] In a parliamentary assembly, 'the character and conduct of the members of the Government, [was] habitually and professionally judged by their declared personal rivals'.[140]

By the late nineteenth century, observers began to argue that MPs no longer had any meaningful independence, that the House of Commons had diminished in importance, and that much of its power was in practice wielded by the cabinet.[141] A series of procedural reforms in the 1880s gave increased power to the government in Parliament and curtailed the ability of the MP to introduce Bills, propose resolutions and even speak.[142] The House of Commons had ceased to be a meaningful law-making body but merely a forum for discussing and implementing the legislative projects of ministers.[143] Only the inner ring of the cabinet had any meaningful power to shape legislation, argued Low:

> nearly one-half of the members at the House are not legislators at all, or only legislators on sufferance and on matters of no moment. They can neither make laws nor prevent laws being made. They can, it is true, talk about them while they are in the process of making; but so can anybody else.[144]

Non-parliamentary platforms were probably just as effective, if not more so, in influencing opinion than a seat in Parliament. The House of Commons had also ceased to play any meaningful role in the task that was traditionally considered to be its most important task, that of selecting the ministry.[145] The choice of the ministry was made by the Prime Minister acting in consultation with his party advisers outside of Parliament; the House merely acquiesced in the choice.[146]

[137] James Fitzjames Stephen, 'Parliamentary Government' (Pt 1) (1873) 23 *Contemporary Review* 1, 7–9, 14; 'Party Government' (1886) 125 *Westminster Review* 429, 441, 444.

[138] Eg, Grey (n 1) ch IX.

[139] Stephen, 'Parliamentary Government' (n 137) 6; 'Party Government' (1886) 125 *Westminster Review* 429, 431, 437.

[140] Cecil, 'Parliamentary Opposition' (n 88) 4.

[141] Anson (n 43) vol II, xxiii–xxix, 134–5; Low, *The Governance of England* (n 26) xx, 19, 54, 68–9, 73–94; R Wallace, 'Single Chamber 'Democrats'' (1895) 37 *Nineteenth Century* 177, 192–3; Hanham (n 26) 163–4.

[142] Fraser (n 26); Redlich (n 26) vol 1, xxxii–iii, 206; Low, *The Governance of England* (n 26) 68–9, 78, 85–7; Hanham (n 26) 148–9.

[143] Low, 'If the House of Commons Were Abolished?' (n 132) 850, 853; Henry Sumner Maine, *Popular Government: Four Essays*, 3rd edn (London, John Murray, 1886) 237.

[144] Low, 'If the House of Commons Were Abolished?' (n 132) 849.

[145] ibid 857.

[146] ibid 855–860.

In theory, one key function of Parliament was to control the executive; the reality was that the executive controlled the House of Commons.[147] Governments were subject to 'unmeasured criticism' in the House of Commons, but not the 'effectual check of an adverse vote' due to the custom of MPs voting with their party.[148] For Low, the source of these problems was plain:

> it will be seen that the comparative weakness and inutility of the House of Commons is due mainly to the increased power of the Cabinet, and to the position of members of Parliament as delegates directed to vote with the party according to the orders of the Caucus, rather than as representatives able to exercise an independent judgment.[149]

Earlier it was noted that parties were considered essential to parliamentary government, providing stability and responsibility. Parties were also subjected to a great deal of criticism. It was frequently asserted that parties compromised the loyalty of MPs and prevented them from acting in the public interest. Parties brought a new set of 'artificial' moral principles into play, which elevated loyalty to the party as the prime consideration. The system of party encouraged disciplined voting and behaviour, and inevitably fettered the judgment and independence of MPs.[150] In addition to party loyalty, the government also retained the threat of a dissolution, which was a potent weapon to compel obedience.[151] Contemporaries believed that parties dominated politics, bringing obedience and bland conformity.[152] As put by Low:

> They [ie political parties] do not send him [ie the MP] to Parliament to exercise his independence; they would be particularly annoyed and irritated if he did; and they scrutinize his votes with jealous care, in order that they may take him to task speedily, and with no superfluous delicacy or reserve, if he shows any dangerous tendency in that direction.[153]

The exigencies of party warfare made it impossible to consider the merits of a measure apart from its political impact.[154] This had the result that the majority of MPs saw their primary duty as being to vote to support a certain ministry, and only secondarily to consider the merits of a Bill.[155]

[147] Syme (n 134) 78.

[148] Low, 'If the House of Commons Were Abolished?' (n 132) 854–6.

[149] ibid 862.

[150] EDJ Wilson, 'The Caucus and its Consequences' (1878) 4 *Nineteenth Century* 695, 697; Low, 'The Decline of the House of Commons' (n 132) 577; Low, 'If the House of Commons Were Abolished?' (n 132) 852; 'The Decline of Parliamentary Government' (1929) 147 *Saturday Review* 33.

[151] 'Party Government' (1858) 69 *Westminster Review* 402, 414.

[152] Ostrogorski (n 25) vol 1, 591, 603–4; 'Party Government' (1886) 125 *Westminster Review* 429, 435; Leonard Courtney, 'The Decline of Parliament' (1904) 17 *Monthly Review* 13, 18; Low, *The Governance of England* (n 26) 63–4; Hanham (n 26) 167.

[153] Low, 'If the House of Commons Were Abolished?' (n 132) 850; also in Low, *The Governance of England* (n 26) 64.

[154] Fisher (n 136) 431.

[155] Low, 'The Decline of the House of Commons' (n 132) 571; 'Party Government' (1858) 69 *Westminster Review* 402, 409.

There were also critiques of the legitimacy of the major British parties. Parties formed on the basis of a political principle were considered legitimate;[156] however, contemporaries argued that there were no longer any real differences of principle between the two major parties in existence in the late nineteenth century.[157] The party system artificially assigned the loyalties of the nation and the MPs to one or the other party: '[w]e must be either hot or cold; Liberal or Conservative; advocates of change or advocates of resistance to change'.[158] However, many important public questions had nothing to do with the distinction – many key questions were not party questions at all.[159] This being the case, it was argued, parties simply existed to maintain MPs in power.[160]

Perhaps the most serious critique of the cabinet system was that it enabled the government to avoid genuine responsibility and scrutiny.[161] When a minister was in danger of censure for the mismanagement of his department, his colleagues were bound to support that minister to the last, so that the cabinet either stood or fell as a whole. This prevented any real responsibility.[162] The stronger a ministry, the less it was accountable; and where a ministry had a majority in both Houses it could do pretty much as it pleased between general elections. Even where the government was turned out of office, the minister would complacently cross the House 'with the full assurance of returning to his old position with the next oscillation of the party see-saw'.[163] The cabinet system thus actively militated against parliamentary control of the executive.[164]

Leading constitutional writers of the late nineteenth century placed important emphasis on parliamentary control,[165] and as explored in later chapters, the concept of parliamentary control of the executive has played a significant role in Australian constitutional jurisprudence. For instance, in the High Court decision *Williams v Commonwealth (No 1)* the High Court was concerned to ensure that the exercise of executive power did not 'undermine the basal assumption of legislative predominance inherited from the United Kingdom'.[166] However, even during the 'golden age of British parliamentary government' there was significant doubt as to whether Parliament actually controlled the executive.

[156] 'Party Government' (1858) 69 *Westminster Review* 402, 412.

[157] ibid; 'The Faction-Fights' (1859) 1 *Bentley's Quarterly Review* 343, 344; K Wilkinson, 'A Plague On Both Your Parties!' (1895) 57 *Fortnightly Review* 757.

[158] 'Party Politics' (1874) 10 *Fraser's Magazine* 1, 3.

[159] Stephen, 'Parliamentary Government' (n 137) 6, 18; 'Party Government' (1886) 125 *Westminster Review* 429, 449.

[160] 'Party Government' (1886) 125 *Westminster Review* 429, 434.

[161] 'Party Government' (1858) 69 *Westminster Review* 402, 410.

[162] 'Responsible Government' (1856) 2 *Saturday Review* 121, 122.

[163] Sidney Low, 'Current Politics' (1901) 49 *Nineteenth Century* 147.

[164] Harrison, 'The Deadlock in the House of Commons' (n 85) 338.

[165] Eg, Dicey (n 38) 310–13.

[166] *Williams v Commonwealth* (2012) 248 CLR 156, 232 [136] (Gummow and Bell JJ). See also 205 [60] (French CJ), 351–2 [516], 358 [544] (Crennan J), 370 [581] (Kiefel J).

V. CONCLUSION

The framers of the Australian Constitution intended to incorporate responsible government modelled on the British system into their Constitution. This chapter has examined key works which were influential for the framers and contributed to their understanding of responsible government. There was no separate Constitution, but merely an aggregation of laws and customs in conformity with which the government was conducted. The 'Constitution' was conceived as being broader than law, including not only customs and conventions but also key norms and assumptions regarding the political system. Being unwritten, the British Constitution was an inherently organic and evolutionary system that was constantly being modified. One key picture that emerges from these writers is that the Constitution was subject to considerable flux and change, and features identified by some writers as essential to parliamentary government were not present after 1884.[167] It is therefore difficult to maintain that certain features were or are inherent to responsible government. Another key aspect of the British Constitution was its contestability. Given that the Constitution was not a set of documents but 'a reading of history',[168] that history could be read in conflicting ways. A level of contestability and uncertainty was therefore inherent in the British Constitution.

The unwritten nature of the British Constitution was to present a crucial dilemma for the framers. It was not seriously in doubt that the Australian Constitution should incorporate responsible government, which, following the British writers, they conceived as inherently organic and impossible to codify. How to graft such a system into a written and legally enforceable Constitution was one of the most difficult challenges facing the framers.

Commentators today often lament executive dominance of the legislature, and it has been argued that the disciplined party system represents a departure from the 'true' principles of parliamentary government.[169] However, in the nineteenth century, political parties were considered essential to responsible government: Bryce could write in the 1890s that party government means 'that one set of men, united, or professing to be united, by holding one set of opinions, have obtained control of the whole machinery of government, and are working it in conformity with those opinions'.[170] Critics of party government often pointed to the absence of stable parties as much as their excessive

[167] See, eg, Anson (n 43) vol 2, xxii–xxiii, xxix, 133–5.
[168] Saunders (n 44).
[169] Eg, David Hamer, 'Senate Committees – Keeping Parliament Responsible' (Papers on Parliament No 12, Parliament of Australia, 1991) 41; Thomas Penberthy Fry, *Australian Contributions to the Evolution of Parliamentary Government* (Brisbane, University of Queensland, 1947) 5; Chandran Kukathas, 'Democracy, Parliament and Responsible Government' (Papers on Parliament No 8, Parliamentary Library, Parliament of Australia, 1990).
[170] Bryce (n 48) vol 1, 285.

discipline. One of the key tensions explored in this chapter is that, on the one hand, responsible government implied control over the government by the House of Commons.[171] And yet paradoxically the government was, at the same time, supposed to lead and direct the Commons.

As noted in chapter one, responsible government must be understood both diachronically and synchronically, given that its principles were drawn from the accumulation of many precedents and rules, but also that it fulfilled certain distinct purposes moulded to the circumstances of the times. As examined later in this book, the framers drew heavily on the tradition of thinking about the British Constitution discussed in this chapter, but also adapted it and gave it a distinctly Australian flavour. In particular, the sovereignty of the people was central to the framers' conception of responsible government and the framers held to a much more democratic view of representation than the British writers, envisaging that the people would exercise an active control over the government.

Works such as those examined in this chapter were well known to the Australian colonies, being noted and discussed in periodicals such as the *Review of Reviews*, which digested articles from the leading English reviews,[172] as well as being cited in parliamentary debates,[173] tracts[174] and newspaper articles.[175] They were important sources for the framers in understanding responsible government. The other principal source of ideas and information about responsible government for the framers was the experience of its functioning in the Australian colonies in the latter decades of the nineteenth century. This is examined in the following chapter.

[171] Bagehot (n 20) 164: 'The House only goes where it thinks in the end the nation will follow; but it takes its chance of the nation following or not following; it assumes the initiative, and acts upon its discretion or its caprice'.

[172] Eg, 'The Future of Party Government' (1893) 7 *Review of Reviews* 625, summarising an article from *Macmillan's Magazine*; 'Can the House of Commons be Saved?' (1893) 8 *Review of Reviews* 407.

[173] Eg, Victoria, *Parliamentary Debates*, Legislative Assembly, 6 September 1893, 1462 (Robert Best).

[174] Eg, *The Evils of Party Government: Proposals for the Elective System of Selecting Cabinet Ministers* (Melbourne, David Syme, 1904) 13.

[175] Eg, 'The September Reviews', *South Australian Register*, 8 November 1881, 6; 'The January Magazines', *The Argus*, 4 March 1882, 13; 'If Parliament Disappeared!', *The Australasian*, 19 January 1895, 29; *The South Australian Advertiser*, 31 March 1874, 2.

3

Responsible Government in the Australian Colonies

[R]esponsible government in the Colonies [is] an arrangement whereby the minimum of legislative result is obtained by the maximum expenditure of time, talk, and trouble.[1]

Sydney Morning Herald (1875)

I. INTRODUCTION

CHAPTER TWO EXAMINED how responsible government was understood by the leading British constitutional writers around the time of Federation. Another important source of ideas and information relating to responsible government for the framers was the working of responsible government in the Australian colonies.[2] Being drawn almost exclusively from the ranks of leading colonial politicians, the framers were well versed in colonial politics, and their experiences inevitably shaped their views of responsible government. In order to understand the framers' views regarding responsible government, an understanding of this context is necessary. This chapter examines how contemporaries understood responsible government, and the development of the political systems under responsible government in the colonies up until the time of Federation.

Throughout the nineteenth century, a desire to ensure popular self-government occupied a central place in the colonial conception of responsible government. Responsible government was introduced into the colonies in the 1850s following agitation from the colonies for local self-government and more accountable government. In the latter decades of the century, attention focused on whether the institutions of government gave effect to the will of the people. Underlying both these developments was a belief in self-government by the people of the Australian colonies.

[1] Editorial, *Sydney Morning Herald*, 17 February 1875, 4.

[2] Following contemporary usage, in this book 'colonies' includes the province of South Australia – see, eg, Australasian Federation Enabling Act 1896 (Vic) s 2, definition of 'Colonies'.

The British Constitution was considered the model for responsible government, with important differences reflecting the different circumstances in the colonies. Chapter two noted that a relatively cohesive party system had developed in Britain by around the mid-nineteenth century. Prior to the 1890s there were no formal political parties (with occasional exceptions) and no developed party system in the Australian colonies: that is, the political parties which were considered essential to parliamentary government did not exist. Throughout much of the nineteenth century, responsible government was carried on in most colonies by means of a factional system whereby governments were formed based on coalitions of independent MPs. Party systems under which two disciplined parties competed for office on the basis of declared policy platforms eventually replaced this factional system, but this transition was by no means complete at the time of Federation. During the period in which Federation was debated, therefore, the political systems of the Australian colonies were in the process of undergoing significant change.

In the late nineteenth century, the merits of the Westminster system of cabinet government were debated robustly in the British colonies. Chapter two explored similar critiques within the UK. Many tracts and articles were written exposing the weaknesses of the working of responsible government and urging reform. The Victorian Parliament set up a royal commission in 1893–4 to report on alternative methods of appointing the executive; in South Australia leading politicians proposed to replace responsible government with a system of 'elective ministries'.

The criticisms of cabinet government were not entirely consistent. Some contemporaries criticised the instability of colonial politics, the weakness of governments and their inability to control Parliament. Others were concerned about the excessive strength of the cabinet, which, they thought, dominated the proceedings of Parliament. Underlying the criticisms was a concern that the need for the ministry to maintain parliamentary majorities to retain office distorted the incentives of MPs, who had regard primarily to the political impact of decisions rather than whether they promoted the public good. This threatened to hinder meaningful responsibility to the people and prevent genuine self-government.

Similar criticisms were voiced during the Federation Conventions, drawing on these debates from the pre-Federation era. As will be considered in chapters four and five, a substantial number of framers criticised responsible government and advocated that the relationship between the legislature and the executive should be modelled on the Swiss system of government, where ministers would be individually elected by Parliament for a fixed term, rather than the British system. How the framers responded to these arguments sheds important light on their views about responsible government.

This chapter examines critiques of the cabinet system in the period leading up to Federation, approximately 1870 to 1900, in the Australian colonies. While of course criticisms were routinely levelled at colonial politicians, parties and the political system in speeches, newspaper articles, cartoons and polemics, the working of responsible government was also subjected to more detailed analysis in leading journals, parliamentary inquiries and debates. This chapter focuses on such sources, including widely read political and current affairs journals,[3] tracts, parliamentary inquiries and parliamentary debates,[4] with the intention of building as complete a picture as possible of those criticisms. This chapter gives particular weight to sources that were known to the framers, or which were likely to have had an influence on them.

II. THE INTRODUCTION OF RESPONSIBLE GOVERNMENT IN THE COLONIES AND ITS TRANSFORMATION INTO A PARTY SYSTEM

The first system of government in Australia has been described as autocratic, with the Governors exercising wide and often arbitrary powers, including legislating, often with little restraint from the British Government.[5] Throughout the 1840s and early 1850s, colonists pressed for constitutional reform, desiring greater autonomy from Britain and more accountable government.[6] Lord Durham recommended in 1837 that Britain grant a larger measure of self-government to the Canadian colonists, as a way of satisfying their desire to stay within the British Empire but also exercise a greater degree of independence.[7] Durham's recommendation was eventually accepted by Earl Grey in 1846 and colonies elsewhere began to call for similar concessions, arguing that subjects of the British Empire were entitled to the same political rights and freedoms as those enjoyed in Britain, including representative institutions and English law.[8]

[3] Such as the *Review of Reviews*, in which numerous framers published articles: eg, Alfred Deakin, 'Federal Council of Australasia' (1895) *Review of Reviews* 154; Sir Philip O Fysh, 'Why Tasmania Should Accept the Federal Bill' (1898) 12 *Review of Reviews* 299; Samuel Walker Griffith, 'The Draft Federal Constitution Framed by the Adelaide Convention of 1897: A Criticism' (1897) 11 *Review of Reviews* 56; FW Holder, 'Why South Australia Should Accept the Bill' (1898) 12 *Review of Reviews* 302; John Quick, 'The Progress and Present Conditions of Federation' (1896) 8 *Review of Reviews* 248; John Quick, 'Why Victoria Should Accept the Bill' (1898) 12 *Review of Reviews* 305; BR Wise, 'Why New South Wales Should Answer "Yes"' (1898) 12 *Review of Reviews* 310.

[4] These were considered an authoritative expression of political ideas: 'Party Politics' (1881) 619 *Fraser's Magazine* 132, 134.

[5] ACV Melbourne, *Early Constitutional Development in Australia*, 2nd edn (St Lucia, University of Queensland Press, 1963) 6–36; W Harrison Moore, *The Constitution of the Commonwealth of Australia*, 2nd edn (Melbourne, Charles F Maxwell, 1910) 10.

[6] John M Ward, 'The Responsible Government Question in Victoria, South Australia and Tasmania, 1851–1856' (1978) 63 *Journal of the Royal Australian Historical Society* 221, 223.

[7] *Report on the Affairs of British North America, from the Earl of Durham* (1839); Benjamin T Jones, *Republicanism and Responsible Government: The Shaping of Democracy in Australia and Canada* (Montreal, McGill–Queen's University Press, 2014) 87.

[8] Ann Curthoys and Jessie Mitchell, 'The Advent of Self-Government, 1840s–1890' in Alison Bashford and Stuart Macintyre (eds), *The Cambridge History of Australia* (Cambridge, Cambridge University Press, 2013) 152; Paul A Pickering, '"The Oak of English Liberty': Popular Constitutionalism in New South Wales, 1848–1856' (2001) 3 *Journal of Australian Colonial History* 1; Peter Cochrane, *Colonial Ambition: Foundations of Democratic Australia* (Melbourne, Melbourne University Press, 2006) 7–10, 53; WC Wentworth, *A Statistical, Historical, and Political Description of the Colony of New South Wales* (London, G and WB Whittacker, 1819) 173–4.

Colonists appealed to key tenets of British constitutionalism in support of their demands and typically viewed the British Constitution as the ideal model.[9]

Initially, it was thought that New South Wales did not possess sufficient political maturity to enable responsible government to function properly;[10] as later put by Governor Denison, 'there would be a good deal of trouble in organizing anything like an effective Government, whoever may be at the head, for in these colonies there is but little instinct of party'.[11] The replacement of Earl Grey by Sir John Pakington as Secretary of State for the Colonies in 1852 led to a more sympathetic reception of the colonists' demands: Pakington informed the colony that the British Government was prepared to grant the concessions sought and that they should submit a draft Constitution for consideration.[12] Draft Constitutions were submitted to Britain for approval and, with some modifications, the Constitutions for New South Wales, Victoria, Tasmania and South Australia were enacted and came into operation in 1855 and 1856, thereby conferring responsible government.[13] As Andrew Inglis Clark colourfully expressed it, the colonial constitutions were 'modified copies of that praise-bespattered idol, the British Constitution'.[14]

All of these Constitutions provided for bicameral legislatures.[15] The major point of difference was that in New South Wales, the members of the upper house were to be appointed by the Governor on the advice of the Executive Council, which meant that appointments would be made on the advice of the ministry.[16] By contrast, in Victoria, South Australia and Tasmania, the Legislative Council was elected, upon a high property qualification for electors in Victoria and a low property qualification in South Australia and Tasmania.[17] All the Constitutions provided that appropriation and taxation Bills must

[9] Edward Silvester (ed), *New South Wales Constitution Bill: The Speeches in the Legislative Council of New South Wales, on the Second Reading of the Bill for Framing a New Sonnnstitution for the Colony* (Sydney, 1853) 51–2, 115, 133, 145–7; WJV Windeyer, 'Responsible Government – Highlights, Sidelights and Reflections' (1957) 42 *Journal of the Royal Australian Historical Society* 257, 278–9, 299; Cochrane (n 8) 93.

[10] WG McMinn, *A Constitutional History of Australia* (Melbourne, Oxford University Press, 1979) 41.

[11] Brian Dickey, 'Responsible Government in New South Wales: The Transfer of Power in a Colony of Settlement' (1974) 60 *Journal of the Royal Australian Historical Society* 217, 224.

[12] CH Currey, 'The Centenary of Responsible Government in New South Wales' (1956) 42 *Journal of the Royal Australian Historical Society* 97, 103–4.

[13] ibid 114–5. New South Wales Constitution Act 1855; Victoria Constitution Act 1855; South Australia Constitution Act 1856; Tasmania Constitution Act 1856. Note that the name of Van Diemen's Land was changed to Tasmania in 1855.

[14] Andrew Inglis Clark, 'Our Australian Constitutions' (Pt 1) (1874) 1 *Quadrilateral* 56, 57.

[15] New South Wales Constitution Act 1855, s 1; Victoria Constitution Act 1855, s 1; South Australia Constitution Act 1856, s 1; Tasmania Constitution Act 1856, s 1.

[16] New South Wales Constitution Act 1855, s 2; Peter Loveday, 'The Legislative Council in New South Wales, 1856–1870' (1965) 11 *Historical Studies* 481.

[17] Victoria Constitution Act 1855, ss 2, 5; South Australia Constitution Act 1856, ss 5, 6; Tasmania Constitution Act 1856, ss 2, 6. In Victoria and Tasmania, entitlement to vote could also be obtained through education, certain professional qualifications or holding certain offices.

originate in the Legislative Assembly; the Victorian Act also provided that the Legislative Council might reject but must not alter such Bills.[18] The intention was for the colonial Constitutions to affirm the principles of ministerial responsibility although they contained no specific reference to the concept, and contained no mention of ministers, the cabinet or the cabinet system of government.[19] It was not considered necessary for the Constitution to spell out the details of ministerial responsibility; as put by McHugh J in *Egan v Willis*, the New South Wales Constitution of 1855 assumed the existence of 'a body of constitutional and political practice which would give meaning to its very sparse provisions'.[20] The incorporation of responsible government was thus a matter of convention rather than statutory prescription.

The full acquisition of self-government occurred gradually as the British Government came to interfere less and less in Australian affairs.[21] Thus, notwithstanding that the Victorian Supreme Court held in 1888 that Victoria had not been given a complete grant of self-government upon the introduction of responsible government, one historian considered that by the 1890s the colonies had virtually 'complete legislative independence'.[22]

Between the late 1880s and 1909, significant changes took place in the Australian political system.[23] Before this period, politics was highly personal and individualistic, lacking stable political parties.[24] By 1909 a party system had developed at the Commonwealth level and in most states, which replaced the old mode of politics with a more formalised and impersonal party organisation.[25] Under the party system, political organisations competed for office on the basis of declared policies and platforms, parties controlled the nomination of candidates and could subject them to discipline, and party cohesion

[18] New South Wales Constitution Act 1855, s 1; Victoria Constitution Act 1855, s 56; South Australia Constitution Act 1856, s 1; Tasmania Constitution Act 1856, s 33.

[19] *Egan v Willis* (1998) 195 CLR 424, 473 (McHugh J); Melbourne (n 5) 400; see also Ward (n 6) 223.

[20] *Egan v Willis* (1998) 195 CLR 424, 473 (McHugh J); Melbourne (n 5) 429; Alpheus Todd, *Parliamentary Government in the British Colonies*, 2nd edn (Longmans, Green, 1894) 28; Zelman Cowen, 'A Historical Survey of the Victorian Constitution, 1856 to 1956' (1957) 1 *Melbourne University Law Review* 9, 21.

[21] ID McNaughtan, 'Colonial Liberalism' in Gordon Greenwood (ed), *Australia: A Social and Political History* (Sydney, Angus & Robertson, 1974) 102; KH Bailey, 'Self-Government in Australia, 1860–1900' in Ernest Scott (ed), *Cambridge History of the British Empire* (Cambridge, Cambridge University Press, 1933) vol 7, pt 1, 398, 411; McMinn (n 10) 54, 87–91; Alex C Castles, *An Australian Legal History* (Sydney, Law Book Co, 1982) 401.

[22] *Chung Teong Toy v Musgrove* (1888) 14 VLR 349; McNaughtan (n 21) 132. See also McMinn (n 10) 89–91.

[23] See generally Ian Campbell, 'Groups, Parties and Federation' in Peter Loveday and Ian Campbell, *Groups in Theory and Practice* (Melbourne, Cheshire, 1962).

[24] Paul Finn, 'Myths of Australian Public Administration' in John Power (ed), *Public Administration in Australia: A Watershed* (Sydney, Hale & Iremonger, 1990) 43.

[25] Tod Moore, Sandra Bourke and Graham Maddox, 'Australia and the Emergence of the Modern Two-Party System' (1998) 44 *Australian Journal of Politics and History* 17, 18.

became the dominant characteristic of political behaviour.[26] The period in which Federation was debated was therefore a very significant period of transition in Australian politics.

The process by which the party system developed varied considerably between the colonies, although there were many similarities in the politics of the colonies prior to the Federation period. The central requirement of responsible government – that majorities be formed and maintained to sustain ministries in power – necessitated the development of systems and techniques to create such majorities.[27] While MPs often fell into distinct camps representing a liberal or conservative approach, these labels did not indicate a coherent set of political principles. In all the colonies there was a prevailing belief that MPs ought to maintain their independence and not bind themselves to particular leaders or parties, and leaders were forced to obtain the support of independent MPs to win and hold on to office. Embryonic political organisations emerged at various points to agitate for causes but few survived for any length of time. Given the lack of parties, MPs would often vote unpredictably; responsible government in the colonies was considered to be 'bewilderingly unstable' and contemporaries often lamented the lack of stable party organisations.[28] Earl Grey had caustically written that in the colonies '[c]hanges of administration have followed each other with almost ludicrous rapidity', so that these 'ephemeral' governments had little opportunity of developing and implementing stable policy.[29]

Unexpectedly, there was a long period of stability in the 1890s.[30] The premiers of New South Wales, Victoria, South Australia, Western Australia and Tasmania held office for unprecedentedly long terms in the mid-1890s, which was crucial to the success of the federal movement. It is also likely that this stability contributed to an optimism in the colonies about responsible government and the working of parliamentary institutions.[31]

[26] AW Martin and Robert S Parker, 'Introduction' in P Loveday, AW Martin and Robert S Parker (eds), *The Emergence of the Australian Party System* (Sydney, Hale & Iremonger, 1977) 1–2.

[27] P Loveday and AW Martin, 'Colonial Politics Before 1890' in P Loveday, AW Martin and Robert S Parker (eds), *The Emergence of the Australian Party System* (Sydney, Hale & Iremonger, 1977) 41–2.

[28] Bailey (n 21) 399; W Harrison Moore, 'Political Systems of Australia' in Meredith Atkinson (ed), *Australia: Economic and Political Studies* (Melbourne, Macmillan, 1920) 97–101; William Pember Reeves, *State Experiments in Australia & New Zealand* (London, Grant Richards, 1902) vol 1, 53–4; Loveday and Martin, 'Colonial Politics Before 1890' (n 27) 12–14.

[29] Earl Grey, *Parliamentary Government Considered with Reference to Reform*, 2nd edn (London, John Murray, 1864) 353.

[30] Helen Irving, 'Making the Federal Commonwealth, 1890–1901' in Bashford and Macintyre (eds), *The Cambridge History of Australia* (Cambridge, Cambridge University Press, 2013) vol 1, 255; LF Crisp, *Federation Fathers* (Carlton, Melbourne University Press, 1990) 317–8; John Bannon, *The Crucial Colony: South Australia's Role in Reviving Federation, 1891 to 1897* (Canberra, Federalism Research Centre, 1994) 4–5.

[31] Moore, *The Constitution of the Commonwealth of Australia* (n 5) 610.

In New South Wales, a parliamentary faction system existed until the late 1880s, when it began to be replaced by a party system. Factional politics was highly personal, consisting of small groups of followers around which leaders built larger parliamentary groups;[32] there were no political parties and no clear divisions on policy and so the Parliament did not contain stable groupings of MPs united by political principles.[33] Historians have expressed divergent views on the effectiveness and stability of the faction system in New South Wales. Loveday and Martin argued that the factional system was 'capable of yielding stable government', even if it did not always do so, and that it provided clear evidence that 'responsible government was a viable form of government despite the absence of political parties'.[34] On their account, parties are not an essential element of responsible government.[35] Not all historians have agreed with Loveday and Martin's argument, with many historians arguing that New South Wales's colonial politics was unstable and disorderly.[36] Bede Nairn argued that the pre-1891 parliamentary system was incoherent, undisciplined and inept, and that 'the words 'cohesion' and 'stability' are hardly relevant to the faction system'.[37] Nairn's view was that greater state intervention was required for the pressing problems of the day, such as labour reform legislation which demanded a more disciplined approach to politics, and that independent MPs led parliamentary proceedings to be uncertain and unpredictable.[38]

In Victoria, the early years of responsible government functioned by means of a factional system. There was no developed party system and no widespread acceptance of the view that responsible government required political parties for its smooth operation; factions and personality rather than parties and ideology were the key determinants of political behaviour.[39] Politicians prized

[32] Gregory Melleuish, 'Personal Politics and Being British: Political Rhetoric, Democracy and their Consequences in Colonial New South Wales' (2013) 39 *Australian Journal of Politics and History* 1, 8.

[33] P Loveday and AW Martin, *Parliament Factions and Parties: The First Thirty Years of Responsible Government in New South Wales, 1856–1889* (Melbourne, Melbourne University Press, 1966) ch 2; Editorial, *Sydney Morning Herald*, 7 December 1874, 4; John Hirst, *Freedom on the Fatal Shore: Australia's First Colony* (Melbourne, Black Inc, 2008) 369.

[34] Loveday and Martin, *Parliament Factions and Parties* (n 33) 1, ch 5, 151–2.

[35] However, Loveday and Martin's argument relies on excluding from consideration the 'four non-faction ministries' and 'the five clearly unstable ministries', which together amount to more than one third of the total number of ministries during that period: Loveday and Martin, *Parliament Factions and Parties* (n 33) 169, fns 3 and 4.

[36] Eg, David Clune and Gareth Griffith, *Decision and Deliberation: The Parliament of New South Wales, 1856–2003* (Sydney, Federation Press, 2006) 49–53; Geoffrey Bolton, *Edmund Barton* (St Leonards, Allen & Unwin, 2000) 39, 49–50; Bruce Mansfield, *Australian Democrat: The Career of Edward William O'Sullivan, 1846–1910* (Sydney, Sydney University Press, 1965) 75–77; JB Hirst, *The Strange Birth of Colonial Democracy* (Sydney, Allen & Unwin, 1988) 175–6, 192.

[37] NB Nairn, 'The Political Mastery of Sir Henry Parkes: New South Wales, 1871–1891' (1967) 53 *Journal of the Royal Australian Historical Society* 1, 5, 9–10.

[38] ibid 20, 26; GN Hawker, *The Parliament of New South Wales, 1856–1965* (Ultimo, Government Printer, 1971) 69; Clune and Griffith (n 36) 39–41; Bolton (n 36) 39.

[39] Geoffrey Serle, *The Golden Age: A History of the Colony of Victoria, 1851–1861* (Parkville, Melbourne University Press, 1963) 249, 253.

their independence; the lack of party organisation created unpredictability and parliamentary disorder which bedevilled Victorian politics for many years.[40] From 1856 to 1890 there were 24 changes of ministry and only 57 per cent of all Bills introduced into Parliament were passed.[41] Coalition governments held office in Victoria from 1883 to 1890, and party seemed largely redundant.[42] In the 1890s, there were no significant differences of belief or opinion between the two major parties; party cohesion remained low and contemporaries complained that there was little validity in the party divisions.[43] Compared with the other colonies, Victorian parties were the least disciplined and the least organised.[44] While this instability was accepted as the norm, and even considered to evidence the successful working of responsible government,[45] it was increasingly subjected to critique during the latter decades of the nineteenth century, as discussed later in this chapter.

Politics was no more stable in South Australia than other colonies, with the average life of a ministry from the advent of responsible government until 1894 just nine months.[46] As with other colonies, prior to the 1890s there were no political parties, but politics was carried on by means of a factional system dominated by the pastoral-mercantile-financial elite.[47] South Australian MPs saw themselves as independent and not committed to programmes or parties; once in Parliament members were free to group and re-group.[48] The result was 'a kaleidoscopic succession of short-lived ministries' which was brought to an end only by the Kingston administration of 1893–99.[49] By the late 1880s three main groups were emerging, each centred around a dominant figure: the radicals around JA Cockburn, the liberals around Thomas Playford and the conservatives

[40] ibid 259; Geoffrey Serle, *The Rush to be Rich: A History of the Colony of Victoria, 1883–1889* (Carlton, Melbourne University Press, 1971) 31.

[41] Thomas Greenlees Watson, *The First Fifty Years of Responsible Government in Victoria: The Role of Parliament and Some Statistics of Progress from 1856 to 1906* (Melbourne, J Kemp, 1906) xxiii; Raymond Wright, *A People's Counsel: A History of the Parliament of Victoria, 1856–1990* (Melbourne, Oxford University Press, 1992) 52.

[42] DW Rawson, 'Victoria' in P Loveday, AW Martin and Robert S Parker (eds), *The Emergence of the Australian Party System* (Sydney, Hale & Iremonger, 1977) 50–2.

[43] ibid 70; SM Ingham, 'Political Parties in the Victorian Legislative Assembly, 1880–1900' (1950) 4 *Historical Studies* 241.

[44] Rawson (n 42) 44–8. One explanation for this was the relative weakness of the Labor Party, which enabled the non-Labor parties to be successful despite their own weakness and factionalism: John Rickard, *Class and Politics: New South Wales, Victoria and the Early Commonwealth, 1890–1910* (Canberra, ANU Press, 1976) 46–48; Lindsay Tanner, 'A Protracted Evolution: Labor in Victorian Politics 1889–1903' (1982) 42 *Labour History* 40.

[45] Wright (n 41) 64.

[46] JC Bannon, 'South Australia' in Helen Irving (ed), *The Centenary Companion to Australian Federation* (Cambridge, Cambridge University Press, 1999) 156.

[47] Loveday and Martin, 'Colonial Politics Before 1890' (n 27) 39.

[48] Dean Jaensch, *The Government of South Australia* (St Lucia, University of Queensland Press, 1977) 2.

[49] Gerald O'Collins, *Patrick McMahon Glynn: A Founder of Australian Federation* (Carlton, Melbourne University Press, 1965) 69.

around John Downer.[50] Independence and faction were slowly subordinated to party as the appearance of the Labor Party in the early 1890s disrupted the old alliances.[51] A hardening of party lines became more and more evident by the mid-1890s; by 1902 organised and relatively stable political parties had come into existence and the faction system was becoming obsolete.[52]

Queensland obtained responsible government in 1859 and its early years have been described as years of great political instability as members seemed unable to formulate common policy or organise stable followings: 'individual interests and the desire for office were the principles that underlay the political activities of the new State'.[53] By the 1880s two parties had formed: the Liberals, led by Samuel Walker Griffith, and the Nationalists or Conservatives, led by Thomas McIlwraith, who together dominated Queensland politics in the 1880s.[54] Both held meetings of parliamentary members, and voting in the Legislative Assembly was relatively cohesive.[55] In 1890 McIlwraith and Griffith formed a coalition government which became known as the 'continuous ministry'. The emergence of the Labor Party prompted the fusion of the liberal and national parties with the result that the basic line of political division became labour and anti-labour.[56] The strength of the continuous ministry meant that the Labor Party was unable to pursue the strategy of support in return for concessions which had been so successful in New South Wales.[57] As such, the Labor Party became in effect a permanent opposition, formally accepting the role of 'Her Majesty's constitutional opposition' in 1898.[58]

Tasmanian politics in the 1870s was very unstable, with the lower house dominated by conservative landowners and merchants. This was followed by a long period of stability between 1879 and 1903, in which there were only

[50] ibid 70; Dean Jaensch, *Political Representation in Colonial South Australia 1857–1901* (PhD Thesis, University of Adelaide, 1973) 473, quoted in Loveday and Martin, 'Colonial Politics Before 1890' (n 27) 41. Richard Chaffey Baker was also a leading conservative figure in the Legislative Council.

[51] John Bannon, *Supreme Federalist: The Political Life of Sir John Downer* (Kent Town, Wakefield Press, 2009) 117; D Jaensch, 'South Australia' in P Loveday, AW Martin and Robert S Parker (eds), *The Emergence of the Australian Party System* (Sydney, Hale & Iremonger, 1977) 257, 261.

[52] 'The Government and Parliament', *South Australian Chronicle* (Adelaide), 22 October 1892, 4; Jaensch, 'South Australia' (n 51) 249.

[53] Loveday and Martin, 'Colonial Politics Before 1890' (n 27) 35; MM Wilson, *The Development of Party Politics in Queensland, 1859–1900* (MA Thesis, University of Queensland, 1938) 21.

[54] PS Callaghan, *Political Alignments in the Queensland Legislative Assembly, 1878–99* (BA (Hons) Thesis, University of Queensland, 1968) 25, 33–9.

[55] Colin A Hughes, *The Government of Queensland* (St Lucia, University of Queensland Press, 1980) 13.

[56] JB Dalton, 'An Interpretative Survey: The Queensland Labour Movement' in DJ Murphy, RB Joyce and Colin A Hughes (eds), *Prelude to Power: The Rise of the Labour Party in Queensland 1885–1915* (Milton, Jacaranda Press, 1970) 10.

[57] Hughes (n 55) 13–4.

[58] Rickard (n 44) 48; Queensland, *Parliamentary Debates*, Legislative Assembly (Government Printer, 1898) vol 79, 252, 365; Ross Fitzgerald, *From the Dreaming to 1915: A History of Queensland* (St Lucia, University of Queensland Press, 1982) 326–7.

five ministries.[59] In the 1880s the assembly became split into two consistent groups; although these groups had distinctive views on the key questions of the day, there were no formal party links, MPs professed to be independent and acknowledged no lasting commitment to any parliamentary group.[60] Party meetings were held to discuss tactics and the voting of members 'was deliberately concerted' which produced cohesion, however, this lacked the rigidity of modern party loyalty and members often changed sides.[61]

Lagging significantly behind the other colonies in population and economic development, Western Australia only became self-governing in 1891. The colony's first premier, John Forrest, dominated the Legislative Assembly for the first decade after responsible government without the need of a political party. He used techniques of leadership similar to those of the New South Wales factional leaders, and although there was considerable fluidity in Parliament, he did not face serious competition for office.[62] Payment of members was introduced in 1900, paving the way for the labour movement to seek representation and Forrest entered the federal Parliament in 1901. A period of unstable government gave way to a clear two-party system, and by 1910 the Western Australian party system mirrored those of the other states.[63]

The Labor Party played a leading role in the development of parties in Australia. After being convincingly defeated in a series of strikes in the early 1890s, the unions concluded that representation in Parliament was needed to achieve improved conditions for workers.[64] The Labor Party achieved spectacular success in New South Wales, winning a third of the seats in Parliament in the 1891 elections and gaining the balance of power.[65] Labor's strategy of support in return for concessions in New South Wales required the party to be both a distinctive political force and to maintain unity and disciplined voting.[66] Labor developed a highly integrated organisation which linked branches, the unions and the parliamentary party through the conference and the executive; it valued solidarity and unity and its distinctive ideal was that authority lay with

[59] WA Townsley, 'The Governor, Cabinet and the Administration' in FC Green (ed), *Tasmania: A Century of Responsible Government 1856–1956* (Hobart, Government Printer, 1956) 246.

[60] Patrick Weller, 'Tasmania' in P Loveday, AW Martin and Robert S Parker (eds), *The Emergence of the Australian Party System* (Sydney, Hale & Iremonger, 1977) 358–9; Patrick Weller, 'Groups, Parliament and Elections: Tasmanian Politics in the 1890s' (1974) 21 *Tasmanian Historical Research Association, Papers and Proceedings* 89, 90.

[61] Weller, 'Groups, Parliament and Elections' (n 60) 94.

[62] Brian de Garis, 'Western Australia' in P Loveday, AW Martin and Robert S Parker (eds), *The Emergence of the Australian Party System* (Sydney, Hale & Iremonger, 1977) 298, 300–2.

[63] ibid 298–9.

[64] *Official Report and Balance Sheet of the New South Wales Labour Defence Committee* (1890), in CMH Clark (ed), *Select Documents in Australian History 1851–1900* (London, Angus and Robertson, 1955) 573–5.

[65] Ray Markey, 'Trade Union Democracy and the Labor Party in New South Wales, 1880–1914' (1986) 22 *Historical Studies* 71.

[66] As George Black famously noted: New South Wales, *Parliamentary Debates*, Legislative Assembly, 16 July 1891, 126–30.

the labour movement outside Parliament.[67] Most notoriously, perhaps, Labor candidates were required to pledge themselves to adhere to decisions of caucus.[68]

Although similar devices existed before Labor came on the scene, Labor made them highly effective, and applied them to a political platform rather than individual issues.[69] Their combined effect was to make the parliamentary party subject to the extra-parliamentary organisation.[70] This reflected a novel understanding of party democracy: Labor MPs were to be delegates implementing the party platform determined collectively at an annual conference rather than exercising their independent judgement.[71] From the outset, the Labor Party was subject to considerable suspicion and hostility, especially from the non-Labor parties, who were 'horrified by Labor's cult of solidarity', believing it would destroy the representative character of Parliament.[72]

There were significant controversies between upper and lower houses in the colonies in the years after responsible government. Under the British Constitution, the two houses of Parliament were theoretically co-equal and co-ordinate branches of the legislature. However, from the mid-nineteenth century the growing power of the House of Commons had lessened the authority of the House of Lords, and it was considered a constitutional principle that the House of Lords ought not to oppose measures passed by the Commons which were clearly supported by public opinion.[73]

Following the British model, the precise relations between the two houses were not specified in any colonial Constitution. The upper houses in Victoria, South Australia and Tasmania were elected on the basis of a property qualification for electors while members of the New South Wales and Queensland Legislative Councils were appointed for life by the Governor (on the advice of the ministry).[74] The more representative lower houses thus possessed a legitimacy that the upper houses did not and were the house in which the government

[67] P Loveday, AW Martin and Patrick Weller, 'New South Wales' in P Loveday, AW Martin and Robert S Parker (eds), *The Emergence of the Australian Party System* (Sydney, Hale & Iremonger, 1977) 203, 246.

[68] WG Spence, *Australia's Awakening: Thirty Years in the Life of an Australian Agitator* (Sydney, Worker Trustees, 1909) 236–7.

[69] JDB Miller, 'Party Discipline in Australia' in Colin A Hughes (ed), *Readings in Australian Government* (St Lucia, University of Queensland Press, 1968) 347, 350.

[70] Ross McMullin, *The Light on the Hill: The Australian Labor Party, 1891–1991* (Melbourne, Oxford University Press, 1991) ch 2.

[71] Frank Bongiorno, 'The Origins of Caucus, 1856–1901' in John Faulkner and Stuart Macintyre (eds), *True Believers: The Story of the Federal Parliamentary Labor Party* (Crows Nest, Allen & Unwin, 2001); Nick Dyrenfurth and Frank Bongiorno, *A Little History of the Australian Labor Party* (Sydney, University of New South Wales Press, 2011) 31.

[72] Dyrenfurth and Bongiorno (n 71) 32; Judith Brett, *Australian Liberals and the Moral Middle Class: From Alfred Deakin to John Howard* (Port Melbourne, Cambridge University Press, 2003) 23–7.

[73] Alpheus Todd, *On Parliamentary Government in England: Its Origin, Development, and Practical Operation*, 2nd edn (London, Longmans Green, 1887) vol 1, 37–41.

[74] Bailey (n 21) 417.

was formed; as a result, premiers and leading politicians typically insisted that an elected government should be able to govern free from upper house interference.[75] However, they never succeeded in having this principle accepted by colonial upper houses. Clashes occurred between the upper and lower houses in the colonies, with the Legislative Councils claiming the right to exercise their legal powers and rejecting any analogy with the House of Lords.[76]

III. COLONIAL CONCEPTIONS OF RESPONSIBLE GOVERNMENT

What did responsible government mean in the Australian colonies around the time of Federation? Few treatises examining the nature of responsible government were published in the colonies during the mid to late nineteenth century. Perhaps this is not surprising, considering that the intention in the colonies was to reproduce the British system of parliamentary government as far as possible. Accordingly, colonists typically looked to the British writers and practice to explain the theory and practice of responsible government, and frequently referred to authors such as Todd, Hearn, Bagehot, Grey and Macaulay.[77]

As noted in chapter two, Alpheus Todd was considered an authoritative writer on the British Constitution. Todd wrote a work entitled *Parliamentary Government in the British Colonies*, which examined the application of the principles of parliamentary government to the British colonies, and which was frequently referred to in the Australian colonies.[78] Todd considered that

[75] Wright (n 41) 76.

[76] McMinn (n 10) 65–78; Bailey (n 21) 419; Wright (n 41) 72–91; Todd, *Parliamentary Government in the British Colonies* (n 20) 720–49; Arthur Berriedale Keith, *Responsible Government in the Dominions* (Oxford, Clarendon Press, 1912) vol 2, 599–625; Dorothy P Clarke, 'The Colonial Office and the Constitutional Crises in Victoria, 1865–68' (1952) 5 *Historical Studies* 160; Alfred Deakin, *The Crisis in Victorian Politics, 1879–1881: A Personal Retrospect* (Carlton, Melbourne University Press, 1957); Geoffrey Serle, 'New Light on the Colonial Office, Sir George Bowen and the Victorian Constitutional Crises' (1969) 13 *Historical Studies* 533; McMinn (n 10) 65–72; Stuart Macintyre, *A Colonial Liberalism: The Lost World of Three Victorian Visionaries* (South Melbourne, Oxford University Press, 1991) 41–54; John Waugh, 'Evading Parliamentary Control of Government Spending: Some Early Case Studies' (1998) 9 *Public Law Review* 28; John Waugh, 'Blocking Supply in Victoria' (2002) 13 *Public Law Review* 241; Paul Strangio, 'Broken Heads and Flaming Houses: Graham Berry, the Wild Colonial' in Paul Strangio and Brian Costar (eds), *The Victorian Premiers 1856–2006* (Annandale, Federation Press, 2006); Greg Taylor, *The Constitution of Victoria* (Annandale, Federation Press, 2006) 41–4.

[77] Eg, *Sydney Mail*, 24 December 1870, 10; *Sydney Morning Herald*, 15 January 1878, 4; *South Australian Chronicle*, 6 July 1889, 6; *The Argus*, 15 August 1870, 6; *Brisbane Courier*, 14 November 1885, 3; *Queensland Times*, 21 April 1877, 3; 'Professor Hearn's Work On Government', *The Age*, 25 May 1867, 6; 'Review: The Government of England: Its Structure, and Its Development', *The Sydney Morning Herald*, 28 September 1886, 5; 'The Commonwealth Bill', *The Tasmanian*, 22 August 1891, 16; 'Queensland Parliament', *Queensland Times, Ipswich Herald and General Advertiser*, 20 July 1876, 4; *The Argus*, 8 June 1868, 7; *The Age*, 12 June 1868, 3; *Sydney Morning Herald*, 8 May 1874, 4; 'Review: Lord Grey on Colonial Responsible Government', *Freeman's Journal*, 16 April 1859, 2; 'Responsible Government', *The Age*, 6 September 1856, 2.

[78] Todd, *Parliamentary Government in the British Colonies* (n 20).

applying the British system of government to the colonies meant recognition and application of the three fundamental maxims of the British Constitution, namely 'the personal irresponsibility of the king; the responsibility of his ministers for all acts of the Crown; and the inquisitorial power and ultimate control of Parliament'.[79] The authority of the Crown was represented in the colonies by the Governor, who exercised important powers and prerogatives such as assembling, proroguing and dissolving Parliament, giving or withholding assent to Bills, appointing the ministry and issuing warrants for the expenditure of funds from the treasury. However, the Governor did not have a plenary delegation of sovereign authority but only possessed those powers which were expressly or impliedly conferred by his commission, and he was required to act in accordance with any instructions given to him by the British Government.[80]

The Crown must act through advisers approved by Parliament and so the introduction of responsible government had the effect that the colonial ministry was responsible for all acts of state, namely framing the policy of the government, introducing Bills into Parliament to give effect to that policy, appointing public officers and controlling all public affairs through government departments.[81] Todd considered that:

> It is of the essence of responsible government that the governor should choose, as his constitutional advisers, persons who already possess, or who can readily obtain, a seat in one or other of the legislative chambers of the colony, in order that they may be the authorised exponents therein of the opinions of government, as well as of the well-understood wishes of the people.[82]

The Governor remained responsible solely to the British Government for the proper discharge of his office and could refuse to accept the advice of his ministers in certain cases, for example where advice was contrary to law or express instructions from the Crown. If the ministry did not accept the Governor's decision, it must resign or be dismissed and the Governor would be obliged to obtain a new ministry which was willing to become responsible for his action. If no such ministry could be found, the Governor would be required to retreat from the position or retire from office.[83] There was, therefore, substantial continuity as well as important points of contrast between the constitutional systems of Britain and Australia.

In 1854 Henry Chapman, then colonial secretary of Van Diemen's Land, published a tract advocating the conferral of responsible government on the Australian colonies.[84] Chapman defined responsible government as a

[79] ibid 3.
[80] ibid 37.
[81] ibid 49.
[82] ibid 55.
[83] ibid 50–1.
[84] HS Chapman, *Parliamentary Government; or, Responsible Ministries for the Australian Colonies* (Hobart, Pratt and Son, 1854). The tract was also printed in instalments in the *Sydney Morning Herald* and the *Launceston Examiner* in September 1854.

ministry responsible to, and removable by, the lower branch of the legislature.[85] Responsible government required, and produced, he argued, harmony between the executive and legislative branches, and also secured accountability to the people. However, the government had been unable to transact business in the Legislative Councils due to the lack of men of suitable calibre to fill the key positions.[86] The introduction of representative legislatures into the colonies was not sufficient to procure parliamentary control over the government because, even though the legislature had the power to withhold supply, this remedy was 'of too extreme and violent a nature to be resorted to in any but extreme cases'.[87] Only responsible government would produce control by Parliament over the actions of the government.[88]

Henry Parkes considered several questions relating to responsible government in an anonymous tract entitled *Responsible Government: What Is It?* published in 1872, which unfortunately did not answer the question posed in the title.[89] Parkes noted that the precedents of British practice should be followed as much as possible, but as the conditions of political life are in many respects different, they cannot be followed in all cases.[90] The need to ensure governmental accountability to Parliament was a key theme of the tract; Parkes was strongly critical of the fact that in 1872 several ministers in New South Wales had held office and enjoyed the privileges of power despite losing their seats in Parliament.[91]

Another significant work was penned by Edward Jenks, a Cambridge-trained professor and Dean of Law at Melbourne University. Jenks published a treatise in 1891 examining the working of government in Victoria[92] which was known to the framers of the Constitution and their contemporaries, although not directly cited in the Convention debates.[93] Jenks noted that Victoria had always had an Executive Council, but that prior to 1855, there was no means of rendering it accountable to the community. Jenks considered that there are dangers with a permanent executive: it may cease to represent the wishes of the community, disagreements may arise with the legislature and it may foster corruption. Britain had solved this problem with the introduction of responsible government, whereby the executive was accountable to the legislature and ultimately to the community.[94]

[85] ibid 3–4.
[86] ibid ch 2.
[87] ibid ch 3.
[88] ibid 5–7.
[89] *Responsible Government: What Is It?* (Sydney, Piddington, 1872). The author listed on the title page is 'Constitutionalist' but the tract has been attributed to Henry Parkes: trove.nla.gov.au/work/19112764/version/275146783.
[90] ibid 10.
[91] ibid 15.
[92] Edward Jenks, *The Government of Victoria (Australia)* (Melbourne, George Robertson & Co, 1897).
[93] See, eg, John Quick and Robert Randolph Garran, *The Annotated Constitution of the Australian Commonwealth* (Sydney, Angus & Robertson, 1901) ix; Moore, *The Constitution of the Commonwealth of Australia* (n 5) 20.
[94] Jenks (n 92) 269.

According to Jenks, the great object of the framers of the Victorian Constitution Act of 1855 was to remedy this state of affairs, and the method employed was the requirement that four members of the ministry must be members of Parliament. The need for the ministry to seek approval by the Parliament for their financial and legislative proposals had the effect that there must be harmony between the legislature and the executive, which could only be achieved by appointing a cabinet approved by Parliament, thus preventing any attempt to carry on government independently of the legislature.[95] As a matter of 'constitutional understanding', even though the Governor's power to appoint the cabinet was unfettered in law, he would only make appointments having regard to the views of Parliament.[96] The importance of the cabinet was underscored in Jenks' statement that the cabinet is 'as nearly as possible, the sovereign power of the community' as it wields 'the whole executive force of the community' and also controls the bent of legislation. It was thus the 'real core and essence of the Government',[97] expressing a view similar to the views of the writers discussed in chapter two.

Under the period of responsible government, the institutions of the Australian colonies consisted of two houses of Parliament, both elective or one elective and one nominee, with the executive consisting of 'officials chosen for their Parliamentary position, and liable to dismissal, like ministers in England, in consequence of an adverse vote of the legislature'.[98] For Jenks, therefore, responsible government and parliamentary control over the executive was designed to ensure that the government was not out of step with the community, alleviate disagreements with the legislature and eliminate or reduce corruption. Jenks also considered that the party system was dying a natural death in Victoria due to the independence of the public service.[99]

In *Chung Teong Toy v Musgrove* the Victorian Supreme Court in 1888 had occasion to consider the extent to which the Constitution Act 1855 had conferred responsible government on Victoria.[100] The majority held that responsible government was a chameleon concept, and that the Constitution Act, despite conferring responsible government, did not confer a complete grant of self-government. Williams J held that 'there may be infinite varieties and infinite degrees of a responsible government', and so merely to state that the purpose of the Act was to confer a system of responsible government on Victoria said little about the content of the powers thereby conferred on the Governor.[101] His Honour held that Victoria had 'merely an instalment of

[95] ibid 209, 270–2.
[96] ibid 216.
[97] ibid 275–6.
[98] ibid 11.
[99] ibid 274.
[100] *Chung Teong Toy v Musgrove* (1888) 14 VLR 349.
[101] ibid 418–9.

responsible government'.[102] Holroyd J considered that there was no universal institution called responsible government, and the scope of the powers conferred must be ascertained from the terms of the statute.[103] A'Beckett J agreed, stating that responsibility may attach to persons whose powers are limited, and the mere existence of responsibility does not indicate the extent of the powers that are conferred.[104]

Powerful dissents were written by Higinbotham CJ and Kerferd J. Higinbotham CJ held that by virtue of the Constitution Act the Governor had powers co-extensive to those of the British Government with regard to its internal affairs and had power to do all acts that were necessary for the proper administration of law and the conduct of public affairs in Victoria.[105] Kerferd J held that the Constitution Act was to be considered to have conferred the prerogative powers of the Crown on the Governor as an incident to the grant of self-government, which were exercisable on the advice of responsible ministers.[106]

The disagreement between the majority and minority relates to the extent of the legal powers conferred on the Governor by the Constitution Act; the judges did not disagree on the conventions of responsible government. That is, whatever were the powers available to the Governor, there was no disagreement with the proposition that those powers must be exercised on the advice on responsible ministers who were accountable to Parliament for that advice.[107]

Responsible government was also discussed in many newspaper articles. In 1857, the *Sydney Morning Herald* opined that '[t]he notion of a responsible Government holding office so long as it retained the confidence of the Legislative Assembly, has for the first time in the present year been brought into practice in the Australian colonies'.[108] The *Freeman's Journal* defined responsible government as a corollary of the maxim, 'the King can do no wrong', whereby 'the responsibility of action is removed from the king and laid upon his ministers'.[109] A lucid definition was also offered by *The Argus* in 1880. The writer noted that Colonial Parliaments do not merely enact laws, but also 'superintend the administration of the Government in all its details'. Her Majesty controls the administration of government, and does so in accordance with the advice of her 'principal servants', the ministry, who are at the head of the various government departments. She appoints or removes the ministry as they possess, or forfeit, 'the general confidence and support of Parliament, or at least of the

[102] ibid 416.
[103] ibid 428.
[104] ibid 434.
[105] ibid 397.
[106] ibid 410.
[107] ibid 386, 398, 407, 409–10, 412, 413, 415, 428, 430, 434, 439.
[108] 'Responsible Government in the Colonies', *Sydney Morning Herald*, 24 March 1857, 2.
[109] *Freeman's Journal*, 28 November 1874, 8.

more popular House of Parliament'. Colonial Governors were likewise bound to follow these principles.[110]

Another definition was offered by the *Sydney Morning Herald* in 1872. Under responsible government the King can do no wrong, and therefore is not responsible. 'His Ministers can do wrong, and they are responsible – first to the law, for the violation of which they may be charged and tried like other men; secondly, to the Parliament, which could once proceed against them by attainder to cut off their heads'. The writer noted regretfully that the latter 'wholesome practice' had been discontinued, leaving the only punishment for corrupt behaviour to be the loss of confidence.[111] Another article defined the essence of responsible government as being that in matters of local politics the Governor acts in accordance with the advice of the ministry who possesses the confidence of the Legislature.[112] One important point made in various articles was that responsible government meant a ministry responsible to the people;[113] responsible government was about ensuring the people retained ultimate control over their government.

The principle that the King can do no wrong was understood to entail that the monarch (and the monarch's representative) was bound to act on the advice of ministers: '[i]n a constitutional country the king can do no wrong, because he acts through responsible ministers, who may be made to pay the penalty for his misdeeds'.[114] This logically entailed that the King's advisers were responsible for all the official acts of the Crown to Parliament, which could express its disapproval of the government's actions by withdrawing its confidence.[115] While the choice of the ministry was the prerogative of the Crown,[116] that choice was limited by the convention that the ministry must possess the confidence of the Legislature.[117] If that confidence was forfeited, the ministry must resign, ensuring that Parliament retained ultimate control over the government.[118]

[110] 'Responsible Government in Australia', *The Argus*, 19 November 1880, 43S.

[111] *Sydney Morning Herald*, 27 March 1872, 4.

[112] 'The Origin of Responsible Government in the Colonies' *West Australian*, 24 September 1880, 2.

[113] *Daily News*, 28 October 1890, 2; 'Constitution Making and Constitution Makers', *Empire*, 9 August 1852, 2; *Western Australian Times*, 18 December 1874, 2; Gordon D Combe, *Responsible Government in South Australia* (Adelaide, Government Printer, 1957) 73.

[114] *Sydney Morning Herald*, 1 December 1892, 5; 'President Lincoln in a "Fix"', *Sydney Morning Herald*, 12 January 1864, 3; *The Age*, 19 April 1865, 4; *Freeman's Journal*, 28 November 1874, 8; 'Responsible or Parliamentary Government', *Launceston Examiner*, 17 June 1856, 2; *The Mercury*, 15 March 1870, 2; 'Colonial Governors, *South Australian Advertiser*, 27 May 1864, 7; *Burrowa News*, 20 February 1875, 2.

[115] *South Australian Weekly Chronicle*, 4 June 1864, 4; *Freeman's Journal*, 28 November 1874, 8; *The Mercury*, 3 April 1862, 2; *Bega Gazette*, 18 August 1866, 2.

[116] 'Her Majesty's Ministers', *Warragul Guardian*, 3 March 1881, 1S.

[117] 'Responsible Government' *Adelaide Observer*, 11 April 1857, 5; 'Responsible Government', *The Age*, 6 September 1856, 2.

[118] *Empire*, 8 September 1856, 6; *Adelaide Observer*, 14 October 1865, 7.

Many articles commented, often unfavourably, on various aspects of the functioning of responsible government.[119] One frequent source of complaint was the instability of colonial Parliaments.[120] Some argued that the cure for this instability was a proper party system, for without parties there would be weak and rapidly changing ministries.[121] Many, if not most, contemporaries argued that responsible government was party government; that is, that responsible government relied on the existence of properly formed parties to provide stable government.[122] Against this, some argued that party should be discarded altogether.[123]

IV. AUSTRALIAN CRITIQUES OF THE CABINET SYSTEM AND EMERGENCE OF PARTY GOVERNMENT

The merits of cabinet government were debated vigorously in the colonies prior to Federation. In Victoria, one prominent critic of the party system was George Higinbotham. In 1875, during debate on a budget presented by the McCulloch ministry, Higinbotham criticised the actions of the ministry for having turned the previous ministry (led by Graham Berry) out of office, with no explanation being given to the House, merely, so it seemed, for the purpose of taking their positions.[124] Higinbotham regarded this incident as symptomatic of deep problems with the working of responsible government:

> [I]t ought to be observed that there are many persons now in this country who have even begun to question the foundations of our Constitution – to ask 'What is the use of responsible government; what good can possibly come out of this House?' These feelings of distrust and disapproval are, if I do not mistake, almost entirely occasioned and generated by the accursed system under which the party on this side

[119] 'The Working of Responsible Government', *Sydney Morning Herald*, 9 January 1858, 11; 'Responsible Government in New South Wales; No 1: Its Parliaments', *Sydney Morning Herald*, 24 November 1863, 5; 'Responsible Government in New South Wales; No II: Its Ministries', *Sydney Morning Herald*, 25 November 1863, 5; 'Victoria and New South Wales Responsible Government in the Colonies', *Sydney Morning Herald*, 18 December 1861, 5; *Sydney Morning Herald*, 20 July 1861, 4; *Brisbane Courier*, 21 February 1871, 7.

[120] 'Responsible Government', *Sydney Morning Herald*, 30 October 1857, 2; *Sydney Morning Herald*, 23 November 1882, 5; *Freeman's Journal*, 16 April 1859, 2–3; *Sydney Morning Herald*, 21 November 1887, 6.

[121] 'Re-election of Ministers', *South Australian Chronicle*, 18 October 1890, 4; 'The Working of Responsible Government', *Sydney Morning Herald*, 9 January 1858, 11.

[122] Eg, Edward Sweetman, *Australian Constitutional Development* (Melbourne, Macmillan, 1925) 316; Chapman, *Parliamentary Government* (n 84) 37; *Sydney Morning Herald*, 31 May 1856, 3; 'Party Government', *The Age*, 4 September 1856, 2; 'Responsible Government in Victoria', *Adelaide Observer*, 19 January 1856, 6; *Sydney Morning Herald*, 11 May 1874, 4; Western Australia, *Parliamentary Debates*, Legislative Assembly, 5 August 1902, 325 (C Harper).

[123] Joy E Mills, 'The Composition of the Victorian Parliament, 1856–1881' (1942) 2 *Historical Studies* 25, 30.

[124] Victoria, *Parliamentary Debates*, Legislative Assembly, 30 November 1875, 1416 (George Higinbotham).

> of the House are always striving to murder the reputation of the party on the other side, in order to leap over the dead bodies of those reputations into the seats on the Treasury bench.[125]

This speech was later quoted by Clark during the 1891 Federal Convention.[126]

Another critic of the party system was Edmund FitzGibbon, who wrote numerous works attacking the party system and proposing reform.[127] In 1875 he castigated the Legislative Assembly for having laboured at nothing else than despatching ministries, leaving it too pre-occupied with the struggle for place to accomplish any business – including dealing with outbreaks of scarlet fever.[128] In 1879 he portrayed the system which in his view had been wrongly named 'Responsible Government' as a system of warfare between two sides, each competing for the spoils of office. The opposition desires to obtain possession of the benefits of office for its leaders and supporters and so opposes every measure proposed by the majority, whom they 'ridicule, malign, and irritate' on every occasion. The majority, likewise, devotes its energies to discrediting the opposition and maintaining itself in power. By virtue of this system, Victoria pays for nearly one-half of its representatives to actively obstruct the business of the colony.[129] FitzGibbon proposed that responsible government should be abandoned, and replaced with a system modelled on that of local government administration.[130] Instead of ministers being chosen with reference to their party allegiances, each department should be managed by a committee of Parliament, with the managers chosen based on their competence, and to hold office for a fixed term such as twelve months. Failure to carry out a department's business properly would subject the managers to censure and loss of position, which would result in genuine accountability.[131]

A consistent theme of FitzGibbon's critiques of responsible government was that the linking of tenure of office with the confidence of Parliament led inevitably to party warfare, and the solution was to break this link. FitzGibbon's arguments and proposals were well known to Victorian parliamentarians. Many contemporaries agreed with his analysis of the problems besetting contemporary politics; however, not all were convinced that his proposals would solve those problems.[132] Others were critical of his proposals on the

[125] ibid 1421.

[126] *Convention Debates* (1891) 245.

[127] See Bernard Barrett, 'FitzGibbon, Edmund Gerald (1825–1905)' in *Australian Dictionary of Biography* (Melbourne, Melbourne University Press, 1972) vol 4.

[128] EG FitzGibbon, *Parliamentary Reform, Permanent Government and Progress* (Melbourne, Samuel Mullen, 1875) 3–4.

[129] EG FitzGibbon, *What Next?* (Melbourne, Fergusson & Moore, 1879) 7–8.

[130] Eg, EG FitzGibbon, *True Coalition* (Melbourne, Fergusson & Moore, 1886) 4, which was addressed to Alfred Deakin; EG FitzGibbon, *Government by Committees* (Melbourne, S Mullen, 1872).

[131] FitzGibbon, *True Coalition* (n 130) 5–6.

[132] See, eg, 'The Defects of Party Government' *Australian Town and Country Journal* (NSW), 1 January 1876, 14.

ground that executive committees under this system would avoid responsibility to Parliament.[133]

The question of cabinet government was also the subject of consideration by a Victorian royal commission. In 1893, MP Robert Best moved for an inquiry into the method of appointing ministers of the Crown, considering that the party system had degenerated into a 'degrading struggle' between the ins and the outs, where one party attempted to govern and the other to prevent them from doing so. The party system necessitated the sacrifice of individual conscience, as each party member was expected to support the policy of the party irrespective of whether they agreed with it or not.[134] In response, the premier, James Patterson, noted that it was much easier to point out defects than to suggest a remedy. He mounted a spirited defence of party government, noting that parties were necessary and desirable to make progress in political matters: 'when you cease to wrangle and to wrestle you are no longer a community with vitality and no longer a Parliament … It is party spirit and fire which you require to do the right thing. It is live political feeling which marks you as a community that can make strides'. Patterson also pointed out that the premier ought to be able to rely on a stable body of support in order to ensure the passage of legislation.[135]

In the result, a royal commission was set up to examine the issue, which included a number of delegates to the 1891 and 1897–98 Federal Conventions.[136] The resulting report noted that much of the Commission's energy had been devoted to consideration of the system under which ministers obtained and held office. Best's proposal to appoint ministers for a fixed period had met with considerable support, but ultimately was not adopted: the Commission noted that it had 'not been able to agree upon any other recommendation which would satisfactorily remove the defects of the present system, and would not at the same time be attended with other defects perhaps equally great'.[137]

In 1904 *The Age* published a work entitled *The Evils of Party Government*, a collection of articles which had originally been published separately in *The Age* newspaper.[138] Although published after Federation, it critiques the working of party government in Australia during the period 1892 to 1904, and so its insights are relevant to the pre-Federation period. The work remarked

[133] *The Australasian* (Melbourne, Australia), 25 November 1893, 36.

[134] Victoria, *Parliamentary Debates*, Legislative Assembly, 6 September 1893, 1460, 1461, 1465 (Robert Best).

[135] ibid, 1467–8 (James Patterson).

[136] These members were Alfred Deakin, a prominent delegate to the 1891 and 1897–8 Conventions, Henry Wrixon, a delegate to the 1891 Convention, and Isaac Isaacs, William Trenwith, George Turner, Alexander Peacock and Graham Berry, who were delegates to the 1897–8 Convention.

[137] *Report of the Royal Commission on Constitutional Reform* (Victorian Government Printer, 1894) 5.

[138] *The Evils of Party Government: Proposals for the Elective System of Selecting Cabinet Ministers* (Melbourne, David Syme, 1904). See further JDB Miller, 'David Syme and Elective Ministries' (1953) 6 *Historical Studies* 1.

that '[t]he evils of the system of Party Government have now become so obvious to everyone who is in any degree acquainted with modern political warfare that no apology is required for entering upon an inquiry as to the best means of remedying them'.[139] Citing authors such as Low, Higinbotham and FitzGibbon, the work considered that the struggles for places on the Treasury benches had brought public business to a standstill and rendered government unworkable. Rather than the Parliament controlling and scrutinising the executive, the ministry was expected to thoroughly dominate the proceedings of Parliament, and any amendment of its proposals was seen as a blow to its authority.[140]

The articles considered that there had been, in the period 1892–1904, 'a noticeable movement of public opinion on the subject', triggered by the 'unseemly scrambles of the outs and the ins'.[141] Party government was a patent absurdity, requiring each party to be continually engaged in party warfare, instead of focusing on the welfare of the state. This had the consequence that half the members in Parliament attempted to carry out the affairs of the nation while the other half did their utmost to oppose them.[142] Party government was in opposition to democratic principles, as it distanced the government from the people. Quoting Low, the work argued that party government concentrated power in the hands of the Prime Minister and inner cabinet, who were the real decision makers, which effectively enabled the executive to ignore the will of the people until the next election. Further, the concentration of power turned party members into mere instruments of their party chiefs.[143] Party government also hindered the maintenance of a consistent policy and instead produced fickleness and instability, as members routinely supported measures as warmly as they formerly opposed them.[144] When voting on measures before Parliament, members were not guided by their merits but party considerations and other matters of expediency. Party was inherently driven to self-interest and corruption, 'the madness of the many for the gain of the few'.[145]

Echoing others who had proposed similar measures, such as Robert Best, Richard Baker and John Cockburn, *The Age* writers proposed a system of elective ministries modelled on the Swiss system in order to rectify the problems with party warfare. An elective system would genuinely make the government the servant, and not the master of the House, not dictating to Parliament the policy that should be followed. Crucially, members would be free to vote in accordance with their consciences, 'as every man in a free Parliament ought always to do'.

[139] *The Evils of Party Government* (n 138) 2.
[140] ibid 3, 12. This was considered contrary to the proper principles of parliamentary government.
[141] ibid 11.
[142] ibid 2, 3, 12, 18, 26.
[143] ibid 5, 10, 13.
[144] On this tendency see also Bannon, *Supreme Federalist* (n 51) 101.
[145] *The Evils of Party Government* (n 138) 14, 24.

The Age writers regretted that the proposals for elective ministries had not received more serious attention at the Federal Conventions.[146]

In 1891 in the South Australian Legislative Assembly John Cockburn moved a motion to replace the system of holding office through maintaining the confidence of the lower house with the system of elective ministries. Cockburn considered the relationship between ministers and Parliament to be 'the most vital point of our Constitution' and that the problems with parliamentary government had begun to be acknowledged throughout the world. Parliamentary government was essentially party government, since it was necessary that ministers should be able to 'guide and control the decisions of Parliament'. However, this led to a paradox at the heart of parliamentary government, for it meant that the government was created by the House, but had the power to terminate its existence by a dissolution: 'it was somewhat extraordinary that the creature should be able to rule its creator'.[147]

Cockburn considered it was necessary to introduce reforms to give the government greater stability and make Parliament a more efficient machine for carrying out the business of the country. Cockburn believed that an elective ministry system modelled on the Swiss system of government would achieve this, remove the need for constant intrigues, and increase the independence of MPs.[148] The Treasurer, Thomas Playford, agreed that fixity of tenure for the executive would have many benefits, including that the government would not be ejected whenever a measure proposed by it was rejected by the legislature. This would remove the constant '[v]iolent and rapid changes of Ministries', which was one of the principal objections to parliamentary government.[149] However, Cockburn's motion did not receive enough support and was dropped.

In 1895, Cockburn published an article analysing the working of the cabinet system.[150] Cockburn noted the difficulties of the view expressed by Alpheus Todd and others that the ministry should be able to guide the decisions of Parliament; for, insofar as the cabinet or any party controls the decisions of Parliament, 'the system falls short of the realisation of Parliamentary government'. He noted that it was frequently the case that cabinets compelled Parliament to arrive at decisions contrary to the wishes of a majority of MPs by means such as threatening to resign, and members were forced into voting against their convictions in order to avoid a crisis. However, 'such triumphs of cabinet over Parliament are manifestly rather destructive of, than essential

[146] ibid 9, 14, 19, 26, 27–8.

[147] South Australia, *Parliamentary Debates*, Legislative Assembly, 9 September 1891, 1068 (Dr Cockburn).

[148] ibid 1070, 1071–2, 1073.

[149] South Australia, *Parliamentary Debates*, Legislative Assembly, 11 November 1891, 1963–4 (T Playford).

[150] JA Cockburn, 'Should the Cabinet System be Changed?' (1895) 6 *Review of Reviews* 399.

to, the principle of government by Parliament'.[151] For Cockburn, Parliament's freedom and control of the government was an indispensable aspect of parliamentary government.

Cockburn also noted that there was growing public discontent with 'the existence of organised bands of members ranged on opposite sides of the House, engaged in a ceaseless struggle for possession of the Treasury benches'. When voting in Parliament, members should be actuated solely by the public welfare, but party government prevented this from occurring. Cockburn echoed the criticisms of other contemporaries of 'government by contradiction'. His proposal was for ministers to be elected by the House as a whole rather than the predominant party in the lower house. Cockburn was optimistic in his predictions, believing that if the elective ministry system was introduced, 'party government would be swept away … and the proper relations between Ministers and parliament established'. This would ensure individual responsibility for ministers in the management of their departments.[152]

During the 1890s, the *Sydney Bulletin* published a series of articles critiquing the party system and proposing instead that the Swiss system of government should be adopted in the Australian colonies and in the Commonwealth. In an article published in August 1890, *The Bulletin* engaged in a stringent critique of the system it dubbed 'Government by Contradiction'. The first principle of government modelled on the British Constitution required that there be an organised opposition, which needed to be ready at all times to rise and contradict the government, and to prove that it was unfit for government. Consequently, argued *The Bulletin*, the system of party government may be defined as 'a system by which two low-minded organisations are hired to expound each other's infamy for the public benefit, and to prove to the country that the other side is an association of grasping brigands'.[153] Rather than striving for political principles, each party devoted its efforts to attain the spoils of office. *The Bulletin* believed that the public was weary of this system and would gladly consign party politics to oblivion if they only knew how to do it.[154]

In *The Bulletin's* view, Switzerland was probably the only state which managed to run a constitutional government irrespective of party considerations. Under this system, the premier and ministry were drawn from Parliament and elected by a direct vote of the Assembly, while the Cabinet held office for three years and was never ejected from office by a failure to win a vote in the Assembly. The government was not required to resign where it was defeated on a proposal, because the House never pledged itself to follow the dictates of the cabinet. This freed the Swiss system from arguably the worst feature of the British and Australian system of government, namely 'that servile obedience

[151] ibid 400.
[152] ibid 401.
[153] 'Party Government', *The Bulletin* (Sydney), 9 August 1890, 6.
[154] See also 'Party Government in the Commonwealth', *The Bulletin* (Sydney), 3 April 1897.

which is the only condition under which an Australian or British government can possibly maintain its position'.[155]

In another article published in 1894 *The Bulletin* continued its attack on party government. In this article, *The Bulletin* argued that party government failed to adequately represent the community, and was an obstacle to popular self-government. In most cases, the ministerial party represented little more than one tenth of the entire community; thus, the government of the day was supported by only 'a miserable fraction of the nation'. The worst feature of the party system, according to *The Bulletin*, was Parliament's lack of control over the ministry. The majority party could not achieve anything in Parliament unless it had the approval and the sanction of the cabinet. The ministry was able, in most cases, to force its party members to vote as it chose: if the party backbenchers failed to support ministerial proposals, the ministry would threaten to resign, or would obtain a dissolution and force the party members to win back their seats. 'Party Government, in short, is a despotism with complications, and about the best thing that can be said for it is that sometimes a Statesman arises and does good in spite of it'.[156]

V. CONCLUSION

This chapter has examined the introduction of responsible government into the Australian colonies, how contemporaries understood responsible government, and the development of the political systems under responsible government in the colonies up until the time of Federation in order to provide context for the framers' views. The framers' views and beliefs in relation to responsible government were shaped by their experiences of the functioning of politics in the colonies, and some understanding of that historical context is necessary to understand the framers' views.

This chapter has argued that the conception held by writers in the nineteenth century drew heavily on the authoritative writings on the British Constitution which were examined in chapter two. As can be seen from the foregoing, the political systems in the colonies under responsible government were not homogenous, but functioned in different ways, despite possessing similar constitutional arrangements. This illustrated a key tenet of British constitutional thought, namely that the British system of government was considered to be an organic Constitution, consisting not simply of a body of laws but also custom, practice and convention. These customs would reflect the relevant circumstances and the political habits of the people, and thus variations were to be expected, consistent with both the diachronic and synchronic nature of responsible government.

[155] 'Party Government', *The Bulletin* (Sydney), 9 August 1890, 6.
[156] 'More Aspects of Party Government', *The Bulletin* (Sydney), 1 December 1894, 6.

Throughout much of the nineteenth century there was significant concern about the instability of colonial politics and many contemporaries wanted stable party groupings to emerge to address this. Historians have often attributed the instability of colonial politics to the absence of political parties.[157] The Federation Conventions which debated the terms of the federal Constitution took place during a period of significant change and ferment in Australian politics. By 1909, a party system existed at the federal level, and in every colony except Victoria, which brought fundamental changes to the political system.[158]

This chapter has also argued that, throughout the nineteenth century, a desire to ensure popular self-government was central to colonial conceptions of responsible government. Responsible government was inherently bound up with questions of self-government,[159] given that a demand for greater local autonomy was a central part of colonists' demands for constitutional reform in the 1850s. In the 1880s and 1890s, increasing attention was being paid to questions of the efficacy of responsible government and the cabinet system and there were often sharp criticisms of the working of responsible government. Underlying both the desire for self-government and concerns about the effectiveness of parliamentary institutions was a belief in popular self-government. The principal source of the problems was the linking of tenure of office with the need to maintain the support of the lower House of Parliament, with its fluctuating majorities and party allegiances, which provoked an ongoing struggle for office between warring parliamentary factions who sought to oust their rivals and secure their own positions on the Treasury benches.[160] Under the system of 'government by contradiction', half the country's politicians attempted to govern the country while the other half strove to prevent them from doing so.[161]

Colonial politics saw frequent changes of ministry and perceptions of instability.[162] Accordingly, some criticised the cabinet system for its instability and weakness. Because the ministry had no certainty of tenure, Parliament spent much time debating no confidence motions rather than accomplishing real

[157] Eg, McMinn (n 10) 58; Clune and Griffith (n 36) 53; Alan J Ward, 'Exporting the British Constitution: Responsible Government in New Zealand, Canada, Australia and Ireland' (1987) 25 *Journal of Commonwealth and Comparative Politics* 3, 9.

[158] P Loveday, 'Emergence: Realignment and Consolidation' in P Loveday, AW Martin and Robert S Parker (eds), *The Emergence of the Australian Party System* (Sydney, Hale & Iremonger, 1977) 453.

[159] See, eg, Moore, *The Constitution of the Commonwealth of Australia* (n 5) 248, 251; Charles Parkinson, 'George Higinbotham and Responsible Government in Colonial Victoria' (2001) 25 *Melbourne University Law Review* 181; Victoria, *Parliamentary Debates*, Legislative Assembly, 2 November 1869, 2123–2141 (George Higinbotham).

[160] South Australia, *Parliamentary Debates*, Legislative Assembly, 9 September 1891, 1074 (Dr Cockburn).

[161] Similar concerns were voiced in New Zealand: *Parliamentary Debates*, House of Representatives, 1 July 1896, 530–1 (Major Steward).

[162] Eg, Nemo, 'Cabinets in Collapse' (1899) 15 *Review of Reviews* 755; Todd, *Parliamentary Government in the British Colonies* (n 20) 61–2; Reeves (n 28) 63–6.

business for the benefit of the country.[163] Others criticised the excessive strength and dominance of cabinet, which reversed the proper constitutional relationship between Parliament and the executive. Rather than Parliament controlling the executive, the executive controlled and dominated Parliament, and only those measures which had the sanction of the ministry had any chance of being passed. When a government measure was threatened, the government could threaten dissolution of Parliament in order to force MPs into subservience. Many criticisms singled out the pernicious effects of cabinet solidarity. If any minister was threatened with censure, his cabinet colleagues closed ranks, preventing Parliament from holding any individual minister accountable. Cabinet solidarity required a false unity, requiring ministers to suppress their own opinions and defend views they did not hold.

It was also thought that the demands of party had a corrupting effect on the behaviour of MPs. MPs who had voted to oust a ministry would often, when in office themselves, adopt the very measures they had previously criticised. Many believed that the combination of executive dominance, party discipline and cabinet unity suppressed the freedom and independence of MPs, forcing them to act as the mere servants of their party. Underlying these criticisms was a concern to ensure genuine accountability and self-government, for both strong and weak ministries could prevent the people properly governing themselves.

Something of the paradox of parliamentary government was captured by Robert Michels, writing in 1915. Michels argued that political parties were a necessity given that organisation was the only means available for the creation of a collective will. Yet, under the 'iron law of oligarchy', this political necessity inevitably led to the leaders assuming control of the organisation, who became largely independent of control from the masses. The upshot was that 'in modern party life aristocracy gladly presents itself in democratic guise, whilst the substance of democracy is permeated with aristocratic elements', where the representatives exercised dominion over the represented.[164]

In South Australia and Victoria, and also during the Federation debates, the system of elective ministries modelled on the Swiss system of government was proposed to remedy the perceived problems with cabinet government. The elective ministry system would give fixity of tenure to the executive for a specified period, preventing fluctuating coalitions from removing the government for party reasons. It was thought that an elective executive would make administration the primary function of the ministry and increase the independence of MPs. However, the elective ministry system was never adopted in any of the colonies.

[163] Victoria, *Parliamentary Debates*, Legislative Assembly, 30 November 1875, 1424 (George Higinbotham).

[164] Robert Michels, *Political Parties: A Sociological Study of the Oligarchical Tendencies of Modern Democracy* (New York, Collier, 1915) 10, 21, 40.

The criticisms of party government were not unanimous, but provoked strong counter-arguments in defence of the status quo, which were principled as well as pragmatic. Contemporaries believed that a stable two-party system was essential to parliamentary government, and that independent groups and coalitions were contrary to the proper working of parliamentary government. While freedom and independence were necessary for MPs, too much independence, or the abuse of that independence, would lead to instability and prevent the transaction of business in Parliament. It was argued that parties were necessary and legitimate; and as long as there were differences of opinion on political matters, parties will form to give expression to those opinions.[165] Party organisation and discipline was necessary to be genuinely effective in politics and implement reforms.[166] It was also considered that there was no satisfactory alternative to responsible government which would not also lead to other problems.[167]

These criticisms and defences of party government were well known to the framers of the Australian Constitution. Some had participated in debates regarding party government and constitutional reform in the colonies; others had themselves published critiques of party government or proposed the adoption of elective ministries. The historical and political context considered in this chapter informed the framers' views about responsible government, and so provides important context to the Federation debates.

[165] For similar debates in New Zealand, see *Parliamentary Debates*, House of Representatives, 1 July 1896, 544–5 (G W Russell), 549 (Mr Collins), 551 (Sir R Stout).
[166] Fisher, 'Party Government'; 'Party Politics' (1881) 619 *Fraser's Magazine* 132; New Zealand, *Parliamentary Debates*, House of Representatives, 1 July 1896, 531 (Mr Seddon).
[167] *Report of the Royal Commission on Constitutional Reform* (n 137) 5.

4

The Framers' Views: Conflict and Resolution

The beauty, the virtue of the English system is its plasticity, its elasticity. Generation after generation introduces some novel feature, and its working conditions again change.[1]

John Winthrop Hackett (1891)

I. INTRODUCTION

CHAPTER ONE NOTED that it is coherent to speak of the concepts of group agency and intention. Adopting that approach, chapters four and five aim to discern the intentions of the framers in relation to the incorporation of responsible government into the Australian Constitution. That is, I aim to ascertain the reasoned conclusion reached by the Federal Conventions in relation to responsible government by examining the views of the framers as articulated in the Federation debates read in light of the historical and intellectual context discussed in earlier chapters, and the impact of those ideas on the drafting of the Constitution. Chapter four examines the framers' views as to responsible government, including how they resolved the conflict of principle arising from the powers of the Senate and proposals to abandon the British system of responsible government. Chapter five examines how they expected the constitutional structure created by the Constitution to function.

These chapters argue that two themes were central to the framers' conception: constitutional evolution and popular self-government. The framers conceived of responsible government as an inherently changeable system whose working could not be prescribed or even predicted in advance. Further, the framers considered that under the system of responsible government, 'the people' would govern themselves through Parliament, and the manner in which they chose to do so would vary from time to time. The two principles dovetailed into a

[1] *Convention Debates* (1891) 279 (Hackett).

dynamic conception of responsible government which drew on British constitutional ideas as well as distinctly Australian concerns relating to self-government.

There were two significant challenges of principle to the incorporation of responsible government into the Constitution. First, a sizable minority of delegates were critical of cabinet government, and wished to abandon it in favour of the Swiss system of 'elective ministries'. Second, the smaller colonies were not prepared to enter the Federation unless the Constitution guaranteed equal representation for the states in the Senate, with the Senate possessing powers co-ordinate or nearly co-ordinate to those of the House of Representatives. This was seen by many framers as being inconsistent with British notions of responsible government, under which the lower house was the predominant house. This book argues that the two themes of constitutional evolution and self-government explain how a majority of the framers conceptualised and resolved these challenges.

There have been many critics of the framers. Among them are those who have argued that the Constitution produced by the framers is profoundly undemocratic, especially with respect to the powers and composition of the Senate.[2] Some have argued that the framers did not, but should have, foreseen the rise of disciplined parties and guarded against them in the Constitution.[3] Others have argued that federalism and responsible government are contradictory, and that the attempt to incorporate both into the Constitution was a direct cause of the 1975 constitutional crisis.[4] It has also been argued that the Constitution is 'hazy' and that the lack of specificity as to the relationship between Parliament and the executive was 'a serious and dangerous mistake'.[5]

[2] Eg, LF Crisp, *Australian National Government*, 5th edn (Melbourne, Longman Cheshire, 1983) 349; David Wood, 'The Senate, Federalism and Democracy' (1989) 17 *Melbourne University Law Review* 292; Helen Coonan, 'Safeguard or Handbrake on Democracy?' in Brian Costar (ed), *Deadlock or Democracy? The Future of the Senate* (Sydney, UNSW Press, 1999) 12–13; Hugh Emy, 'The Mandate, the Senate and Responsible Government' (1996) 30 *Australia and World Affairs* 5; Gareth Evans, 'Labor and the Constitution' (1976) 35 *Meanjin* 3; Geoffrey Sawer, 'Towards a New Federal Structure?' in Gareth Evans (ed), *Labor and the Constitution, 1972–1975: Essays and Commentaries on the Constitutional Controversies of the Whitlam Years in Australian Government* (Richmond, Heinemann Educational Australia, 1977) 15–16; EG Whitlam, *On Australia's Constitution* (Camberwell, Widescope, 1977) 229–50, 251–7.

[3] GS Reid, 'Parliamentary-Executive Relations: The Suppression of Politics' in Henry Mayer, (ed), *Australian Politics: A Second Reader* (Melbourne, Cheshire, 1970); Jim Chalmers and Glyn Davis, 'Power: Relations Between the Parliament and the Executive' (Research Paper No 14, Parliamentary Library, Parliament of Australia, 2000); Ian Marsh, *Beyond the Two Party System: Political Representation, Economic Competitiveness, and Australian Politics* (Cambridge, Cambridge University Press, 1995); Harry Evans, 'Reflections on the Founders', *The House Magazine*, 1 March 1995.

[4] Colin Howard and Cheryl Saunders, 'The Blocking of the Budget and Dismissal of the Government' in Gareth Evans (ed), *Labor and the Constitution, 1972–1975* (Melbourne, Heinemann, 1977) 286; Geoffrey Sawer, *Federation Under Strain: Australia 1972–1975* (Carlton, Melbourne University Press, 1977) 121–3; George Winterton, *Parliament, the Executive and the Governor-General: A Constitutional Analysis* (Melbourne, Melbourne University Press, 1983) 5–11.

[5] Chalmers and Davis (n 3) 6; Winterton (n 4) 3–4.

Chapters four and five offer a corrective to these criticisms. They argue that a belief in popular self-government led the framers to draft what they considered to be a democratic Constitution, which enabled the people to govern themselves through the institutions of government. Under this structure the Senate was not intended to be an obstacle to the enactment of the people's will but instead another means of ascertaining that will. Chapter two noted that parties were considered necessary for the functioning of parliamentary government; consistent with this constitutional orthodoxy, chapters four and five argue that the framers did recognise that parties would exist in the Commonwealth. Further, the problems with parties and cabinet government were well known to the framers and a number of the framers had themselves penned critiques of that system, but they did not consider that a mere paper Constitution could eradicate those problems. Finally, the framers believed that the people should have the right to govern themselves through Parliament in the manner they saw fit, and that it was not their role, or even possible, to attempt to limit or prescribe how they would do so. As such, it was illegitimate, or impossible, to mandate key aspects of the relationship between Parliament and the executive such as how governments were formed and held accountable.

Two competing views of responsible government vied for acceptance throughout the Conventions. Framers from New South Wales and Victoria including Parkes, Reid, Gillies, Munro, Isaacs, Higgins and Trenwith advocated a strongly normative or prescriptive view, arguing that lower house dominance was of the essence of responsible government and that the Constitution should explicitly require the ministry to possess the confidence of the House of Representatives. Other framers advocated a more descriptive and evolutionary view which accepted that lower house dominance was a feature of the British Constitution as at the time of Federation, but saw this as a historically contingent stage in the development of responsible government rather than an inherent or essential feature. Following British conceptions of the Constitution as organic and living, these framers expected that the functioning of responsible government would continue to evolve after Federation, especially with a democratically elected federal upper house, and that to entrench lower house dominance would have been to ossify a particular development of responsible government.[6]

This book argues that the latter view prevailed. The picture that emerges from a careful reading of the Convention debates in their historical and intellectual context is of a belief shared by all of the framers (including those who advocated the normative view) that responsible government was a dynamic and constantly evolving set of practices that could not be prescribed or fully predicted in advance but whose functioning would be determined by the people. The framers intended to create a government and a Parliament for a sovereign

[6] Note that s 128 enables formal changes to be made to the text of the Constitution and ss 51(xxxvi)–(xxxviii) also contemplate changes to the operation of the Constitution and the powers exercisable by the Commonwealth.

people, and created a deliberately elastic form of executive so that those people could shape their institutions to govern themselves as they saw best.[7]

II. RELEVANT ASPECTS OF THE FEDERATION PROCESS

The terms of the Constitution were debated during two Conventions held in the 1890s. At both Conventions debate followed an agreed process closely modelled on contemporary parliamentary procedure. The first Convention was held in Sydney in 1891 and was attended by representatives of the six Australian colonies chosen by the colonial Parliaments, together with two delegates from New Zealand, all of whom were experienced parliamentarians. Debate was conducted based on a series of preliminary resolutions moved by Henry Parkes. Parkes proposed that the Convention should approve the drafting of a federal Constitution which would establish a bicameral federal Parliament, with a Senate consisting of an equal number of members from each province, and a House of Representatives to be elected by districts formed on a population basis, and which was to possess the sole power of originating and amending Bills appropriating revenue or imposing taxation. Parkes also proposed that there should be a federal Supreme Court to function as a final court of appeal for Australia and that the Constitution should enshrine the principles of responsible government, establishing a Governor-General to be advised by ministers possessing the confidence of the lower house.[8]

These proposed resolutions exposed significant divisions among delegates, especially relating to the composition and powers of the Senate. Delegates from the smaller colonies[9] considered that the essence of Federation was that the people of the states, as well as the people of the nation as a whole, should assent to the passage of all legislation by the federal Parliament.[10] This required that all states should be equally represented in the upper house and that the upper house should powers equal to those of the House of Representatives. However, as discussed in more detail below, it was considered that an upper house constituted in this way would be inconsistent with responsible government according to the British model.[11] Thus, delegates from the larger colonies[12] strongly resisted the proposal to establish an upper house with co-equal power, considering that this would result in the minority governing the majority.[13]

[7] *Cf*, BR Wise, *The Commonwealth of Australia* (London, Pitman, 1909) 193–4.
[8] *Convention Debates* (1891) 23.
[9] That is, South Australia, Queensland, Tasmania and Western Australia.
[10] *Convention Debates* (1891) 31 (Griffith).
[11] *Convention Debates* (1891) 33, 35, 38 (Griffith), 56–8 (Playford).
[12] That is, Victoria and New South Wales.
[13] *Convention Debates* (1891) 47–8 (Munro).

This controversy was resolved by what became known as the '1891 compromise', which survived, with some modifications, in the later drafts of the Constitution. In summary, this compromise gave the House of Representatives the sole power to initiate appropriation and taxation Bills, and prohibited it from 'tacking' additional matters onto a taxation Bill. The Senate had power to affirm or reject, but not amend, laws imposing taxation and laws appropriating 'the necessary supplies for the ordinary annual services of the Government', although it could suggest amendments. In all other respects the Senate had equal legislative power.[14]

After debating Parkes' resolutions, the Convention appointed three committees to deliberate and provide instructions for the preparation of a draft Constitution.[15] A drafting committee consisting of Sir Samuel Walker Griffith, Andrew Inglis Clark and Charles Cameron Kingston was appointed to draft a Constitution giving effect to the decisions reached by the committees and the resolutions of the Convention. Their draft was debated and revised by the constitutional committee before being reported to the Convention for consideration and debate;[16] after surprisingly little debate, and surprisingly few amendments, the Constitution was adopted by the Convention.[17]

The intention was that the Constitution would be taken to the colonial Parliaments for adoption, and ultimately enacted by the imperial Parliament. However, the 1891 Bill was soon shelved due to lack of interest, as well as 'political vicissitudes and the stress of urgent local issues' including strong opposition in New South Wales.[18] Following a period of stagnation and public indifference,[19] the premiers of the colonies decided that Federation was a pressing issue, and agreed to convene a second Convention to frame a federal Constitution. The second federal Convention was held over three sessions in 1897–98 with delegates sent by New South Wales, South Australia, Tasmania, Victoria and Western Australia. As with the earlier Convention, all delegates save one were experienced parliamentarians.[20] Delegates were directly elected by the people and voted as individuals.[21] The 1897 Convention commenced in

[14] *Convention Debates*, Adelaide (1897) 441–2 (Barton); Draft Constitution, Chapter I, clause 55, in *Convention Debates* (1891) 953–4.

[15] *Convention Debates* (1891) 500–10.

[16] ibid 521–34.

[17] John Quick and Robert Randolph Garran, *The Annotated Constitution of the Australian Commonwealth* (Sydney, Angus & Robertson, 1901) 130.

[18] 'Intercolonial Federation', *Sydney Morning Herald*, 25 August 1894, 9; George Houstoun Reid, 'The 'Commonwealth of Australia'' (1891) 173 *Nineteenth Century* 145, 150.

[19] John Bannon, *The Crucial Colony: South Australia's Role in Reviving Federation, 1891 to 1897* (Canberra, Federalism Research Centre, 1994) 27–38.

[20] Helen Irving, 'Making the Federal Commonwealth, 1890–1901' in Alison Bashford and Stuart Macintyre (eds), *The Cambridge History of Australia* (Melbourne, Cambridge University Press, 2013) vol 1, 260.

[21] For discussion see Peter Loveday, 'The Federal Convention, An Analysis of the Voting' (1972) 18 *Australian Journal of Politics and History* 169.

familiar fashion by debating a series of resolutions put by Edmund Barton, in similar terms to those moved by Parkes in 1891. Barton emphasised that the establishment of the federal government was for the purpose of enlarging the powers of self-government of the people of Australia.[22] Although the framers resolved to start afresh, the 1891 Bill was essentially the starting point for the later draft Constitution, and many aspects of the earlier Bill were replicated along with some significant modifications.[23] A drafting committee consisting of Barton, Richard O'Connor and Sir John Downer prepared a draft Constitution which was laid before the Convention, almost immediately provoking a crisis about the powers of the Senate in relation to money Bills. The resulting discussion retraced much of the ground that had been traversed in 1891, and after significant debate in substance re-affirmed the 1891 compromise by a narrow margin.[24]

After the first session the Convention adjourned for the draft Constitution to be considered by the colonial Parliaments. Two further sessions were necessary to finalise consideration of the Bill and reach agreement; after long debate, the draft Bill was eventually approved by the Convention on 17 March 1898. The 1898 Bill differed in important respects from the 1891 Bill, and delegates considered the later Bill much more liberal and democratic.[25] After a somewhat tortuous process the Constitution was approved by the required majorities in referendums in each of the colonies and enacted by the British Parliament.[26]

The framers conceived the Federation process as a negotiation among contracting partners. Each delegate had been elected to represent the interests of his colony and secure the best terms possible, with the resulting product requiring the approval by the people of the colonies and Australia as a whole.[27] As a result, the framers considered their task to be to frame a workable Constitution that

[22] *Convention Debates*, Adelaide (1897) 17, 366 (Barton). See also 86, 94 (Carruthers).

[23] ibid 433 (Barton); JA La Nauze, 'Federal Conventions – The 1890s and Now' (1973) 45 *Australian Quarterly* 52; Quick and Garran (n 17) 165; Robert Randolph Garran, 'The Making and Working of the Constitution' (1932) 4(15) *Australian Quarterly* 5, 5.

[24] See *Convention Debates*, Adelaide (1897) 548.

[25] *Convention Debates* (1898) 2467 (Barton). Key differences included election of senators rather than appointment by state Parliaments; additional legislative powers including the power to legislate with reference to invalid and old-age pensions and conciliation and arbitration for the prevention and settlement of industrial disputes which extend beyond the limits of one state; a provision for the resolution of deadlocks and amendment of the Constitution by dual referendum.

[26] For interesting contemporaneous discussions of the Federation process see 'Australian Federation: The Story of a Great Fight' (1898) 12 *Review of Reviews* 690; ENC Braddon, 'The Federation Movement in Australasia' (1896) 233 *Nineteenth Century* 156; Alfred Deakin, 'The Present Federal Crisis' in *Proceedings, People's Federal Convention, Bathurst, November, 1896* (Sydney, Gordon and Gotch, 1897) 177–80; George Houstoun Reid, 'The Outlook of Federation' (January 1897) *Review of Reviews* 33; BR Wise, *The Struggle for Union: Episodes in the Movement for Australian Federation* (Sydney, 1912); 'The Commonwealth of Australia' (Jul 1899) *Review of Reviews* 48.

[27] *Convention Debates* (1891) 199 (Moore), 353, 451 (Gordon), 480 (Cockburn); *Convention Debates*, Sydney (1897) 493 (Cockburn, Downer), 563 (Holder), 603 (Lyne), 634 (Turner), 861 (Carruthers).

was acceptable to the majority in each of the colonies.[28] The resultant Bill was a compromise between the competing views and interests of the various colonies rather than a Constitution that any one or more of the framers considered ideal.[29] Further, the framers had a strong sense that they met only in an advisory capacity and that the people had to approve the terms of any Federation, which inevitably constrained what the individual delegates could agree to.[30] As they were elected by the people of the colonies and the Constitution was submitted to the electors at a referendum, the framers believed that the Constitution emanated from the people and was consistent with their wishes;[31] as put by Cockburn, '[n]ever before has the instrument of government of a nation been so entirely the handiwork of the people themselves'.[32]

III. HOW THE FRAMERS UNDERSTOOD RESPONSIBLE GOVERNMENT

This section outlines the fundamental elements of the framers' view of responsible government. The overwhelming majority of the delegates to the Federation

[28] *Convention Debates*, Adelaide (1897) 650–1 (Deakin).

[29] *Convention Debates* (1898) 2478 (Barton). See also *Convention Debates* (1891) 45 (Fysh), 69 (Deakin), 242 (Clark); *Convention Debates*, Adelaide (1897) 665–6 (Higgins); Alfred Deakin, 'The Federation of Australia' (1891) 10 *Scribner's Magazine* 549, 550; BR Wise, *The Making of the Australian Commonwealth, 1889–1900: A Stage in the Growth of the Empire* (London, Longmans Green, 1913) 259; Alfred Deakin and Lord Brassey (eds), *Speeches on Australian Federation by the Premiers of Victoria, South Australia, Queensland, Tasmania, and Western Australia* (Melbourne, G Robertson & Co, 1899) 5–6.

[30] *Convention Debates* (1891) 19 (Baker), 21 (Smith), 27 (Parkes), 70 (Deakin), 104 (Thynne), 189, 902 (Munro), 211 (Brown), 224 (Gillies), 335 (Deakin), 390–1 (Munro), 419 (Wrixon), 732 (Forrest), 902 (Dibbs), 902 (Fitzgerald).

[31] John Quick, 'The Progress and Present Conditions of Federation' (1896) 8 *Review of Reviews* 248; John Quick, 'Why Victoria Should Accept the Bill' (1898) 12 *Review of Reviews* 305; John A Cockburn, 'The Commonwealth of Australia' (1901) 49 *Journal of the Society of Arts* 381, 384; John A Cockburn, *Australian Federation* (London, Horace Marshall, 1901) 25–6, 73; *Convention Debates* (1898) 2480 (Barton); Henry Wrixon, *The Constitution of the Commonwealth of Australia: An Address* (Melbourne, Melville, Mullen & Slade, 1901) 1, 3; BR Wise, 'The Commonwealth of Australia' (1899) 33 *National Review* 823, 829; Charles Cameron Kingston, *The Democratic Element in Australian Federation* (Adelaide, L Bonython & Co, 1897) 6.

[32] Cockburn, *Australian Federation* (n 31) 73. See also JH Symon, *The Australian Commonwealth Bill: The Spectator's Criticism: A Reply* (Adelaide, Hussey & Gillingham, Printers, 1900) 6; Anonymous, *Is Federation Our True Policy? The Politician Revealed To Himself* (Melbourne, George Robertson and Company, 1898) 6. There has been debate about the extent to which Federation was truly a popular process: Brian De Garis, 'How Popular was the Popular Federation Movement?' (Papers on Parliament No 21, Parliament of Australia, 1993) 105; Stuart Macintyre, 'Corowa and the Voice of the People' (Papers on Parliament No 32, Parliament of Australia, 1998); Stuart Macintyre, 'Some Absentees from Adelaide' (1998) 1 *New Federalist* 16; Stuart Macintyre, 'The Fortunes of Federation' in David Headon and John Williams (eds), *Makers of Miracles: The Cast of the Federation Story* (Carlton, Melbourne University Press, 1999); John Hirst, 'Federation and the People: A Response to Stuart Macintyre' (Papers on Parliament No 32, Parliament of Australia, 1998); Helen Irving, 'Introduction' in Helen Irving (ed), *The Centenary Companion to Australian Federation* (Melbourne, Cambridge University Press, 1999) 10; Marian Quartly, 'Victoria' in Helen Irving (ed), *The Centenary Companion to Australian Federation* (Melbourne, Cambridge University Press, 1999) 241–2; Brian Galligan and Winsome Roberts, 'The People's Constitution?

Conventions were experienced politicians, thoroughly conversant with the practice of responsible government.[33] Many of the framers were familiar with the leading British writings on the British Constitution,[34] and their conception of responsible government drew strongly on these writings. The British Constitution was considered the authoritative model for the principles of responsible government, although the framers acknowledged that it was impossible to reproduce the British Constitution in its entirety.[35] The terms 'British Constitution', 'English form of government' and 'responsible government' were used largely synonymously by the framers, with responsible government being taken to mean the stage in the development of the British Constitution as at the time of Federation.[36]

Chapter two noted that the British Constitution was conceived as organic and inherently changeable, and that 'the Constitution' included the practices and conventions which gave life to the institutions of government.[37] The framers conceived of responsible government consistently with this understanding. Responsible government, for the framers, was not primarily a set of constitutional rules or conventions (for example, that the ministry must maintain the confidence of the lower house of Parliament), but an understanding of how the British Constitution, and the colonial governments which were modelled on the British system, functioned. Responsible government was therefore broader than the legal rules of the Constitution; the framers spoke of the Constitution as a 'skeleton' that the people would breathe into life, and considered that the way the system of government would work in practice would be determined by the people, not the text of the Constitution.[38] Conventions were an essential part of the 'constitution'.[39] 'Responsible government' therefore can be understood

Exploring Australia's Popular Democracy 1885–1901: A Research Study' (2000) 5 *New Federalist* 87; George Williams and David Hume, *Human Rights under the Australian Constitution*, 2nd edn (South Melbourne, Oxford University Press, 2013) 56–7; Rosemary Pringle, 'The Federation Issue in New South Wales Politics 1891–99' (2008) 21 *Australian Journal of Politics & History* 1; Alastair Davidson, *The Invisible State: The Formation of the Australian State 1788–1901* (Cambridge, Cambridge University Press, 1991) 233–38.

[33] GW McDonald, 'The Eighty Founding Fathers' (1968) 1 *Queensland Historical Review* 38.

[34] Eg, *Convention Debates* (1891) 105 (Thynne, quoting Hearn), 543 (Baker, referring to Bagehot); *Convention Debates*, Adelaide (1897) 912 (Barton, quoting Bagehot), 915 (Glynn, referring to Todd as the 'leading authority on parliamentary government in the colonies'), 948 (Isaacs, quoting Todd); *Convention Debates* (1898) 2250 (Deakin, quoting Todd), 2293 (Abbott, quoting Todd); Cockburn, *Australian Federation* (n 31) 100.

[35] *Convention Debates* (1891) 50 (Munro), 242–3, 245 (Clark), 401 (Douglas), 417–8, 456–7 (Parkes), 456 (Griffith). See also Andrew Inglis Clark, 'Our Australian Constitutions' (Pt 1) (1874) 1 *Quadrilateral* 56, 58.

[36] Eg, *Convention Debates* (1891) 419 (Wrixon).

[37] See, eg, RC Baker, *Notes on the Constitution of South Australia* (Hussey & Gillingham, 1899) ii, xxxi.

[38] *Convention Debates*, Adelaide (1897) 86–7 (Carruthers), 511 (Deakin); Andrew Inglis Clark, *Studies in Australian Constitutional Law* (Melbourne, Charles F Maxwell, 1901) 6.

[39] *Convention Debates* (1891) 715 (Downer).

to have meant something like the way the British Constitution, and the colonial systems modelled on that Constitution, functioned at the time of Federation.[40]

Responsible government had evolved over a long period, being the 'growth of centuries'.[41] As a 'codeless myriad of precedents',[42] responsible government was not a strictly logical system; rather, as argued by Glynn, it was a 'combination of compromises and contradictions' and there was not a single principle or tenet of the British Constitution that could stand the 'strictly logical test'.[43] Cockburn wrote that the essential feature of the British Constitution is 'its power of adaptation to suit the requirements and pressure of the times. Its plasticity is its perfection'.[44] The principles of responsible government consisted of unwritten conventions and were not defined in any of the colonial constitutions.[45] The framers recognised that accurately and comprehensively defining responsible government would have been a difficult exercise, not because the framers were 'afraid of appearing gauche and uneducated in British eyes',[46] but due to the 'studied vagueness' of the British Constitution.[47]

Despite this difficulty, scattered throughout the debates are many competent and concise definitions of both the theory and practical operation of responsible government. As understood by the framers, responsible government meant principally that the head of state acted on the advice of the ministry;[48] as explained by Clark, every executive act must be performed in accordance with the advice of responsible ministers.[49] An equally important feature of responsible government at the time of Federation was the requirement for the ministry to possess the confidence of the lower house of Parliament, so that the ministry was responsible to Parliament for its actions, especially the lower house.[50] The rationale for this was that 'parliament represents and is responsible to the people', given that

[40] See, eg, *Convention Debates* (1891) 527 (Griffith); Samuel Walker Griffith, *Notes on Australian Federation: Its Nature and Probable Effects: A Paper Presented to the Government of Queensland* (Brisbane, Government Printer, 1896) 6.

[41] *Convention Debates*, Adelaide (1897) 118 (Henry), 180 (Isaacs), 388, 391 (Barton).

[42] ibid 244 (Fysh).

[43] ibid 276 (Glynn).

[44] John A Cockburn, 'Should the Cabinet System be Changed?' (1895) 6 *Review of Reviews* 399, 399.

[45] *Convention Debates* (1891) 162 (Kingston), 280 (Hackett), 471 (Gillies), 727 (Thynne).

[46] As argued by Winterton (n 4) 3.

[47] Émile Boutmy, *Studies in Constitutional Law: France, England, United States* (EM Dicey tr, London, Macmillan, 1891) 24; *Convention Debates* (1891) 306 (Suttor), 727 (Thynne); William Reynell Anson, *The Law and Custom of the Constitution*, 3rd edn (Oxford, Clarendon Press, 1897) vol 1, 39; GS Reid, 'Responsible Government and Ministerial Responsibility' (1980) 39 *Australian Journal of Public Administration* 301, 301.

[48] *Convention Debates* (1891) 85, 570–1 (Deakin), 105 (Thynne, quoting Hearn), 575 (Baker); *Convention Debates*, Adelaide (1897) 909 (Reid), 910 (Barton).

[49] Clark, *Studies in Australian Constitutional Law* (n 38) 257; see also *Convention Debates* (1898) 2250 (Deakin, quoting Todd), 2252–4 (Barton).

[50] *Convention Debates* (1891) 85, 571 (Deakin), 105 (Thynne); 162 (Kingston), 240 (Gillies), 472 (Downer), 544 (Baker); *cf* 431 (Griffith); *Convention Debates*, Adelaide (1897) 44, 909 (Reid), 493 (Higgins), 911 (Barton).

'the end and object of responsible government is that the will of the people shall prevail'.[51] Thus, the conventions of responsible government were intended to ensure self-government by the people. Consistent with the descriptions of Bagehot and Todd, the cabinet united the legislature and executive, as ministers would lead and guide the legislature as well as administering departments.[52]

Following standard conceptions of the British Constitution, the framers saw responsible government as an inherently evolutionary system. Griffith was the most articulate proponent of this conception. As noted earlier, at the outset of debate in the 1891 Federal Convention, Parkes moved a series of proposed resolutions which were intended to frame the debate and provide a series of principles which would be reflected in a federal Constitution. One of Parkes's proposed resolutions included the proposition that the Constitution should establish:

> An executive, consisting of a Governor-General and such persons as may from time to time be appointed as his advisers, such persons sitting in Parliament, and whose term of office shall depend upon their possessing the confidence of the house of representatives, expressed by the support of the majority.[53]

This assumed the requirement for the ministry to maintain the confidence of the lower house to be a key feature of responsible government.[54] Griffith challenged this view, arguing that the essence of responsible government was not that the ministers must possess the confidence of the lower house of Parliament. Instead, Griffith considered that its essence was that the head of state administered the government through ministers who were responsible to Parliament. The linking of the ministry's tenure with the confidence of the lower house of Parliament was merely the present stage of development; significant changes had taken place in the working of responsible government up until the 1890s and changes would continue to occur in the future.[55] Griffith wanted the nature of the relationship between Parliament and the executive to be left open for further development, contending that the Convention 'should not make our constitutions so rigid as to insist upon any particular form of … relationship between the executive and parliament'.[56] Griffith expressed some disapproval of party government, which was becoming 'somewhat discredited' in the colonies, and anticipated its replacement with something better; however, he did not consider it was possible to predict the working of the government established by the

[51] *Convention Debates*, Sydney (1897) 665 (Isaacs).

[52] Henry Bournes Higgins, 'The Rigid Constitution' (1905) 20 *Political Science Quarterly* 203, 208; Robert Randolph Garran, *The Coming Commonwealth: An Australian Handbook of Federal Government* (Sydney, Angus & Robertson, 1897) 148.

[53] *Convention Debates* (1891) 23.

[54] ibid 26–7, 447 (Parkes), *cf* 46 (Munro).

[55] *Convention Debates* (1891) 34–5, 37, 767 (Griffith); see also 298 (Douglas); Griffith (n 40) 6–7; GB Barton, *Notes on Australian Federation and the Draft Constitution Bills Framed by the Conventions of 1891 and 1897* (Sydney, Government Printer, 1897) 32.

[56] *Convention Debates* (1891) 467.

Constitution.[57] Early in debate in 1891, Munro attributed to Griffith the view that 'he does not think the government or the executive should be responsible to the house of representatives'. Griffith retorted: 'I said nothing of the kind. I said I did not think it should be a rigid rule of the constitution that it must be responsible to one house only'.[58]

While Griffith's view has been taken as a challenge to or redefinition of responsible government,[59] it is more accurate to see it as a historically attuned conception which drew on familiar themes relating to the British Constitution, which allowed for further development and evolution in the functioning of responsible government. Griffith thus proposed that the Constitution should not mandate that the ministry must possess the confidence of the House of Representatives, which the Convention accepted.[60] Following Griffith's view, the 1891 Bill contained no requirement for ministers to hold seats in Parliament. Notwithstanding that significant changes were made to the draft Constitution, it is argued below that Griffith's view survived relatively intact in the 1897–98 Convention.

In contrast to the picture painted by some writers,[61] popular self-government was a key element of the framers' conception of responsible government.[62] Chapter three noted that self-government was a key theme of nineteenth century colonial conceptions of responsible government and that many in the late nineteenth century were concerned that the cabinet system and political parties hindered accountability to the people. These emphases were reflected in the framers' views: for the framers, responsible government was designed to ensure government by the people. Under the system of representative and responsible government the people did not govern directly, but through the institution of Parliament, and so responsible government combined the legal sovereignty of Parliament with the political supremacy of the electorate.[63] The British system

[57] ibid 40, 431, 527, 714.

[58] ibid 48.

[59] Eg, Brian Galligan, 'The Founders' Design and Intentions Regarding Responsible Government' (1980) 15 *Politics* 1, 2; Frank Roland McGrath, *The Intentions of the Framers of the Commonwealth of Australia Constitution* (PhD Thesis, University of Sydney, 2006) 37.

[60] *Convention Debates* (1891) 467, 473.

[61] Eg, Crisp (n 2) 14–17.

[62] Richard Waterhouse argued that in the 1890s 'most politicians embraced the notion that federation was a people's movement and that the constitution should be based on the notion of popular sovereignty': '... a bastard offspring of tyranny under the guise of liberty': Liberty and Representative Government in Australia, 1788–1901' in Jack P Greene (ed), *Exclusionary Empire: English Liberty Overseas, 1600–1900* (Cambridge, Cambridge University Press, 2010) 244.

[63] William McMillan, *Speech on the Referendum as a Mode of Settling Disputes Between the Two Houses of Parliament* (Sydney, Angus & Robertson, 1896) 9–10; W Harrison Moore, *The Constitution of the Commonwealth of Australia*, 2nd edn (Melbourne, Charles F Maxwell, 1910) 248. See also Jeffrey Goldsworthy, *The Sovereignty of Parliament: History and Philosophy* (Oxford, Clarendon Press, 1999) 219–20.

of government embodied the principle of popular sovereignty by ensuring that the institutions of government gave effect to the will of the people.[64]

The vast majority of the framers believed that under responsible government the people must rule and that the institutions of government ought to give effect to the will of the people.[65] Barton's resolutions in Adelaide in 1897 proposed that the establishment of the federal government was intended 'to enlarge the powers of self-government of the people of Australia'.[66] Trenwith considered the genius of the British Constitution to be 'that the people must govern themselves', and Barton said that '[w]e regard public opinion as our master'.[67] There was a strong belief that the force of public opinion ought to, and would, shape and control the institutions of government, and that it was not possible to resist the will of the people for long.[68] As put by Wise, behind every political measure is 'the vitalising or destructive force of public opinion' without which no ministry or Parliament could exercise the least of its powers.[69] Lyne argued that '[w]e want in this democratic country to lay the foundation of a constitution on which ultimately the voice of the people must be heard and must predominate'.[70] Others agreed that the Constitution should create a democratic government.[71] Cockburn considered that '[t]he voice of the people must prevail' and that '[t]he people can be trusted to manage their own affairs, because they know what their own interests are'.[72] O'Connor noted that public opinion 'always enforces, in a self-governing community, that the will of the majority shall prevail'.[73]

It was not just 'liberals' or 'democrats' who affirmed this. Conservative states' rights advocates such as Baker considered that 'all forms of government are machines to bring into effect the wishes of the people, or, at all events, they ought to be machines to bring into operation and to give effect to the wishes and opinions of the people of the country'.[74] Downer, another conservative, said

[64] McMillan, *Speech on the Referendum* (n 63) 9–10; Wrixon, *The Constitution of the Commonwealth of Australia* (n 31) 6.

[65] In addition to the other sources cited in this paragraph see *Convention Debates* (1891) 735 (Playford); *Convention Debates*, Adelaide (1897) 178 (Isaacs), 542 (Carruthers), 1167 (Symon); *Convention Debates*, Sydney (1897) 271 (Carruthers), 537 (Cockburn), 649–50 (Reid); *Convention Debates* (1898) 2198–9 (Wise); see also the quotations in Anonymous, 'The Federal Bill' (1898) 12 *Review of Reviews* 297, 298–9.

[66] Barton's resolutions, *Convention Debates*, Adelaide (1897) 17.

[67] *Convention Debates*, Adelaide (1897) 525 (Trenwith), 559 (Barton).

[68] *Convention Debates*, Adelaide (1897) 511 (Deakin); *Convention Debates*, Sydney (1897) 324 (Wise); *Convention Debates* (1898) 2216 (Trenwith).

[69] Wise, *The Making of the Australian Commonwealth* (n 29) 240. See also *Convention Debates*, Sydney (1897) 660 (Isaacs).

[70] *Convention Debates*, Sydney (1897) 600.

[71] *Convention Debates*, Adelaide (1897) 144 (Holder), 185 (Quick), 651 (Deakin).

[72] *Convention Debates*, Sydney (1897) 673 (Cockburn); to like effect see also *Convention Debates* (1891) 747 (Downer). Cf John A Cockburn, 'The Sphere of State Activity in Australia' (1901) 50 *Journal of the Society of Arts* 589, 590.

[73] *Convention Debates*, Sydney (1897) 574; see also 665 (Isaacs).

[74] *Convention Debates*, Sydney (1897) 784; RC Baker, *A Manual of Reference to Authorities for the Use of the Members of the National Australasian Convention* (Adelaide, WK Thomas & Co, 1891) 60. See also *Convention Debates*, Sydney (1897) 684 (Higgins).

that '[o]f course, the people's voice will rule' and believed that if 'we ... make both Houses liberal, and trust the people, the result will be that our Federation will work out with that fairness and peace that every one of us desire'.[75] Braddon argued that '[n]othing can be done under the Constitution which is contrary to the will of the people' and Symon considered that a leading characteristic of the British Constitution was that it was 'susceptible to the expression of the people's will'.[76] In addition to an aspirational political principle, this belief in self-government was also an empirical expectation that the people would, in fact, govern, and that the manner in which they chose to do so would vary from time to time. The framers were not naïvely optimistic about the wisdom of the people but recognised that that politics did not always function well.[77]

Although the framers frequently referred to 'the people' and the 'will of the people', they did not articulate precisely what they meant by these terms.[78] At the time of Federation there were differences in the franchise among the colonies, and the framers held competing views as to which categories of people should be entitled to vote. Notwithstanding these differences, for the most part they agreed on the fundamental principle that the chief purpose of responsible government was to realise self-government by the people, but without entrenching any particular conception of 'the people'. In this way, the framers' views concerning popular self-government reflected widespread agreement about the purpose of government while also masking important differences of principle.

The framers conceived the people federally, contemplating local, provincial and national groupings constituting, and being represented in, different levels of government.[79] The new Commonwealth was to be a composite state, formed by a federal union of the colonies, in which there was 'a divided sovereignty' and 'a double citizenship'.[80] The framers' conception of 'the people's will' did not imply a single, unified national will[81] but allowed scope for regional differences between states, as well as contested and competing political views advocated by different political parties. The framers' therefore conceived self-government federally, emphasising local self-government and self-determination.[82] Accordingly, when the framers referred to 'the people' governing themselves, they meant the people participating in their own self-government through state and

[75] *Convention Debates*, Adelaide (1897) 216; see also *Convention Debates* (1898) 725 (Downer).

[76] ibid 1167 (Symon); 'The Federal Bill' (1898) 12 *Review of Reviews* 297, 298 (Braddon).

[77] See, eg, *Convention Debates*, Adelaide (1897) 126 (Symon).

[78] These are some of the most contested concepts in political theory: see, eg, Robert A Dahl, *Democracy and its Critics* (New Haven, Yale University Press, 1989) 3–5; Duncan Ivison, 'Democracy' in Mark Bevir (ed), *Encyclopedia of Political Theory* (Thousand Oaks, Sage, 2010); Joseph A Schumpeter, *Capitalism, Socialism and Democracy* (London, Routledge, 2010) ch 20.

[79] Nicholas Aroney, *The Constitution of a Federal Commonwealth: The Making and Meaning of the Australian Constitution* (Cambridge, Cambridge University Press, 2009) 123–4, 318–9, 344.

[80] Quick and Garran (n 17) 333.

[81] Nicholas Aroney, 'Four Reasons for an Upper House: Representative Democracy, Public Debate, Legislative Outputs and Executive Accountability' (2008) 29 *Adelaide Law Review* 205, 214–6.

[82] Aroney, *The Constitution of a Federal Commonwealth* (n 79) 157, 197, 221.

Commonwealth institutions of government. The primary referent of 'the people' was of course the electors who chose their representatives: the references to 'the people' in the Constitution are to "the people' acting as and through electors', who therefore represent the people more broadly.[83] However, those who were not electors were still politically relevant; those who were not able to vote could express their views through the media and thus contribute to informed public opinion.[84]

The establishment of the architecture of the federal Commonwealth did not require the framers to definitively reach a consensus on who, precisely, 'the people' were; their approach reflects an understanding that the concepts of 'the people' and their 'will' were contested political concepts whose meaning would evolve over time. 'The people' were incorporated into key provisions of the Constitution but not defined, leaving questions of the extent of the franchise to be dealt with by the Commonwealth Parliament.[85] The concept of 'the people' was thus an ambulatory concept, intended to reflect, and allow for diversity in, prevailing views of political representation among the colonies, as well as further development in political thinking.[86]

Delegates from the larger colonies (especially Victoria and New South Wales) were under a particular burden to demonstrate to their colonies that the principle of the rule of the majority was not significantly interfered with, so that their colonies' interests were not overtaken by those of the small colonies,[87] and so it is not surprising that those delegates argued that self-government should mean majority rule.[88] With his customary eloquence Deakin noted that '[t]he sole arbiter, the sole Court of Appeal, which constitutionally we have come to recognise in this country, or in the mother-country, is the rule of the majority. Upon the ultimate rule of the majority the British Constitution swings as upon a pivot'.[89] Berry argued that the trend of modern thought and political

[83] Elisa Arcioni, 'The Core of the Australian Constitutional People – 'The People' as 'The Electors'' (2016) 39 *University of New South Wales Law Journal* 421, 425, 427.

[84] See, eg, Susan Magarey, *Unbridling the Tongues of Women: A Biography of Catherine Helen Spence*, rev edn (Adelaide, University of Adelaide Press, 2010) 119–121 (describing Spence's influence on South Australian public life in the 1890s).

[85] Especially the preamble and ss 7 and 24 of the Constitution.

[86] See also Arcioni (n 83) 435, 442.

[87] See, eg, 'The Attainment of Federation: What was Lacking in the Convention Bill, Being a Reprint of Eight Articles from the *Sydney Daily Telegraph*' (Sydney, 1898); Wise, *The Making of the Australian Commonwealth* (n 29) 239.

[88] *Convention Debates*, Adelaide (1897) 525 (Trenwith), 667 (Reid), 309 (Walker), 499 (O'Connor), 509 (Deakin), 642 (Higgins); *Convention Debates*, Sydney (1897) 330 (Deakin), 687 (Higgins), 857 (Carruthers).

[89] *Convention Debates*, Adelaide (1897) 289. He went on to say: 'Our whole history is the history of a struggle to give more and more effect to that principle, and the whole occasion of the existence of our parties, whether in the colonies or in the mother-country, is the division between those who frankly and fully accept the principle of the rule of the majority, and those who, for one reason or another, accept it only with qualification'.

developments has affirmed 'the theory that the majority must rule, based upon the widest possible adult suffrage'.[90]

Federation necessarily entailed a departure from a purely majoritarian conception of the people's will as argued for by the likes of Deakin, Isaacs and Higgins,[91] and this was reflected in the views of delegates from the smaller colonies. It is not to be thought, however, that such framers were committed to a conservative or undemocratic view of government. As will be discussed in more detail in this chapter and chapter five, both houses of Parliament were structured so as to represent the people, although on different bases. The framers had been elected to represent the interests of their colonies in the Federation negotiations, and these political realities could not be ignored. Theirs was the democracy of elected parliamentarians sent to accomplish a specific goal on behalf of their colonies, to whom they must give an account. There was widespread agreement that the purpose of representative and responsible government was to give effect to 'the will of the people' and that the Constitution was designed to do the same.[92] The differences among the framers, with some exceptions, related to the proper way to give effect to this rather than the principle of rule by the people.[93]

How to translate the will of the people into legislative outcomes, and whether in fact parliamentary systems effectively achieved this, are of course difficult questions, and the framers held divergent views. Deakin wrote in 1891 that under responsible government public opinion 'takes a much more precise shape, takes it much more rapidly, and is enabled to compel its leaders in the popular house'.[94] However, chapters two and three noted that there were significant concerns with the functioning of the parliamentary system in the late nineteenth century which focused on the extent to which the people were in reality able to control the institutions of government. Echoing these concerns, some of the framers acknowledged that the parliamentary process did not always accurately reflect the people's wishes.[95] Holder wrote that it was 'nearly impossible to ascertain what the mind of the people is on any one question from the men returned to Parliament' and Wise considered that public opinion was not a powerful restraining force on individual MPs.[96] These views do not sit

[90] *Convention Debates*, Sydney (1897) 341 (Berry).

[91] Moore, *The Constitution of the Commonwealth of Australia* (n 63) 78; Aroney, *The Constitution of a Federal Commonwealth* (n 79) 196.

[92] FW Holder, 'Why South Australia Should Accept the Bill' (1898) 12 *Review of Reviews* 302; 303; Henry Wrixon, *Self-Government in Victoria: Its Present Condition and the Questions it has to Deal With: Addressed to the Electors of Belfast* (Melbourne, George Robertson, 1876) 8.

[93] The differences are well illustrated by the contrasting speeches in *Convention Debates* (1898) 2172–87 (Isaacs), 2187–2203 (Wise).

[94] Alfred Deakin, 'The Federation of Australia' (1891) 10 *Scribner's Magazine* 549, 558.

[95] AV Dicey raised a similar concern: 'Will the Form of Parliamentary Government be Permanent?' (1899) 13 *Harvard Law Review* 67, 77.

[96] FW Holder, 'The Sydney Convention of 1897' (15 October 1897) *Review of Reviews* 441, 444; BR Wise, 'Australian Politics' (1889) 50 *Macmillan's Magazine* 183, 184. See also BR Wise, *An Australian Appeal to the English Democracy* (Sydney, William Dymock, 1885).

easily with a belief in rapid and compelling popular control of the institutions of government.

British writers such as Todd, Hearn and Bagehot considered that the government must be responsive to public opinion, but they did not conceive the British Constitution in fully democratic terms. The framers' emphasis on self-government represents a distinctive Australian view of responsible government, reflecting concern in the Australian colonies to ensure local autonomy. As put by Deakin: '[w]e cannot afford to have in our constitution any man exercising authority, unless he derives it from the people of Australia'.[97] The Victorian Supreme Court had held in 1888 that the Victorian Constitution conferred only an instalment of self-government.[98] The framers intended to ensure that the Constitution would confer not merely an 'instalment' of self-government, but the fullest measure of self-government that was consistent with maintaining the unity of the British Empire.[99]

Accountability was also a crucial part of the framers' conception of responsible government; indeed, 'responsible' was largely synonymous with 'accountable'.[100] For Griffith, 'responsible' simply meant that ministers take the blame for the advice they give when exercising executive powers.[101] Responsible government allowed blame to be fixed on the right shoulders: where the ministry acted in a way contrary to the wishes of the people, the people possessed the 'sacred privilege' of turning it out of office.[102] Accordingly, the essence of responsible government was that the ministry would be accountable to Parliament, who would in turn be accountable to the people.[103] An effective opposition played an important role in ensuring this accountability. McMillan expressed the hope that there would 'always be an opposition, sturdy, critical, and independent, so that the ministry may always feel the breath of the people, and be turned out as soon as they cease to represent the people'.[104]

Bryce's treatise *The American Commonwealth*, whose influence on the framers is well known, confirmed for the framers the wisdom of parliamentary

[97] *Convention Debates* (1891) 571 (Deakin). See also *Convention Debates*, Adelaide (1897) 178 (Isaacs), 332 (Trenwith); also *Convention Debates* (1898) 2205 (Reid), 2477 (Barton).

[98] *Chung Teong Toy v Musgrove* (1888) 14 VLR 349. According to GB Barton, this ruling created a 'scare' among Melbourne politicians: Barton, *Notes on Australian Federation* (n 55) 58.

[99] *Convention Debates* (1891) 85 (Deakin), see also 105 (Thynne); John Waugh, 'Chung Teong Toy v Musgrove and the Commonwealth Executive' (1991) 2 *Public Law Review* 160, 172.

[100] Richard Baker, *The Executive in a Federation* (Adelaide, Government Printer, 1897) 17; *Convention Debates* (1891) 441 (Thynne), 710 (Deakin), 740 (Jennings), 748 (Downer), 767, 774 (Griffith); *Convention Debates*, Adelaide (1897) 54 (O'Connor, Barton), 133–4 (Symon), 211 (Downer), 243 (Fysh), 334 (Trenwith), 511 (Deakin), 916–7 (Turner); *Convention Debates*, Sydney (1897) 624 (Barton).

[101] *Convention Debates* (1891) 774 (Griffith).

[102] *Convention Debates*, Adelaide (1897) 382 (Barton); *Convention Debates* (1891) 238 (Gillies), 767, 774 (Griffith).

[103] *Convention Debates*, Adelaide (1897) 135 (Symon), 389–90 (Isaacs and Barton); *Convention Debates*, Sydney (1897) 883 (O'Connor).

[104] *Convention Debates* (1891) 273, 431.

systems of government. Rather than an attempt to 'anglicise' the American Government,[105] Bryce's treatise can more accurately be understood as a critique of the American system from a British perspective. Bryce had argued that under the American system there was little effective accountability for leaders and members of Congress, due to the separation of executive and legislative powers, and other features such as the committee system, which meant that it was not clear who should shoulder the blame for the conduct of government. By contrast, the British cabinet system enabled clear responsibility for both legislation and administration.[106] The framers were keen to ensure that key features of the Constitution they drafted did not detract from this fundamentally important feature of responsible government; according to Reid, the virtue of the British Constitution was that it enabled 'firm, flexible, incessant, popular control over the instruments of executive power'.[107]

IV. CHALLENGES OF PRINCIPLE TO RESPONSIBLE GOVERNMENT

As noted earlier, at the commencement of debate in 1891, Parkes proposed that the Constitution should explicitly recognise that the ministry must possess the confidence of the lower house.[108] Parkes' resolution provoked two significant challenges of principle: first, proposals to abandon the British system of responsible government in favour of the Swiss system of electing the executive; second, the demand from the smaller colonies for the Constitution to guarantee equal representation for the states in a Senate possessing powers co-ordinate to those of the House of Representatives. This section examines these challenges and how they were resolved.

A. Criticisms of Responsible Government

As discussed in chapters two and three, numerous criticisms were levelled at responsible government in the late nineteenth century, some penned by the framers themselves. Similar criticisms were voiced during the Conventions. Shiels noted that complaints had been made in the colonies that parliamentary government led to much talk but little action.[109] New Zealand delegate Russell noted that many in New Zealand were beginning to doubt the wisdom of responsible

[105] As argued by John SF Wright, 'Anglicizing the United States Constitution: James Bryce's Contribution to Australian Federalism' (2001) 31 *Publius* 107.

[106] James Bryce, *The American Commonwealth*, 2nd edn (London, Macmillan, 1891) vol 1, 156–7, 167–8, 209–10.

[107] *Convention Debates*, Adelaide (1897) 274.

[108] *Convention Debates* (1891) 23, 321. See also 46 (Munro).

[109] ibid 17.

government, because it subordinated all public questions to the fight for office and did not give effect to public opinion.[110] Kingston echoed the fears of many that responsible government distorted the proper working of Parliament, preventing the consideration of legislation on its merits.[111] Clark quoted Higinbotham to the effect that MPs were pre-occupied only with seeking to murder the reputations of the other party in order to leap into their seats.[112] Dobson considered that they had all felt at times ashamed of the party system; he wished to prevent party government from operating in the Commonwealth.[113] Bray noted, in similar fashion to the pre-Federation criticisms, that under responsible government the proposals of the ministry were routinely torn to pieces by the other side. Accordingly, he queried:

> Is it necessary to have men on the one side proposing what they believe to be best for the state, and men on the other side who advocate an opposite course, and who can only carry out their views by removing those who compose the government? It does not appear to me to be absolutely necessary to have a responsible government and an opposition.[114]

Hackett argued that responsible government had 'distinctly proved a failure' in Canada and even in the UK.[115] O'Connor noted that responsible government had 'many imperfections',[116] while Donaldson considered that responsible government was on its trial, and that it led to uncertainty and rapid changes of ministry.[117] Baker noted that the constant quarrels between the 'ins' and the 'outs' forced the ministry to fight constantly to hold on to office, preventing it from carrying on the business of the country.[118]

Stemming partly from these concerns, and partly from federalist motivations, a sizeable minority of framers argued that the cabinet form of government should be abandoned and that the relationship between the government and the legislature should be modelled on the Swiss form of government rather than the cabinet system. Under this system, ministers would be elected individually by both houses of Parliament for a fixed term and individually responsible for administering their departments, with Parliament responsible for determining matters of policy.[119] It was argued that this would alleviate the problems with

[110] ibid 65.
[111] ibid 162. See also 441 (Baker).
[112] ibid 245. See also Andrew Inglis Clark, *Australasian Federation* (Hobart, 1891) 5–6; Clark, 'Our Australian Constitutions' (n 35) 59.
[113] *Convention Debates*, Adelaide (1897) 195–6; *Convention Debates*, Sydney (1897) 185; *cf Convention Debates*, Adelaide (1897) 345 (Cockburn). See also *Convention Debates*, Sydney (1897) 1109 (Forrest).
[114] *Convention Debates* (1891) 259.
[115] ibid 280 (Hackett).
[116] *Convention Debates*, Adelaide (1897) 51 (O'Connor). See also 133 (Symon), 334 (Trenwith), 532 (Dobson).
[117] *Convention Debates* (1891) 309 (Donaldson).
[118] ibid 440–1 (Baker).
[119] *Convention Debates* (1891) 198 (Cockburn), 440 (Baker); *Convention Debates*, Adelaide (1897) 334 (Trenwith); *Convention Debates*, Sydney (1897) 787 (Baker).

parties and cabinet dominance, especially by giving the ministry the freedom to govern without needing constantly to fight to retain their seats, and would also resist the encroachment of the lower house and the dwindling of the Senate.[120] For these framers, the demands of federalism required an executive moulded to the powers of Parliament and not vice versa; as put by Downer, 'the executive must be made for the parliament, and not the parliament for the executive'.[121]

B. Responsible Government, Lower House Pre-dominance and the Senate

The tension between responsible government and the Senate was one of the most hotly contested issues to be resolved at the Conventions and nearly derailed Federation.[122] For the small colonies, it was essential that the Senate have powers co-ordinate to, or nearly co-ordinate to, those of the lower house, and that the states be equally represented in that house, to ensure that any measures passed by Parliament would have the assent of both the majority of the people and a majority of the states.[123] Many of the framers considered that a Senate established in this way would be inconsistent with responsible government, which entailed the dominance of the lower house.[124] There were several inter-related elements of this perceived incompatibility.

First, many framers considered lower house dominance to be an essential feature of responsible government.[125] Under the British Constitution, the lower house was the dominant house because it was the more representative chamber, it was the house in which the government was formed, and as a result it was the house that controlled public finance. Thus, many framers, especially those from larger colonies, considered that responsible government necessarily required a dominant lower house. However, delegates from the smaller colonies proposed to create a Senate with powers that were practically equal to those of the lower

[120] *Convention Debates* (1891) 438–41 (Baker); *Convention Debates*, Adelaide (1897) 324 (Gordon), 344–6 (Cockburn).

[121] *Convention Debates* (1891) 102, 443 (Downer), 438–41, 465 (Baker); *Convention Debates*, Adelaide (1897) 148 (Holder), 213 (Downer), 324 (Gordon); 334–5 (Trenwith); *Convention Debates*, Sydney (1897) 782–9 (Baker).

[122] Note also JA La Nauze, *The Making of the Australian Constitution* (Carlton, Melbourne University Press, 1972) 139–149.

[123] Richard Baker, *Federation* (Adelaide, 1897) 3–5, 10, 19; *Convention Debates* (1891) 31–2 (Griffith); *Convention Debates*, Sydney (1897) 291 (Symon), 338 (Deakin), 342 (Berry), 349 (Isaacs).

[124] *Convention Debates* (1891) 50, 468 (Munro), 58, 424 (Playford), 102, 472 (Downer), 280 (Hackett), 284 (Moore), 384, 710 (Deakin), 419–21 (Wrixon), 435 (Macrossan), 465 (Baker); *Convention Debates*, Adelaide (1897) 28 (Baker), 96, 492 (Higgins), 106–7 (Wise), 134, 136 (Symon), 146 (Holder), 499–500 (O'Connor), 511 (Deakin), 526 (Trenwith). See also Howard Willoughby, *Australian Federation: Its Aims and its Possibilities* (Sandy & McDougall, 1891) 64.

[125] *Convention Debates* (1891) 26 (Parkes), 58, 424 (Playford), 296 (Douglas); *Convention Debates*, Adelaide (1897) 52–3 (O'Connor); Winterton (n 4) 5.

house, and which would be powerful due to its representative character.[126] It was widely believed that such an upper house could not be reconciled with the 'omnipotence' of one chamber.[127]

Under the conventions of the British Constitution, the ministry was required to possess the confidence of the lower house, and so that house was 'the arbiter of the fate of the Executive Government'.[128] In addition, it was thought that one house must predominate in relation to money Bills, that is, taxation and appropriation Bills. As noted by Griffith, the real basis of the power of the popular house over the executive government was due to the exclusive right of originating supply Bills and the power to refuse supply.[129] The house that controls finance 'unquestionably controls the government', and so responsible government necessarily meant that one house had to prevail in matters of finance and appropriation.[130] This entailed that the lower house must have the 'sole power of the purse', including power to initiate money Bills.[131] A government could still function if the Senate rejected one of its legislative measures, but if the Senate refused to pass an appropriation Bill, this would effectively deprive the government of the finances necessary to govern.[132] Wrixon observed that '[f]inance is government, and government is finance', as finance was necessary to ensure that government could be carried on.[133] Conferring power on the Senate to withhold supply created the risk of serious deadlocks and that its powers could be used so as to prevent the working of government.[134] Further, conferring power on the Senate to amend (or 'veto in detail') money Bills would give the Senate the power to interfere with the government's financial policy.[135] On the other hand, if the Constitution were to give effect to responsible government according to the British model, the inevitable result would be 'that the powers of the

[126] *Convention Debates* (1891) 146 (Rutledge), *cf* 31, 456–7 (Griffith), 277–8 (Hackett); *Convention Debates* (1898) 2033, 2036 (Downer).

[127] Baker, *Federation* (n 123) 4–5, 19; Baker, *The Executive in a Federation* (n 100) 9; *Convention Debates*, Sydney (1897) 782–9.

[128] *Convention Debates*, Adelaide (1897) 52 (O'Connor).

[129] Samuel Walker Griffith, 'The Draft Federal Constitution Framed by the Adelaide Convention of 1897: A Criticism' (1897) 11 *Review of Reviews* 56, 57.

[130] *Convention Debates* (1891) 215, 419–20 (Wrixon), 544 (Baker); *Convention Debates*, Adelaide (1897) 52–3 (O'Connor), 92 (Carruthers), 97 (Higgins), 107 (Wise), 222, 505 (McMillan), 275, 485 (Reid), 295 (Deakin), 523 (Leake); *Convention Debates*, Sydney (1897) 882 (O'Connor).

[131] *Convention Debates*, Adelaide (1897) 97 (Higgins), 92 (Carruthers), 222 (McMillan).

[132] *Convention Debates*, Adelaide (1897) 54 (O'Connor), 72 (Glynn). See also Walter Bagehot, *The English Constitution* (London, Chapman and Hall, 1867) 127–128.

[133] *Convention Debates* (1891) 214 (Wrixon); see also *Convention Debates* (1891) 284 (Moore); *Convention Debates*, Adelaide (1897) 97 (Higgins), 441 (Barton), 568 (Moore); John Quick, *The Federation Bill: Complete Official Text; Full Explanation by Dr Quick, Delegate to Convention* (Melbourne, Wilson and MacKinnon, 1898) 7.

[134] *Convention Debates* (1891) 246 (Clark), 717 (Munro); *Convention Debates*, Adelaide (1897) 22–3 (Barton), 485, 609 (Reid), 507 (Deakin), 526 (Trenwith).

[135] *Convention Debates*, Adelaide (1897) 107 (Wise), 295, 507–8 (Deakin), 554–5 (Barton).

Senate will wane until it becomes only a dignified appendage of the House of the Representatives'.[136]

A concern for accountability also underlay the dispute about the Senate's powers. The framers considered that a powerful upper chamber would destroy or weaken the responsibility of the government to Parliament, because it potentially divided responsibility between two equal houses.[137] Reid most clearly articulated this concern, noting that '[d]ivided control means weakened responsibility', and that the power of controlling the government must be clearly vested somewhere in order for there to be effective responsibility. Blending responsible government and federalism would make the government responsible for administering the affairs of the country but enable the upper chamber to deny the government the ability to carry out its policy.[138] Similarly, if the Senate had power to reject or amend the government's financial measures, it would not be clear who was responsible for the financial policy of the country.[139]

Finally, there was concern that conferring power on the Senate to reject legislation passed by the lower house would enable the minority of the Commonwealth to dictate to the majority. Delegates from the larger colonies argued that it was necessary to entrench the responsibility of the lower house so as to prevent the minority from overruling the majority.[140] Munro, the Victorian premier, argued in 1891 that the lower house must be responsible for the finances and therefore have the 'ultimate power'; the minority should not have power to govern the majority of questions of finance.[141] Conferring equal power on the Senate would be to confer 'the right of an absolute veto to the House which may, in its majority, represent a small minority of the people'.[142]

It should be noted that the framers' concerns did not simply arise as a result of the proposed co-ordinate legal powers of the Senate, as sometimes asserted.[143] The colonial upper houses had powers comparable to, or in some cases more extensive than, those of the Senate and the majority of the framers did not consider that the colonies lacked true responsible government because of this.[144] The concern also arose due to the fact that it was proposed to create

[136] ibid 29 (Baker).

[137] ibid 508 (Deakin), 526 (Trenwith), 554–5, 557 (Barton).

[138] ibid 275; *Convention Debates*, Sydney (1897) 658. See also *Convention Debates* (1891) 48 (Munro); *Convention Debates*, Adelaide (1897) 554 (Barton).

[139] *Convention Debates* (1891) 49, 53 (Munro); *Convention Debates*, Adelaide (1897) 507 (Deakin), 554 (Barton).

[140] ibid 48 (Munro), 215 (Wrixon); *Convention Debates*, Adelaide (1897) 169 (Isaacs), 380 (Barton); see also 66 (Braddon); *Convention Debates*, Sydney (1897) 881 (O'Connor); see also 596 (Symon).

[141] *Convention Debates* (1891) 50, 53; see also *Convention Debates*, Adelaide (1897) 92 (Carruthers).

[142] *Convention Debates*, Adelaide (1897) 510 (Deakin).

[143] Elaine Thompson, 'The 'Washminster' Mutation' (1980) 15 *Politics* 32, 33; Paul Kelly, 'Reflections on 1975: The Dismissal and Australian Democracy' in Michael Coper and George Williams (eds), *Power, Parliament and the People* (Leichhardt, Federation Press, 1997) 128.

[144] Munro argued that the colonies lacked true responsible government on this account: *Convention Debates* (1891) 50. See also Stuart Macintyre, *A Colonial Liberalism: The Lost World of Three Victorian Visionaries* (South Melbourne, Oxford University Press, 1991) 45.

a Senate which was representative of the people and therefore would possess democratic legitimacy. For the framers, especially those from the smaller colonies, Federation necessarily entailed that the Senate was to be 'a body of dignity and power and authority',[145] a 'strong, a powerful, and a living house' and not 'an entirely subsidiary house' as the colonial legislative councils were.[146] As a representative and democratically legitimate upper chamber it would be an equal partner with the lower house, although representing a different constituency.[147] The Senate would have a solid backing from the people and there was no guarantee that it would always give way in a conflict with the lower house. As Hackett said, 'if we get a strong senate and a good senate, which again depends upon the powers and rights which we give to that body, it will make its will known. There can be no doubt about that'.[148] In such a Federation the centre of gravity would not be exclusively in the House of Representatives.[149] The framers expected that the Senate was to be very different from colonial upper houses and the House of Lords, which some framers considered to be a 'mere appendage to the House of Commons'.[150] The clash between a Senate constituted in this way and responsible government can readily be appreciated:

> The essence of federation is the existence of two houses, if not of actually co-equal power, at all events of approximately co-equal power. The essence of responsible government is the existence of one chamber of predominant power. Now, how are we to reconcile two irreconcilable propositions?[151]

For these reasons, many framers considered that responsible government and federalism were incompatible.[152] Attempting to incorporate both would either result in responsible government killing Federation, by diminishing the role of the Senate, or Federation killing responsible government by eliminating lower house dominance.[153]

As well as exposing competing conceptions of democracy and federalism, these debates also reveal different understandings of the nature of responsible government. It is true that all framers accepted that, at the time of Federation,

[145] *Convention Debates*, Adelaide (1897) 510 (Deakin).
[146] *Convention Debates*, Sydney (1897) 784.
[147] *Convention Debates*, Adelaide (1897) 41 (Turner), 146 (Holder), 502 (O'Connor).
[148] *Convention Debates*, Sydney (1897) 516–7. See also *Convention Debates* (1891) 280.
[149] *Convention Debates* (1891) 710 (Deakin).
[150] *Convention Debates* (1891) 146 (Rutledge), see also 31, 456–7 (Griffith), 102 (Downer), 146 (Rutledge), 278 (Hackett), 298 (Douglas), 465–6 (Baker); Bagehot (n 132) 128–135, 145.
[151] *Convention Debates*, Sydney (1897) 784 (Baker).
[152] Eg, *Convention Debates* (1891) 58 (Playford), 419–21 (Barton), 435 (Macrossan), 468 (Munro), 472 (Playford); *Convention Debates*, Adelaide (1897) 96, 492 (Higgins), 134 (Symon), 146 (Holder), 193, 532 (Dobson), 211 (Downer), 499–500 (O'Connor), 511 (Deakin). Some saw no difficulty in having responsible government with accountability to both houses: *Convention Debates* (1891) 161 (Kingston); *Convention Debates*, Adelaide (1897) 345 (Cockburn), 487 (Downer).
[153] *Convention Debates* (1891) 102 (Downer), 280 (Hackett); *Convention Debates*, Adelaide (1897) 28 (Baker); *cf Convention Debates*, Sydney (1897) 529 (Barton).

responsible government on the lines of the British Constitution meant the dominance of the lower house, as the constitutional conventions required the executive to hold the confidence of the lower house of Parliament.[154] The framers were, however, divided as to whether this feature was of the essence of responsible government. Both sides of this debate could claim precedent in British constitutional thinking. Delegates who saw the supremacy of the lower house as an inherent feature of responsible government considered that their approach was more faithful to the British Constitution in the form it took at the time of Federation. However, in doing so they ignored the diachronic context of responsible government and underplayed its evolutionary nature, thus advocating for the adoption of a static and idealised understanding of responsible government. By contrast, delegates who took a different view wanted to see politics in the Federation depart in important respects from the way responsible government functioned prior to Federation, but considered this to be consistent with an inherently changeable constitution whose working was given a distinctive cast by each generation.

C. Resolving the Conflict of Principle

The framers who advocated the Swiss form of government were not able to persuade the majority: despite its known problems, a majority of the framers considered that responsible government was a highly successful form of government which had the sanction of long experience.[155] The period of stability which occurred in the 1890s made reform to the cabinet system seem less urgent than it had seemed before this period.[156] Most of the framers agreed that the British Constitution should be the model. Barton declared: 'I for one, as I do not wish my boots made in Germany, do not want my Constitution made in Switzerland. I think our British forms of Government, those we have adopted and adapted, are best fitted for ourselves'.[157] Deakin described criticisms of responsible government as 'heresies', and Brown argued that the institution of responsible government has, on the whole, worked fairly well, 'notwithstanding the carping, and sneering, and adverse criticisms to which it has been subjected from

[154] As put by Isaacs: 'Responsible government, as has been admitted on all hands, means the responsibility of the Ministry of the day to the Lower Chamber' (*Convention Debates*, Adelaide (1897) 1170).

[155] *Convention Debates* (1891) 36 (Griffith), 60 (Playford), 84, 85 (Deakin), 99 (Barton), 210 (Brown), 213, 214 (Wrixon), 222 (Forrest), 238–9 (Gillies), 272–3 (McMillan), 317–8, 447–8, 450 (Parkes), 466 (Baker), 468 (Wrixon), 470 (Kingston); *Convention Debates*, Adelaide (1897) 96–7 (Higgins), 133 (Symon), 169 (Isaacs), 649 (Higgins).

[156] W Harrison Moore, 'Constitution Making in Australia' (1898) 31 *National Review* 269, 278.

[157] *Convention Debates*, Adelaide (1897) 24 (Barton); *Convention Debates* (1891) 213 (Wrixon), 239 (Gillies).

time to time'.[158] More effusively, Isaacs described responsible government as 'the noblest child of our constitutional system' which had preserved the liberties of the people, and which it was 'utterly impossible' to abandon.[159]

Given that elective ministries or the Swiss system had not been introduced in any Australian colony prior to Federation, it is not surprising that the proposal was unsuccessful. Most of the framers considered that responsible government was more likely to be accepted by the people because they were familiar with that system.[160] Baker argued with some realism that many of the delegates had attained prominence under responsible government and that it would be a difficult task to persuade them that there were problems with that system.[161] The framers were successful and experienced politicians who had been put in positions of power and elected to the Conventions through a process that was both parliamentary and popular, and it is unlikely that they would have sought to abandon the system to which they owed their places.

Accepting the reality that responsible government was likely to be the only system that was acceptable to the people[162] forced the framers to grapple with its compatibility with federalism. For those framers who saw a direct contradiction, resolving that contradiction was a question of the starting point. If the essential condition of Federation was a strong Senate in which the colonies were equally represented, then responsible government should be moulded to adapt to the powers of the Senate. Thus, Baker argued that responsible government and federalism were not compatible and concluded that responsible government should give way; if it was necessary to kill one or the other, then responsible government should be the victim.[163] Higgins and others drew precisely the opposite conclusion, namely that there should not be responsibility to two houses. They argued that responsible government and lower house dominance should be the starting point, and that the powers of the Senate must be moulded to fit with responsible government, as they conceived it.[164]

The framers considered that the people demanded equal representation in a powerful Senate, yet also would not accept any system other than responsible government. As such, the compromise reached was that the 1898 Bill did not choose between federalism and responsible government but attempted to give

[158] *Convention Debates* (1891) 69 (Deakin), 210 (Brown).

[159] *Convention* Debates, Adelaide (1897) 169 (Isaacs).

[160] *Convention Debates* (1891) 84 (Deakin), 213 (Wrixon), 228, 239 (Gillies), 427 (Playford), 447 (Parkes), 470 (Kingston); *Convention Debates*, Adelaide (1897) 51 (O'Connor), 96 (Higgins), 118–9 (Henry), 255 (Solomon), 287 (Deakin), 334 (Trenwith).

[161] *Convention Debates* (1891) 466; Wise, *The Commonwealth of Australia* (n 7) 194.

[162] *Convention Debates* (1891) 85, 571 (Deakin), 427 (Playford); *Convention Debates*, Adelaide (1897) 51 (O'Connor), 96 (Higgins), 118–9 (Henry), 287 (Deakin), 334 (Trenwith).

[163] *Convention Debates*, Adelaide (1897) 28–31 (Baker), 148 (Holder).

[164] *Convention Debates* (1891) 215 (Wrixon); *Convention Debates*, Adelaide (1897) 51 (O'Connor), 96 (Higgins), 106 (Wise), 169 (Isaacs). See Aroney, *The Constitution of a Federal Commonwealth* (n 79) 211–12, 218–22.

effect to both as far as possible.[165] The Constitution reflects the principles of federalism in conferring significant powers on the Senate, including the power to reject the financial measures of the lower house, and providing for equal representation of the states.[166] The Constitution reflects the principles of responsible government by requiring ministers to hold seats in Parliament and establishes the priority of the lower house with respect to money Bills.[167] Beyond this, the Constitution does not seek to entrench or prescribe the features of responsible government, leaving considerable flexibility for future development.

This was not simply the mashing together of irreconcilable principles:[168] the position reflected an underlying shared conception of responsible government of which the principles of constitutional evolution and popular self-government were the key elements, and which enabled the framers to consider the resulting compromise a workable one. Rather than a static set of constitutional rules or requirements, the framers conceived responsible government as an inherently changeable system whose working could not be prescribed or predicted in advance, and which adapts to changing circumstances. The framers saw their role as establishing the legal framework within which responsible government would operate, but the way it functioned would be determined by the people.

As noted above, Griffith was the most articulate proponent of an evolutionary conception of responsible government, believing that the dominance of the lower house was a historically contingent feature that reflected the evolution of responsible government in Britain and the colonies as at the time of Federation. Accordingly, he argued persuasively that responsibility to one house should not be 'a rigid rule of the constitution'.[169] Griffith's evolutionary conception was not exceptional but was the dominant way of conceiving responsible government in the 1890s, even for those who wished to enshrine lower house dominance in the Constitution. It was widely held that the British Constitution was evolutionary; as put by Douglas, the Constitution of England was a 'continually changing one'.[170] Clark, Wrixon, Downer and Lyne all wanted an elastic Constitution[171] and Wise argued that the Constitution should 'contain within itself great possibilities of growth'.[172] In 1888 Quick had written that the Victorian Constitution

[165] *Convention Debates*, Sydney (1897) 529 (Barton); *Convention Debates*, Adelaide (1897) 148 (Holder); *Convention Debates* (1898) 2060, 2066, 2102, 2109 (Barton).

[166] Constitution, ss 7, 53.

[167] Constitution, ss 53–56, 64; Wise, 'The Commonwealth of Australia' (n 31) 831.

[168] *Cf* Michael Crommelin, 'The Executive' in Gregory Craven (ed), *The Convention Debates 1891–1898: Commentaries, Indices and Guide* (Sydney, Legal Books, 1986) 140–1.

[169] *Convention Debates* (1891) 31, 48.

[170] *Convention Debates* (1891) 401 (Douglas), also 229, 239 (Gillies), 410 (Barton); *Convention Debates*, Adelaide (1897) 1167 (Symon).

[171] *Convention Debates* (1891) 244 (Clark), 468 (Wrixon), 716 (Downer); *Convention Debates*, Adelaide (1897) 162 (Lyne). See also Clark, *Australasian Federation* (n 112) 6.

[172] *Convention Debates*, Sydney (1897) 648 (Wise).

was 'still yielding to the laws of growth and evolution' and was 'founded on the sovereignty of the people'.[173] Commenting on the 1898 Bill, Quick considered that the Constitution will be capable of evolution 'arising from the altered conditions of the people, whom it is designed to govern'.[174]

Other leading framers held a similar conception. Thynne noted that 'responsible government is one of those things that will adapt itself to almost any circumstances which may arise', arguing that it would be unwise 'to impose any fetter that is not absolutely necessary upon the free and full development of the future constitution'.[175] Kingston argued that it is highly desirable 'to allow the greatest elasticity, so that from time to time such amendments may be made in the practical working of the constitution as may be found to be necessary'.[176] Hackett agreed that to make the requirement for the ministry to hold the confidence of the lower house into a legally enforceable rule would have been to ossify a particular development of responsible government, to 'fix the changeable, and to make the unalterable the alterable': '[t]he beauty, the virtue of the English system is its plasticity, its elasticity. Generation after generation introduces some novel feature, and its working conditions again change'.[177] These arguments all assumed that the legal framework within which responsible government operated would remain stable, but that the way it functioned in practice would change significantly. As Reid put it:

> We have endeavoured to deal with broad principles, irrespective of the way in which they may affect this or that part of Australia. For the sake of these broad principles we have all been willing to leave the actual working of the Constitution, in any precise direction, to the fortune of party warfare in the constituencies after federation is accomplished.[178]

Griffith exercised a significant influence over the 1891 Convention as leader and main drafter, and his view was accepted by the delegates to that Convention.[179] The draft Constitution produced by the 1891 Convention merely provided that ministers may sit in Parliament but contained no requirement that they do so.[180] This allowed both 'rigid adherence to the doctrine of responsible government, or a practice at variance with it'.[181] It is true that there was a stronger emphasis on responsible government in the 1897–98 Convention, which Moore attributed

[173] John Quick, *The Inauguration of the Parliamentary Government in Victoria* (Sandhurst, JW Burrows, 1888) 22.

[174] Quick, 'Why Victoria Should Accept the Bill' (n 31) 307.

[175] *Convention Debates* (1891) 104, 727 (Thynne). See also 151 (Rutledge).

[176] ibid 162 (Kingston).

[177] ibid 279 (Hackett). See also 468 (Wrixon).

[178] *Convention Debates* (1898) 1465 (Reid).

[179] Griffith, *Notes on Australian Federation* (n 40) 1.

[180] John M Williams, *The Australian Constitution: A Documentary History* (Carlton, Melbourne University Press, 2005) 425.

[181] Reid, 'The 'Commonwealth of Australia'' (n 18) 148. As noted, the 1891 Bill did contain some acknowledgment of lower house supremacy by providing that money Bills must originate in the House of Representatives: Chapter I, clause 54: Williams (n 180) 447.

to the long period of political stability in the colonies in the 1890s,[182] as well as a more 'democratic' and 'nationalistic' focus.[183] These resulted in important changes to the draft Constitution. However, these differences should not be overstated. A challenge to the 1891 compromise was unsuccessful, with the Convention rejecting a proposal to give the Senate power to amend taxation Bills.[184] Thus, the provisions giving effect to the 1891 compromise were in substance re-affirmed,[185] as was a strongly evolutionary conception of responsible government. The Constitution adopted by the 1897–98 Convention included a requirement that ministers must hold a seat in either house of Parliament, and because of this change it has been argued that the 1897–98 Convention abandoned the earlier view of responsible government. In Paul Strangio's view, at the later Convention, the framers entrenched responsible government into the Constitution, abandoning the elastic approach which was adopted in 1891.[186] Brian Galligan drew a similar contrast, arguing that '[w]hereas the 1891 Bill was flexible about the executive, the 1897 Bill required responsible government'.[187] These arguments, however, rest on a misunderstanding of the framers' views.

Section 64 was interpreted by contemporaries as embedding responsible government into the Constitution;[188] however, its principal purpose was not to ensure lower house dominance, but ministerial accountability. Introducing the Constitution Bill into the New South Wales Parliament, Barton noted that section 64 requires ministers to hold seats in either house of Parliament so that they can be called to account, rather than leaving this to the insistence of Parliament.[189] Further, section 64 leaves a great deal of freedom in relation to

[182] Moore, *The Constitution of the Commonwealth of Australia* (n 63) 610.

[183] Aroney, *The Constitution of a Federal Commonwealth* (n 79) 206. See also George Houstoun Reid, 'The Conference of Premiers at Hobart' (February 1895) *Review of Reviews* 149.

[184] Some framers considered the distinction between amendment and suggestion a distinction without a difference. However, it was considered there was a real difference between amendment and suggestion, because under the latter approach the House of Representatives would retain the responsibility for the Bill as a whole: eg, *Convention Debates*, Adelaide (1897) 507–8 (Deakin), 554–5, 557 (Barton).

[185] Changes including re-wording and re-ordering of the provisions, and the extension of the prohibition on 'tacking' to laws imposing duties of customs and excise. Note that it has been argued that the omission of the words 'which the Senate may affirm or reject' from subsequent drafts of the Constitution deny the Senate the power to reject money Bills: Sir Richard Eggleston's Commentary on Colin Howard and Cheryl Saunders, 'The Blocking of the Budget and Dismissal of the Government' in Evans (ed) (n 2) 297–301.

[186] Paul Strangio, 'The Ancestry of the Australian Prime Ministership: "The Blue Ribbon of the Highest Possible Ambition"' (2015) 61 *Australian Journal of Politics and History* 19, 20–1, 31. See also Paul Strangio, Paul Hart and James Walter, *Settling the Office: The Australian Prime Ministership from Federation to Reconstruction* (Carlton, Miegunyah Press, 2016) 9.

[187] Galligan, 'The Founders' Design and Intentions Regarding Responsible Government' (n 59) 6.

[188] *Convention Debates*, Adelaide (1897) 443 (Barton); Robert Randolph Garran, *Draft Bill to Constitute the Commonwealth of Australia* (Sydney, Government Printer, 1898) 17; Quick, *The Federation Bill* (n 133) 7; New South Wales, *Parliamentary Debates*, Legislative Council, 14 July 1897, 1896 (Barton).

[189] New South Wales, *Parliamentary Debates*, Legislative Council, 14 July 1897, 1897 [sic]; John A Cockburn, 'The Biology of Federation' (1903) 52 *Journal of the Society of Arts* 272, 278.

matters such as how the government is to be formed and held to account, and what role the Senate has to play in this. Contemporaries recognised that the Constitution left considerable scope for further evolution;[190] as put by Wise, section 64 is sufficiently wide to allow for systems other than responsible government, should the latter prove unsuited to a federation:

> Except that Ministers must sit in Parliament, there seems no limit to the changes which might be made with the acquiescence of the Governor-General, in the method of appointment, tenure of office, or function. No part of the Constitution evinces greater sagacity and foresight.[191]

The degree to which the Constitution mandates or prescribes responsible government should therefore not be overstated. Further, it is not the case that the belief in the evolutionary nature of responsible government was abandoned in the 1897–98 Convention; there is ample evidence of such a view in the Convention debates and contemporary writings. Consistent with standard accounts of the British Constitution and the colonial systems modelled on that Constitution, there was a widespread belief that the Australian Constitution should be flexible and allow scope for future development.[192] Garran wrote in 1897 that the Constitution should not 'attempt to fix the present pattern of responsible government as a thing to be clung to for all time' but must allow scope for development, so that it could be 'moulded to fit the political ideas of each generation'.[193] George Barton wrote that 'no Constitution, which is not elastic enough to adapt itself to circumstances, can hope to survive "the sad vicissitude of things"'.[194]

Downer, discussing responsible government, considered that 'Constitutions must be a growth', and cannot be statute made.[195] Carruthers noted in Sydney that '[w]e have always expressed our admiration for the British Constitution because it has been of such a character that it has adapted itself at all times to the circumstances of the people and to their growing aspirations'.[196] Baker said: 'I do not care in what way you frame the constitution, the people of Australia will mould and modify it in accordance with their ideas and sentiments for the

[190] Note also Barton's comments in *Convention Debates*, Adelaide (1897) 443–4.

[191] Wise, *The Commonwealth of Australia* (n 7) 193–5.

[192] *Convention Debates*, Adelaide (1897) 45 (Turner), 94 (Carruthers), 271 (Reid), 534 (Glynn); *Convention Debates*, Sydney (1897) 369 (McMillan), 404 (Trenwith); *Convention Debates* (1898) 344, 613, 1787 (Symon), 503, 1985 (Barton), (Symon), 737, 739, 740 (Glynn), 904 (McMillan), 2239 (Higgins). See also Cockburn, 'The Biology of Federation' (n 189) 275.

[193] Garran, *The Coming Commonwealth* (n 52) 149, also 150–1. Compare Quick and Garran (n 17) 706–7.

[194] GB Barton, *The Draft Bill to Constitute the Commonwealth of Australia: As Adopted by the Convention of 1891* (Chapman, 1891) 50.

[195] *Convention Debates*, Adelaide (1897) 214, 478 (Downer). See also Baker, *A Manual of Reference* (n 74) 46; Cockburn, 'The Biology of Federation' (n 189) 277.

[196] *Convention Debates*, Adelaide (1897) 275 (Carruthers), 194, 531 (Dobson).

moment, although its form may remain the same'.[197] Matthew Clarke, Symon and Dobson argued for sufficient flexibility to allow for future development in relation to responsible government and the executive;[198] and Lyne and Reid more generally wanted the Constitution to be flexible.[199] Glynn considered that the Constitution included 'that principle of elasticity which is a peculiarity, if not one of the glories of the British Constitution'.[200] Symon argued that the Constitution was 'an elastic Constitution … saturated with those principles of free government which are inherent in the British race'.[201]

Holder considered that the draft Constitution was a 'people's Constitution, which conserves everything that is good, and yet provides ample scope for natural growth' and Quick argued that 'we want to provide reasonable scope for the growth and evolution of national life'.[202] Wrixon wrote that 'nothing is more certain than that a free people will insensibly mould any constitution which they may live under, by the mere attrition of its daily working, to suit their own wants and wishes'.[203] Barton considered that the people of Australia would adapt and work the institutions of federal government as they saw fit, arguing that '[w]e cannot predict how this constitution will work. We can only form, from our experience of political and constitutional matters, a reasonable judgment as to how it will work'.[204] The precise allocation of responsibility between the two houses would be worked out by the Commonwealth Parliament after Federation.[205]

Even those framers who disagreed with the approach taken in the Bill shared a similar underlying conception of responsible government. Introducing the Constitution Bill into the Victorian Legislative Assembly, Isaacs referred to the 'beneficent elasticity of the British Constitution' and argued that '[w]e must have responsible government, with every opportunity for its growth and its advancement. We desire indeed that it shall take its natural course, that natural course being, I presume, the fullest exercise of national power by the people themselves'.[206]

[197] *Convention Debates* (1891) 545.

[198] *Convention Debates*, Adelaide (1897) 194 (Dobson), 307 (Clarke); *Convention Debates* (1898) 2262 (Symon).

[199] *Convention Debates*, Adelaide (1897) 161–2 (Lyne), 274, 280, 284 (Reid); *Convention Debates* (1898) 2350 (Reid).

[200] *Convention Debates* (1898) 2514.

[201] ibid 2508.

[202] Holder, 'Why South Australia Should Accept the Bill' (n 92) 303; Quick, 'Why Victoria Should Accept the Bill' (n 31) 306. See also Cockburn, *Australian Federation* (n 31) 27 (discussed in 'Personal Notes from London', *The Advertiser*, 6 February 1901, 6); Patrick McMahon Glynn, *Federation* (Adelaide, WK Thomas & Co, 1897) 5.

[203] Wrixon, *The Constitution of the Commonwealth of Australia* (n 31) 9. See also Henry Wrixon, *Democracy in Australia: Being a Consideration of the Cause of our Present Political Difficulties and Their True Remedy* (Melbourne, Heath & Cordell, 1868) 16.

[204] *Convention Debates*, Sydney (1897) 628.

[205] *Convention Debates*, Adelaide (1897) 443–4 (Barton).

[206] Victoria, *Parliamentary Debates*, Legislative Assembly, 20 July 1897, 526, also 542 (Isaacs).

Learned contemporaries considered that the later drafts of the Constitution gave effect to an evolutionary conception of responsible government. Harrison Moore wrote that the provisions of the Constitution relating to the ministers of state were made 'with a view to the Cabinet System' but did 'not preclude very extensive modifications of that system': the 1898 Bill established no more than a parliamentary executive, and left the rest to custom and convention.[207] He thought it was not possible to predict how the Senate's power would be exercised, but considered that it was certain that responsible government would suffer modifications as a result of the powers of the Senate: 'its powers are too great for it not to claim some share in the making and unmaking of Cabinets'.[208]

In the late 1890s Griffith (who was absent from the 1897–98 Convention) penned a series of pamphlets commenting on the Constitution produced by the Convention. These writings are significant, because they reflect Griffith's assessment of the Bill removed from the heat of battle. While Griffith was unsurprisingly critical of section 64, he nevertheless saw the final Constitution as largely consistent with his views. Although requiring ministers to sit in Parliament, the draft Bill remained open as to the mode of appointment of the government. The extent to which the Senate would use its powers to claim a share in the appointment of the ministry would depend on the resoluteness with which the Senate was prepared to insist on its powers, which in turn would depend upon public opinion.[209] If it proved necessary to modify the present system of responsible government, Griffith considered that there was 'ample power in the Constitution to make the necessary alterations without undue friction or difficulty'.[210]

[207] Moore, *The Constitution of the Commonwealth of Australia* (n 63) 168–9. See also Lord Brassey, 'Australian Federation' (1899) 266 *Nineteenth Century* 548, 550–1.

[208] W Harrison Moore, *The Commonwealth of Australia: Four Lectures on the Constitution Bill 1897* (Melbourne, George Robertson and Co, 1897) 81–2.

[209] Samuel Walker Griffith, *Notes on the Draft Federal Constitution Framed by the Adelaide Convention of 1897* (Brisbane, Government Printer, 1897) 4; Griffith (n 129) 57.

[210] Samuel Walker Griffith, *Australian Federation and the Draft Commonwealth Bill* (Brisbane, Government Printer, 1899) 16.

5

The Framers' Views: The Functioning of a Federal Commonwealth

[W]e are now simply making a mask and form of government into which life has yet to be breathed, and which the great force of national will will hereafter shape into its own form and expression.[1]

Alfred Deakin (1897)

I. INTRODUCTION

CHAPTER FOUR EXAMINED the framers' conception of responsible government and how they resolved, at the level of principle, the challenges arising from proposals to adopt the Swiss system of electing the executive rather than the British system of responsible government, and the demand from the smaller colonies for a strong Senate. It argued that the framers were able to accept both federalism and responsible government because they accepted that responsible government was an inherently evolutionary system and would adapt to the circumstances of a federal Commonwealth. This chapter examines how they expected that structure to function, arguing that constitutional evolution and popular sovereignty were central to their expectations.

II. HOW THE FRAMERS EXPECTED THE CONSTITUTION TO FUNCTION

A. The Constitution as a Skeleton

The framers considered their role to be to create the structure within which government would be conducted, but not to attempt to prescribe how government would function. That would be determined by the character of the people and their representatives. The framers' views can therefore be seen to reflect a distinctly political model of constitutionalism. Deakin said that '[t]he forces of national life are not to be confined by artificial forms' and considered that

[1] *Convention Debates*, Adelaide (1897) 511 (Deakin).

in drafting a Constitution the delegates were 'simply making a mask and form of government into which life has yet to be breathed' which 'the great force of national will' would 'hereafter shape into its own form and expression'.[2] Barton considered that the people of Australia would work the institutions of government as they saw fit.[3] In Adelaide, Carruthers said that the Constitution would be 'the dry bones of a Constitution into which the people themselves will breathe the breath of life'.[4] McMillan said: 'I always look to men to do things, and not to institutions'.[5] Clark wrote in 1901 that it is 'the present inheritors and possessors of sovereign power' that 'make a living force of that which would otherwise be a silent and lifeless document'.[6] Wrixon wrote that '[a]lmost as much depends upon how we work the Constitution as upon what is in the Constitution itself'.[7] Harrison Moore was later to write that 'constitutions are merely the machine; the motive power is human intelligence and character'.[8]

The way the Constitution functioned would be determined by the habits and views of the people rather than the text of the Constitution. A mere change to the legal rules would not alter this, because it was not possible for paper requirements to alter the political spirit of a people.[9] As Western Australian delegate Walter James argued colourfully:

> It amuses me almost to hear some members of this Convention endeavoring to wetnurse responsible government. That institution is of such a vigorous growth that if we in this Convention dared to place undue restriction on it, it would sweep us away like cobwebs. Let us adopt the true principle, being assured that responsible government is so much a part of us, and of the atmosphere we have always breathed in our political life, that no Constitution we can frame can interfere with the essential principles of its growth.[10]

Contemporaries expected, as a practical reality, that the 'mere force of habit' would lead to an executive responsible to the lower house.[11] Accordingly, the functioning of Parliament would be determined by the character of its members: as McMillan noted, '[a] great deal must depend upon the judgment and wisdom

[2] ibid 511.

[3] *Convention Debates*, Sydney (1897) 628.

[4] *Convention Debates*, Adelaide (1897) 86–7 (Carruthers). See also 511 (Deakin).

[5] ibid 505 (McMillan).

[6] Andrew Inglis Clark, *Studies in Australian Constitutional Law* (Melbourne, Charles F Maxwell, 1901) 21.

[7] Henry Wrixon, *The Constitution of the Commonwealth of Australia: An Address* (Melbourne, Melville, Mullen & Slade, 1901) 13.

[8] W Harrison Moore, 'Constitutional Development in Australia' (1931) 3 *Australian Quarterly* 16, 35.

[9] *Convention Debates*, Adelaide (1897) 288 (Deakin). See also Andrew Inglis Clark, 'The Commonwealth of Australia', *Daily Telegraph*, 31 October 1900, 6 (Pt 2).

[10] *Convention Debates*, Adelaide (1897) 548, see also *Convention Debates*, Sydney (1897) 522.

[11] AB Piddington, *Popular Government and Federation* (Sydney, Angus & Robertson, 1898) 14; BR Wise, *The Making of the Australian Commonwealth, 1889–1900: A Stage in the Growth of the Empire* (London, Longmans Green, 1913) 240.

of the men who form the first Federal Parliament'.[12] Cockburn considered that the 'surest guarantee of its success' was the knowledge that the practical working of the Constitution rested in the hands of a people who were 'saturated with the British genius for self-government'.[13] Deakin noted that '[i]f this Senate strain its power to the utmost it can of course render government impossible'.[14] An expectation that senators would behave, to some degree, honourably, presumed nothing further than the typical belief that responsible government depended for its working upon 'mutual conciliation, mutual compromise and patriotism on the part of all'.[15]

B. Parties and Party Discipline

As noted in chapter one, some scholars have argued that the framers intended a 'liberal ideal' of parliamentarism to operate in the federal government, and failed to predict that parties would exist.[16] The same scholars have argued that the formation of the disciplined party system in 1909 defeated the intentions of the framers, and that the framers should have guarded against parties in the Constitution.[17] These critiques misunderstand both the 'liberal ideal' and the framers' intentions. As argued in chapter two, it was an established axiom of British constitutional thinking that a stable two-party system was essential to the working of responsible government. Consistent with this, as will be seen, the framers by and large expected party government to operate in the Federation, rather than a mythical ideal of parliamentary government, even if they did not specifically predict the precise form of the disciplined two-party system which arose in the early twentieth century.

It is sometimes argued that only some framers predicted the rise of parties. This argument is based on the fact that the majority of the framers intended

[12] *Convention Debates*, Adelaide (1897) 222. See also John A Cockburn, 'The Commonwealth of Australia' (1901) 49 *Journal of the Society of Arts* 381, 386; John Henry, *Address to the Electors of Tasmania on the Federal Constitution Bill* (Devonport, Printed at 'The North-West Post' office, 1898) 4.

[13] John A Cockburn, *Australian Federation* (London, Horace Marshall, 1901) 74.

[14] *Convention Debates*, Adelaide (1897) 510–11 (Deakin).

[15] *Convention Debates*, Sydney (1897) 547 (McMillan). See also *Convention Debates*, Adelaide (1897) 306 (Clarke); Robert Randolph Garran, *The Coming Commonwealth: An Australian Handbook of Federal Government* (Sydney, Angus & Robertson, 1897) 129–30, cited in *Convention Debates*, Sydney (1897) 689 (Walker).

[16] GS Reid and Martyn Forrest, *Australia's Commonwealth Parliament 1901–1988: Ten Perspectives* (Carlton, Melbourne University Press, 1989) 12; Jim Chalmers and Glyn Davis, 'Power: Relations Between the Parliament and the Executive' (Research Paper No 14, Parliament of Australia, 2000); Harry Evans, 'Reflections on the Founders', *The House Magazine* (1 March 1995) 8.

[17] See also Jack Richardson, 'Resolving Deadlocks in the Australian Parliament' (Research Paper 9, Parliament of Australia, 2000) i, 6; John M Williams, 'A Toast to Absent Friends' (1998) 1 *New Federalist* 23, 24; Department of the Prime Minister and Cabinet, *Resolving Deadlocks: A Discussion Paper on Section 57 of the Australian Constitution* (Canberra, Commonwealth of Australia, 2003) 13.

the Senate to be a states' house, representing the interests of the states. Framers such as Deakin questioned the reasoning underlying this, pointing out that the Senate would divide on party, not state, lines, as the American Senate had done. Despite this, framers from the smaller colonies insisted that the Senate should be established to protect state interests, which has led some scholars to argue that the majority of framers ignored the predictions of Deakin and others and did not anticipate the rise of parties in the early twentieth century.[18] However, this argument misreads the Convention debates. While most of the framers certainly expected the Senate to be a states' house, at the same time, as will be seen, they did not doubt that government in the new Federation would be a party government. That is, the framers considered that the Senate would have a role to play in protecting state interests, but also understood that parties would exist in the Federation.

It is true that, as Deakin later reflected, the framers initially 'overlooked or under-estimated' the influence of party in the 1891 Convention.[19] It is unclear why this should have been the case, given that parties were considered necessary for the functioning of responsible government; it is possible that the framers believed that the proposal that senators should be elected by state Parliaments would break the typical mould of party politics. Whatever the reason, Macrossan warned the Convention not to 'forget the action of party':

> We have been arguing all through as if party government were to cease immediately we adopt the new constitution. Now, I really do not see how that is to be brought about. The influence of party will remain much the same as it is now, and instead of members of the senate voting, as has been suggested, as states, they will vote as members of parties to which they will belong. … Parties have always existed, and will continue to exist where free men give free expression to their opinions.[20]

Macrossan had not been the first to refer to parties. Gillies had noted that MPs would naturally form into a government and an opposition as naturally 'as they would take their breakfasts if they were hungry'. In response to a taunt that he was 'reckoning them very low', Gillies replied that his comment simply reflected the reality that MPs held different political views.[21] Jennings also clearly acknowledged that '[t]here will be parties in the senate, as there will be parties in the house of representatives'.[22]

[18] Reid and Forrest (n 16) 12; LF Crisp, *Australian National Government*, 5th edn (Melbourne, Longman Cheshire, 1983) 20; JA La Nauze, *The Making of the Australian Constitution* (Carlton, Melbourne University Press, 1972) 119; Nicholas Aroney, *The Constitution of a Federal Commonwealth: The Making and Meaning of the Australian Constitution* (Cambridge, Cambridge University Press, 2009) 197–8.

[19] Alfred Deakin, *'And Be One People': Alfred Deakin's Federal Story*, 3rd edn (Carlton South, Melbourne University Press, 1995) 37.

[20] *Convention Debates* (1891) 434; Deakin (n 19) 37.

[21] ibid 240–1 (Gillies). See also 245, 259, 441.

[22] ibid 740 (Jennings).

In any case, there is no question that, at the 1897–98 Convention, the framers were clearly aware that parties would exist in the Federation, and that direct election of senators removed any basis for thinking otherwise. Deakin, whose predictions are well-known, argued that:

> we shall never find in the future federation certain states ranked against certain other states, or that party lines will be drawn between certain states which happen to be the more populous … this appears to me a wholly mistaken reading of the situation. What is absolutely certain is that, as soon as this federation is formed, parties will begin to declare themselves in every state. Every state will be divided. Our form of government is not susceptible of continuous or successful working without parties.[23]

This was not a particularly prescient prediction, but merely echoed constitutional orthodoxy about the role of parties. Deakin considered that, upon the enactment of the Constitution, the people would naturally divide themselves into two great national parties, the party of 'more progress and faster', and the party of 'less progress and slower'.[24] The adoption of responsible government necessarily implied the adoption of party government:

> Our system, even more that the American system, implies government by party. It is an important fact that we propose to adopt in this federal constitution the same form of responsible government that we employ in these colonies. That in itself is a guarantee that party government must be introduced here.[25]

Deakin was not alone in his prediction. Barton, Kingston, Carruthers and Trenwith argued that differing political views would divide the Commonwealth rather than geographical differences.[26] Cockburn considered that parties would divide on the lines of existing party divisions in the colonies,[27] and in 1901 he wrote that '[j]udging by analogy, political parties, with all their advantages and drawbacks, will be formed in the Commonwealth as elsewhere'.[28] O'Connor noted that 'you may be very well assured that in the Parliament of the Commonwealth we shall have parties upon some lines'. Baker, an ardent advocate of states' rights, acknowledged that parties would exist: '[t]here can be no doubt that, at all events for some time to come, we shall have party government'.[29] Wise later wrote that responsible government depends on a party

[23] *Convention Debates*, Sydney (1897) 335, 585. He expressed similar views at *Convention Debates*, Adelaide (1897) 297–8.

[24] *Convention Debates*, Adelaide (1897) 297–8.

[25] *Convention Debates*, Sydney (1897) 584–5.

[26] *Convention Debates*, Adelaide (1897) 381 (Barton); *Convention Debates*, Sydney (1897) 857 (Carruthers), 870 (Kingston), 947 (Trenwith). See also *Convention Debates*, Sydney (1897) 185 (Dobson).

[27] *Convention Debates*, Sydney (1897) 951. Crisp selectively misquoted Cockburn to prove that 'States' rights' advocates such as Cockburn were 'blind' to the 'rising significance of party': Crisp (n 18) 20. However, Crisp's quotation omits crucial parts of Cockburn's remarks such as his statement that '[p]arties will be clearly defined' in Australia.

[28] Cockburn, *Australian Federation* (n 13) 32.

[29] *Convention Debates* (1898) 1498–9 (O'Connor), 2483–4 (Baker).

system.[30] There were also specific predictions about the influence of party in the Senate. Barton noted that we must imagine 'that elections for the States Assembly will be conducted on party lines'.[31] Lewis predicted that '[i]n the future, party politics may run very high in the Senate as well as the House of Representatives', and Holder considered that parties would exist in the Senate.[32]

Accordingly, it is difficult to sustain the argument that the framers did not predict the existence of parties in the Commonwealth,[33] although it is unlikely that they specifically predicted the form of the disciplined two-party system which prevailed from 1909. This is not to say that the framers all welcomed the rise of parties. Many expressed criticisms of party government, some of which have already been noted, mirroring criticisms of the cabinet system prior to Federation. Deakin conceded that party spirit sometimes runs to an extreme, and that parties 'will even endanger great public objects to gain their own ends'.[34] Dobson was a strong critic of responsible government and hoped that the federal government would develop a better form of government that avoided 'the evils that attend our party systems'.[35] Cockburn, while acknowledging that parties would exist in the Commonwealth, wanted to do away with them, continuing a theme of his pre-Federation writings. He considered that the cabinet system 'makes Ministers responsible to the Cabinet instead of to their real masters – Parliament' and wanted to adopt the Swiss form of government, which, he thought, would preserve the accountability of ministers to Parliament but eliminate government by party.[36] George Barton, Edmund Barton's brother, wrote an article in 1901 warning of the havoc that the labour movement was about to inflict in the new Federation.[37] He claimed that because the Labor Party held the balance of power in the New South Wales Parliament, it was able to dictate policy to Parliament and the government. Worse still, according to Barton, the party had proclaimed its intention to repeat this behaviour in the federal Parliament.[38]

Given that many of the framers were distrustful of parties, why did the framers not seek to eliminate them? Options for doing so certainly existed. Colonel

[30] BR Wise, *The Commonwealth of Australia* (London, Pitman, 1909) 225. See also Henry Wrixon, *Democracy in Australia: Being a Consideration of the Cause of our Present Political Difficulties and Their True Remedy* (Melbourne, Heath & Cordell, 1868) 40.

[31] *Convention Debates*, Adelaide (1897) 457 (Barton).

[32] ibid 682 (Lewis); *Convention Debates* (1898) 2021 (Holder). See also *Convention Debates*, Sydney (1897) 574 (O'Connor); *Convention Debates* (1898) 2196–7 (Wise).

[33] Brian Galligan, *A Federal Republic: Australia's Constitutional System of Government* (Melbourne, Cambridge University Press, 1995) 83; John Uhr, *Deliberative Democracy in Australia: The Changing Place of Parliament* (Melbourne, Cambridge University Press, 1998) 110.

[34] *Convention Debates*, Sydney (1897) 585 (Deakin).

[35] *Convention Debates*, Adelaide (1897) 194, 195–6; *Convention Debates*, Sydney (1897) 185.

[36] ibid 345; *Convention Debates*, Sydney (1897) 678; John A Cockburn, 'Should the Cabinet System be Changed?' (1895) 6 *Review of Reviews* 399.

[37] Eg, GB Barton, 'The Troubles of Australian Federation' (1901) 11 *Imperial and Asiatic Quarterly Review* 303.

[38] ibid 309–10.

Smith proposed that after each election the houses of Parliament should jointly appoint a government for a three-year term, which, he thought, would eliminate party government.[39] From the late nineteenth century many American states began introducing laws mandating systems of direct primary election, which effectively extended the franchise back into the candidate nomination process, weakening party discipline and the ability of party leaders to control candidate selection.[40]

However, mechanisms such as this were not seriously entertained by the framers, and their reasons for rejecting such proposals shed important light on their conception of responsible government. The first reason related to the standard constitutional orthodoxy that parties were necessary for the working of responsible government.[41] Deakin declared that '[o]ur form of government is not susceptible of continuous or successful working without parties'.[42] Parties were essential for stability, providing the necessary working majorities for governments to be formed, and were also the engine room of parliamentary government, essential for getting legislation passed. In a Parliament with no parties, there was no guarantee that a ministry's measures would be successful; party provided the assurance that Bills could be passed and a government's objectives attained.[43] Most of the framers themselves were affiliated with political parties at some point in their careers and could hardly have been successful politicians without a mastery of political arts. They had also seen the destructive consequences of the lack of parties in the instability of colonial Parliaments.[44] Proposals for eradicating the party system had not met with any success prior to Federation; it was thus considered safest to have responsible government with its known weaknesses than institute a new system with as yet unknown problems.[45]

The second reason related to the nature of responsible government, as conceived by the framers. The framers saw responsible government as an inherently unconstrainable system of government which the people would work to their own ends. As noted earlier, James Bryce's treatise *The American Commonwealth* had a significant influence on the Australian framers. In that work Bryce described the practical operation of the American political system frustrating the intentions of its framers, especially in the domination of the party system. According to Bryce, the framers of the American Constitution

[39] *Convention Debates* (1891) 135 (Smith).

[40] Graeme Orr, 'Party Primaries for Candidate Preselection? Right Question, Wrong Answer' (2011) 34 *University of New South Wales Law Journal* 964.

[41] *Convention Debates*, Adelaide (1897) 297–8 (Deakin); *Convention Debates*, Sydney (1897) 335 (Deakin).

[42] *Convention Debates*, Sydney (1897) 335.

[43] *Convention Debates*, Adelaide (1897) 381 (Barton).

[44] Trenwith noted a standard complaint of parliamentary behaviour, namely that Bills would get mangled in committee 'as to dissatisfy in some measure almost every member in the House': *Convention Debates* (1898) 2215.

[45] *Convention Debates*, Adelaide (1897) 255 (Solomon).

were suspicious of parties and had designed the method of electing the President to ensure that he would be 'outside and above party'. In practice, the system of party completely dominated all aspects of the American political system, dictating the outcome of elections and concentrating power in hidden party leaders. The demands of party made the President a wirepuller, and in the election of senators, the legislatures did little more than give effect to choices made by the party managers. Even the election of state judges was controlled by the parties.[46]

One key lesson from Bryce's account was that the working of a Constitution would not necessarily conform to the intentions of its framers and that there was little that constitutional drafters could do to prevent this. A Constitution is nothing more than paper, and the practical character of a system of government depends on the party system under which it functions, and on 'the political habits of the people'.[47] Thus, '[t]o expect any form of words, however weightily conceived, with whatever sanctions enacted, permanently to restrain the passions and interests of men is to expect the impossible'.[48] The people would govern themselves in the way they chose, regardless of institutional structures or well-intentioned constitutional requirements. Accordingly, and consistent with their views of responsible government as an inherently evolutionary system, the framers considered it would not be possible to do away with party government. Barton argued that incorporating elements from the Swiss or the US Constitution would not achieve that end, 'because the conditions under which you live would assert themselves', namely the habits of the people accustomed to party government.[49] Downer said that, 'as to limiting the manner in which the constitution will evolve itself, we are absolutely powerless'.[50] Symon likewise considered that 'try as we may, and animated as we are by a federal spirit or by a spirit of compromise, you cannot eradicate party spirit or government by party in these days from the political life of the British race. It is a system with which we have grown up'.[51] In response to the arguments of framers who wished to get rid of the party system by means of a Senate with co-ordinate powers, Deakin argued:

> no change of form … can confine, or is capable of seriously altering, the political spirit under which the inhabitants elect to work it. … We all recognise that, not only would it be impossible for us to frame an ideally-perfect, and scientifically-flawless Constitution, but that if we did devise it any people would speedily reduce it in its

[46] James Bryce, *The American Commonwealth*, 2nd edn (London, Macmillan, 1891) vol 1, 41, 61, 87, 95–6, 113, 485. Reid voiced similar concerns: *Convention Debates*, Adelaide (1897) 275 (Reid).

[47] Bryce, *The American Commonwealth* (n 46) 270, 291.

[48] ibid 396.

[49] *Convention Debates*, Adelaide (1897) 381 (Barton). See also *Convention Debates*, Sydney (1897) 628 (Barton).

[50] *Convention Debates*, Sydney (1897) 496–7 (Downer).

[51] *Convention Debates*, Adelaide (1897) 133 (Symon).

> operation to their own level. Be the form adopted what we will, the reliance which we place upon the future of Australia will never be based upon the form of its Government, but always upon the intelligence, the conscience, and the judgment of the people.[52]

Deakin rebuked those who sought to force the Swiss form of government upon the people of Australia, which would not achieve its object, but a 'mere paper constitution would be twisted between their fingers in twelve months back into its present shape'.[53]

The evidence presented in this section enables the arguments of scholars such as Reid and Forrest, Marsh, and Chalmers and Davis to be evaluated. As noted in chapter one, these scholars argued that the framers incorporated the liberal ideal of Parliament into the Constitution, that the disciplined party system changed the nature of politics in ways not intended or desired by the framers and that the framers ought to have done more to check the influence of political parties in the Commonwealth.[54] However, these views rest on a misunderstanding of the British tradition of constitutionalism and the framers' views. As noted in chapter two, the standard constitutional orthodoxy was that responsible government required a stable two-party system to make it effective. Complaints in the colonies about responsible government often related to the weakness of the party system rather than its strength.[55] Consistent with these views, the framers expected parties to exist and most of them welcomed this as a normal part of responsible government. It is true the framers may not have predicted the precise form of the disciplined party system; even if they had, the framers would not have considered that they could do much to prevent it from developing.[56] The majority of framers did not accept that formal changes such as introducing the Swiss system into the Constitution would minimise or eliminate the problems with parties: they thought that the people would govern themselves through Parliament as they chose, and there was little the framers could do to guard against such problems.

C. A Senate for a Sovereign People

It is necessary to consider how the Senate was expected to function within the federal framework established by the framers given that its compatibility with

[52] *Convention Debates*, Adelaide (1897) 288. See also Wise, *The Commonwealth of Australia* (n 30) 227.

[53] *Convention Debates*, Adelaide (1897) 287. See also Alfred Deakin, 'The Federation of Australia' (1891) 10 *Scribner's Magazine* 549, 549.

[54] Reid and Forrest (n 16) 12; Chalmers and Davis (n 16); Ian Marsh, *Beyond the Two Party System: Political Representation, Economic Competitiveness, and Australian Politics* (Melbourne, Cambridge University Press, 1995).

[55] Eg, Barton, 'The Troubles of Australian Federation' (n 37) 308.

[56] *Cf* Aroney, *The Constitution of a Federal Commonwealth* (n 18) 198.

responsible government was such a controversial issue at the Conventions.[57] It has often been argued that the Constitution is conservative, that the Senate was intended as a check on democracy, and that it was ideological conservatism that led to the framers' desire for a strong upper house.[58] Against these views, I argue that the framers intended to create a Senate which, as well as defending the interests of the states, would promote self-government by providing another means of giving expression to the public will.[59]

The smaller colonies' demand for equal representation would mean that small states were represented in the Senate on an equal basis with the larger states, which was challenged by delegates from the larger colonies as infringing the principle of majority rule.[60] This argument certainly had force in relation to the 1891 Bill, which proposed that senators would be chosen by the state Parliaments rather than elected,[61] and prompted a concern that the Senate would be able to thwart the will of the people.[62] However, the argument that the Senate was undemocratic had less force in 1897–98.[63] The Constitution approved at the second Convention provided that the senators would be directly elected by the people;[64] as a result, it was considered that the Senate would be representative of the people, perhaps even as representative as the lower house,[65] and therefore would be in touch with the people.[66] Cockburn, a radical, considered that the Senate would be just as democratic as the house of representatives and had little patience with arguments that the Senate would be conservative:

[57] See generally Brian Galligan and James Warden, 'The Design of the Senate' in Gregory Craven (ed), *The Convention Debates 1891–1898: Commentaries, Indices and Guide* (Sydney, Legal Books, 1986).

[58] Eg, Manning Clark, *A History of Australia, Volume 5: The People Make Laws 1888–1915* (Carlton, Melbourne University Press, 1981) ch 5; Sylvia Marchant, *The Historical Traditions of the Australian Senate: The Upper House We Had to Have* (PhD Thesis, Australian National University, 2009) 270, 275; Crisp (n 18) 18, 349; RL Reid, 'South Australian Politicians and the Proposals for Federation' (1960) 4 *Melbourne Studies in Education* 204, 207.

[59] Cockburn, *Australian Federation* (n 13) 174. See also John W Russell, 'Australian Federation' (1898) 167 *North American Review* 27, 34.

[60] *Convention Debates* (1891) 233 (Gillies), 710 (Deakin); *Convention Debates*, Adelaide (1897) 663 (Trenwith); *Convention Debates*, Sydney (1897) 657 (Reid), 858 (Carruthers), 947 (Trenwith); *Convention Debates* (1898) 1831, 1834 (Isaacs).

[61] John M Williams, *The Australian Constitution: A Documentary History* (Carlton, Melbourne University Press, 2005) 416.

[62] *Convention Debates* (1891) 384–5 (Deakin). *Cf* A McLaren, *Federation: The Draft Bill Exposed* (Sydney, Sir Robert Bear, 1891) 7–8.

[63] It was certainly pressed: *Convention Debates*, Adelaide (1897) 92, 657 (Carruthers), 101–2 (Higgins), 489 (Kingston), 510 (Deakin), 652–4, 667 (Lyne), 663 (Trenwith). See also Henry Bournes Higgins, *The Convention Bill of 1898: Address Delivered by HB Higgins to His Constituents in Geelong, April 18th, 1898* (Melbourne, Atlas Press, 1898) 12.

[64] See Aroney, *The Constitution of a Federal Commonwealth* (n 18) 208–9, 217–8.

[65] *Convention Debates*, Sydney (1897) 736 (Kingston), 819–21 (Deakin), 868 (Kingston), 883 (O'Connor), 890 (Higgins), 905 (Barton), 939–40 (Carruthers); *Convention Debates* (1898) 2060 (Barton).

[66] *Convention Debates*, Sydney (1897) 821–3 (Deakin); *Convention Debates*, Adelaide (1897) 386 (Barton).

'[t]he hon. member [Higgins] talks about the senate as if it were going to be a rigidly conservative house. How can a house that is elected by manhood votes be a conservative house? The thing is too preposterous, and the hon. member must know it'. Indeed, the state governments, by virtue of their closer proximity, were more likely to be in closer contact with their constituents than a distant central government.[67] For the majority of delegates, the Senate was not intended to be a bastion of property nor a bulwark against democracy.[68]

While the framers' views of democracy may be different to views held today, they did not see their Constitution as conservative.[69] Barton considered that the liberal nature of the 1898 Constitution 'speaks for itself'; Deakin, a leading liberal, said that 'there is no Federal Constitution in the world so liberal', and Symon considered that the Bill produced at the Adelaide Convention 'was the finest and the most democratic instrument of federal government ever framed'.[70] Kingston, considered a radical liberal, wrote a paper in 1897 arguing that the Constitution was consistent with democratic ideals.[71] Harrison Moore argued that 'the prevalence of the democratic principle' was a dominant feature of the Constitution and that 'the rights of individuals are sufficiently secured by ensuring as far as possible to each a share, and an equal share, in political power'.[72]

The framers intended that the Senate should be a strong, independent and effective body, which could only be the case if it was democratically elected.[73] The Senate, therefore, was to be genuinely representative,[74] and as such would be radically different, in both composition and function, from the House of

[67] *Convention Debates*, Sydney (1897) 537, 680 (Cockburn).

[68] *Convention Debates*, Adelaide (1897) 502 (O'Connor), 531 (Dobson), 570 (Solomon), 649 (Higgins), 1167 (Symon); *Convention Debates*, Sydney (1897) 483 (Forrest), 544, 859 (Carruthers), 566 (Fraser), 569 (Abbott); *Convention Debates* (1898) 725 (Downer). Carruthers even said that the Senate could be the more democratic body: *Convention Debates*, Adelaide (1897) 544, 859. See also W Harrison Moore, *The Constitution of the Commonwealth of Australia*, 2nd edn (Melbourne, Charles F Maxwell, 1910) 152. Higgins conceded that the Senate would be democratic (*Convention Debates*, Sydney (1897) 894), although he later retreated from this: Higgins, *The Convention Bill of 1898* (n 63) 12–13, 21.

[69] *Convention Debates*, Adelaide (1897) 144 (Holder), 651 (Deakin).

[70] *Convention Debates* (1898) 2467 (Barton), 2502 (Deakin); *Convention Debates*, Sydney (1897) 300 (Symon). See also *Convention Debates*, Sydney (1897) 821 (Deakin arguing that the draft Bill 'enshrined the principle of the rule of the majority') and 'The Federation of Australia' (Nov 1891) *Review of Reviews* 494.

[71] Charles Cameron Kingston, *The Democratic Element in Australian Federation* (Adelaide, L Bonython & Co, 1897) 6.

[72] Moore, *The Constitution of the Commonwealth of Australia* (n 68) 612, 616, quoted in *McCloy v New South Wales* (2015) 257 CLR 178, 202 [27]–[28] (French CJ, Kiefel, Bell and Keane JJ), 226 [110] (Gageler J).

[73] *Convention Debates*, Adelaide (1897) 521 (Symon), 523 (Leake); 531 (Dobson); *Convention Debates*, Sydney (1897) 430–5 (O'Connor), 497, 765 (Downer), 514 (Carruthers), 552 (Quick), 575 (O'Connor), 718 (Forrest), 735 (Symon), 765 (Downer), 870 (Kingston); *Convention Debates* (1898) 2007 (Quick), 2031 (Reid), 2066 (Barton), 2479 (Braddon). See also Bryce, *The American Commonwealth* (n 46) vol 1, 112.

[74] *Convention Debates*, Sydney (1897) 483 (Forrest), 507 (Braddon), 868 (Kingston).

Lords and the colonial upper houses.[75] The majority of framers were concerned to defend the Senate against accusations from Isaacs and Higgins that it was not democratic and intended that the Senate should not be an obstacle to the will of the people.[76] Kingston, a states' rights advocate, considered that the Senate should be under the control of their constituents just as much as the lower house, and only have a right to speak 'as the mouthpiece of their constituents'.[77] It was therefore not intended that the Senate be more conservative than the lower house; as put by Playford, '[d]emocracy and state rights are synonymous terms!'[78] Symon, an ardent advocate of states' rights, argued that 'the people should exercise their just influence in every respect, and I say that it is the duty of the representatives of the people in the senate and in the house of representatives to bow to the will of the people'.[79] Braddon argued that the Senate 'should be a body representative to the very fullest extent of the popular will'.[80] Under the Constitution there would be 'two sets of public opinion', namely, 'the public opinion which upholds the House of Representatives solid and inflexible', and also 'the public opinion of the state, which supports the senate equally solid and equally inflexible'.[81] As a representative body the Senate would not be able to withstand the force of public opinion for long.[82]

The framers recognised that it was often difficult to determine the 'will of the people';[83] indeed, identifying the 'people's will' or 'voice' will always be politically contested.[84] Elections could be clouded by many considerations and the results unclear.[85] While the views of 'democrats' such as Higgins and Isaacs rested on the assumption that the lower house would be more likely to accurately reflect the 'people's will', at times it could fail to do so.[86] The Senate would be entitled, therefore, in appropriate cases, to put the burden on the House to go back to its constituents to ascertain whether it really was acting in accordance with the people's wishes.[87] Delay for consideration by the Senate was not considered undemocratic, but an opportunity to debate proposals in the light of public

[75] *Convention Debates*, Adelaide (1897) 146 (Holder).

[76] Dobson was an outlier in arguing that upper houses could be acting legitimately in opposing the people's wishes: *Convention Debates* (1898) 2130.

[77] *Convention Debates*, Sydney (1897) 580 (Kingston).

[78] *Convention Debates* (1891) 433 (Playford). See also 'The Last Resort in Political Warfare', *The Spectator*, 25 September 1897, 397.

[79] *Convention Debates*, Sydney (1897) 592.

[80] ibid 507.

[81] ibid 574 (O'Connor).

[82] Eg, ibid 324 (Wise).

[83] ibid 518, 636 (Dobson), 549–50 (McMillan), 562 (Holder), 666 (Isaacs), 729 (Glynn), 826 (Deakin), 838–9 (Reid).

[84] Nicholas Aroney et al, *The Constitution of the Commonwealth of Australia: History, Principle and Interpretation* (Port Melbourne, Cambridge University Press, 2015) 58.

[85] *Convention Debates*, Adelaide (1897) 333 (Trenwith); *Convention Debates*, Sydney (1897) 580 (Kingston).

[86] *Convention Debates*, Sydney (1897) 544 (Carruthers).

[87] ibid 735 (Symon), 868 (Kingston).

scrutiny and thereby gain a better understanding of the public will.[88] This was important, because under the realities of political life governments could usually get the lower house to pass a measure without much difficulty.[89] Accordingly, dialogue, deliberation and conflict between the houses was considered a means of testing proposals and more accurately determining the will of the people. If democratic decision-making should not be merely an exercise in crude majoritarianism or preference aggregation but should result instead from informed and reflective discussion,[90] the framers' intentions for the Senate can be seen as a mechanism for improving democratic deliberation.

The framers intended the Senate to have two principal functions: it would act as the states' house and second, be a house of review. As the states' house, it would represent the states, thereby ensuring that they played an important constitutive role in the federal Parliament,[91] although in so doing it was to represent 'the people of the states rather than the political institution of the states'.[92] In practice, the Senate has not operated as a states' house, but rather as a party house, and so it is commonly thought that the actual functioning of the Senate has defeated the framers' intentions.[93] The framers had been warned of this. Bryce had noted that the American Senate had not acted as a states' house because there had never been any division of interests between the great states and the small ones, and this was pointed out in the Conventions on several occasions.[94] Similarly, some framers argued that the key lines of division in the Federation era would most likely be social and party questions.[95]

[88] ibid 325 (Wise), 606 (Trenwith), 716 (Fraser). See also Howard Willoughby, *Federation: The Hope and the Danger: A Lecture, 24th March, 1896* (Melbourne, Australasian National League, 1896) 6.

[89] *Convention Debates*, Sydney (1897) 732 (Fraser).

[90] See Ron Levy and Graeme Orr, *The Law of Deliberative Democracy* (London, Routledge, 2016) ch 2.

[91] *Convention Debates* (1891) 31 (Griffith); *Convention Debates*, Adelaide (1897) 65 (Braddon), 146 (Holder), 256 (Solomon), 326 (Gordon), 338–9, 343 (Cockburn), 356 (Howe), 377 (Barton), 501 (O'Connor), 517 (Symon), 531 (Dobson), 547 (James); *Convention Debates*, Sydney (1897) 361 (Barton), 384 (Symon), 387–8 (Holder), 425 (Isaacs), 436–7 (McMillan), 445 (Reid), 507 (Braddon), 598 (Downer); *Convention Debates* (1898) 1836, 1923 (Barton).

[92] Aroney et al (n 84) 49.

[93] James Bryce, *Modern Democracies* (London, Macmillan, 1921) vol II, 187; Stanley Bach, *Platypus and Parliament: The Australian Senate in Theory and Practice* (Canberra, Department of the Senate, Parliament of Australia, 2003) 143–4; David Butler, 'Australia's Contribution to Political Institutions' (2001) 7 *New Federalist* 47; Jacqueline Lipton, 'Responsible Government, Representative Democracy and the Senate: Options for Reform' (1997) 19 *University of Queensland Law Journal* 194; Geoffrey Lindell, 'Advancing the Federal Principle Through the Intergovernmental Immunity Doctrine' in HP Lee and Peter Gerangelos (eds), *Constitutional Advancement in a Frozen Continent* (Annandale, Federation Press, 2009) 25; Elaine Thompson, 'The Constitution and the Australian System of Limited Government, Responsible Government and Representative Democracy: Revisiting the Washminster Mutation' (2001) 24 *University of New South Wales Law Journal* 657, 657; Campbell Sharman, 'The Australian Senate as a States House' (1977) 12 *Politics* 64 (noting but not endorsing this view).

[94] Bryce, *The American Commonwealth* (n 46) vol 1, 94, 182; *Convention Debates*, Adelaide (1897) 100 (Higgins), 536–7 (Glynn), 646 (Higgins).

[95] *Convention Debates* (1891) 250 (Clark), 405 (Russell), 434 (Macrossan); *Convention Debates*, Adelaide (1897) 107–8, 487, 1151 (Wise), 493 (Higgins); *Convention Debates*, Sydney (1897) 262,

Despite this, the small colonies were not prepared to enter the Federation without the protection of a strong Senate in which each state was equally represented, considering that in a Federation both the people and the states must be represented and both must agree in matters of government and legislation.[96] This was the price of Federation for the larger colonies.[97] Hackett explained the purpose of the Senate as being:

> to cement these isolated communities together, to make a dismembered Australia into a single nation … to convert the popular will into the federal will – to allow the popular body all the power to which it is entitled – to allow it, in the first and in the last resort, to give full voice to the wishes of the populace, but, at the same time, to take care before that voice issues forth as the voice of Australia that it shall be clothed with all the rights and duties of the federal will.[98]

From the framers' perspective, it appeared that there would be several questions for resolution in the Commonwealth which were likely to be matters of crucial contention between the states. This included pre-eminently the question of the tariff; as Reid observed, 'in no case could a state interest be more vitally at stake than in connexion with matters of Tariff and trade'.[99] Other such issues included the distribution of the income of the Commonwealth among the states in an equitable manner and questions of railway construction in a state. Where the interests of the small states were seriously threatened in such matters, they would be entitled to resist the larger states.[100] Thus, the framers seem to have expected that, most of the time, the Senate would be a party house, following the normal course of political life, but where matters affecting a state came up for consideration, senators would be expected to defend the interests of their state. These need not have been frequent; Kingston and Symon acknowledged that the majority of cases would not be state questions.[101] The states' rights view was well summarised by Trenwith as a belief that 'there may arise contingencies in which distinctly state interests are involved, and upon which, therefore, the states have a right to speak as states, without regard to their numerical condition'.[102] Although the Senate has not generally performed this function,

265 (Higgins), 584–6, 820 (Deakin), 840 (Reid), 888 (O'Connor), 899 (Holder); *Convention Debates* (1898) 2168 (Dobson).

[96] *Convention Debates*, Sydney (1897) 557 (Downer); *Convention Debates* (1898) 1835–6 (Barton); Aroney, *The Constitution of a Federal Commonwealth* (n 18) 155–7.

[97] Victoria, *Parliamentary Debates*, Legislative Assembly, 20 July 1897, 523 (Isaacs).

[98] *Convention Debates* (1891) 280.

[99] *Convention Debates* (1898) 2208–9. See also *Convention Debates*, Sydney (1897) 881 (O'Connor).

[100] ibid 2123–4 (Kingston); *Convention Debates*, Sydney (1897) 324 (Wise). Reid challenged this: 657.

[101] *Convention Debates*, Sydney (1897) 765 (Downer), 870 (Kingston), 953 (Symon).

[102] ibid 947 (Trenwith). This was not Trenwith's view, but is an able summary of the states' rights view.

the framers' twin expectation both that parties would arise, and that there was a role for the Senate in upholding state interests, was not an incoherent one.

The Senate was also intended to be a house of review along the lines of traditional upper houses,[103] introducing a methodological, if not ideological, conservatism into the functioning of Parliament. In fulfilling its functions, the Senate would be democratically elected and accountable to the people of the states and thus 'a totally different institution, and created for different purposes and different functions altogether, from those performed by the second chambers in the colonies'.[104] Delaying legislation passed by the lower house for further consideration was not considered undemocratic; even 'democrats' supported the Senate playing such a role.[105] It was also envisaged that the Senate would play an important role in holding the government to account. Some delegates expressed concern at the excessive power wielded by the lower house.[106] Baker wished to avoid the concentration of power in the lower house of the legislature, and Deakin expressed the hope that the upper house would be able to 'exercise a very large and salutary power indeed in controlling legislation, and in controlling even the executive government',[107] thus playing an important role in holding the executive to account.

Accordingly, the framers' intentions for the Senate were consistent with their conception of responsible government. The Senate was to be representative of the people, although on a different basis than the House of Representatives; it would be a means of determining the people's will and therefore an instrument of self-government. Disputes between the two houses in the colonies prior to Federation were often considered to arise due to upper house intransigence. In the federal Parliament, however, disputes between the two houses were expected to occur where one house considered that a Bill proposed by the other house did not represent the wishes of the people.[108] This, of course, was most likely to occur where there were different majorities in the houses; as noted by Deakin, '[c]ontests between the two houses will only arise when one party is in possession of a majority in the one chamber, and the other in the possession of a majority in the other chamber'.[109] It may, therefore, be entirely legitimate for the Senate to oppose the House of Representatives. A strong Senate, representative of the people, and with the authority to reject measures proposed by the

[103] ibid 606 (Trenwith), 715 (Fraser), 717 (Forrest), 733 (Henry), 770, 830 (Symon), 812 (McMillan), 898 (Holder).

[104] *Convention Debates* (1891) 244 (Clark).

[105] Eg, *Convention Debates*, Sydney (1897) 606 (Trenwith), 733 (Henry).

[106] *Convention Debates* (1891) 298 (Douglas); *Convention Debates*, Adelaide (1897) 222 (McMillan).

[107] ibid 385–6 (Deakin), 544 (Baker); *Convention Debates*, Adelaide (1897) 222 (McMillan).

[108] *Convention Debates*, Sydney (1897) 813 (McMillan), 819 (Deakin), 870 (Kingston); *Convention Debates* (1898) 723 (Isaacs), 725–6 (Downer).

[109] *Convention Debates*, Sydney (1897) 584. *Cf* 947 (Trenwith).

lower house, could enable alternative views to be agitated.[110] Wise argued that if public opinion was behind a measure the Senate would not be able to long withstand that measure, but would eventually be forced to give way.[111] Deliberation, debate and even conflict between the houses was to be welcomed as a means of refining and ascertaining the will of the people, so that it would ultimately prevail, with the deadlock mechanism intended to ensure this where the houses of Parliament could not agree.

As the functioning of responsible government was not something that the Constitution could mandate but would depend on the people and their representatives, the framers did not consider it to be possible to prescribe how the Senate would exercise its powers. The precise manner in which the Senate exercised its powers would 'depend upon the strength of the body which has the authority to exercise it', which would be related to its representativeness and consistency with public opinion.[112]

Under the British Constitution as it functioned at the time of Federation, the centre of gravity was the lower house and the upper house was a mere house of review and delay.[113] This was not the framers' intention for the Senate: they intended the Senate to be an active, powerful and legitimate part of the federal legislature, representative and accountable to the people. Giving effect to the principles of federalism meant consciously departing from the British Constitution as it functioned at Federation in key respects.[114]

III. ASSESSING THE FRAMERS' ACHIEVEMENT

Many criticisms have been levelled at the framers and their Constitution. The framers have sometimes been criticised for failing to anticipate the development of political parties and the cabinet dominance that characterises modern politics.[115] Others have criticised the framers for incorporating contradictory principles into the Constitution, which has been seen as a direct cause of the 1975 crisis.[116] Are the framers to be praised or criticised for their Constitution?

[110] ibid 735–7, 761. See also Greg Taylor, *The Constitution of Victoria* (Annandale, Federation Press, 2006) 252–5.

[111] *Convention Debates*, Sydney (1897) 324.

[112] *Convention Debates*, Adelaide (1897) 486–7 (Downer); *Convention Debates*, Sydney (1897) 514 (Carruthers).

[113] AH Birch, *Representative and Responsible Government: An Essay on the British Constitution* (London, Allen & Unwin, 1964) 65.

[114] *Convention Debates* (1891) 114–5 (Baker), 122 (Bird), 230–1 (Gillies), 243–4 (Clark), 298 (Douglas), 464 (Baker); *Convention Debates*, Adelaide (1897) 276 (Reid); *Convention Debates*, Sydney (1897) 333 (Deakin).

[115] Chalmers and Davis (n 16); Reid and Forrest (n 16) 12; GS Reid, 'Parliamentary-Executive Relations: The Suppression of Politics' in Henry Mayer (ed), *Australian Politics: A Second Reader* (Melbourne, Cheshire, 1970) 502.

[116] Brian Galligan, *A Federal Republic: Australia's Constitutional System of Government* (Melbourne, Cambridge University Press, 1995) 47; Brian Galligan, 'The Kerr-Whitlam Debate

It is certainly true that the Constitution leaves many questions unanswered. Further, the conduct of politics since Federation has often left a lot to be desired. Are the framers to be blamed for this?

It is first to be noted that constitutional conventions are central to the functioning of responsible government, and uncertainty is inherent to the nature of convention. Conventions are framed in general terms and have contested exceptions and limitations, and disputes about their existence are often inconclusive.[117] Further, there is no agreed method for determining the source or content of conventions and the application of constitutional conventions 'has often been a matter of sharp political controversy'.[118] Uncertainty is an inevitable feature of the British system of government[119] and it is not possible to attain precise certainty about every aspect of the functioning of responsible government.

In assessing the framers' achievement it must be recognised that Federation was a compromise between competing views, and that the delegates considered they were bound to advocate positions that would benefit their colonies. The most prominent example of this was the question of the structure and powers of the Senate. Representatives from the smaller colonies considered that their colonies would only accept Federation on terms that guaranteed equal representation in the Senate, and where the Senate possessed powers co-ordinate (or nearly co-ordinate) with those of the House of Representatives, notwithstanding large differences in the populations of the colonies.[120] By contrast, many representatives from the large colonies considered that the demands of the small

and the Principles of the Australian Constitution' (1980) 18 *Journal of Commonwealth and Comparative Politics* 247; George Winterton, *Parliament, the Executive and the Governor-General: A Constitutional Analysis* (Melbourne, Melbourne University Press, 1983) 3–5, 6; Colin Howard and Cheryl Saunders, 'The Blocking of the Budget and Dismissal of the Government' in Gareth Evans (ed), *Labor and the Constitution, 1972–1975: Essays and Commentaries on the Constitutional Controversies of the Whitlam Years in Australian Government* (Melbourne, Heinemann Educational Australia, 1977) 286; Joan Rydon, 'Some Problems of Combining the British and American Elements in the Australian Constitution' (1985) 23 *Journal of Commonwealth & Comparative Politics* 67; Geoffrey Sawer, *Federation Under Strain: Australia 1972–1975* (Melbourne, Melbourne University Press, 1977) 121–3; Paul Kelly, *November 1975: The Inside Story of Australia's Greatest Political Crisis* (St Leonards, Allen & Unwin, 1995) 15–17.

[117] Geoffrey Marshall, *Constitutional Conventions: The Rules and Forms of Political Accountability* (Oxford, Clarendon Press, 1984) 2–4, 10, 19, 55–61, 210–2.

[118] ibid 2.

[119] At the time of Federation, constitutional writers debated issues such as the legitimacy of swamping the House of Lords, the consistency of independent boards with responsible government and whether confidence in the ministry extended to administration or policy. See William Edward Hearn, *The Government of England: Its Structure, and Its Development*, 2nd edn (Melbourne, George Robertson, 1886) 188, 241; William Reynell Anson, *The Law and Custom of the Constitution*, 3rd edn (Oxford, Clarendon Press, 1897) vol 1, 260–1, 291; Alpheus Todd, *On Parliamentary Government in England: Its Origin, Development, and Practical Operation*, 2nd edn (London, Longmans, Green and Co, 1887) vol 1, 205–6, vol 2, 221–2.

[120] *Convention Debates*, Adelaide (1897) 65 (Braddon), 145–6 (Holder), 255–6 (Solomon), 326 (Gordon), 343 (Cockburn), 356 (Howe), 377–8 (Barton), 517–19 (Symon), 547 (James), 655 (Quick), 661 (Isaacs), 666 (Reid).

colonies would result in the minority dictating to the majority, and that their colonies would not accept any proposal that did not allow the will of the majority to prevail, given their experiences with constitutional conflicts between the houses.[121] Thus, delegates from the larger colonies pressed for a Constitution that was more nationalistically majoritarian than that which was ultimately adopted, while delegates from the smaller colonies pressed for a strong Senate and a conscious departure from the British model. No colony was entirely satisfied with the compromise which resulted from the Federal Conventions.[122]

If the Constitution evidences design flaws due to the resultant compromises, to whom should responsibility be attributed for these flaws? All delegates were motivated by a mixture of political principle together with a belief that these positions were what the people of their colonies wanted. The framers were embedded within the parliamentary and political systems of their day and can hardly be expected to have radically transcended those systems and structures. To the extent that the framers' views were deficient they reflected the limitations and deficiencies of the electoral and parliamentary system of their time. Although no delegate was completely satisfied with its final form, the Constitution represented a compromise that the delegates and their colonies could accept. It is difficult to conceive of alternatives that were realistically open to the framers and that would have harmonised their competing views.

The Constitution reflects and implements the conception that responsible government was an inherently evolutionary form of government which would be adapted and worked by each generation to meet their own needs. The framers did not consider they could predict the needs of future generations, let alone prescribe how the Constitution was to be worked by those generations. As Higgins later wrote, 'as it is human to err, it is human also to be ever trying to impose our wisdom on the future'.[123] Isaacs argued that the purpose of the Constitution was to lay down 'merely fundamental principles, which will be suitable to and adapt themselves to every phase and stage of the nation's life; and every step we go beyond that puts fetters on our future progress'.[124]

Those who have criticised the framers for the brinkmanship or the failings of government in the time since Federation[125] thus evince a fundamentally different conception of what it is possible for a Constitution to achieve. The framers would no doubt be surprised to learn that they have been criticised for those failings. They believed that it was not possible to create a structure in which

[121] Ibid 91–2 (Carruthers), 102 (Higgins), 500 (O'Connor), 509–10 (Deakin), 652 (Lyne).

[122] See, eg, John Forrest, *Speech by the Right Honourable Sir John Forrest, on the Federation of Australia, on the terms proposed in the Commonwealth Bill passed by the Federal Convention, 1898* (Perth, Government Printer, 1898) 8; Lord Brassey, 'Australian Federation' (1899) 266 *Nineteenth Century* 548, 555.

[123] Henry Bournes Higgins, 'The Rigid Constitution' (1905) 20 *Political Science Quarterly* 203, 204.

[124] Victoria, *Parliamentary Debates*, Legislative Assembly, 20 July 1897, 542 (Isaacs).

[125] Eg, Chalmers and Davis (n 16); Winterton (n 116) 5–11; Kelly (n 114) 15–17.

the 1975 crisis could not occur. The view that a written Constitution could prevent the rise of the disciplined party system, or could guarantee constitutional propriety, betrays considerable naivety. Needless to say, it is not suggested that the framers were a source of infallible wisdom or that the age of Federation was a golden age which we must attempt to recover. Clearly not; that age had its failings, and the framers themselves were fallible men, subject to the norms and prejudices of their own day. They had the humility, however, to see that they could not predict the needs of the future, and so bequeathed a Constitution which devolved the responsibility onto each generation to work out its own federal salvation.[126]

IV. CONCLUSION: THE FRAMERS' INTENTIONS AND EXPECTATIONS

Chapters four and five enable the intentions of the framers of the Constitution relating to responsible government to be discerned. The Constitution reflects a compromise between the views of those framers who wanted a federal government chosen by and accountable solely to the lower house, and the views of those framers who wanted two chambers of co-equal power. The reasoned conclusion reached by the Federal Conventions was a compromise position whereby the framers attempted to give effect to both federalism (as they conceived it) and responsible government as far as possible. The Constitution guarantees equal representation of each original state in the Senate, and the Senate has equal legislative power with the House of Representatives, subject to some exceptions in relation to money Bills, which contemplate lower house predominance in the formation of the government.[127] The Constitution requires ministers to hold seats in Parliament.[128] The deadlock procedure effectively presupposes that the House of Representatives will ultimately prevail if the joint sitting mechanism is triggered after a deadlock between the houses.[129] However, the Constitution does not entrench the features of responsible government beyond this, and confers power on the Senate to reject appropriation Bills, and contemporaries recognised that in doing so the Senate may force a dissolution or change of ministry.[130]

This compromise reflected an underlying shared conception of responsible government of which the ideas of constitutional evolution and popular sovereignty were the key elements. While the framers may not have been 'progressivists',[131] they accepted that responsible government was an evolutionary form

[126] Eg, *Convention Debates*, Sydney (1897) 581 (Kingston), 793 (Holder).
[127] Constitution, ss 7, 53–56; Wise, 'The Commonwealth of Australia' (n 30) 831.
[128] Constitution, s 64.
[129] Constitution, s 57; see *Convention Debates* (1898) 2468–9 (Barton).
[130] Moore, *The Constitution of the Commonwealth of Australia* (n 68) 144.
[131] Greg Craven, 'Heresy as Orthodoxy: Were the Founders Progressivists?' (2003) 31 *Federal Law Review* 87.

of government and expected further development in the functioning of government. In articulating their views about responsible government, the framers drew from a shared constitutional vocabulary informed by the common law and the British tradition of constitutionalism as expounded in leading works by writers such as Hearn, Todd, Bagehot, Grey and Anson, who had depicted the British Constitution as organic and in constant flux. The framers employed these principles to resolve the conflict of principle which arose for resolution at the Federal Conventions. While it would be simplistic to think that an evolutionary conception of responsible government removed any tension with federalism, it explains how the framers thought the two principles could be reconciled. As argued strongly by Griffith, lower house dominance was not an inherent feature of responsible government or the British Constitution, but the particular stage in the evolution of responsible government in Britain and the colonies as at the time of Federation. Giving effect to the principles of federalism meant consciously departing from the British Constitution as it functioned at Federation, but within the framework of an inherently evolutionary system of government. It was possible to give effect both to responsible government and federalism because the institutions they established would evolve to accommodate both.

The framers believed that the people would adapt to find a way of making the system work.[132] Griffith maintained that 'the genius of the English people' has shown itself to be capable of 'moulding the constitution ... to suit it to the exigencies of the times' and would be able to find a solution to the difficulties this posed.[133] Thynne said 'that responsible government is one of those things that will adapt itself to almost any circumstances which may arise', and that even with co-equal houses, a system of responsible government would exist in a better condition than in the colonies.[134] Clarke considered that the genius of the Australian people would evolve what is necessary 'to make the principles of responsible government and of two almost co-ordinate Houses work well together'.[135] Carruthers noted that the British Constitution 'has adapted itself at all times to the circumstances of the people and to their growing aspirations'.[136] Hackett agreed, noting that the political genius of the English people 'will discover a way out of any difficulty that may arise, and our business is to impose as few obstacles as possible in the path of its freest development'.[137]

The framers' conception of responsible government was a strongly political one, believing that the way the system functioned could not be prescribed or

[132] *Convention Debates*, Adelaide (1897) 324 (Gordon); *Convention Debates*, Sydney (1897) 516 (Hackett). See also 'The Federation of Australia' (1899) 87 *Saturday Review* 516, 517.
[133] *Convention Debates* (1891) 467 (Griffith).
[134] ibid 727 (Thynne).
[135] *Convention Debates*, Adelaide (1897) 307; *Convention Debates*, Sydney (1897) 512.
[136] *Convention Debates*, Sydney (1897) 275 (Carruthers).
[137] ibid 516 (Hackett).

even predicted in advance, but would depend upon the character of the people and their representatives.[138] As such, it was not advisable or even possible to attempt to prevent the rise of disciplined political parties. These views were consistent with standard constitutional orthodoxy about the nature of responsible government. The framers frequently stated that, in creating the framework for a federal Commonwealth, they trusted to the good sense of the people to ensure that it functioned well.[139] If these sentiments were naive or unrealistic, they were no more so than standard views about the functioning of political institutions which prevailed at the time of Federation. It was commonplace for contemporaries to consider that moderation and common sense were necessary for the functioning of British parliamentary institutions;[140] WE Gladstone said that the British Constitution presumed 'the good sense and the good faith of those who work it'.[141]

If the evolutionary nature of responsible government was crucial for the framers in reconciling responsible government and federalism, equally important was the creation of both houses as accountable to the people. The Senate was not established as an obstacle to the democratic will of the people as expressed in the lower house, but was representative of the people and designed to give effect to their wishes, although elected on a different basis to the House of Representatives. Underlying all the institutions established by the Constitution were the people, who would determine how the institutions of government were worked. The lower house did not have a monopoly on the people's will; and the representatives in either house 'may not faithfully represent the wishes of their constituents'.[142] The Senate would also represent the people and thus have a duty to ensure that the House of Representatives gave effect to the will of the people, including by rejecting measures proposed by the lower house.[143]

How, precisely, the system of government created by the Constitution would function given these constraints would depend on the people. The framers intended to create a Constitution whose 'guiding law' was government by the

[138] Jeffrey Archer and Graham Maddox, 'The 1975 Constitutional Crisis in Australia' (1976) 14 *Journal of Commonwealth and Comparative Politics* 141, 148.

[139] *Convention Debates*, Adelaide (1897) 72 (Glynn), 110 (Wise), 125–6, 516–7 (Symon), 307 (Clarke), 357 (Howe), 387–8 (Barton); *Convention Debates*, Sydney (1897) 276–7 (Carruthers), 512 (Clarke), 609 (Forrest), 618–9 (Leake).

[140] Eg, Patrick McMahon Glynn, *Federation: Speech by P McM Glynn* (Adelaide, WK Thomas & Co, 1897) 7.

[141] WE Gladstone, *Gleanings of Past Years, 1843–1878* (London, J Murray, 1879) vol 1, 245, quoted in *Convention Debates* (1891) 409 (Barton); see also Alpheus Todd, *Parliamentary Government in the British Colonies*, 2nd edn (London, Longmans, Green, 1894) 754; Walter Bagehot, *The English Constitution* (London, Chapman and Hall, 1867) 177, 181–4; Hearn (n 119) 190; *Convention Debates*, Adelaide (1897) 306 (Clarke), 387–8 (Barton), 516, 630 (Symon), 523 (Leake), 526 (Dobson and Forrest); RC Baker, *Notes on the Constitution of South Australia* (Adelaide, Hussey & Gillingham, 1899) xxiii.

[142] *Convention Debates*, Sydney (1897) 580 (Kingston).

[143] ibid 830 (Symon).

people.[144] In contrast to the American Constitution, whose foundational principle was '[t]rust in no man', the foundation of the Australian Constitution was '[t]rust in the people'.[145] Under the Constitution, Wrixon wrote that the people of Australia were given 'free power to mould our own destiny in our own way, for our own purposes, in full reliance upon the British political prudence of our people'.[146]

For the most part, it seems that these predictions have proven accurate. The system of government created by the Constitution has, in general, been remarkably stable. In 1919 John Quick, with the benefit of 18 years of experience, considered that the functioning of the Constitution had proved the 'extreme' predictions of the likes of Higgins (who feared that the Senate would control the public finance of Australia and thereby control the executive) and Baker (who feared that responsible government would obliterate the Senate) incorrect: he wrote that 'Federation has not killed the Cabinet nor has the Cabinet System killed Federation. Both are surviving and none the worse for their association'.[147]

[144] Wrixon, *The Constitution of the Commonwealth of Australia* (n 6) 5.

[145] 'Draft of a Bill to Constitute the Commonwealth of Australia, 1898' (1899) 190 *Quarterly Review* 289, 315. See also Moore, *The Constitution of the Commonwealth of Australia* (n 68) 613, 616; *Convention Debates* (1898) 2181 (Isaacs).

[146] Wrixon, *The Constitution of the Commonwealth of Australia* (n 6) 6.

[147] John Quick, *The Legislative Powers of the Commonwealth and the States of Australia with Proposed Amendments* (Melbourne, Maxwell, 1919) 17–18.

6

A Theory of Responsible Government under the Australian Constitution

> To the people we come sooner or later: it is upon their wisdom and self-restraint that the stability of the most cunningly devised scheme of government will in the last resort depend.[1]
>
> James Bryce (1891)

I. INTRODUCTION

CHAPTERS TWO TO five of this book examined the incorporation of responsible government into the Australian Constitution by exploring the historical and constitutional background, including the intentions of the framers of the Constitution. Chapters six and seven draw on this historical material to develop an account of responsible government and consider its implications for the interpretation of the Constitution.

This chapter develops a theory of responsible government which draws from the historical material in chapters two to five as well as High Court jurisprudence since Federation and explores the specific provisions of the Constitution which give effect to or assume responsible government. There are valuable discussions of responsible government in the literature.[2] This chapter supplements those accounts by providing a broader account which identifies key constitutional values drawn from the history of Australian constitutionalism as central to responsible government, including accountability, popular sovereignty and evolutionary change.

[1] James Bryce, *The American Commonwealth*, 2nd edn (London, Macmillan, 1891) vol 1, 270, 291.

[2] Eg, AH Birch, *Representative and Responsible Government: An Essay on the British Constitution* (London, Allen & Unwin, 1964); Patrick Weller and Dean Jaensch (eds), *Responsible Government in Australia* (Richmond, Australasian Political Studies Association, 1980); George Winterton, *Parliament, the Executive and the Governor-General: A Constitutional Analysis* (Melbourne, Melbourne University Press, 1983) 71–85; Geoffrey Lindell, 'Responsible Government' in PD Finn (ed), *Essays on Law and Government, Volume 1: Principles and Values* (North Ryde, Law Book Co, 1995).

II. RESPONSIBLE GOVERNMENT AND THE CONSTITUTION: A THEORY

A. Fundamental Feature of the Constitution

The Constitution contains little express recognition of responsible government. Nevertheless, responsible government is a fundamental constitutional principle.[3] The High Court has described responsible government as 'the central feature of the Australian constitutional system'.[4] When the Commonwealth of Australia Constitution Bill was debated in the House of Commons in 1900, Mr Haldane said, in words later quoted by the High Court:

> This Bill is permeated through and through with the spirit of the greatest institution which exists in the Empire, and which pertains to every Constitution established within the Empire – I mean the institution of responsible government, a government under which the Executive is directly responsible to – nay, is almost the creature of – the legislature.[5]

The centrality of responsible government is evident from the fact that it governs some of the most fundamental matters relating to the functioning of government, namely the formation of the ministry and the manner in which key powers are exercised. The Constitution was drafted on the assumption that its provisions will function in accordance with the conventions of responsible government[6] and many High Court cases have noted that responsible government is one of the central features of the Australian Constitution.[7] Responsible government 'is part of the fabric on which the written words of the Constitution are superimposed';[8] it is 'invisibly but none the less inextricably and powerfully

[3] John Quick and Robert Randolph Garran, *The Annotated Constitution of the Australian Commonwealth* (Sydney, Angus and Robertson, 1901) 706–7; Winterton, *Parliament, the Executive and the Governor-General* (n 2) 1, 71–85.

[4] *R v Kirby; Ex parte Boilermakers' Society of Australia* (1956) 94 CLR 254, 275 (Dixon CJ, McTiernan, Fullagar and Kitto JJ).

[5] United Kingdom, *Parliamentary Debates*, House of Commons, 14 May 1900, vol 83, 98–9 (Richard Haldane), quoted in *Williams v Attorney-General (NSW)* (1913) 16 CLR 404, 459 (Isaacs J) and *Amalgamated Society of Engineers v Adelaide Steamship Co Ltd* (1920) 28 CLR 129, 147 (Knox CJ, Isaacs, Rich and Starke JJ).

[6] *Convention Debates*, Adelaide (1897) 443 (Barton); *Convention Debates*, Sydney (1897) 229, 795 (Barton); *Convention Debates* (1898) 2469–70 (Barton). See also *Victoria v Commonwealth* (1975) 134 CLR 81, 156 (Gibbs J); *Victoria v Commonwealth* (1975) 134 CLR 338, 405–406 (Jacobs J).

[7] *Amalgamated Society of Engineers v Adelaide Steamship Co Ltd* (1920) 28 CLR 129, 146–7 (Knox CJ, Isaacs, Rich and Starke JJ); *Victorian Stevedoring & General Contracting Co Pty Ltd v Dignan* (1931) 46 CLR 73, 114 (Evatt J); *R v Kirby; Ex parte Boilermakers' Society* (1956) 94 CLR 254, 275 (Dixon CJ, McTiernan, Fullagar and Kitto JJ); *Lange v Australian Broadcasting Corporation* (1997) 189 CLR 520, 557–558 (Brennan CJ, Dawson, Toohey, Gaudron, McHugh, Gummow and Kirby JJ); *McCloy v New South Wales* (2015) 257 CLR 178, 224 [106] (Gageler J), 279 [301] (Gordon J); *Murphy v Electoral Commissioner* (2016) 261 CLR 28, 112 [260] (Gordon J); *Comcare v Banerji* (2019) 267 CLR 373, 437 [149] (Gordon J).

[8] *Commonwealth v Kreglinger & Fernau Ltd* (1926) 37 CLR 393, 413 (Isaacs J).

interwoven with the texture of the written word'.[9] Responsible government is 'not merely an assumption upon which the actual provisions are based; it is an integral element in the Constitution'.[10] The system of responsible government has been 'embedded in the federal Constitution and cannot now be disturbed without amendment to that Constitution'.[11] Responsible government also applies throughout the states and territories and the principles of responsible government as they apply throughout the various Australian constitutional systems have much in common.[12]

Notwithstanding its centrality to the Australian system of government, the text of the Constitution contains limited recognition of responsible government. The inclusion of responsible government in the Australian constitutional framework is therefore something that can only be inferred historically, based on the framers' intentions and a knowledge of the constitutional background to Federation. A further consequence is that responsible government is better seen as being assumed rather than prescribed.[13] The High Court's description of the relationship between responsible government and the Constitution in this regard is not always consistent. In some decisions responsible government has been described as being 'provided for' or 'established' by the Constitution.[14] More often, however, the High Court prefers to speak of responsible government being 'prescribed' or 'mandated' by the Constitution.[15] The difficulty with this is that there is little in the Constitution that prescribes or mandates any aspect of responsible government other than the requirement that ministers must be a member of either house of Parliament.[16] Very little else relating to responsible

[9] *Commonwealth v Colonial Combing, Spinning and Weaving Co Ltd* (1922) 31 CLR 421, 446 (Isaacs J).

[10] *Australian Capital Television Pty Ltd v Commonwealth* (1992) 177 CLR 106, 135 (Mason CJ).

[11] *Williams v Commonwealth* (2012) 248 CLR 156, 204 [58] (French CJ), referring to Quick and Garran (n 3) 706–7.

[12] See, eg, *Mann v Carnell* (1999) 201 CLR 1, 28–9 (McHugh J); *Egan v Willis* (1998) 195 CLR 424, 446 [27], 451 [42] (Gaudron, Gummow and Hayne JJ), 502 [154] (Kirby J); *Williams v Commonwealth* (2012) 248 CLR 156, 211–12 [74] (French CJ); *Palmer v Western Australia* (2021) 272 CLR 505, 557 [155] (Gageler J).

[13] *Cf Egan v Willis* (1998) 195 CLR 424, 473 [95]–[96] (McHugh J). This is analogous to the relationship between the Constitution and the rule of law: *Australian Communist Party v Commonwealth* (1951) 83 CLR 1, 193 (Dixon J).

[14] *Lange v Australian Broadcasting Corporation* (1997) 189 CLR 520, 557, 561 (Brennan CJ, Dawson, Toohey, Gaudron, McHugh, Gummow and Kirby JJ); *Kruger v Commonwealth* (1997) 190 CLR 1, 91 (Toohey J), 156 (Gummow J).

[15] *Lange v Australian Broadcasting Corporation* (1997) 189 CLR 520, 561, 562, 567, 569 (Brennan CJ, Dawson, Toohey, Gaudron, McHugh, Gummow and Kirby JJ); *Egan v Willis* (1998) 195 CLR 424, 451 [42] (Gaudron, Gummow and Hayne JJ); *Brown v Tasmania* (2017) 261 CLR 328, 363–4 [102]–[104] (Kiefel CJ, Bell and Keane JJ), 376 [156] (Gageler J), 413 [271] (Nettle J); *Clubb v Edwards* (2019) 267 CLR 171, 194 [44] (Kiefel CJ, Bell and Keane JJ), 223–4 [157] (Gageler J), 259 [256] (Nettle J), 295 [355] (Gordon J); *Comcare v Banerji* (2019) 267 CLR 373, 395 [20], 399 [29] (Kiefel CJ, Bell, Keane and Nettle JJ).

[16] Constitution, s 64. Note also s 53, which confers greater powers on the House of Representatives in relation to taxation and appropriation Bills than the Senate, thus contemplating lower house

government is prescribed or mandated; for instance, the Constitution does not require that the Governor-General must act on the advice of the ministry, it confers power on the Governor-General to appoint ministers but says nothing about the basis on which those ministers are selected, and it does not require the ministry to hold the confidence of the House of Representatives.

Thus, the extent to which the Constitution prescribes responsible government should not be overstated. Recognising this, Harrison Moore wrote in 1910 that the provisions of the Constitution relating to the ministers of state were made 'with a view to the Cabinet System' but did 'not preclude very extensive modifications of that system': the 1898 Bill established no more than a parliamentary executive, and left the rest to custom and convention.[17] In short, few of the main features of responsible government are prescribed by the Constitution: the concept of responsible government 'is not one which is elaborated in the Constitution'.[18] While insisting that the Constitution assumes rather than prescribes responsible government may seem a fine distinction, it reflects a fundamentally different conception of the relationship between responsible government and the Constitution, with potentially significant implications for the interpretation of the Constitution.

B. Law, Convention and Constitution

In the Australian constitutional system, 'the Constitution' and constitutional law are typically conceived as something separate from the rest of the law, and possessing a superior authority. This is not surprising, given the written and entrenched nature of the Australian Constitution. However, as noted, responsible government has been described as a central feature of the Australian Constitution, but it is not expressly recognised by the Constitution and its conventions are not legally enforceable. John Gardner forcefully argued that '[n]o constitution is exhausted by its law' and that even a formal written Constitution 'only adds another fragment to its constitution'.[19] In Australia, 'the constitution' consists not only of the written text of the Constitution, but includes judicial decisions (especially decisions interpreting the Constitution), statutes (such as the Australia Act 1986 (Cth)) and constitutional conventions,[20] as well as a body

predominance in public finance and the formation of government; s 83 provides that '[n]o money shall be drawn from the Treasury of the Commonwealth except under appropriation made by law'.

[17] W Harrison Moore, *The Constitution of the Commonwealth of Australia*, 2nd edn (Melbourne, Charles F Maxwell, 1910) 168–9.

[18] *Re Patterson; Ex parte Taylor* (2001) 207 CLR 391, 415 [63] (Gaudron J).

[19] John Gardner, 'Can There Be a Written Constitution?' in Leslie Green and Brian Leiter (eds), *Oxford Studies in Philosophy of Law* (Oxford, Oxford University Press, 2011) vol 1, 168.

[20] Brendan Lim, *Australia's Constitution After Whitlam* (Cambridge, Cambridge University Press, 2017) 19–22.

of constitutional law which gives content to the sparse text of the Constitution. Indeed, as chapters four and five argued, the Australian Constitution did not attempt to codify our constitutional law or practice, but simply to set out the architecture of the constitutional system, drawing on the pre-existing body of common law, as well as constitutional convention, custom and practice. Many of the key principles and institutions of Australian constitutionalism therefore pre-date the formal enactment of the written Constitution.

As is often noted, the framers intended to incorporate responsible government modelled on the principles of the British Constitution into the Australian Constitution.[21] As discussed in chapter two, the British Constitution was conceived as something which resulted from the general law and included the manner in which it functioned. Dicey argued that the Constitution is simply 'the result of the ordinary law of the land'[22] and Bryce wrote that:

> there is in England no such thing as a constitution apart from the rest of the law: there is merely a mass of law, consisting partly of statutes and partly of decided cases and accepted usages, in conformity with which the government of the country is carried on from day to day, but which is being constantly modified by fresh statutes and cases.[23]

Thus, for the framers, 'the Constitution' was the totality of law, custom and convention according to which the business of government was carried out. As such, responsible government is not primarily a constitutional doctrine but includes the way the system of government functions in practice. It would be an overstatement to say, as Professor John Griffith famously said, that the Constitution 'is no more and no less than what happens'.[24] Nevertheless, it is true that the non-legal aspects of responsible government such as convention and practice are fundamental to the idea of responsible government.

Herein lies arguably the fundamental tension relating to responsible government under the Australian Constitution.[25] Under a written Constitution, there is necessarily a strong distinction between that which is law and that which is not, and a greater prominence given to that which is law. A written Constitution is the paramount embodiment of legal constitutionalism under which the written text and the interpretation of that text have primacy in what is considered to be constitutional. And one of the most fundamental features of our Constitution is responsible government, which is an inherently political and changeable system

[21] Eg, *Williams v Commonwealth* (2012) 248 CLR 156, 204 [58] (French CJ), 349 [508] (Crennan J); Quick and Garran (n 3) 706–7.

[22] AV Dicey, *Introduction to the Study of the Law of the Constitution*, 6th edn (London, MacMillan, 1902) 85, 199.

[23] Bryce (n 1) vol 1, 237. To similar effect see Dicey, *Introduction to the Study of the Law of the Constitution* (n 22) 22–4, 191–201; Moore, *The Constitution of the Commonwealth of Australia* (n 17) 83.

[24] JAG Griffith, 'The Political Constitution' (1979) 42 *Modern Law Review* 1, 19.

[25] *Convention Debates* (1891) 197, 199 (Cockburn).

of constitutionalism whose primary features are not legally enforceable[26] and where the 'constitution' is not something separate from its functioning.

The incorporation of responsible government within a constitutional system where the written, enforceable legal text is primary raises difficult tensions. The inherently political nature of responsible government suggests that the role of the courts is somewhat circumscribed; and yet the fact that responsible government is a central feature of the Constitution suggests that it cannot be ignored when the courts interpret the Constitution. In so doing, 'much will turn on the definition of responsible government and how that concept is judicially interpreted'.[27]

C. Parliament, the Sovereign and the Executive

Under the British theory of government, every act of government was in law the act of the Crown, but the acts of the Crown had to be carried out by authorised officers.[28] As Samuel Griffith put it:

> The system called Responsible Government is based on the notion that the head of the State can himself do no wrong, that he does not do any act of State of his own motion, but follows the advice of his ministers, on whom the responsibility for acts done, in order to give effect to their volition, naturally falls. They are therefore called Responsible Ministers. If they do wrong, they can be punished or dismissed from office without effecting any change in the Headship of the State.[29]

The Constitution united the Australian colonies under the Crown and expressly constituted the Queen as an element of the Australian legislature and executive.[30] As such, the Australian Constitution replicates many aspects of the traditional British conception of government:

> In the theory of our government the Sovereign is the source of all authority, legislative, executive and judicial. The British Constitution requires that practically in all cases the Sovereign's authority shall be exercised in the prescribed manner, with the prescribed advice and consent, and by the prescribed agents.[31]

[26] *Cf Commonwealth v Kreglinger & Fernau Ltd* (1926) 37 CLR 393, 412 (Isaacs J).

[27] Geoffrey Lindell, *Responsible Government and the Australian Constitution – Conventions Transformed into Law?* (Leichhardt, Federation Press, 2004) 4.

[28] William Edward Hearn, *The Government of England: Its Structure, and Its Development*, 2nd edn (Melbourne, George Robertson, 1886) 10, 16–18, 118, 124, 126, 162.

[29] Samuel Walker Griffith, *Notes on Australian Federation: Its Nature and Probable Effects: A Paper Presented to the Government of Queensland* (Brisbane, Government Printer, 1896) 17–18.

[30] *Constitution* preamble, ss 1, 2, 61.

[31] *R v Boston* (1923) 33 CLR 386, 399 (Isaacs and Rich JJ); see also *Ryder v Foley* (1906) 4 CLR 422, 432 (Griffith CJ). It should be noted that not every aspect of the British Constitution was replicated in Australia: *Plaintiff M68/2015 v Minister for Immigration and Border Protection* (2016) 257 CLR 42, 94 [125] (Gageler J).

Under the conventions of responsible government the head of state acts on the advice of ministers.[32] Thus, while the acts of the executive are in law those of the Crown, in practice the work of government is carried on by ministers and other executive officers.[33] Chapter II of the Constitution 'left, as a matter of law, the means and method of executing and maintaining the laws entirely to the Sovereign's discretion, and tacitly subjected the exercise of the power only to the conventions of responsible government'.[34]

Responsible government is the principle of a parliamentary executive. Brennan J, quoting Alpheus Todd and Earl Grey, described the 'distinguishing feature' of Parliamentary government as the practice 'which requires the powers belonging to the Crown to be exercised by ministers who possess the confidence of Parliament'.[35] 'The essence of responsible government is that the Legislature has full confidence in the Executive, just as those who assented to the Constitution had full confidence in their Parliament'.[36] Thus, the executive is drawn from Parliament rather than being directly elected, and is 'almost the creature of' the legislature.[37] As such, in the long run Parliament 'is in a position to control the Executive Government'.[38]

Parliamentary control of the executive is therefore fundamental to responsible government, being the primary mechanism by which the executive is held to account for the actions of government. That supremacy is both legal and political. By retaining the ultimate power to determine the composition of the ministry, Parliament can check or reverse any improper exercise of power by an executive officer.[39] Parliament's role is oversight, not administration: that is, significant discretion is conferred on the executive to manage the business of government, and the Parliament's role is to oversee the executive, rather than

[32] *Theodore v Duncan* [1919] AC 696, 706 (Viscount Haldane); *New South Wales v Bardolph* (1934) 52 CLR 455, 517, 525 (McTiernan J); *New South Wales v Commonwealth* (1975) 135 CLR 337, 365 (Barwick CJ); *Victoria v Commonwealth* (1975) 134 CLR 81, 156 (Gibbs J); *FAI Insurances Ltd v Winneke* (1982) 151 CLR 342, 349 (Gibbs CJ), 352 (Stephen J), 373 (Murphy J), 414 (Brennan J); *Sue v Hill* (1999) 199 CLR 462, 494 [70] (Gleeson CJ, Gummow and Hayne JJ).

[33] *New South Wales v Bardolph* (1934) 52 CLR 455, 481 (Evatt J), 495 (Rich J), 501, 503 (Starke J), 507 (Dixon J), 518 (McTiernan J); *Re Residential Tenancies Tribunal (NSW) and Henderson; Ex parte Defence Housing Authority* (1997) 190 CLR 410, 438 (Dawson, Toohey and Gaudron JJ); *Ryder v Foley* (1906) 4 CLR 422, 432 (Griffith CJ); *Plaintiff M68/2015 v Minister for Immigration and Border Protection* (2016) 257 CLR 42, 95 [128] (Gageler J); *Western Australia v Commonwealth* (1975) 134 CLR 201, 278 (Jacobs J); *Chung Teong Toy v Musgrove* (1888) 14 VLR 349, 373–5 (Higinbotham CJ), 412–3 (Kerferd J).

[34] *New South Wales v Commonwealth* (1915) 20 CLR 54, 89 (Isaacs J).

[35] *FAI Insurances Ltd v Winneke* (1982) 151 CLR 342, 414–5 (Brennan J). See also *Mann v Carnell* (1999) 201 CLR 1, 26 (McHugh J).

[36] *Le Mesurier v Connor* (1929) 42 CLR 481, 505 (Isaacs J).

[37] *Williams v Attorney-General (NSW)* (1913) 16 CLR 404, 459 (Isaacs J); *Amalgamated Society of Engineers v Adelaide Steamship Co Ltd* (1920) 28 CLR 129, 147 (Knox CJ, Isaacs, Rich and Starke JJ).

[38] *New South Wales v Commonwealth* (1975) 135 CLR 337, 365 (Barwick CJ); *Plaintiff M68/2015 v Minister for Immigration and Border Protection* (2016) 257 CLR 42, 96 [128] (Gageler J).

[39] *Nott Bros & Co Ltd v Barkley (Collector of Customs (NSW))* (1925) 36 CLR 20, 29 (Isaacs J).

to directly exercise governmental functions.[40] This means that MPs are under an obligation to conscientiously scrutinise the actions of the government, free from any interests which would cloud their judgement.[41] Further, 'it is of the very nature of executive power in a system of responsible government that it is susceptible to control by the exercise of legislative power by Parliament';[42] the Australian Constitution imports 'the basal assumption of legislative predominance inherited from the United Kingdom'.[43] This is a fundamental constitutional principle which is not expressly stated in the Constitution,[44] which highlights the limitations of the text in understanding the Australian constitutional system. An essential aspect of this control is parliamentary control over public finance, which means that public funds cannot be levied or spent without parliamentary approval.[45] Taxation may only be imposed by parliamentary authority, and funds expended by the executive must be appropriated by law, as reflected in the terms of the Constitution.[46] As put by French CJ, '[t]he principle that the Executive draws money from Consolidated Revenue only upon statutory authority is central to the idea of responsible government'.[47]

Parliamentary control of the executive is, however, largely a myth. In the modern regulatory state, parliamentary control of the executive no longer accurately describes the relationship between Parliament and the executive – assuming it ever did. The need to maintain stable majorities means that the party which wins the majority of the seats in the lower house of Parliament wins office, and therefore controls that house: 'the Crown and the executive have come to represent the same forces as control a majority in the lower house'.[48] Rather than this being a corruption of parliamentary government as argued by some scholars,[49] this has long been a feature of responsible government. As discussed

[40] *New South Wales v Bardolph* (1934) 52 CLR 455, 472–3 (Evatt J).

[41] *Wilkinson v Osborne* (1915) 21 CLR 89, 98–100, 102 (Isaacs J); *Horne v Barber* (1920) 27 CLR 494, 499–500 (Knox CJ and Gavan Duffy J, Isaacs J); *Re Lambie* (2018) 263 CLR 601, 615–6 [22]–[24] (Kiefel CJ, Bell, Gageler, Keane, Nettle and Gordon JJ). See also *Re Day (No 2)* (2017) 263 CLR 201, 226 [72] (Kiefel CJ, Bell and Edelman JJ).

[42] *Re Residential Tenancies Tribunal (NSW) and Henderson; Ex parte Defence Housing Authority* (1997) 190 CLR 410, 441 (Dawson, Toohey and Gaudron JJ); *Brown v West* (1990) 169 CLR 195, 202 (Mason CJ, Brennan, Deane, Dawson and Toohey JJ).

[43] *Williams v Commonwealth* (2012) 248 CLR 156, 232 [136] (Gummow and Bell JJ).

[44] Nicholas Aroney, 'The High Court on Constitutional Law: The 2012 Term – Explanatory Power and the Modalities of Constitutional Reasoning' (2013) 36 *University of New South Wales Law Journal* 863, 881. But see *Victoria v Commonwealth* (1975) 134 CLR 338, 406 (Jacobs J); *Plaintiff M68/2015 v Minister for Immigration and Border Protection* (2016) 257 CLR 42, 93 [121]–[122] (Gageler J).

[45] *Commonwealth v Colonial Combing, Spinning and Weaving Co Ltd* (1922) 31 CLR 421, 434 (Isaacs J).

[46] *Williams v Commonwealth* (2012) 248 CLR 156, 259 [219] (Hayne J).

[47] *Pape v Federal Commissioner of Taxation* (2009) 238 CLR 1, 37–8 [58] (French CJ).

[48] *Victoria v Commonwealth (AAP Case)* (1975) 134 CLR 338, 384 (Stephen J); *Brown v West* (1990) 169 CLR 195, 201 (Mason CJ, Brennan, Deane, Dawson and Toohey JJ).

[49] GS Reid and Martyn Forrest, *Australia's Commonwealth Parliament 1901–1988: Ten Perspectives* (Carlton, Melbourne University Press, 1989) 12; GS Reid, 'Parliamentary-Executive Relations: The

in chapter two, from around the mid nineteenth century, the leading constitutional writers considered a two-party system to be essential for the proper working of responsible government and cabinet largely dominated Parliament. Under responsible government, the legislature legally controls the executive but the executive controls the legislature (at least, the lower house) politically.[50]

While Parliament formally enacts legislation, the vast majority of laws enacted by Parliament originate from the executive, which controls the policy-making process.[51] The introduction of legislation into Parliament is the culmination of a long process of formulating policy, consultation and legislative drafting, all of which occur within the executive. In the realm of public finance, executives have 'vast institutional expertise' which far surpasses the expertise of Parliament.[52] Executives possess the initiative in financial proposals and Parliament has little meaningful role in financial legislation. As several commentators have noted, Parliament ratifies (or rejects) the financial legislation developed by the executive and exercises 'a weak form of ex post review of public spending'.[53] Parliament has thus been described as a gatekeeper, whereby parliamentary powers and procedures set narrow gateways 'through which it is essential for executive policies to pass if they are to be effective'.[54] It may be better, therefore, to conceive the relationship between Parliament and the executive as one of interdependence rather than hierarchy.[55]

Is this lack of parliamentary control in relation to the executive a concern? Is there a need to seek to elevate the role of Parliament from mere ratifier and gatekeeper? Perhaps not. This chapter discusses below the detailed mechanisms that exist for scrutiny and accountability in relation to the modern executive and how this affects our conception of responsible government. Posner and Vermeule have argued that executive governments have a strong incentive to fill

Suppression of Politics' in Henry Mayer (ed), *Australian Politics: A Second Reader* (Melbourne, Cheshire, 1970) 502; Jim Chalmers and Glyn Davis, 'Power: Relations Between the Parliament and the Executive' (Research Paper No 14, Parliament of Australia, 2000) 1–2, 11, 21; Ian Marsh, *Beyond the Two Party System: Political Representation, Economic Competitiveness, and Australian Politics* (Melbourne, Cambridge University Press, 1995) 272.

[50] Margit Cohn has recently argued that analyses of the executive branch tend to oscillate between 'visions of legal subservience and political dominance': Margit Cohn, *A Theory of the Executive Branch: Tension and Legality* (Oxford, Oxford University Press, 2021) 25.

[51] *The Pilbara Infrastructure Pty Ltd v Australian Competition Tribunal* (2012) 246 CLR 379, 431 [138] (Heydon J); *Public Service Association and Professional Officers' Association Amalgamated (NSW) v Director of Public Employment* (2012) 250 CLR 343, 372 [69] (Heydon J).

[52] Will Bateman, *Public Finance and Parliamentary Constitutionalism* (Cambridge, Cambridge University Press, 2020) 210.

[53] ibid 1, 206, 222; Charles Lawson, 'Re-Invigorating the Accountability and Transparency of the Australian Government's Expenditure' (2008) 32 *Melbourne University Law Review* 879, 916; *Victoria v Commonwealth* (1975) 134 CLR 338, 384 (Stephen J).

[54] Terence Daintith and Alan Page, *The Executive in the Constitution: Structure, Autonomy, and Internal Control* (Oxford, Oxford University Press, 1999) 396.

[55] ibid 107, 201.

the accountability gap left by the failure of the legislature and the judiciary to provide effective checks by developing intra-executive constraints which, paradoxically, serve to strengthen the executive's powers by increasing its credibility.[56] Similarly, Daintith and Page argue that there is 'little or no difference between the interests of Parliament in financial control and those of the people within government entrusted with these tasks'.[57] That is, executives have an incentive to self-regulate and in so doing may exercise much more effective supervision than Parliament could.[58]

D. A Flexible, Evolutionary Institution

Crucial to understanding responsible government is the fact that it evolved and developed over time rather than being created. The framers incorporated into the Constitution responsible government modelled on the British Constitution as it functioned as at Federation, which was considered to have developed through a long process of evolution.[59] This remains true notwithstanding its incorporation into a written Constitution: responsible government derives its fundamental features and content through a process of historical evolution.

There are two principal implications of this. The first is that responsible government must be understood historically, in light of its historical development. The principles of responsible government were not determined in advance and prescriptively set out in a written document. The features of responsible government are not self-contained within the text of the Constitution; as noted, the text of the Constitution contains little express recognition of responsible government. The Constitution assumes a constitutional background which is necessary to understand in order to make sense of its text[60] and its content therefore must be determined by means of sources external to the Constitution.[61] As McHugh J said in *Egan v Willis*, in words that apply with equal force to the Commonwealth Constitution:

> the powers and privileges of each of the Houses of the Parliament of New South Wales can only be understood by reference to the powers and privileges of the House of Commons and the great constitutional conflicts between the House of Commons

[56] Eric A Posner and Adrian Vermeule, *The Executive Unbound: After the Madisonian Republic* (Oxford, Oxford University Press, 2010) ch 4.

[57] Daintith and Page (n 54) 105.

[58] See also ibid 396.

[59] Walter Bagehot, *The English Constitution* (London, Chapman and Hall, 1867) 254.

[60] See, eg, *Ryder v Foley* (1906) 4 CLR 422, 448 (O'Connor J); *Commissioner of Taxation (Cth) v Munro* (1926) 38 CLR 153, 187–8 (Isaacs J).

[61] See *Egan v Willis* (1998) 195 CLR 424, 447 [29] (Gaudron, Gummow and Hayne JJ); *Plaintiff M68/2015 v Minister for Immigration and Border Protection* (2016) 257 CLR 42, 96 [129] (Gageler J).

> on the one hand and the Crown, the House of Lords and the courts of law on the other which remained unsettled until the 19th century.[62]

The second key implication is that responsible government is inherently evolutionary: because its core content is not fixed, it continues to change. As put by JA Cockburn, the essence of the British Constitution is 'elasticity and development'.[63] In 1888 Holroyd J wrote that '[t]here is no cut-and-dried institution called responsible government, identical in all countries where it exists'.[64] This flexibility enables responsible government, chameleon-like, to adapt to a wide variety of circumstances.[65] It should be appreciated that this is more than simply to say that responsible government is subject to change; rather, change is of the essence of responsible government; change is a constitutional principle. Gaudron, Gummow and Hayne JJ wrote in *Egan v Willis* that '[i]t should not be assumed that the characteristics of a system of responsible government are fixed or that the principles of ministerial responsibility which developed in New South Wales after 1855 necessarily reflected closely those from time to time accepted at Westminster'.[66] The framers consciously adopted a flexible conception of responsible government and drafted the Constitution to enable it to adapt to changing circumstances and societal attitudes.[67]

Gleeson CJ's judgment in *Re Patterson; Ex parte Taylor* contains perhaps the clearest judicial recognition of this, where his Honour noted that the provisions of chapter II of the Constitution are brief and 'expressed in a form which allows the flexibility that is appropriate to the practical subject of governmental administration, consistent with the basic requirements of responsible government'.[68] Further, '[f]or the framers of the Constitution to have descended into greater specificity would have imposed an unnecessary and inappropriate degree of inflexibility upon constitutional arrangements that need to be capable of development and adaptability'.[69] The Constitution 'was framed to endure and to be capable of application to changing circumstances which the framers of the Constitution could not be expected to foresee, and it would be contrary to all principle to confine the operation of any of its provisions to matters known

[62] *Egan v Willis* (1998) 195 CLR 424, 459 [63], 473 [95] (McHugh J).

[63] John A Cockburn, *Australian Federation* (London, Horace Marshall, 1901) 100.

[64] *Chung Teong Toy v Musgrove* (1888) 14 VLR 349, 428 (Holroyd J). See also RAW Rhodes, John Wanna and Patrick Weller, *Comparing Westminster* (Oxford, Oxford University Press, 2011) 1–2, 221–2.

[65] *Commonwealth v Colonial Combing, Spinning and Weaving Co Ltd* (1922) 31 CLR 421, 438–9 (Isaacs J); *Marks v Commonwealth* (1964) 111 CLR 549, 557–58 (Kitto J).

[66] *Egan v Willis* (1998) 195 CLR 424, 451 [41] (Gaudron, Gummow and Hayne JJ).

[67] See, eg, *Combet v Commonwealth* (2005) 224 CLR 494, 522 [4] (Gleeson CJ); *Sue v Hill* (1999) 199 CLR 462, 496 [78] (Gleeson CJ, Gummow and Hayne JJ); *McGinty v Western Australia* (1996) 186 CLR 140, 201 (Toohey J); *Mulholland v Australian Electoral Commission* (2004) 220 CLR 181, 189 [9] (Gleeson CJ), 237 [154] (Gummow and Hayne JJ).

[68] *Re Patterson; Ex parte Taylor* (2001) 207 CLR 391, 401 [11] (Gleeson CJ).

[69] ibid 402–3 [14] (Gleeson CJ).

to exist in 1901'.[70] A key theme of the Coombs *Royal Commission on Australian Government Administration* completed in 1976 was that the structures of public administration needed to be capable of adapting to the changing needs of contemporary government.[71]

Responsible government therefore needs to be understood both synchronically and diachronically: its principles evolved over a long period and it also adapts itself to the circumstances of the time, such that the particular form it takes in a particular context is shaped by the prevailing circumstances and political realities.[72] Unsurprisingly, there have been many changes in the nature and conduct of government since Federation.[73] These include the following. There have been significant changes in society's expectations of the role of government, with a corresponding increase in the size of government.[74] Australian Parliaments have come to be dominated by parties with very high levels of party discipline, although, as explored in chapter two, this is much more consistent with traditional parliamentary government than often realised. There has been continued growth of non-departmental agencies, such as statutory agencies and government corporations, who exercise significant functions, sometimes with legislatively conferred independence.[75] Significant policy decisions are made by individual ministers and even by public servants rather than cabinet.[76]

This suggests that the traditional Westminster model, which contemplates government being carried out by ministers who are responsible to Parliament, is increasingly at odds with the reality of modern government.[77] However, it is not to be thought that changes in the structure of government since Federation are a departure from the 'true' principles of responsible government which must be recovered, but rather a legitimate evolution in circumstances and societal values which the Constitution is deliberately structured to provide for. The modern executive is vastly different from that which existed in 1901 and the significant changes that have occurred in the nature of government could not have been

[70] *Brown v R* (1986) 160 CLR 171, 183 (Gibbs CJ).

[71] *Royal Commission on Australian Government Administration* (Canberra, Australian Government Publishing Service, 1976) 3, 5, 66, 68.

[72] *Egan v Willis* (1998) 195 CLR 424, 449 [38] (Gaudron, Gummow and Hayne JJ).

[73] *Williams v Commonwealth* (2012) 248 CLR 156, 204 [59] (French CJ).

[74] *Re Residential Tenancies Tribunal (NSW) and Henderson; Ex parte Defence Housing Authority* (1997) 190 CLR 410, 438 (Dawson, Toohey and Gaudron JJ).

[75] *Deputy Commissioner of Taxation v State Bank (NSW)* (1992) 174 CLR 219, 230–1 (Mason CJ, Brennan, Deane, Dawson, Toohey, Gaudron and McHugh JJ); *Federated Amalgamated Government Railway and Tramway Service Association v NSW Railway Traffic Employes Association (the Railway Servants Case)* (1906) 4 CLR 488, 535 (Griffith CJ).

[76] Colin Turpin, 'Ministerial Responsibility' in Jeffrey Jowell and Dawn Oliver (eds), *The Changing Constitution*, 3rd edn (Oxford, Clarendon Press, 1994) 118–23.

[77] *Royal Commission on Australian Government Administration* (n 71) 11–12; Terence Daintith and Yee-Fui Ng, 'Executives' in Cheryl Saunders and Adrienne Stone (eds), *The Oxford Handbook of the Australian Constitution* (Oxford, Oxford University Press, 2018) 596; *Ansett Transport Industries (Operations) Pty Ltd v Commonwealth* (1977) 139 CLR 54, 87 (Murphy J).

predicted at Federation. The Constitution has been expressly designed to be flexible so as to accommodate such changes and to enable the people of Australia to govern themselves in the manner they see fit.

E. Popular Sovereignty

A fundamental feature of the Australian conception of responsible government is popular sovereignty: that is, the Australian Constitution is designed to ensure self-government by the people of Australia. As put by Justice Gageler, 'the Constitution sets up a system to enlarge the powers of self-government of the people of Australia through institutions of government that are structured to be politically accountable to the people of Australia'.[78]

It might be thought surprising to argue that popular sovereignty is central to responsible government given that some aspects of Australia's constitutional system are considered to militate against such an argument. The Australian constitutional tradition has been deeply influenced by parliamentary sovereignty, and parliamentary sovereignty and popular sovereignty are sometimes thought to be in sharp contrast.[79] The Constitution took its legal force through an enactment of the Imperial Parliament rather than an exercise of the legal sovereignty of the people, and there are difficulties with arguing that the legal basis of the authority of the Constitution now rests in popular sovereignty.[80] Prominent scholars have also questioned the democratic credentials of the Australian constitutional system. LF Crisp described the Constitution as a 'splendid bastion of property' and argued that it 'is impossible to reconcile sound democratic principles' with the structure and power of the Senate.[81] In 1993 Paul Finn wrote that the Australian people 'seem often enough to be an afterthought in discussion of

[78] Stephen Gageler, 'Beyond the Text: A Vision of the Structure and Function of the Constitution' (2009) 32 *Australian Bar Review* 138, 152.

[79] See, eg, Wilson R Huhn, 'Constantly Approximating Popular Sovereignty: Seven Fundamental Principles of Constitutional Law' (2010) 19 *William & Mary Bill of Rights Journal* 291, 296–7; Morton J Horwitz, 'A Historiography of the People Themselves and Popular Constitutionalism' (2006) 81 *Chicago-Kent Law Review* 813, 817; Stuart Wilks-Heeg, Andrew Blick and Stephen Crone, *How Democratic is the UK? The 2012 Audit* (Liverpool, Democratic Audit, 2012) 10; AR Blackshield, 'The Implied Freedom of Communication' in Geoffrey Lindell (ed), *Future Directions in Australian Constitutional Law: Essays in Honour of Professor Leslie Zines* (Sydney, Federation Press, 1994) 235, 240, 242.

[80] GJ Lindell, 'Why Is Australia's Constitution Binding? – The Reason in 1900 and Now, and the Effect of Independence' (1986) 16 *Federal Law Review* 29; John Daley, *The Bases for the Authority of the Australian Constitution* (Dphil Thesis, Oxford University, 1999); Anthony Dillon, 'A Turtle by Any Other Name: The Legal Basis of the Australian Constitution' (2001) 29 *Federal Law Review* 241; Simon Evans, 'Why Is the Constitution Binding? Authority, Obligation and the Role of the People' (2004) 25 *Adelaide Law Review* 107.

[81] LF Crisp, *Australian National Government*, 5th edn (Melbourne, Longman Cheshire, 1983) 14–21, 349. See also Manning Clark, *A History of Australia, Volume 5: The People Make Laws 1888–1915* (Carlton, Melbourne University Press, 1981) 139.

this country's system of government' and that ideas of popular sovereignty have had limited influence on the Australian constitutional tradition.[82]

Contrary to these views, I argue that popular sovereignty is a key element of the Australian conception of responsible government, and has been so from the enactment of the Constitution. Throughout western political thought, popular sovereignty has been conceived in two principal ways, which are compatible rather than mutually exclusive. The first is that of a founding moment whereby a people create a new polity through a sovereign act of self-constitution. The second is concerned with the relationship between the people and the institutions of government, and stipulates that those institutions should give effect to the will of the people.[83] As briefly explored in chapter two, in the British constitutional tradition, thinkers such as AV Dicey distinguished between political and legal conceptions of sovereignty, arguing that although Parliament was legally sovereign, the electorate in Great Britain possessed political sovereignty given that its will ultimately prevailed in the system of government.[84] As put by Todd, under responsible government, 'rule and authority must receive the sanction of popular consent, though it does not necessarily emanate from the will of the people'.[85]

Although the British tradition did not recognise a concept of legal sovereignty similar to that which animated the founding of the US, it strongly upheld a political concept of popular sovereignty whereby the institutions of government exercised their powers in accordance with the will of the electorate.[86] Parliamentary and popular sovereignty are thus compatible: the legal sovereignty of Parliament co-exists alongside a political conception of popular sovereignty whereby the legal powers of Parliament are exercised by elected representatives who are accountable to the people, whose will ultimately prevails politically.

The location of legal sovereignty (assuming that is a coherent concept) within the Australian legal system is contested and it is beyond the scope of this book to explore these questions.[87] The Australian constitutional tradition of responsible government is closely aligned with both of the conceptions of popular sovereignty which have been emphasised throughout history.[88] Responsible government is the principle that the people are politically sovereign. Sir Samuel Griffith pointed out that the effect of responsible government 'is that the actual

[82] Paul Finn, 'Public Trust and Public Accountability' (1993) 65 *Australian Quarterly* 50, 50.

[83] Benjamin B Saunders and Simon Kennedy, 'Popular Sovereignty, 'the People', and the Australian Constitution: A Historical Reassessment' (2019) 30 *Public Law Review* 36.

[84] Dicey, *Introduction to the Study of the Law of the Constitution* (n 22) 70–3.

[85] Alpheus Todd, *On Parliamentary Government in England: Its Origin, Development, and Practical Operation*, 2nd edn (London, Longmans,Green and Co, 1887) vol 1, 2.

[86] See further Saunders and Kennedy (n 83) 44–48.

[87] See further Nicholas Aroney, *The Constitution of a Federal Commonwealth: The Making and Meaning of the Australian Constitution* (Cambridge, Cambridge University Press, 2009) 345–51.

[88] See further Saunders and Kennedy (n 83) 48–56.

government of the State is conducted by officers who enjoy the confidence of the people'.[89] Under the Australian Constitution, the people of the Commonwealth are 'the sovereign political authority'.[90]

Even though the Constitution took its force from its enactment by the Imperial Parliament, its foundation politically can be said to be 'popular sovereignty implied in the agreement of the 'people' of the pre-Federation colonies 'to unite in one indissoluble federal Commonwealth''.[91] The basis of the principle of representative government is that 'all powers of government ultimately belong to, and are derived from, the governed'.[92] As put by Alfred Deakin: '[w]e cannot afford to have in our constitution any man exercising authority, unless he derives it from the people of Australia'.[93] Under the Australian constitutional tradition of representative and responsible government, the people are the legitimating agents for government, legislative and executive powers ought to be exercised on their behalf, and 'all powers of government ultimately belong to, and are derived from, the governed'.[94]

This political sovereignty is exercised through the mechanisms of representative and responsible government. In *Australian Capital Television Pty Ltd v Commonwealth* ('*ACTV*') Mason CJ said: '[t]he very concept of representative government and representative democracy signifies government by the people through their representatives. Translated into constitutional terms, it denotes that the sovereign power which resides in the people is exercised on their behalf by their representatives'.[95] Thus, 'unlike the case of the American Constitution, the Australian Constitution is built upon confidence in a system of parliamentary Government with ministerial responsibility',[96] because the Parliament is an emanation of the will of the people. Inherent in the concept of responsible government is the view that, '[f]ar from being something to be feared and contained, ordinary politics was seen as the primary means by which people exerted real, tangible and ongoing control over government'.[97]

This implies that MPs have a duty to exercise their powers for the benefit of the people.[98] As Harrison Moore put it: '[t]he great underlying principle [of the

[89] Griffith, *Notes on Australian Federation* (n 29) 17, quoted in *Lange v Australian Broadcasting Corporation* (1997) 189 CLR 520, 559 (Brennan CJ, Dawson, Toohey, Gaudron, McHugh, Gummow and Kirby JJ), *McCloy v New South Wales* (2015) 257 CLR 178, 225 [107] (Gageler J); *Comcare v Banerji* (2019) 267 CLR 373, 410 [59] (Gageler J).

[90] *Clubb v Edwards* (2019) 267 CLR 171, 191 [29] (Kiefel CJ, Bell and Keane JJ).

[91] *Ruddock v Vadarlis* (2001) 110 FCR 491, 542–3 [192] (French J).

[92] *Nationwide News Pty Ltd v Wills* (1992) 177 CLR 1, 70 (Deane and Toohey JJ); *McGinty v Western Australia* (1996) 186 CLR 140, 199 (Toohey J).

[93] *Convention Debates* (1891) 571 (Deakin). See also *Convention Debates*, Adelaide (1897) 178 (Isaacs), 332 (Trenwith); also *Convention Debates* (1898) 2205 (Reid), 2477 (Barton).

[94] *Nationwide News Pty Ltd v Wills* (1992) 177 CLR 1, 70 (Deane and Toohey JJ).

[95] *Australian Capital Television Pty Ltd v Commonwealth* (1992) 177 CLR 106, 137 (Mason CJ).

[96] *A-G (Cth) ex rel McKinlay v Commonwealth* (1975) 135 CLR 1, 58 (Stephen J).

[97] Stephen Gageler, 'Foundations of Australian Federalism and the Role of Judicial Review' (1987) 17 *Federal Law Review* 162, 173.

[98] *Australian Capital Television Pty Ltd v Commonwealth* (1992) 177 CLR 106, 138 (Mason CJ).

Constitution] is that the rights of individuals are sufficiently secured by ensuring as far as possible to each a share, and an equal share, in political power'.[99] Gaudron J rightly noted that ultimate responsibility rests with the people:

> Although it is for the Parliament to make proper provision for the government of the territories of the Commonwealth, responsibility for their government and, thus, for the welfare of those who reside in them ultimately rests with the people to whom the Constitution entrusts the responsibility of choosing the Members of Parliament.[100]

In *ACTV* Mason CJ said that the Australia Act 1986 'marked the end of the legal sovereignty of the Imperial Parliament and recognized that ultimate sovereignty resided in the Australian people'.[101] In recent cases the High Court has retreated from more contentious assertions about the legal basis of sovereignty and has placed increasing emphasis on a political concept of sovereignty, arguing that the concept of representative government gives effect to the principle that the Australian people are politically sovereign. As French CJ, Kiefel, Bell and Keane JJ wrote in *McCloy*, '[e]quality of opportunity to participate in the exercise of political sovereignty is an aspect of the representative democracy guaranteed by our Constitution'.[102] This resonates strongly with the British constitutional tradition which the framers drew upon, and the views of the framers themselves. "Political sovereignty' in this sense means the freedom of electors, through communication between themselves and with their political representatives, to implement legislative and political changes'.[103] Further, 'equality of political power … is at the heart of the Australian constitutional conception of political sovereignty'.[104]

The principles of responsible government, and the provisions of the Constitution which assume the operation of responsible government, are also a crucial expression of popular sovereignty. Section 64 requires that the ministry must be composed of members of Parliament, and so must be elected, and under the conventions of responsible government they must also hold the confidence of the House of Representatives, thereby ensuring accountability to both Parliament and the people. Sections 7 and 24 of the Constitution, which mandate the direct popular election of the members of the Senate and House of Representatives, provide for the exercise of this sovereignty.[105] These provisions

[99] Moore, *The Constitution of the Commonwealth of Australia* (n 17) 616.

[100] *Kruger v Commonwealth* (1997) 190 CLR 1, 120 (Gaudron J).

[101] *Australian Capital Television Pty Ltd v Commonwealth* (1992) 177 CLR 106, 138 (Mason CJ). This was considered to constitute a 'revolutionary change to traditional legal theory': Leighton McDonald, 'The Denizens of Democracy: The High Court and the Free Speech Cases' (1994) 5 *Public Law Review* 160, 177.

[102] *McCloy v New South Wales* (2015) 257 CLR 178, 207 [45] (French CJ, Kiefel, Bell and Keane JJ).

[103] ibid 257 [216] (Nettle J).

[104] ibid 274 [271] (Nettle J).

[105] *Gerner v Victoria* (2020) 270 CLR 412, 426 [24] (Kiefel CJ, Gageler, Keane, Gordon and Edelman JJ); *Rowe v Electoral Commissioner* (2010) 243 CLR 1, 46 [117], 48 [121] (Gummow and Bell JJ), 107 [330], 108–112 [333]–[347] (Crennan J).

'guarantee the political sovereignty of the people of the Commonwealth by ensuring that their choice of elected representatives is a real choice'.[106] Voting in Commonwealth elections 'lies at the very heart of the system of government for which the Constitution provides'.[107] The High Court has also held that the free flow of information concerning politics and the institutions of government is necessary to ensure that the people are sufficiently informed so as to be able to exercise a meaningful choice as electors, and so it is necessary to safeguard the political sovereignty of the people by means of a judicially enforceable freedom of political communication.[108]

The creation of the Senate with nearly coordinate powers to those of the House of Representatives has been thought to pose challenges for a principle of popular sovereignty. Many have held the view that the Senate is a handbrake on democracy, and an obstacle to the realisation of popular sovereignty.[109] It remains true that the Senate is founded on a principle of popular election,[110] although on a different basis to that of the lower house, which necessarily entails a modification of traditional lower house majoritarian conceptions of popular sovereignty. Brendan Lim has argued that the Australian constitutional tradition represents 'an uneasy expression of popular sovereignty' characterised by 'competing institutional claims to speak for a legally sovereign people'. That is, no one institution can claim to speak exclusively on behalf of the people but authority to do so must be earned through institutional conflict and the electoral process.[111] The Senate, as a popularly elected body, 'has its own claim to democratic legitimacy' and therefore may claim its own right to speak for the people.[112] Rather than a handbrake on the expression of popular sovereignty, the Senate functions as another organ of political responsibility, giving effect to the popular will and making the government subject to that will.

[106] *Unions NSW v New South Wales* (2019) 264 CLR 595, 614 [40] (Kiefel CJ, Bell and Keane JJ); *Murphy v Electoral Commissioner* (2016) 261 CLR 28, 86 [176] (Keane J).

[107] *Roach v Electoral Commissioner* (2007) 233 CLR 162, 198 [81] (Gummow, Kirby and Crennan JJ).

[108] *Clubb v Edwards* (2019) 267 CLR 171, 196 [51] (Kiefel CJ, Bell and Keane JJ); *LibertyWorks Inc v Commonwealth* (2021) 95 ALJR 490, 503–4 [44] (Kiefel CJ, Keane and Gleeson JJ); *Unions NSW v New South Wales* (2013) 252 CLR 530, 571 [104], 578 [135] (Keane J).

[109] See, eg, Crisp (n 81) 349; David Wood, 'The Senate, Federalism and Democracy' (1989) 17 *Melbourne University Law Review* 292; Helen Coonan, 'Safeguard or Handbrake on Democracy?' in Brian Costar (ed), *Deadlock or Democracy? The Future of the Senate* (Sydney, UNSW Press, 1999) 12–13; Hugh Emy, 'The Mandate, the Senate and Responsible Government' (1996) 30 *Australia and World Affairs* 5; Gareth Evans, 'Labor and the Constitution' (1976) 35 *Meanjin* 3; Geoffrey Sawer, 'Towards a New Federal Structure?' in Gareth Evans (ed), *Labor and the Constitution, 1972–1975: Essays and Commentaries on the Constitutional Controversies of the Whitlam Years in Australian Government* (Richmond, Heinemann Educational Australia, 1977) 15–16.

[110] Quick and Garran (n 3) 418; *Rowe v Electoral Commissioner* (2010) 243 CLR 1, 47 [119] (Gummow and Bell JJ).

[111] Lim (n 20) 31–4.

[112] ibid 76, 84–5. See also Bryce (n 1) vol 1, 183, *Convention Debates* (1891) 151 (Rutledge).

F. The Senate and the House of Representatives: An Uneasy Compromise

The relative roles of the Senate and the House of Representatives have been controversial, both at and since Federation.[113] The tension is well known: as at Federation, under the principles of the British Constitution, the government held office by virtue of maintaining the confidence of the lower house of Parliament. The lower house was therefore the centre of gravity in the political system. Establishing a Senate with powers nearly equal to those of the lower house posed a risk of a deadlock between the two houses, which would be especially problematic for supply Bills: if the Senate rejects or fails to pass a money Bill this would result in the dismissal or resignation of the government or dissolution of Parliament.[114] As Sir Richard Baker put it: '[i]f we adopt this Cabinet system of Executive it will either kill Federation or Federation will kill it; because we cannot conceal from ourselves that the very fundamental essence of the Cabinet system of Executive is the predominating power of one Chamber'.[115] While the High Court has described the successful combination of both responsible government and federalism in the Constitution as the framers' most 'striking achievement',[116] others have lamented the tension introduced into the Constitution.[117]

Many have questioned the democratic legitimacy of the Senate and its compatibility with responsible government,[118] and governments from both sides of politics are quick to label any interference with their policy proposals by the Senate as obstructive and contrary to the principles of responsible government, especially where minor parties or independent senators hold the balance of power.[119] Attitudes such as these underlie proposals to curtail the

[113] John Uhr, 'Explicating the Australian Senate' (2002) 8 *Journal of Legislative Studies* 3.

[114] RD Lumb, *Australian Constitutionalism* (Sydney, Butterworths, 1983) 90–1.

[115] *Convention Debates*, Adelaide (1897) 28, quoted in *Williams v Commonwealth* (2012) 248 CLR 156, 203 [58] (French CJ).

[116] *R v Kirby; Ex parte Boilermakers' Society of Australia* (1956) 94 CLR 254, 275 (Dixon CJ, McTiernan, Fullagar and Kitto JJ); Cheryl Saunders, 'Future Prospects of the Australian Constitution' in Robert French, Geoffrey Lindell and Cheryl Saunders (eds), *Reflections on the Australian Constitution* (Annandale, Federation Press, 2003) 219. See also Gordon Greenwood, *The Future of Australian Federalism: A Commentary on the Working of the Constitution*, 2nd edn (St Lucia, University of Queensland Press, 1976) 55.

[117] Eg, Brian Galligan, *A Federal Republic: Australia's Constitutional System of Government* (Melbourne, Cambridge University Press, 1995) 47; Winterton, *Parliament, the Executive and the Governor-General* (n 2) 3–4; Colin Howard and Cheryl Saunders, 'The Blocking of the Budget and Dismissal of the Government' in Evans (ed) (n 109) 286.

[118] See n 109.

[119] Brian Costar, 'Introduction' in Costar (ed) (n 109) 10; Stanley Bach, *Platypus and Parliament: The Australian Senate in Theory and Practice* (Canberra, Department of the Senate, 2003) 275–6, 278, 280, 283; Department of the Prime Minister and Cabinet, *Resolving Deadlocks: A Discussion Paper on Section 57 of the Australian Constitution* (Canberra, Commonwealth of Australia, 2003) 31–3; John Uhr, *Deliberative Democracy in Australia: The Changing Place of Parliament* (Melbourne, Cambridge University Press, 1998) 106–9; Harry Evans, 'The Case for Bicameralism'

Senate's powers, for example proposals to prevent the Senate from rejecting appropriation Bills or make it easier to convene a joint sitting.[120] While formal constitutional amendment to implement such reforms is unlikely, commentators have argued that the unwritten conventions of responsible government should be construed as strong normative constraints on the exercise of the Senate's legal power to refuse supply.[121]

It has been said that Federation 'was an essentially practical and political affair, achieved after much negotiation and the outcome of extensive compromise'.[122] Nowhere is this more apparent than in relation to the respective powers of the two houses of Parliament, an issue which was settled by a compromise position whereby the Senate was given co-ordinate legislative power to the House of Representatives, except in relation to money Bills.[123] The compromise struck by the framers means that the Constitution does not attempt to replicate the British Constitution in all its particulars, which means that traditional conceptions of responsible government are likely to have suffered modification in their translation to the Australian federal context.[124] The creation of the Senate as an elected body with co-ordinate powers to those of the House of Representatives, accountable in its own right to the Australian people, means that traditional assumptions regarding the respective roles of the two houses may no longer apply. Responsible government therefore must adapt to the text of the Constitution as enacted and the changed circumstances of the Australian Federation.

The Australian Senate seems perpetually caught between the Scylla of impotence and the Charybdis of perceived democratic illegitimacy.[125] On the one hand, it seems generally true that the Senate has not proven to be an equal partner

in Nicholas Aroney, Scott Prasser and JR Nethercote (eds), *Restraining Elective Dictatorship: The Upper House Solution?* (Crawley, University of Western Australia Press, 2008) 73; John Hogg, 'An Opposition View of the Australian Senate' in Aroney, Prasser and Nethercote (eds) *Restraining Elective Dictatorship: The Upper House Solution?* (Crawley, University of Western Australia Press, 2008) 94–5; Narelle Miragliotta, Wayne Errington and Nicholas Barry, *The Australian Political System in Action*, 2nd edn (South Melbourne, Oxford University Press, 2013) 85.

[120] Eg, John Faulkner, 'A Labor Perspective on Senate Reform' (Papers on Parliament No 34, Parliament of Australia, 1999) 119, 125; Winterton, *Parliament, the Executive and the Governor-General* (n 2) 147–9; Department of the Prime Minister and Cabinet, *Resolving Deadlocks* (n 119).

[121] Jeffrey Archer and Graham Maddox, 'The 1975 Constitutional Crisis in Australia' (1976) 14 *Journal of Commonwealth and Comparative Politics* 141, 147–52; Howard and Saunders (n 117) 265–6; LJM Cooray, *Conventions, the Australian Constitution and the Future* (Sydney, Legal Books, 1979) 157. See also Winterton, *Parliament, the Executive and the Governor-General* (n 2) 5–9.

[122] *A-G (Cth) ex rel McKinlay v Commonwealth* (1975) 135 CLR 1, 58 (Stephen J).

[123] Susan Crennan, 'Federation' in Cheryl Saunders and Adrienne Stone (eds), *The Oxford Handbook of the Australian Constitution* (Oxford, Oxford University Press, 2018) 88–9.

[124] *Commissioner of Taxation (Cth) v Munro* (1926) 38 CLR 153, 185 (Isaacs J); W Harrison Moore, *The Commonwealth of Australia: Four Lectures on the Constitution Bill 1897* (Melbourne, George Robertson and Co, 1897) 81–2. See also *McGinty v Western Australia* (1996) 186 CLR 140, 270 (Gummow J).

[125] See Miragliotta, Errington and Barry (n 119) 83.

in the Parliament. Governments are formed in the House of Representatives and the vast majority of legislation emanates from the government and is initiated in the lower house.[126] The combination of disciplined party politics and responsible executive government has had the effect of overshadowing the Senate.[127] As such, the locus of power is very much the lower house. On the other hand, the Senate has enjoyed something of a revival since the mid-twentieth century.[128] The introduction of proportional representation in 1948 has made it difficult for major parties to win majorities in the Senate,[129] and the establishment of the Senate's committee system has led to increased involvement in the legislative process and oversight of the executive.[130] These developments have led to a more assertive Senate, although this should not be exaggerated.[131]

I argue that it is simplistic and inaccurate to argue that the structure and powers of the Senate are straightforwardly incompatible with responsible government as adopted into the Australian constitutional framework.[132] Greater intrusion by the Senate into government decision-making is not contrary to responsible government, but was expected as a necessary corollary of the modification to British traditions of responsible government effected by the framers' conception of federalism. Responsible government is not fixed and immutable, and so it is misguided to simplistically resolve any tension between responsible government and the Senate in favour of a particular, historically contingent conception of responsible government. It is equally misguided to appeal to the framers in support of such a conception.[133] The framers' expectations for the Senate are – as they themselves would have been the first to acknowledge – not determinative for how it should function today.

The political conditions prevailing today are very different from those on which the nineteenth century conception of responsible government rested.

[126] Alan J Ward, *Parliamentary Government in Australia*, rev edn (North Melbourne, Australian Scholarly Publishing, 2012) 210; Bach, *Platypus and Parliament* (n 119) 241.

[127] Brian Galligan, 'The Kerr-Whitlam Debate and the Principles of the Australian Constitution' (1980) 18 *Journal of Commonwealth and Comparative Politics* 247, 261; Galligan, *A Federal Republic* (n 117) 63.

[128] Brenton Prosser and Richard Denniss, 'Lobbying and Minority Government in Australia: The Concept of the Marginal Member' (2015) 50 *Australian Journal of Political Science* 496; John Summers, 'Parliament and Responsible Government' in Dennis Woodward, Andrew Parkin and John Summers (eds), *Government, Politics, Power and Policy in Australia*, 9th edn (Frenchs Forest, Pearson Australia, 2010) 86.

[129] Liz Young, 'Parliament and the Executive' in Paul Boreham, Geoffrey Stokes and Richard Hall (eds), *The Politics of Australian Society: Political Issues for the New Century*, 2nd edn (Frenchs Forest, Pearson Education, 2004) 121.

[130] George Brandis, 'The Australian Senate and Responsible Government' in Aroney, Prasser and Nethercote (eds) (n 119) 86–7; On the effectiveness of Senate committees see Ian Holland, 'Senate Committees and the Legislative Process' (Research Paper No 7, Parliamentary Studies Centre); Martin Indyk, 'Making Government Responsible: The Role of Parliamentary Committees' (1980) 15 *Politics* 93.

[131] See Bach, *Platypus and Parliament* (n 119) 161–2.

[132] See also ibid 103.

[133] Eg, Winterton, *Parliament, the Executive and the Governor-General* (n 2) 9–10.

As at Federation, the lower house prevailed, because it was the popular house. Today, both houses of Parliament are popular houses. John Uhr has argued that 'the institution of parliament has no fixed place' within the Australian conception of responsible government but 'is liable to movement according to the tug of power and argument over changing institutional priorities'.[134] While this may be an overstatement,[135] it remains true that the respective roles of the houses of Parliament, within the limits mandated by the Constitution, must be continually tested and asserted through institutional competition and the electoral process.[136]

Indeed, there are numerous benefits to a strong Senate.[137] If the inherent tendency of the Westminster system of government is towards executive dominance of Parliament, especially the lower house, that house is unlikely to function as a meaningful source of executive accountability.[138] By contrast, the government does not typically hold a majority in the Senate, and so the upper house provides the most likely source of meaningful parliamentary oversight for the executive.[139] As discussed in chapters four and five, the Senate allows for greater diversity of representation than is possible in the lower house, being another organ for the representation of the people. As put by Galligan, the Senate 'is not less democratic or legitimate than the House of Representatives; the two houses are simply constituted according to different principles of representation of the people'.[140]

G. Politics, Government and the People

The Constitution's lack of specificity as to the principles of responsible government has often been a source of confusion and criticism.[141] Underlying the approach adopted by the Australian framers was a belief that the conduct and practice of responsible government is inherently unconstrainable and that it could not be prescribed or even predicted in advance. One element of this was the framers' views about the relationship between government and governed, namely

[134] Uhr, *Deliberative Democracy in Australia* (n 119) 58.

[135] See Galligan, 'The Kerr-Whitlam Debate' (n 127) 261.

[136] Lim (n 20) 31–4.

[137] Nicholas Aroney, 'Four Reasons for an Upper House: Representative Democracy, Public Debate, Legislative Outputs and Executive Accountability' (2008) 29 *Adelaide Law Review* 205.

[138] Campbell Sharman, 'Reforming Executive Power' in George Winterton (ed), *We the People: Australian Republican Government* (St Leonards, Allen and Unwin, 1994) 114, 116.

[139] Stanley Bach, 'Crisp, the Senate, and the Constitution' (2008) 54 *Australian Journal of Politics and History* 545, 559, 561; see also *Egan v Willis* (1998) 195 CLR 424, 453 [45]–[46] (Gaudron, Gummow and Hayne JJ).

[140] Galligan, *A Federal Republic* (n 117) 74.

[141] See, eg, Winterton, *Parliament, the Executive and the Governor-General* (n 2) 3–5, 6; Chalmers and Davis (n 49).

that the functioning of responsible government is dependent on the character of the people and their representatives. 'Frogs must have their storks'.[142]

In 1978 Quentin Skinner observed that there have been two main approaches in western political theory to the question of the proper functioning of political institutions. The first stresses that 'government is effective whenever its institutions are strong, and corrupt whenever its machinery fails to function adequately'. The second approach stresses the 'proper *spirit* of the rulers, the people, and the laws': if those who control the institutions of government are corrupt, 'the best possible institutions cannot be expected to shape or constrain them', while if the rulers are virtuous, 'the health of the institutions will be a matter of secondary importance'.[143]

Arguably, most constitutional scholarship today reflects the first approach. A common response to the challenges facing governments today is to propose that the answers lie in reforms to laws, institutions and structures.[144] To fix the problems of constitutional democracy, it is thought, we need to reform our Parliaments and electoral systems such as by amending campaign financing rules, introduce more accountability institutions and mechanisms such as ombudsmen, independent electoral commissions and counter-corruption agencies,[145] and ensure that national courts perform their role more effectively.[146] These proposals – which may of course lead to beneficial results – reflect an underlying assumption that good governance is first and foremost a matter of establishing good institutions. Australian constitutional scholarship often evinces a similar tendency. A notable illustration of this is the academic response to the 1975 constitutional crisis, which typically emphasised questions of institutional design as being the source of the crisis.[147]

Underlying the Australian Constitution is a very different approach, which more closely aligns with the second approach identified by Skinner. As explored in chapters four and five, the framers were well aware of the problems with the functioning of responsible government which existed in the late nineteenth

[142] Quoted in Martin Luther, 'Temporal Authority: To What Extent It Should be Obeyed' (1523), tr JJ Schindel, in Theodore G Tappert (ed), *Selected Writings of Martin Luther: 1520–1523* (Minneapolis, Fortress Press, 2007) 304.

[143] Quentin Skinner, *The Foundations of Modern Political Thought* (Cambridge, Cambridge University Press, 1978) vol 1, 44–5.

[144] Eg, Peter Shergold et al, 'Reforming Our Democracy: Options for Renewing Democracy in Australia' (University of Melbourne, The New Democracy Foundation and the Susan McKinnon Foundation, 2019).

[145] Eg, Tom Ginsburg and Aziz Z Huq, *How to Save a Constitutional Democracy* (Chicago, University of Chicago Press, 2018) 194–6.

[146] Eg, Daniel Epps and Ganesh Sitaraman, 'How to Save the Supreme Court' (2019) 129 *Yale Law Journal* 148.

[147] See, eg, Winterton, *Parliament, the Executive and the Governor-General* (n 2) 3–6; George Winterton, '1975: The Dismissal of the Whitlam Government' in HP Lee and George Winterton (eds), *Australian Constitutional Landmarks* (Port Melbourne, Cambridge University Press, 2003); Howard and Saunders (n 117).

century, such as cabinet dominance and the rise of political parties, but did not consider that they were able to prevent such problems. The framers' views can be well summarised by James Bryce, who wrote that the practical character of a system of government depends on the party system under which it functions, and on 'the political habits of the people'. As a result, '[t]o expect any form of words, however weightily conceived, with whatever sanctions enacted, permanently to restrain the passions and interests of men is to expect the impossible'.[148] As put by Bagehot, '[n]o polity can get out of a nation more than there is in the nation'.[149] This does not mean that questions of institutional design are unimportant, but it does mean that the good functioning of a constitutional system cannot be mandated by the written terms of a Constitution. The High Court noted in *Lange* that confidence in the government 'is ultimately expressed or denied by the operation of the electoral process, and the attitudes of electors to the conduct of the Executive may be a significant determinant of the contemporary practice of responsible government'.[150]

This understanding of responsible government resonates with several aspects of Australian constitutionalism. Australian law retains a strong distinction between law and policy, with the political branches responsible for determining and implementing policy.[151] The conduct of politics is within the political realm, with the government accountable to the electorate for the conduct of government, and the court's role confined to questions of law. It is for Parliament to determine what is in the public interest and the courts ought not to declare legislation invalid lightly.[152] As Brennan J noted in *ACTV*:

> The Parliament chosen by the people – not the courts, not the Executive Government – bears the chief responsibility for maintaining representative democracy in the Australian Commonwealth. Representative democracy, as a principle or institution of our Constitution, can be protected to some extent by decree of the Courts and can be fostered by Executive action but, if performance of the duties of members of the Parliament were to be subverted by obligations to large benefactors or if the parties to which they belong were to trade their commitment to published policies in exchange for funds to conduct expensive campaigns, no curial decree could, and no executive action would, restore representative democracy to the Australian people.[153]

[148] Bryce (n 1) vol 1, 270, 291, 396. See also Hearn (n 28) 116, 176, 190.

[149] Bagehot (n 59) 251; see also 198, 271, 334.

[150] *Lange v Australian Broadcasting Corporation* (1997) 189 CLR 520, 559 (Brennan CJ, Dawson, Toohey, Gaudron, McHugh, Gummow and Kirby JJ).

[151] *Australian Communist Party v Commonwealth* (1951) 83 CLR 1, 142, 144–6, 148–9 (Latham CJ), 223 (Williams J), 272 (Kitto J); *Bennett v Commonwealth* (2007) 231 CLR 91, 107 [32] (Gleeson CJ, Gummow, Hayne, Heydon and Crennan JJ); *Muldowney v South Australia* (1996) 186 CLR 352, 375 (Toohey J); *Western Australia v Commonwealth* (1975) 134 CLR 201, 293 (Murphy J).

[152] *Commissioner of Taxation (Cth) v Munro* (1926) 38 CLR 153, 180 (Isaacs J); *Comcare v Banerji* (2019) 267 CLR 373, 457 [205] (Edelman J); *Clubb v Edwards* (2019) 267 CLR 171, 239 [207] (Gageler J), 265 [267], 266 [269] (Nettle J).

[153] *Australian Capital Television Pty Ltd v Commonwealth* (1992) 177 CLR 106, 156 (Brennan J).

This view of responsible government is also relevant to the interpretation of the Constitution. The High Court noted in *Gerner* that '[t]he interpretation of the Constitution is not to be approached with a jaundiced view of the integrity or wisdom or practical competence of the representatives chosen by the people'[154] and typically refuses to read down constitutional power on the basis that such power might be misused. Under responsible government the functioning of Parliament, and the mechanisms of accountability, are inherently political. Electoral choice 'constitutes the principal constraint on the constitutional exercise by the Parliament of the legislative power of the Commonwealth, and on the lawful exercise by Ministers and officers within their departments of the executive power of the Commonwealth', and is the principal 'ordinary constitutional means' by which that constraint occurs.[155] A strong theme of Australian constitutionalism is that the principal remedies for poor governmental performance and even abuse of power are political rather than legal.[156]

H. Accountability

At the heart of responsible government is accountability. I noted earlier that under the British Constitution, all acts of government were acts of the Crown, and the Crown could do no wrong. Responsible government was considered to fill this accountability gap by prescribing that the executive is politically accountable to Parliament, and each individual MP and Parliament as a whole are accountable to the people of Australia. The conventions and principles of responsible government, therefore, are intended to make government and Parliament accountable to the people.[157] As Gordon J wrote in *Comcare*, '[s]ecuring accountability of government activity is the very essence of 'responsible government' – the system of government by which the executive is responsible to the legislature'.[158] Responsible government 'is the constitutional check on arbitrary administration'.[159] Responsible government ensures that the executive

[154] *Gerner v Victoria* (2020) 270 CLR 412, 424 [18] (Kiefel CJ, Gageler, Keane, Gordon and Edelman JJ).

[155] *McCloy v New South Wales* (2015) 257 CLR 178, 226–7 [111]–[113] (Gageler J); *Marks v Commonwealth* (1964) 111 CLR 549, 557–558 (Kitto J); Gageler, 'Foundations of Australian Federalism' (n 97) 173.

[156] *Amalgamated Society of Engineers v Adelaide Steamship Co Ltd* (1920) 28 CLR 129, 151–2 (Knox CJ, Isaacs, Rich and Starke JJ); *Australian Communist Party v Commonwealth* (1951) 83 CLR 1, 152–4 (Latham CJ), 242 (Webb J); *Theodore v Duncan* [1919] AC 696, 706 (Viscount Haldane).

[157] *Australian Capital Television Pty Ltd v Commonwealth* (1992) 177 CLR 106, 138, 139 (Mason CJ), 230–1 (McHugh J); *Nationwide News Pty Ltd v Wills* (1992) 177 CLR 1, 47 (Brennan J), 70 (Deane and Toohey JJ).

[158] *Comcare v Banerji* (2019) 267 CLR 373, 436 [146] (Gordon J).

[159] *Williamson v Ah On* (1926) 39 CLR 95, 103 (Isaacs J).

is accountable to Parliament,[160] and ultimately to the Australian people.[161] This accountability is both political and legal: every action of the executive is open to criticism and censure by Parliament;[162] the Parliament also has power to regulate the exercise of executive power through legislation[163] and may subject the executive to specific forms of accountability in law.[164] Ministerial responsibility is central to accountability under responsible government, but this does not preclude other forms of accountability.[165]

Given the central role of Parliament, MPs have a duty to scrutinise the acts of the executive and are not permitted to enter into dealings which impair their ability to exercise independent oversight.[166] Isaacs J wrote that the duty of the MP includes:

> that of watching on behalf of the general community the conduct of the Executive, of criticizing it, and, if necessary, of calling it to account in the constitutional way by censure from his place in Parliament – censure which, if sufficiently supported, means removal from office. That is the whole essence of responsible government, which is

[160] *Comcare v Banerji* (2019) 267 CLR 373, 436–7 [146]–[148] (Gordon J); *Williams v Commonwealth* (2012) 248 CLR 156, 349–50 [509], 51 [515] (Crennan J); *Egan v Willis* (1998) 195 CLR 424, 451 (Gaudron, Gummow and Hayne JJ); *Victorian Stevedoring & General Contracting Co Pty Ltd v Dignan* (1931) 46 CLR 73, 123 (Evatt J); *Commonwealth v Colonial Combing, Spinning and Weaving Co Ltd* (1922) 31 CLR 421, 449 (Isaacs J).

[161] *Comcare v Banerji* (2019) 267 CLR 373, 410 [59]–[60] (Gageler J); *Hughes Aircraft Systems International v Airservices Australia* (1997) 76 FCR 151, 245 (Finn J); *FAI Insurances Ltd v Winneke* (1982) 151 CLR 342, 366 (Mason J), 396, 400 (Wilson J); *Egan v Willis* (1998) 195 CLR 424, 502, 504 (Kirby J).

[162] *R v Boston* (1923) 33 CLR 386, 394 (Knox CJ), 399, 401 (Isaacs and Rich JJ); *Nott Bros & Co Ltd v Barkley (Collector of Customs (NSW))* (1925) 36 CLR 20, 29 (Isaacs J).

[163] *Re Richard Foreman & Sons Pty Ltd; Uther v Commissioner of Taxation (Cth)* (1947) 74 CLR 508, 514 (Latham CJ), 523 (Rich J), 531 (Dixon J); *Barton v Commonwealth* (1974) 131 CLR 477, 488 (Barwick CJ), 491 (McTiernan and Menzies JJ), 501 (Mason J); *Victoria v Commonwealth* (1975) 134 CLR 338, 406 (Jacobs J); *Brown v West* (1990) 169 CLR 195, 202 (Mason CJ, Brennan, Deane, Dawson and Toohey JJ); *Ling v Commonwealth* (1994) 51 FCR 88, 92 (Gummow, Lee and Hill JJ); *Re Residential Tenancies Tribunal (NSW); Ex parte Defence Housing Authority* (1997) 190 CLR 410, 459 (McHugh J); *Ruddock v Vadarlis* (2001) 110 FCR 491, 501 [33], 507 [61] (Black CJ), 539 [181] (French J); *Jarratt v Commissioner of Police for New South Wales* (2005) 224 CLR 44, 69–70 [85] (McHugh, Gummow and Hayne JJ); *Northern Territory v Arnhem Land Trust* (2008) 236 CLR 24, 58 [27] (Gleeson CJ, Gummow, Hayne and Crennan JJ); *Cadia Holdings Pty Ltd v New South Wales* (2010) 242 CLR 195, 204 [14] (French CJ), 228 [94] (Gummow, Hayne, Heydon and Crennan JJ); *CPCF v Minister for Immigration and Border Protection* (2015) 255 CLR 514, 600–1 [277], [279], 602 [284] (Kiefel J).

[164] *Plaintiff M79/2012 v Minister for Immigration and Citizenship* (2013) 252 CLR 336, 353 [40] (French CJ, Crennan and Bell JJ); *Plaintiff S10/2011 v Minister for Immigration and Citizenship* (2012) 246 CLR 636, 656 [55] (Gummow, Hayne, Crennan and Bell JJ); *Minister for Immigration and Multicultural Affairs v Jia Legeng* (2001) 205 CLR 507, 539 [102] (Gleeson CJ and Gummow J).

[165] *Hughes Aircraft Systems International v Airservices Australia* (1997) 76 FCR 151, 245–6 (Finn J).

[166] *Wilkinson v Osborne* (1915) 21 CLR 89, 98–9, 100, 102 (Isaacs J); *Horne v Barber* (1920) 27 CLR 494, 499, 500 (Knox CJ and Gavan Duffy J, Isaacs J); *Re Day (No 2)* (2017) 263 CLR 201, 226 [72] ((Kiefel CJ, Bell and Edelman JJ); *Re Lambie* (2018) 263 CLR 601, 615–6 [22]–[25] (Kiefel CJ, Bell, Gageler, Keane, Nettle and Gordon JJ). Isaacs also expressed similar views in *Convention Debates*, Adelaide (1897) 1037–8.

> the keystone of our political system, and is the main constitutional safeguard the community possesses.[167]

The High Court has also described an apolitical public service as essential to the working of responsible government; in the words of Gordon J, an apolitical public service is a 'defining characteristic of the constitutionally prescribed system of responsible government'.[168] The public service assists ministers to carry out the work of government departments and is responsible to those ministers, who in turn are accountable to Parliament.[169] In theory, therefore, ministerial responsibility encompasses the entirety of the executive branch and is a central means of ensuring accountability: '[i]t is through ministers that the whole of the administration – departments, statutory bodies and agencies of one kind and another – is responsible to the Parliament and thus, ultimately, to the people'.[170]

However, the traditional model of accountability is increasingly unrealistic and even misleading as a depiction of modern government.[171] The size and complexity of modern government and government bureaucracies has inevitably challenged what formerly was a 'pretty precise' conception of accountability and responsibility under the Westminster system.[172] As has been noted, the executive controls Parliament due to party discipline and its greater institutional resources and competence, and it is unfeasible to expect Parliament to exercise meaningful scrutiny of the activities of the entire executive. It is often argued that individual ministerial responsibility has been eroded in Australia.[173] While ministers are in theory responsible for all actions of their department, in practice ministers will rarely take responsibility for matters which they did not personally know about.[174] Ministers are personally accountable for their own actions, but there does not appear to be a clearly accepted principle as to when a minister will

[167] *Horne v Barber* (1920) 27 CLR 494, 500 (Isaacs J).

[168] *Comcare v Banerji* (2019) 267 CLR 373, 439 [155]–[156] (Gordon J).

[169] *Comcare v Banerji* (2019) 267 CLR 373, 423 [100]–[101] (Gageler J), 455–6 [202]–[203] (Edelman J). See further RW Cole, 'Responsible Government and the Public Service' (1980) 15 *Politics* 168.

[170] *Royal Commission on Australian Government Administration* (n 71) 59; Senate Legal and Constitutional References Committee, Parliament of Australia, *Administration and Operation of the Migration Act 1958* (Report, March 2006) 8.

[171] *Royal Commission on Australian Government Administration* (n 71) 12, 26, 276.

[172] RS Parker, 'The Meaning of Responsible Government' (1976) 11 *Politics* 178, 179, 181.

[173] See, eg, Lindell, 'Responsible Government' (n 2) 78, 94–5; Luke Raffin, 'Individual Ministerial Responsibility During the Howard Years: 1996–2007' (2008) 54 *Australian Journal of Politics and History* 225; Judy Maddigan, 'Ministerial Responsibility: Reality or Myth?' (2011) 26 *Australasian Parliamentary Review* 158; IDF Callinan, 'Responsible Government – in Dilution' (2008) 52:4 *Quadrant* 16.

[174] *Royal Commission on Australian Government Administration* (n 71) 59–60; Senate Legal and Constitutional References Committee (n 170) 8–9; Keith Dowding, Chris Lewis and Adam Packer, 'The Pattern of Forced Exits from the Ministry' in Keith Dowding and Chris Lewis (eds), *Ministerial Careers and Accountability in the Australian Commonwealth Government* (Acton, ANU E Press, 2012) 115, 116.

resign or be sacked for personal failures[175] and some consider that there has been a dilution of ministerial standards.[176] There is extensive use of politicised ministerial advisers which has enabled ministers to evade accountability.[177]

The weakening of parliamentary and ministerial responsibility might be thought to create an accountability gap in relation to the executive and a corresponding need to strengthen the conventions of ministerial responsibility. Ministerial responsibility has been supplemented with mechanisms to hold the executive to account such as administrative law, watchdogs such as ombudsmen and auditors-general, freedom of information, and an extensive centralised system of public service regulation and financial accountability.[178] Sometimes these changes are seen as evidence of the failure or inadequacy of responsible government.[179] As will be seen in chapter seven, in recent cases the High Court has sought to address such perceived failures through restricting the scope of non-statutory executive power so as to force the executive to engage more meaningfully with the parliamentary process.

I argue that these views are misguided. It would be misguided to seek to return to an outdated model of ministerial responsibility, and the development of additional mechanisms of accountability are not evidence of the failure of responsible government. I argued above that the Constitution deliberately includes a high level of flexibility so as to enable the people of Australia to govern themselves as they see fit. There have inevitably been significant changes in the structure of government since Federation, which necessitates significant changes in the accountability arrangements for scrutiny of the executive. The enormous size of modern government departments means that it is impossible for ministers to be aware of everything that occurs in their department, and so making ministers responsible for actions which they did not participate in and of which they were unaware would be unreasonable and may create perverse outcomes and incentives.[180] I have argued that responsible government creates an agency

[175] Richard Mulgan, 'Assessing Ministerial Responsibility in Australia' in Dowding and Lewis (eds) (n 174) 177. Barbara Page argued that media reaction is 'a more consistently reliable indicator of a minister's fate than either the minister's compliance or party support': 'Ministerial Resignation and Individual Ministerial Responsibility in Australia 1976–1989' (1990) 28 *Journal of Commonwealth & Comparative Politics* 141, 156.

[176] See, eg, Senate Finance and Public Administration References Committee, Parliament of Australia, *Compliance by Former Ministers of State with the Requirements of the Prime Minister's Statement of Ministerial Standards* (Report, September 2019).

[177] Phil Larkin, 'Ministerial Accountability to Parliament' in Dowding and Lewis (eds) (n 174) 95, 109. See also Yee-Fui Ng, *Ministerial Advisers in Australia: The Modern Legal Context* (Annandale, Federation Press, 2016).

[178] Yee-Fui Ng, 'Political Constitutionalism: Individual Responsibility and Collective Restraint' (2020) 48 *Federal Law Review* 455, 460, 464.

[179] See, eg, Ian Thynne and John Goldring, 'Government 'Responsibility' and Responsible Government' (1981) 16 *Politics* 197, 205; Gabrielle Appleby, 'Unwritten Rules' in Cheryl Saunders and Adrienne Stone (eds), *The Oxford Handbook of the Australian Constitution* (Oxford, Oxford University Press, 2018) 229–30.

[180] *Royal Commission on Australian Government Administration* (n 71) 59–60; Senate Legal and Constitutional References Committee (n 170) 8–9.

problem with respect to non-departmental statutory bodies, centred in the role of the minister, which may hinder effective accountability in relation to those types of entities.[181] Thus, it may be unhelpful and even counter-productive to insist today that it is solely or primarily through ministers that the entirety of the executive is responsible to Parliament and the people. Returning to outdated conceptions of responsible government may hinder rather than promote effective accountability.

If it is true that government has become increasingly decentralised given that significant functions are routinely exercised and decisions made by government departments and public servants,[182] then this suggests that more direct forms of accountability ought to be developed to hold the executive to account, including parliamentary, executive and judicial. The structure of the modern Australian executive is consistent with this. At the Commonwealth level, there is an extensive system of intra-executive scrutiny and accountability. Reforms introduced since the late 1990s have seen the devolution of important responsibilities to agency heads subject to significant levels of ministerial oversight and control.[183] Legislation imposes duties on Commonwealth public servants and entities, including governance duties modelled on the duties applicable to company directors.[184] Commonwealth public servants are subject to the APS Code of Conduct, and the Australian Public Service Commissioner has power to investigate potential breaches of the Code.[185] Commonwealth entities are subject to significant levels of oversight in relation to their activities and expenditure, with detailed budgeting, reporting and audit requirements, supervised by the Minister and Department of Finance.[186] Central departments also exercise policy control over the Commonwealth public sector[187] and there are many centralised policies that apply to Commonwealth agencies relating to such things as procurement, purchasing legal services, the administration of grants[188] and directions relating to the employment of public sector staff.[189] The Ombudsman

[181] Benjamin B Saunders, 'Ministers, Statutory Authorities and Government Corporations: The Agency Problem in Public Sector Governance' (2022) 45 *Melbourne University Law Review* 695.

[182] Turpin (n 76) 118–23.

[183] Charles Lawson, 'The Legal Structures of Responsible Government and Ministerial Responsibility' (2011) 35 *Melbourne University Law Review* 1005.

[184] Public Governance, Performance and Accountability Act 2013 (Cth) ss 15–29. For analysis see Benjamin B Saunders, 'The Public Sector Duty of Care and Diligence' (2019) 42 *University of New South Wales Law Journal* 652.

[185] Public Service Act 1999 (Cth) ss 13, 41A, 41B.

[186] Public Governance, Performance and Accountability Act 2013 (Cth) pts 2-3–2-4.

[187] The Minister for Finance has power to implement policy directives which Commonwealth entities are required to comply with: *Public Governance, Performance and Accountability Act 2013* (Cth) ss 21, 22, 93.

[188] Department of Finance, *Department of Finance, Commonwealth Procurement Rules 1 July 2022: Achieving Value for Money (Commonwealth of Australia, 1 July 2022)*; Department of Finance, *Commonwealth Grants Rules and Guidelines* (Commonwealth of Australia, 2017).

[189] Australian Public Service Commissioner, *Australian Public Service Commissioner's Directions 2022* (31 January 2022).

has power to investigate complaints in relation to administrative action.[190] Commonwealth entities are subject to audit by the Auditor-General, although the Auditor-General is deemed to be an independent officer of Parliament, and so is not strictly part of the executive branch.[191] The provision for the review of administrative decisions by the Administrative Appeals Tribunal could also be seen as a form of intra-executive accountability.[192] Parliaments have developed a more sophisticated committee system for scrutiny of the executive.[193]

These mechanisms of scrutiny, which include parliamentary, executive and judicial mechanisms, are together much more effective than a single model of ministerial responsibility to Parliament. Given that 'Parliament alone is incapable of effecting a system of governmental accountability' and that the potential for a systematic regime of governmental accountability through the judicial branch is limited,[194] the clear implication is that mechanisms of effective accountability are to be sought elsewhere. Daintith and Page argued that:

> In the long run it is more important for Parliament to ensure that these gateways are not enlarged or circumvented than itself to determine what passes through them, since real control, generally in a sense sympathetic to Parliament's concerns, is exercised centrally within the executive by reference to the gateways.[195]

The additional mechanisms for scrutiny of the executive which now exist are best seen not as challenges to responsible government, but as 'valuable additions' which help 'responsible government' to function more effectively and which are also an appropriate response to the volume and complexity of government' which developed in the twentieth century.[196]

I. Convention

Geoffrey Marshall wrote that constitutional conventions 'play a central part in the theory of British Government'.[197] It is of the essence of the British Constitution that it is unwritten and conventional: convention is central to the British conception of constitutionalism. Conventions are 'as important

[190] Ombudsman Act 1976 (Cth) s 5.

[191] Auditor-General Act 1997 (Cth) s 8.

[192] Administrative Appeals Tribunal Act 1975 (Cth) Part IV.

[193] See House of Representatives Standing Committee on Procedure, Parliament of Australia, *Building a Modern Committee System: An Inquiry into the Effectiveness of the House Committee System* (Report, June 2010).

[194] David Kinley, 'Governmental Accountability in Australia and the United Kingdom: A Conceptual Analysis of the Role of Non-Parliamentary Institutions and Devices' (1995) 18 *University of New South Wales Law Journal* 409, 409–10.

[195] Daintith and Page (n 54) 396.

[196] Lindell, 'Responsible Government' (n 2) 102.

[197] Geoffrey Marshall, *Constitutional Conventions: The Rules and Forms of Political Accountability* (Oxford, Clarendon Press, 1984) 3.

and sometimes more important than law',[198] given that the actual day-to-day functioning of the system of government is governed by convention and that constitutional questions are infrequently adjudicated by the courts in Australia.

It is also the case that uncertainty is inherent to the nature of convention. Conventions are general rules whose outer limits may not have been explored, and conventions may conflict.[199] While the core of responsible government is accepted, many aspects of responsible government are uncertain and contested. Given that the British Constitution 'was not a set of documents but a reading of history',[200] competing interpretations of that history are possible. This chapter has emphasised that the conventions of responsible government evolved over time and may continue to evolve and change, and as such, absolute certainty is not attainable.

The Australian Constitution reflects this conception of constitutionalism by containing minimal requirements regarding the structure and functioning of the executive branch; as put by Harrison Moore, the Constitution establishes no more than a parliamentary executive, and left the rest to custom and convention.[201] The working of responsible government is expressed in certain conventions, as a result of which government functions in practice in a manner at variance from strict legal theory. These conventions facilitate the political accountability of the ministry both individually and collectively.[202] The conventions are well known: the head of state is bound to act on the advice of his or her ministers;[203] those ministers must hold the confidence of Parliament and are accountable to it for the conduct of government.[204] Ministers are also the heads of government departments and are individually responsible for their own actions and the actions of their departments, although the precise extent to which ministers are (or ought to be) responsible for departmental actions is contested.

Responsible government is not readily susceptible of codification or judicial enforcement. William Hearn noted that it 'has been a subject of no small surprise and remark that our modern system of government is not expressed, and seems incapable of being expressed, in a legal form'.[205] This follows from the

[198] ibid 12.
[199] ibid 2, 5.
[200] Robert Saunders, 'Parliament and People: The British Constitution in the Long Nineteenth Century' (2008) 6 *Journal of Modern European History* 72.
[201] Moore, *The Constitution of the Commonwealth of Australia* (n 17) 168–9.
[202] *Comcare v Banerji* (2019) 267 CLR 373, 410 [60] (Gageler J).
[203] *New South Wales v Commonwealth* (1975) 135 CLR 337, 365 (Barwick CJ); *Sue v Hill* (1999) 199 CLR 462, 494 [70] (Gleeson CJ, Gummow and Hayne JJ); *FAI Insurances Ltd v Winneke* (1982) 151 CLR 342, 349 (Gibbs CJ), 352 (Stephen J), 373 (Murphy J), 414 (Brennan J).
[204] *Egan v Willis* (1998) 195 CLR 424, 453 [45] (Gaudron, Gummow and Hayne JJ), 476 [102] (McHugh J); *Comcare v Banerji* (2019) 267 CLR 373, 436–7 [146]–[148] (Gordon J).
[205] Hearn (n 28) 124.

principles discussed in this chapter. Responsible government is inherently political, unconstrainable and its functioning depends on the character of the people and their representatives; further, its functioning is encapsulated in conventions rather than a written document such as the Constitution. In *Williams v Attorney-General (NSW)* Isaacs J described constitutional conventions as 'those practical constitutional understandings not reducible to written law which go to form responsible government'.[206] As such, it is not surprising that proposals to codify the conventions of responsible government have not met with unanimous approval[207] and the courts have resisted the judicial enforcement of the conventions of responsible government.[208]

III. RESPONSIBLE GOVERNMENT AND THE CONSTITUTION: THE TEXT

This section briefly explains the provisions of the Constitution in light of the principles outlined in this chapter. In summary, the Commonwealth Constitution 'created a system of government which is representative (ss 1, 7, 8, 13, 24, 25, 28 and 30), in which the executive is responsible to Parliament (ss 6, 49, 62, 64 and 83), and which is unalterable save by democratic means (s 128)'.[209] The principles of constitutional evolution and popular sovereignty were central to the framers' conception of responsible government, and these principles also explain the framers' approach to the drafting of key features of the Constitution. In drafting the Constitution, the framers conceived their task as providing the architecture of the new Commonwealth such that the Constitution should contain the minimum number of provisions necessary to establish the federal government, and leave considerable freedom to the federal Parliament to make whatever laws were considered necessary.[210] In part this constitutional restraint arose because the framers did not believe they could predict the conditions of the future.[211]

Section 1 establishes the federal Parliament consisting of the Queen, the Senate and House of Representatives, and section 2 provides that a Governor-General is 'Her Majesty's representative in the Commonwealth'. Following the British theory that the Crown is the repository of all executive power, the Constitution

[206] *Williams v Attorney-General (NSW)* (1913) 16 CLR 404, 457 (Isaacs J).

[207] Anne Twomey, *The Veiled Sceptre: Reserve Powers of Heads of State in Westminster Systems* (Cambridge, Cambridge University Press, 2018) 38.

[208] *Cf* Farrah Ahmed, Richard Albert and Adam Perry, 'Judging Constitutional Conventions' (2019) 17 *International Journal of Constitutional Law* 787.

[209] *Coleman v Power* (2004) 220 CLR 1, 120 [320] (Heydon J).

[210] *Convention Debates*, Adelaide (1897) 745 (Barton), 708 (Trenwith), 747–8 (Holder), 752 (Reid). See also 919–20; *Convention Debates*, Sydney (1897) 113 (O'Connor), 418 (Barton), 1002 (Isaacs), 1013–14 (Glynn), 1032 (Holder).

[211] *Convention Debates*, Sydney (1897) 368 (McMillan).

recognises that legal power is vested in the Queen and provides for its exercise by the Governor-General, the Queen's representative.[212] These provisions import the concept of the Crown and adapt the principles of the British Constitution into the Australian context.[213]

Responsible government is closely related to representative government, reflecting the centrality of the principle of popular sovereignty. The provisions of Chapter I of the Constitution, especially sections 7 and 24, create a system of representative government,[214] by providing that members of the Senate and House of Representatives are to be 'directly chosen by the people'.[215] These provisions are deliberately non-prescriptive: the High Court has held that representative government is inherently evolutionary,[216] and so, '[w]hile concepts such as self-government, representative government, and democratic process have a minimum content, standards as to their most appropriate forms of expression vary with time and place'.[217] As such, Parliament has substantial freedom to determine the nature of the electoral system,[218] within some limits, including direct popular choice and a 'requirement that the electoral system as a whole provide for ultimate control by periodic popular election'.[219] The Court has held that compulsory voting is constitutionally valid;[220] that a compulsory system of preferential voting is consistent with the requirements of sections 7 and 24 of the Constitution;[221] that section 24 of the Constitution does not require the number of people or the number of electors in electoral divisions to be equal;[222] and has upheld requirements relating to the registration of political parties.[223] Sections 8 and 30 'contain specific limitations upon the power of the

[212] Constitution, ss 2 and 61.

[213] See *Sue v Hill* (1999) 199 CLR 462, 497–503 [83]–[94] (Gleeson CJ, Gummow and Hayne JJ).

[214] *Lange v Australian Broadcasting Corporation* (1997) 189 CLR 520, 558 (Brennan CJ, Dawson, Toohey, Gaudron, McHugh, Gummow and Kirby JJ): '[t]he effect of ss 1, 7, 8, 13, 24, 25, 28 and 30 therefore is to ensure that the Parliament of the Commonwealth will be representative of the people of the Commonwealth'.

[215] Barwick CJ explained the purpose of s 24 in *A-G (Cth) ex rel McKinlay v Commonwealth* (1975) 135 CLR 1, 20.

[216] *Roach v Electoral Commissioner* (2007) 233 CLR 162, 186–7 [45] (Gummow, Kirby and Crennan JJ); *Mulholland v Australian Electoral Commission* (2004) 220 CLR 181, 237 [155]–[156]; *McGinty v Western Australia* (1996) 186 CLR 140, 280, 283 (Gummow J).

[217] *Bennett v Commonwealth* (2007) 231 CLR 91, 107 [32] (Gleeson CJ, Gummow, Hayne, Heydon and Crennan JJ); *A-G (Cth) ex rel McKinlay v Commonwealth* (1975) 135 CLR 1, 56–7 (Stephen J).

[218] *A-G (Cth) ex rel McKinlay v Commonwealth* (1975) 135 CLR 1, 35–6 (McTiernan and Jacobs JJ), 46 (Gibbs J); *Mulholland v Australian Electoral Commission* (2004) 220 CLR 181, 188–9 [7]–[9] (Gleeson CJ), 206 [63], 217 [86] (McHugh J); *Roach v Electoral Commissioner* (2007) 233 CLR 162, 173 [4] (Gleeson CJ); *Rowe v Electoral Commissioner* (2010) 243 CLR 1, 49–50 [125] (Gummow and Bell JJ), 68 [194]–[195] (Hayne J).

[219] *Roach v Electoral Commissioner* (2007) 233 CLR 162, 187–8 [49] (Gummow, Kirby and Crennan JJ).

[220] *Judd v McKeon* (1926) 38 CLR 380.

[221] *Langer v Commonwealth* (1996) 186 CLR 302.

[222] *A-G (Cth) ex rel McKinlay v Commonwealth* (1975) 135 CLR 1. See also *McGinty v Western Australia* (1996) 186 CLR 140.

[223] *Mulholland v Australian Electoral Commission* (2004) 220 CLR 181.

Parliament to prescribe the franchise. There can be no plural voting (for example, by reference to the location of several parcels of real property owned by the elector) and the qualifications of electors cannot differ between the two legislative chambers'.[224] Section 28 provides that the maximum duration for each Parliament is three years, thus ensuring regular elections.

Chapter II of the Constitution, consisting of 10 meagre provisions, deals with the structure and powers of the executive branch. Its purpose is to 'establish the Executive Government as a national responsible government'.[225] The sparsity of these provisions results from the framers' belief that the way the government was to be worked by the people was not something that a Constitution should attempt to prescribe. Accordingly, the Constitution requires ministers to sit in Parliament and assumes that the head of state will act on the advice of the ministry, but otherwise leaves the relationship between Parliament and the executive free to develop. The framers considered that responsible government would operate along the lines of the British Constitution in the manner carried on in the colonies prior to Federation, and so it was not necessary to prescribe the conventions of responsible government.[226] When introducing clause 64 to the Convention, Barton argued that the requirement of the presence of ministers in Parliament would remove any doubt as to whether the Bill incorporated responsible government, and that clauses 62 and 64 could only function under the British cabinet system. Barton expected that every executive power would be exercised on the advice of a responsible minister, and, importantly, that it would be for the Parliament to determine the precise manner in which responsibility would be divided between the two houses.[227]

Section 61 recognises that executive power is vested in the Queen and provides that it is exercisable by the Governor-General as the Queen's representative. Section 61 describes rather than defines Commonwealth executive power, providing that it 'extends to the execution and maintenance of this Constitution, and of the laws of the Commonwealth'.[228] The reference to the Queen has been taken to import those prerogative powers of the Crown which are apposite to the Commonwealth,[229] demonstrating the need to read the Constitution in light

[224] *Roach v Electoral Commissioner* (2007) 233 CLR 162, 187 [47] (Gummow, Kirby and Crennan JJ).

[225] *Plaintiff M68/2015 v Minister for Immigration and Border Protection* (2016) 257 CLR 42, 99 [138] (Gageler J).

[226] *Convention Debates* (1891) 240 (Gillies), 273 (McMillan), 296 (Douglas), 306 (Suttor), 576–7 (Playford).

[227] *Convention Debates*, Adelaide (1897) 443–4, 910–13; *Convention Debates* (1898) 2252–3, 2255. See also Moore, *The Constitution of the Commonwealth of Australia* (n 17) 103.

[228] Constitution, s 61; *Commonwealth v Colonial Combing, Spinning and Weaving Co Ltd* (1922) 31 CLR 421, 437 (Isaacs J); *Davis v Commonwealth* (1988) 166 CLR 79, 92–3 (Mason CJ, Deane and Gaudron JJ); *Pape v Commissioner of Taxation* (2009) 238 CLR 1, 62 [131] (French CJ); *Williams v Commonwealth* (2012) 248 CLR 156, 372 [588] (Kiefel J); *Plaintiff M68/2015 v Minister for Immigration and Border Protection* (2016) 257 CLR 42, 96 [129] (Gageler J).

[229] *Barton v Commonwealth* (1974) 131 CLR 477, 498 (Mason J); *Victoria v Commonwealth* (1975) 134 CLR 338, 405–6 (Jacobs J); *Cadia Holdings Pty Ltd v New South Wales* (2010) 242 CLR 195,

of its constitutional background. The provisions of Chapter II assume rather than prescribe responsible government, assuming for instance that the executive power described in section 61 would ordinarily be exercised on the advice of responsible ministers.[230]

The extent to which the Constitution prescribes responsible government should not be overstated. Perhaps the only direct recognition of responsible government is section 64, which provides that all ministers must be a member of one of the Houses of Parliament. Section 64 makes plain that the design of Chapters I and II of the Constitution is to facilitate the application of responsible government to the federal Commonwealth.[231] Section 64 makes ministers answerable in Parliament for the conduct of the administration of government,[232] thus facilitating 'the political accountability of Ministers to the House of Representatives and to the Senate'[233] and giving effect to both collective and individual responsibility, which correspond to the conventions of responsible government.[234] It is 'through ministers that the whole of the administration – departments, statutory bodies and agencies of one kind and another – is responsible to the Parliament and thus, ultimately, to the people',[235] which is secured 'because Ministers sit in, and are answerable to, Parliament'.[236]

Section 62, which provides for the establishment of a Federal Executive Council to advise the Governor-General, has also been seen as introducing responsible government.[237] As the Court held in *Lange*, sections 62 and 64:

> combine to provide for the executive power of the Commonwealth, which is vested in the Queen and exercisable by the Governor-General, to be exercised 'on the initiative and advice' of Ministers and limit to three months the period in which a Minister of State may hold office without being or becoming a senator or member of the House of Representatives.[238]

Sections 65 and 66 enhance the political accountability of ministers by enabling the Parliament 'to have legislative control over the number and salaries of

226 [86] (Gummow, Hayne, Heydon and Crennan JJ); *Pape v Federal Commissioner of Taxation* (2009) 238 CLR 1, 61–62 [130] (French CJ), 83 [214] (Gummow, Crennan and Bell JJ); *Williams v Commonwealth* (2012) 248 CLR 156, 184–5 [22]–[24] (French CJ), 227–8 [123] (Gummow and Bell JJ), 342 [484] (Crennan J).

[230] *Victoria v Commonwealth* (1975) 134 CLR 338, 405–406 (Jacobs J); *New South Wales v Commonwealth* (1915) 20 CLR 54, 89 (Isaacs J).

[231] *McCloy v New South Wales* (2015) 257 CLR 178, 224 [106] (Gageler J); *Church of Scientology Inc v Woodward* (1980) 154 CLR 25, 64 (Murphy J).

[232] *Re Patterson; Ex parte Taylor* (2001) 207 CLR 391, 402 [13] (Gleeson CJ), 415 [64] (Gaudron J); 464 [220] (Gummow and Hayne JJ).

[233] *Comcare v Banerji* (2019) 267 CLR 373, 410 [59] (Gageler J).

[234] ibid 410 [60] (Gageler J).

[235] *Royal Commission on Australian Government Administration* (n 71) 59.

[236] *Comcare v Banerji* (2019) 267 CLR 373, 437 [148]–[149] (Gordon J).

[237] *New South Wales v Commonwealth* (1975) 135 CLR 337, 364–365 (Barwick CJ).

[238] *Lange v Australian Broadcasting Corporation* (1997) 189 CLR 520, 558 (Brennan CJ, Dawson, Toohey, Gaudron, McHugh, Gummow and Kirby JJ, footnote omitted).

Ministers'.[239] Section 67 authorises the appointment of public servants, and the power conferred by section 51(xxxvi) enables the Parliament to regulate the terms of their appointment. Under section 44(iv) public servants are unable to hold a seat in Parliament, thereby contributing to an impartial and apolitical public service.[240] The Constitution contemplates that ministerial responsibility is the prime means of holding the executive to account.

A cluster of provisions ensure parliamentary control in relation to the executive. Section 44 disqualifies certain classes of people from sitting or being chosen as a member of Parliament, including any person who 'holds any office of profit under the Crown'.[241] This serves an important function 'in protecting the framework for responsible government' by safeguarding the 'capacity for the Houses of Parliament to act as a check on executive action' which is essential to responsible government.[242] Section 49 provides for the 'powers, privileges, and immunities' of the Houses of Parliament to be those of the House of Commons as at Federation, which would include the power to summon witnesses and compel information, which, historically was a powerful means of holding the executive to account.[243] By conferring power on the Commonwealth Parliament to make laws with respect to 'matters incidental to the execution of any power' vested by the Constitution 'in the Government of the Commonwealth' and 'in any department or officer of the Commonwealth', section 51(xxxix) has been seen as extending to 'legislative regulation of the manner and circumstances of the execution of the executive power of the Commonwealth', thus securing legislative supremacy over the executive.[244]

Sections 81 and 83 also enshrine the principle of parliamentary control of the executive.[245] They require prior parliamentary approval by law for the expenditure of public money but are not a source of power to spend.[246] Under

[239] *Comcare v Banerji* (2019) 267 CLR 373, 410 [61] (Gageler J).

[240] ibid 410–13 [62]–[65] (Gageler J), 455–6 [202] (Edelman J); *Sykes v Cleary (No 2)* (1992) 176 CLR 77, 96 (Mason CJ, Toohey and McHugh JJ).

[241] Constitution, s 44(iv).

[242] *Re Lambie* (2018) 263 CLR 601, 615 [23] (Kiefel CJ, Bell, Gageler, Keane, Nettle and Gordon JJ).

[243] *Lange v Australian Broadcasting Corporation* (1997) 189 CLR 520, 558–9 (Brennan CJ, Dawson, Toohey, Gaudron, McHugh, Gummow and Kirby JJ).

[244] *Plaintiff M68/2015 v Minister for Immigration and Border Protection* (2016) 257 CLR 42, 93 [121]–[122] (Gageler J).

[245] *Brown v West* (1990) 169 CLR 195, 205, 207 (Mason CJ, Brennan, Deane, Dawson and Toohey JJ); *Victoria v Commonwealth* (1975) 134 CLR 338, 384 (Stephen J); *Combet v Commonwealth* (2005) 224 CLR 494, 595 [227] (Kirby J); *Pape v Federal Commissioner of Taxation* (2009) 238 CLR 1, 43–44 [77] (French C), 105 [294] (Hayne and Kiefel JJ); *Williams v Commonwealth* (2012) 248 CLR 156, 259 [219] (Hayne J); *Wilkie v Commonwealth* (2017) 263 CLR 487, 523 [61] (Kiefel CJ, Bell, Gageler, Keane, Nettle, Gordon and Edelman JJ).

[246] *Pape v Federal Commissioner of Taxation* (2009) 238 CLR 1, 23 [8], 36 [53], 55–56 [111]–[113] (French CJ), 72–75 [176], [178], [180], [183]–[184] (Gummow, Crennan and Bell JJ), 100–101 [283], 105 [296], 113 [320] (Hayne and Kiefel JJ), 210 [600], 212–213 [606]–[607] (Heydon J); *ICM Agriculture Pty Ltd v Commonwealth* (2009) 240 CLR 140, 169 [41] (French CJ, Gummow and

section 81, all moneys received by the Commonwealth form one Consolidated Revenue Fund, to be appropriated 'for the purposes of the Commonwealth'. Section 83 provides that: [n]o money shall be drawn from the Treasury of the Commonwealth except under appropriation made by law.[247] In the *Surplus Revenue Case* Isaacs J noted:

> 'Appropriation of money to a Commonwealth purpose' means legally segregating it from the general mass of the Consolidated Fund and dedicating it to the execution of some purpose which either the Constitution has itself declared, or Parliament has lawfully determined, shall be carried out.[248]

Section 83 ensures control of public finance by the legislature, and it does so by 'requiring parliamentary authority for the expenditure by the Executive Government of any fund or sum of money standing to the credit of the Crown in right of the Commonwealth'.[249]

Parliamentary control over public finance is further regulated by other provisions of the Constitution, including sections 53, 54 and 55 which specify the respective powers of the Houses of Parliament in relation to taxation and appropriation Bills.[250] The respective powers of the two houses of Parliament reflect the compromise position reached at the Federal Conventions, which forged an uneasy path between lower house supremacy and upper house equality.[251]

The Senate has equal power with the House of Representatives in respect of all proposed laws other than money Bills.[252] Appropriation and taxation Bills may only originate in the lower house, and the Senate can affirm or reject but not amend laws imposing taxation and laws appropriating the necessary supplies for the ordinary annual services of government. The Senate can, however, propose amendments to such Bills by suggestion. The Constitution prohibits 'tacking'[253] and prohibits the Senate from amending any Bill in such a manner as to increase a proposed charge or burden on the people. Any Bill appropriating money must

Crennan JJ); *Williams v Commonwealth* (2012) 248 CLR 156, 193 [39] (French CJ), 224 [114] (Gummow and Bell JJ), 248 [191] (Hayne J), 341 [478] (Crennan J), 362 [559] (Kiefel J).

[247] Constitution, s 83.

[248] *New South Wales v Commonwealth (Surplus Revenue Case)* (1908) 7 CLR 179, 200 (Isaacs J).

[249] *Lange v Australian Broadcasting Corporation* (1997) 189 CLR 520, 558 (Brennan CJ, Dawson, Toohey, Gaudron, McHugh, Gummow and Kirby JJ); *Northern Suburbs General Cemetery Reserve Trust v Commonwealth* (1993) 176 CLR 555, 572–573 (Mason CJ, Deane, Toohey and Gaudron JJ), 580–581 (Brennan J), 590–591 (Dawson J), 597–598 (McHugh J).

[250] *Williams v Commonwealth* (2012) 248 CLR 156, 260 [220] (Hayne J); *Wilkie v Commonwealth* (2017) 263 CLR 487, 523 [62] (Kiefel CJ, Bell, Gageler, Keane, Nettle, Gordon and Edelman JJ).

[251] According to Barton, the Constitution does not choose between the principles of Federation and responsible government but attempts to conserve both as far as possible: *Convention Debates*, Sydney (1897) 529 (Barton); *Convention Debates*, Adelaide (1897) 148 (Holder); *Convention Debates* (1898) 2060, 2066, 2109 (Barton).

[252] *Convention Debates* (1891) 714–5 (Griffith). Quoted in *Convention Debates*, Adelaide (1897) 501 (O'Connor).

[253] That is, including matters unrelated to taxation or appropriation in a taxation or appropriation Bill.

first be recommended by message of the Governor-General, which preserves the exclusive right of the executive in matters of finance.[254]

The provisions of the Constitution relating to money Bills (section 53), and the deadlock procedure (section 57) were crafted on the assumption that the government would be formed in the lower house.[255] As section 53 requires that appropriation and taxation Bills must originate in the House of Representatives, it would be impossible for a government to carry on without a majority in the lower house.[256] The greater powers of the House of Representatives ensure that the control of the government's financial policy would be in the hands of the government. The Constitution in effect recognises lower house supremacy in matters of finance while also giving extensive powers to the upper house to reconsider.[257]

The mechanism for resolving deadlocks between the two houses reflects the Federation Convention's eventual acceptance that a safety valve was necessary, but in a way which, they thought, best preserved the proper working of responsible government. Reflecting the framers' views about self-government, the double dissolution was intended to ensure that, in case of a conflict, the people were the final court of appeal.[258] Where one house considers that a Bill proposed by the other house did not represent the wishes of the people[259] a dissolution would enable the people to determine the matter, while retaining the accountability which was so essential to responsible government.[260]

The Constitution confers some powers and functions on the Governor-General and others on the 'Governor-General in Council'.[261] The distinction between the two was obscure even for many of the framers.[262] Barton explained that the difference reflected contemporary statutory usage: where a prerogative power was placed on a statutory footing, the power would be described in the relevant statute as exercisable by the 'Governor in Council'. However, some powers had not been displaced or regulated by statute, such as the power to summon and

[254] Constitution, s 56; *Combet v Commonwealth* (2005) 224 CLR 494, 595 [227] (Kirby J). See also Moore, *The Commonwealth of Australia: Four Lectures on the Constitution Bill 1897* (n 124) 76.

[255] Moore, *The Constitution of the Commonwealth of Australia* (n 17) 140.

[256] Geoffrey Sawer, *Federation Under Strain: Australia 1972–1975*, 3rd edn (Carlton, Melbourne University Press, 1977) 122.

[257] BR Wise, *The Commonwealth of Australia* (London, Pitman, 1909) 208–9.

[258] *Convention Debates*, Adelaide (1897) 657 (Carruthers); Sydney (1897) 580, 736–7 (Kingston), 740 (Lyne), 761 (Holder), 841 (Reid), 858 (Carruthers), 882 (O'Connor), 948 (Trenwith).

[259] *Convention Debates*, Sydney (1897) 813 (McMillan), 819 (Deakin), 870 (Kingston); (1898) 723 (Isaacs), 725, 735.

[260] *Convention Debates*, Sydney (1897) 556 (Brown), 576 (O'Connor), 595–6 (Symon), 622, 624–5 (Barton), 680 (Braddon).

[261] For the former: ss 5, 28, 56, 57, 58, 61, 64, 65, 68, 69, 126, 128. For the latter: ss 32, 33, 63, 64, 67, 72, 85, 103. See also s 70.

[262] *Convention Debates* (1898) 1929–30, 2250–64. Clark devoted a whole chapter to this issue: Andrew Inglis Clark, *Studies in Australian Constitutional Law* (Melbourne, Charles F Maxwell, 1901) ch 13.

dissolve Parliament and the right to declare war and peace, which remained exclusively prerogative powers.[263] The Constitution reflects this usage by providing that powers were exercisable by the 'Governor-General in Council' where the equivalent power under statute was exercisable by the Governor in Council; all other powers were exercisable by the 'Governor-General'. Although the Constitution in this way contains differing legal requirements relating to the exercise of the various classes of power, the conventions of responsible government operate in relation to both types of power.[264]

The Constitution in several other ways contemplates that its provisions and operation will not be static. Section 51(xxxvi) contemplates legislative changes to the operation of specified provisions of the Constitution[265] and section 51(xxxvii) empowers the Commonwealth to legislate with respect to matters referred by the states.[266] The framers' emphasis on evolutionary self-government is also reflected in the mechanism for amending the Constitution, which gives power to the people of successive generations to retain ultimate control over their Constitution, and make such changes as they believe necessary.[267]

The provisions of the Constitution reflect the framers' understanding of responsible government as giving effect to the principle of popular sovereignty. As put by Deakin, '[o]ur constitution embodies the principle of the rule of the majority, not as its working principle or method, but as its final and ultimate test of the work done'.[268]

IV. CONCLUSION

Responsible government is often articulated as a static set of constitutional and political rules.[269] This chapter has endeavoured to develop an account or a 'constitutive theory' of responsible government,[270] aiming to show that

[263] *Convention Debates* (1898) 2252–5; Quick and Garran (n 3) 406.

[264] Barton stated that it was widely acknowledged that 'every prerogative of the Crown is now administered in trust for the people' and must be exercised on the advice of a responsible minister: *Convention Debates* (1898) 2252–5. See also *Australian Communist Party v Commonwealth* (1951) 83 CLR 1, 179 (Dixon J); *New South Wales v Commonwealth* (1975) 135 CLR 337, 364–5 (Barwick CJ); *FAI Insurances Ltd v Winneke* (1982) 151 CLR 342, 373 (Murphy J), 382 (Aickin J), 400 (Wilson J), 415 (Brennan J).

[265] The precise wording is as follows: 'under s 51(xxxvi), the Parliament has power to make laws with respect to 'matters in respect of which this Constitution makes provision until the Parliament otherwise provides'.

[266] See also s 51(xxxviii).

[267] David Hume and George Williams, *People Power: The History and Future of the Referendum in Australia* (Sydney, University of New South Wales Press, 2010) 3–4.

[268] *Convention Debates*, Sydney (1897) 331.

[269] Eg, RS Parker, 'Responsible Government in Australia' (1980) 15 *Politics* 11, 13–14; Lindell, 'Responsible Government' (n 2) 76–9.

[270] Luke Beck, *Religious Freedom and the Australian Constitution: Origins and Future* (London, Routledge, 2018) 114.

responsible government is a complex, dynamic doctrine which drew from a rich political and constitutional tradition, and which cannot be reduced to a set of rules. Consistent with colonial precedent,[271] the text of the Constitution contains little by way of express recognition of responsible government: '[a] notable feature of our system of representative and responsible government is how little of the detail of that system is to be found in the Constitution, and how much is left to be filled in by Parliament'.[272] The principles discussed in this chapter explain why this is so.

Responsible government under the Australian Constitution is intended to enable the sovereign people to govern themselves in the manner they see fit, through the political mechanisms of the Constitution. The manner in which the people choose to govern themselves will change over time, as circumstances change, and as the people themselves change. There is an important need to preserve flexibility to enable this to happen. Responsible government is also a fundamentally political system of government, such that certain questions are not thought suitable for judicial resolution. As John Gardner wrote, 'something is amiss in the public life of a society when constitutional questions often have to be settled in the courtroom'.[273]

Responsible government represents a hybrid of two arguably inconsistent approaches to constitutionalism. Central to the Australian constitutional tradition is a written, judicially enforceable Constitution which is inherently rigid, defining the limits of Commonwealth power.[274] As Dicey wrote, federalism 'means legalism – the predominance of the judiciary in the constitution – the prevalence of a spirit of legality among the people'.[275] A written Constitution emphasises stability and predictability, and may also encourage the tendency to give greater emphasis to law and the Constitution, and to downplay the importance of convention. By contrast, responsible government, one of the architectonic features of the Constitution, is inherently flexible and political. Convention and practice are fundamental to the functioning of responsible government, and they are not readily susceptible to codification or judicial enforcement. Although it is an exaggeration to say that these approaches are incompatible, it is certainly true that the incorporation of responsible government which is largely unwritten and conventional within a constitutional system whose principal feature is a written, rigid Constitution, is an awkward fit.

[271] *Chung Teong Toy v Musgrove* (1888) 14 VLR 349, 391–2 (Higinbotham CJ).

[272] *Mulholland v Australian Electoral Commission* (2004) 220 CLR 181, 188 [6] (Gleeson CJ); *Re Patterson; Ex parte Taylor* (2001) 207 CLR 391, 415 [63] (Gaudron J).

[273] Gardner (n 19) 169.

[274] *R v Kirby; Ex parte Boilermakers' Society of Australia* (1956) 94 CLR 254, 267 (Dixon CJ, McTiernan, Fullagar and Kitto JJ).

[275] AV Dicey, 'Federal Government' (1885) 1 *Law Quarterly Review* 80, 97.

7

Implications for the Interpretation of the Constitution

We should be careful not to suffer the wisdom of the present to determine the actions of the Commonwealth for many years to come.[1]

Patrick McMahon Glynn (1898)

I. INTRODUCTION

CHAPTERS TWO TO five of this book undertook a detailed examination of the history relevant to the inclusion of responsible government into the Constitution and chapter six drew on this to develop a constitutive theory of responsible government under the Australian Constitution. This chapter considers the implications of the account of responsible government developed in this book for the interpretation of the Constitution. It discusses how the Constitution may be illumined by history and then considers several specific areas of constitutional doctrine which may be impacted by the arguments made in this book.

It is not the intention of this chapter to lay out a fully developed theory of constitutional interpretation. The modest argument I advance here is that the Constitution must be interpreted in light of its historical context. This is a stronger claim than simply that history is one of the many factors that may be taken into account. Rather, I argue that historical context is a necessary starting point when interpreting the Constitution, and that the text of the Constitution cannot be understood without an understanding of that context. My argument is not originalist; I do not argue that development in the meaning of constitutional provisions is impermissible.

In an article published in 2020, Simon Kennedy and I articulated an approach to constitutional interpretation which drew from the methodology of intellectual history, especially the 'Cambridge school' of textual interpretation.

[1] *Convention Debates* (1898) 737.

This approach argues that all historical texts are written against the background of particular language contexts, and that these contexts are partly determinative of the meaning of the text. Further, texts are actions, written within a context for particular purposes. As such, historical texts can only be understood by reading them in light of their background and the purpose for which they were written. These things are true of Constitutions: every Constitution is written within a particular legal and historical context, and is designed to achieve particular purposes. As a result, we argued that a Constitution must first be considered as a historical text in light of its historical context and purpose, and that the meaning derived in this way ought to be the starting point when interpreting a Constitution.[2]

This book aims to show how interpreting the Australian Constitution in this way can shed valuable light on its provisions, especially the sparse provisions which relate to responsible government, and can assist in uncovering key constitutional values. In this chapter I aim to explain how my proposed approach is consistent with orthodox interpretive principles endorsed by the High Court.

II. INTERPRETING THE CONSTITUTION IN THE LIGHT OF HISTORY

It is widely accepted within the Australian constitutional tradition that history is relevant to constitutional interpretation. Even those who do not wish to be bound by the 'dead hands of those who framed it'[3] accept that history is relevant when interpreting the Constitution, even if it is not determinative or controlling.[4] As with any historical text, Constitutions are documents written within a particular context, which includes the social and historical context as well as the particular legal and constitutional doctrines and ideas which informed the specific wording of the text. Further, Constitutions are not contextless statements of constitutional principles, but are written to achieve specific purposes,[5] which, in the case of the Australian Constitution, was to unite the

[2] Benjamin B Saunders and Simon P Kennedy, 'History and Constitutional Interpretation: Applying the 'Cambridge School' Approach to Interpreting Constitutions' (2020) 40 *Oxford Journal of Legal Studies* 591.

[3] *Theophanous v Herald & Weekly Times Ltd* (1994) 182 CLR 104, 171 (Deane J); *Re Wakim; Ex parte McNally* (1999) 198 CLR 511, 600 [186] (Kirby J); Michael Kirby, 'Constitutional Interpretation and Original Intent: A Form of Ancestor Worship?' (2000) 24 *Melbourne University Law Review* 1.

[4] Eg, *Re Patterson; Ex parte Taylor* (2001) 207 CLR 391, 426 [106]–[107] (McHugh J), 479 [266] (Kirby J); *Roach v Electoral Commissioner* (2007) 233 CLR 162, 188–9 [53] (Gummow, Kirby and Crennan JJ).

[5] David S Law and Mila Versteeg argue that there is a 'growing generic component to global constitutionalism': 'The Declining Influence of the United States Constitution' (2012) 87 *New York University Law Review* 762; note also David S Law, 'Generic Constitutional Law' (2005) 89 *Minnesota Law Review* 652.

Australian colonies into one federal Commonwealth.[6] A Constitution is necessarily the product of its time and authorship. Therefore, in order to understand and interpret a Constitution, it is necessary to understand both its historical context, especially the legal and constitutional context, and the purpose for which it was written.

This is apparent from the terms of the Australian Constitution. The Constitution is not a self-contained document whose meaning can be wholly gleaned from its text.[7] It employs many terms and concepts without defining them, thus assuming a pre-existing body of legal and constitutional doctrine which gives content to those terms. As discussed in chapter six, the principles of responsible government are not defined in the Constitution, and the expected functioning of the executive government is not apparent from its text. If responsible government 'is part of the fabric on which the written words of the Constitution are superimposed',[8] then an understanding of that fabric is necessary to understand the Constitution itself. Bernhard Wise wrote that, in order to understand the Constitution, 'an American or foreigner would search the text in vain, unless he were acquainted with the practical working of British Government'.[9] Alfred Deakin argued that the Constitution pre-supposed a 'considerable amount of constitutional knowledge' without which it could not be understood.[10] A knowledge of that constitutional background is a necessary pre-condition to an understanding of the Constitution; in other words, the Constitution must be read in light of its historical context.

There remains controversy about the use of history in constitutional interpretation. In *Permewan Wright Consolidated Pty Ltd v Trewhitt* Mason J saw 'no compelling reason why we should interpret section 92 by reference to doctrines which were current at the end of the nineteenth century'.[11] Notwithstanding this apparent reluctance, many cases have noted that the Constitution needs to be interpreted according to its text understood in light of the history, and in numerous cases the Court has drawn on historical materials when interpreting the Constitution.[12] The reluctance to employ history is perhaps best understood

[6] Constitution, preamble; Nicholas Aroney, *The Constitution of a Federal Commonwealth: The Making and Meaning of the Australian Constitution* (Cambridge, Cambridge University Press, 2009).

[7] *Commonwealth v Colonial Combing, Spinning and Weaving Co Ltd* (1922) 31 CLR 421, 442, 446 (Isaacs J); Justice Stephen Gageler, 'Beyond the Text: A Vision of the Structure and Function of the *Constitution*' (2009) 32 *Australian Bar Review* 138, 140–1.

[8] *Commonwealth v Kreglinger & Fernau Ltd* (1926) 37 CLR 393, 413 (Issacs J).

[9] BR Wise, *The Commonwealth of Australia* (London, Pitman, 1909) 193. See also Commonwealth of Australia, *Final Report of the Constitutional Commission 1988* (Canberra, Australian Government Publishing Service, 1988) [2.191]; W Harrison Moore, *The Commonwealth of Australia: Four Lectures on the Constitution Bill 1897* (Melbourne, George Robertson and Co, 1897) 79.

[10] *Convention Debates* (1898) 1064 (Deakin).

[11] *Permewan Wright Consolidated Pty Ltd v Trewhitt* (1979) 145 CLR 1, 35. See also *North Eastern Dairy Co Ltd v Dairy Industry Authority of NSW* (1975) 134 CLR 559, 615 (Mason J).

[12] *Amalgamated Society of Engineers v Adelaide Steamship Co Ltd* (1920) 28 CLR 129, 152 (Knox CJ, Isaacs, Rich and Starke JJ); *Commonwealth v Kreglinger & Fernau Ltd* (1926) 37 CLR 393, 411–412 (Issacs J); *Victoria v Commonwealth* (1975) 134 CLR 338, 354 (Barwick CJ), 385–6 (Stephen J), 394 (Mason J); *A-G (Cth) ex rel McKinlay v Commonwealth* (1975) 135 CLR 1, 17, 19 (Barwick CJ);

as a reluctance to limit the meaning of the Constitution to its meaning as at Federation,[13] rather than an absolute rule that history or historical context have no place in determining the meaning of the Constitution.

In 1907 the High Court held that, when interpreting the Constitution, it is necessary to understand the 'mischief and defect' to which the constitutional provision in question was directed as ascertained from the relevant historical facts, the 'object of the advocates of Australian federation', and those things that the framers of the Constitution 'may be supposed to have known'.[14] It is well known that in *Cole v Whitfield* the High Court held that reference to the history of constitutional provisions may be made:

> not for the purpose of substituting for the meaning of the words used the scope and effect – if such could be established – which the founding fathers subjectively intended the section to have, but for the purpose of identifying the contemporary meaning of language used, the subject to which that language was directed and the nature and objectives of the movement towards federation from which the compact of the Constitution finally emerged.[15]

The High Court in *Cheatle* held that it is well settled that the provisions of the Constitution 'are framed in the language of the English common law, and are to be read in the light of the common law's history'.[16] In *Singh v Commonwealth*

Cole v Whitfield (1988) 165 CLR 360, 385, 407 (Mason CJ, Wilson, Brennan, Deane, Dawson, Toohey and Gaudron JJ); *Australian Capital Television Pty Ltd v Commonwealth* (1992) 177 CLR 106, 230 (McHugh J); *Cheatle v The Queen* (1993) 177 CLR 541, 552, 562 (Mason CJ, Brennan, Deane, Dawson, Toohey, Gaudron and McHugh JJ); *Theophanous v Herald & Weekly Times Ltd* (1994) 182 CLR 104, 143, 147 (Brennan J), 196–7 (McHugh J); *McGinty v Western Australia* (1996) 186 CLR 140, 230, 239 (McHugh J); *Re Patterson; Ex parte Taylor* (2001) 207 CLR 391, 426 [106]–[107] (McHugh J), 479 [266] (Kirby J); *Mulholland v Australian Electoral Commission* (2004) 220 CLR 181, 234 [150] (Gummow and Hayne JJ), see also 189 [9] (Gleeson CJ); *Combet v Commonwealth* (2005) 224 CLR 494, 535–6 [44]–[45] (McHugh J); *Roach v Electoral Commissioner* (2007) 233 CLR 162, 188–9 [53] (Gummow, Kirby and Crennan JJ), 206 [111]–[112], 208–212 [121]–[133] (Hayne J); *Pape v Federal Commissioner of Taxation* (2009) 238 CLR 1, 36–45 [53]–[81], 56–8 [115]–[122] (French CJ), 75–81 [187]–[205] (Gummow, Crennan and Bell JJ), 106–8 [298]–[306] (Hayne and Kiefel JJ); *Williams v Commonwealth* (2012) 248 CLR 156, 179 [4], 194–206 [40]–[61] (French CJ); *Williams v Commonwealth (No 2)* (2014) 252 CLR 416, 468–9 [80]–[81] (French CJ, Hayne, Kiefel, Bell and Keane JJ); *Plaintiff M68/2015 v Minister for Immigration and Border Protection* (2016) 257 CLR 42, 96 [129], 99 [138]–[139] (Gageler J);

[13] See, eg, *Commonwealth v Australian Capital Territory* (2013) 250 CLR 441, 456 [16] (French CJ, Hayne, Crennan, Kiefel, Bell and Keane JJ), where the High Court held that s 51(xxi) is not to be construed 'with respect only to the status of marriage, the institution reflected in that status, or the rights and obligations attached to it, as they stood at federation'.

[14] *Baxter v Commissioners of Taxation (NSW)* (1907) 4 CLR 1087, 1104–6 (Griffith CJ, Barton and O'Connor JJ).

[15] *Cole v Whitfield* (1988) 165 CLR 360, 385 (Mason CJ, Wilson, Brennan, Deane, Dawson, Toohey and Gaudron JJ).

[16] *Cheatle v The Queen* (1993) 177 CLR 541, 552 (Mason CJ, Brennan, Deane, Dawson, Toohey, Gaudron and McHugh JJ), referring to *Australian Communist Party v Commonwealth* (1951) 83 CLR 1, 193 (Dixon J); *Re Richard Foreman & Sons Ply Ltd; Uther v Federal Commissioner of Taxation* (1947) 74 CLR 508, 521 (Latham CJ); *Commonwealth v Kreglinger & Fernau Ltd* (1926) 37 CLR 393, 411–412 (Issacs J); *R v Snow* (1915) 20 CLR 323, 322–3 (Griffith CJ).

Gummow, Hayne and Heydon JJ wrote that 'to identify the meaning conveyed, at the time of Federation, by the words used in the Constitution is more than a matter of historical interest. It is an essential step in the task of construction'.[17] In *Australian Capital Television Pty Ltd v Commonwealth* McHugh J argued that the Constitution should be 'read as a whole and in the light of the history of constitutional government in Great Britain and the Australian colonies before federation'.[18] In important recent cases the High Court has shown a willingness to examine both the framers' intentions and the historical context relevant to various provisions of the Constitution.[19] More recently in *Gerner v Victoria* the Court noted that it would be 'a distinctly unsound approach' to adopt an interpretation of the Constitution that the framers were 'united in rejecting'.[20]

At the very least, therefore, according to orthodox principles of interpretation endorsed by the High Court, history is relevant in construing the provisions of the Constitution. Thus, the evidence presented in this book provides important historical background and is a necessary starting point when considering the provisions of the Constitution that relate to responsible government.

Although it might be said that a theory of interpretation is logically anterior to the actual task of interpreting the Constitution,[21] no one theory of interpretation has commanded the assent of the High Court or accurately reflects what High Court justices actually do.[22] As Justice Gummow wrote, '[q]uestions of construction of the Constitution are not to be answered by the adoption and application of any particular all-embracing and revelatory theory or doctrine of interpretation', in words that were approved by a unanimous decision of the High Court.[23] Thus, I do not attempt to propose any such revelatory theory of interpretation. Instead, the approach I advocate is a focus on the text of the Constitution as both a historical enactment and an instrument of contemporary government. In particular, I argue the Constitution must first be construed as a text authored by a specific group of people in a specific historical context, which was intended to achieve certain purposes.

[17] *Singh v Commonwealth* (2004) 222 CLR 322, 385 [159] (footnote omitted).

[18] *Australian Capital Television Pty Ltd v Commonwealth* (1992) 177 CLR 106, 227 (McHugh J).

[19] Eg, *Pape v Federal Commissioner of Taxation* (2009) 238 CLR 1, 41–5 [68]–[80], 56–8 [115]–[122] (French CJ), 75–81 [187]–[205] (Gummow, Crennan and Bell JJ), 106–8 [298]–[306] (Hayne and Kiefel JJ); *Williams v Commonwealth* (2012) 248 CLR 156, 194–206 [40]–[61] (French CJ), 296–7 [346]–[347] (Heydon J).

[20] *Gerner v Victoria* (2020) 270 CLR 412, 429 [34] (Kiefel CJ, Gageler, Keane, Gordon and Edelman JJ), citing *Codelfa Construction Pty Ltd v State Rail Authority (NSW)* (1982) 149 CLR 337, 353. See also *Duncan v Queensland* (1916) 22 CLR 556, 605 (Barton J).

[21] Jeremy Kirk, 'Constitutional Interpretation and a Theory of Evolutionary Originalism' (1999) 27 *Federal Law Review* 323, 323.

[22] Cheryl Saunders, 'Interpreting the *Constitution*' (2004) 15 *Public Law Review* 289, 291.

[23] *SGH Ltd v Commissioner of Taxation* (2001) 210 CLR 51, 75 [41] (Gummow J); approved in *Wong v Commonwealth* (2009) 236 CLR 573, 582 [20] (French CJ and Gummow J) and *Commonwealth v Australian Capital Territory* (2013) 250 CLR 441, 455 [14] (French CJ, Hayne, Crennan, Kiefel, Bell and Keane JJ).

While a focus on the text of the Constitution understood in light of its historical context may seem an unremarkable starting point, it has important implications. There is debate as to which aspects of the historical context are relevant to the question of constitutional interpretation and some approaches propose giving greater or even exclusive weight to certain types of sources rather than others.[24] Some scholars argue that certain approaches to constitutional interpretation (such as originalism) are to be preferred because they best promote values such as popular sovereignty or the rule of law, or minimise the ability of unelected judges to implement constitutional change.[25] Some argue that a Constitution should be interpreted in accordance with its original public meaning, because that 'better captures the public authority of the text'.[26] Others argue that a Constitution should be interpreted in accordance with the understandings held by the ratifiers, because the Constitution owes its authority to the consent of the people.[27]

I argue that it is preferable not to conflate questions such as the basis of the authority of the Constitution with questions of its interpretation, as such questions are liable to distort the interpretive process. Whether the framers were bigoted or sexist by today's standards is irrelevant to the meaning of the Constitution. The voters who ratified the Constitution at popular referendums did so after the text of the Constitution had been drafted by the framers and so their intentions are only relevant to the extent that they had an impact on the text of the Constitution. The individual intentions of any one of the framers are irrelevant unless those intentions had a demonstrable impact on the Constitution. The Constitution employs terms with particular legal and specialised meanings, and so the meaning of those terms may be very different to the dictionary meaning or original public meaning. Therefore, it is not a helpful approach to insist that the Constitution should be interpreted solely by reference to one particular type of source, whether original public meaning, ratifiers' intentions or framers' intentions. A focus on the text explains which historical sources are relevant and which are not: only sources which influenced the text of the Constitution are relevant to its interpretation.

In interpreting the Constitution no type of source should be a priori excluded or privileged; rather, each piece of historical evidence ought to be weighed for

[24] Donald L Drakeman, *The Hollow Core of Constitutional Theory: Why We Need the Framers* (Cambridge, Cambridge University Press, 2020) 8–14.

[25] See, eg, Jeffrey Goldsworthy, 'Constitutional Interpretation: Originalism' (2009) 4 *Philosophy Compass* 682, 687–8; Robert N Clinton, 'Original Understanding, Legal Realism and the Interpretation of "This *Constitution*"' (1987) 72 *Iowa Law Review* 1177, 1185; Eric A Posner and Adrian Vermeule, *The Executive Unbound: After the Madisonian Republic* (Oxford, Oxford University Press, 2010) 64.

[26] Keith E Whittington, 'Originalism: A Critical Introduction' (2013) 82 *Fordham Law Review* 375, 381.

[27] See, eg, Helen Irving, 'Constitutional Interpretation, the High Court, and the Discipline of History' (2013) 41 *Federal Law Review* 95, 119.

its relevance and evidential value. For instance, the general social, political and religious views of the Australian people during the 1890s no doubt impacted the Federation process and the general outlook of the framers, but may not have had a direct impact on the text of the Constitution. By contrast, during the Federation Convention debates, section 116 and the acknowledgment of God in the preamble were inserted into the Constitution after urging by religious leaders and church groups who reflected the broader wishes of the people.[28] As such, the intentions of those groups, and their views as to the relationship between religion and government, may be relevant in illuminating the meaning of those provisions.

In construing the Australian Constitution it is necessary to pay close attention to historical context and interpret it in light of that context. It is often said that the task of constitutional interpretation is to determine the intention of the provision in question objectively from the language used.[29] The Court held in *Engineers* that 'it is the chief and special duty of this Court faithfully to expound and give effect to it according to its own terms, finding the intention from the words of the compact, and upholding it throughout precisely as framed'.[30] Barwick CJ said that '[t]he words of the Constitution are to be read in that natural sense they bore in the circumstances of their enactment by the Imperial Parliament in 1900'.[31] Constitutional interpretation in Australia is typically 'firmly grounded in the 'text and structure' of the Constitution'.[32]

As a result of this emphasis on the primacy of the text of the Constitution, there has sometimes been resistance to the use of contextual materials in its interpretation.[33] However, it is not possible to completely exclude reference to contextual materials when interpreting the Constitution, as the High Court itself has recognised. McHugh J noted that '[t]he true meaning of a legal text almost always depends on a background of concepts, principles, practices,

[28] Luke Beck, *Religious Freedom and the Australian Constitution: Origins and Future* (London, Routledge, 2018) chs 2–3; Alex Deagon and Benjamin B Saunders, 'Principles, Pragmatism and Power: Another Look at the Historical Context of Section 116' (2020) 43 *Melbourne University Law Review* 1033.

[29] *Re Wakim; Ex parte McNally* (1999) 198 CLR 511, 549 [35], 551 [40] (McHugh J); *Eastman v R* (2000) 203 CLR 1, 45–47 [145]–[147], 49 [154] (McHugh J); *Singh v Commonwealth* (2004) 222 CLR 322, 336 [19] (Gleeson CJ), 348 [52] (McHugh J), 413 [247] (Kirby J), 425 [295] (Callinan J); *Al-Kateb v Godwin* (2004) 219 CLR 562, 622 [167] (Kirby J); Andrew Inglis Clark, *Studies in Australian Constitutional Law* (Melbourne, Charles F Maxwell, 1901) 19.

[30] *Amalgamated Society of Engineers v Adelaide Steamship Co Ltd* (1920) 28 CLR 129, 142, 149 (Knox CJ, Isaacs, Rich and Starke JJ).

[31] *King v Jones* (1972) 128 CLR 221, 229 (Barwick CJ).

[32] Rosalind Dixon and Gabrielle Appleby, 'Constitutional Implications in Australia: Explaining the Structure – Rights Dualism' in Rosalind Dixon and Adrienne Stone (eds), *The Invisible Constitution in Comparative Perspective* (Cambridge, Cambridge University Press, 2018) 363. See, eg, *Lange v Australian Broadcasting Corporation* (1997) 189 CLR 520, 566–7 (Brennan CJ, Dawson, Toohey, Gaudron, McHugh, Gummow and Kirby JJ).

[33] James A Thomson, 'Constitutional Interpretation: History and the High Court: A Bibliographical Survey' (1982) 5 *University of New South Wales Law Journal* 309, 310–11. See, eg, *Municipal Council of Sydney v Commonwealth* (1904) 1 CLR 208, 213–4 (Griffith CJ).

facts, rights and duties which the authors of the text took for granted or understood, without conscious advertence, by reason of their common language or culture', and this was especially true of a Constitution.[34] And as Gleeson CJ and McHugh J noted, '[a]n understanding of the context in which an instrument was written is ordinarily useful, and sometimes essential, for an understanding of its meaning'.[35] The High Court has permitted reference to extrinsic materials in interpreting the Constitution in many cases.[36]

It is common for legal documents to contain ellipses, and there are many examples of this in the Constitution.[37] The Australian Constitution is not a self-contained document, but assumes the existence of a body of constitutional and common law concepts which give content to its text.[38] In the well-known words of Griffith CJ, Barton and O'Connor JJ, '[i]t is true that what has been called an 'astral intelligence', unprejudiced by any historical knowledge, and interpreting a Constitution merely by the aid of a dictionary, might arrive at a very different conclusion as to its meaning from that which a person familiar with history would reach'.[39] Isaacs J referred to the 'impossibility of regarding the mere written words of the Constitution as affording the only test of validity' of the exercise of executive power[40] and declared that it was the duty of the court, when interpreting the Constitution, to take judicial notice 'of every fundamental constitutional doctrine existing and fully recognized at the time the Constitution was passed, and therefore to be taken as influencing the meaning in which its words were used by the Imperial Legislature'.[41]

The Constitution employs a wide range of specialised legal concepts which it does not define, such as 'executive power', 'judicial power', 'jurisdiction', 'jury' and many others.[42] It also uses terms such as 'Queen', 'Minister of State', 'representative' and 'elector' which carry considerable constitutional baggage based on the history of the British Constitution and the constitutional systems

[34] *Theophanous v Herald & Weekly Times Ltd* (1994) 182 CLR 104, 196 (McHugh). See also *Singh v Commonwealth* (2004) 222 CLR 322, 332 [12] (Gleeson CJ), 349–50 [54] (McHugh J); JGA Pocock, *Virtue, Commerce and History* (Cambridge, Cambridge University Press, 1985) 7–8.

[35] *Brownlee v R* (2001) 207 CLR 278, 285 [8] (Gleeson CJ and McHugh J); *Roach v Electoral Commissioner* (2007) 233 CLR 162, 188 [53] (Gummow, Kirby and Crennan JJ).

[36] J D Heydon, 'Theories of Constitutional Interpretation: A Taxonomy' (2007) *Bar News* 12, 16; *Cole v Whitfield* (1988) 165 CLR 360, 385 (Mason CJ, Wilson, Brennan, Deane, Dawson, Toohey and Gaudron JJ).

[37] Richard Ekins and Jeffrey Goldsworthy, 'The Reality and Indispensability of Legislative Intentions' (2014) 36 *Sydney Law Review* 39, 55.

[38] *Australian Communist Party v Commonwealth* (1951) 83 CLR 1, 193 (Dixon J); *Federal Commissioner of Taxation v Official Liquidator of EO Farley Ltd (in liq)* (1940) 63 CLR 278, 304 (Dixon J). See also *Convention Debates* (1891) 767 (Wrixon), 769 (Deakin).

[39] *Baxter v Commissioners of Taxation (NSW)* (1907) 4 CLR 1087, 1106 (Griffith CJ, Barton and O'Connor JJ).

[40] *Commonwealth v Colonial Combing, Spinning and Weaving Co Ltd* (1922) 31 CLR 421, 442, 446 (Isaacs J).

[41] *Commonwealth v Kreglinger & Fernau Ltd* (1926) 37 CLR 393, 411–12 (Isaacs J). See also *Commonwealth v Colonial Combing, Spinning and Weaving Co Ltd* (1922) 31 CLR 421, 433–4 (Isaacs J).

[42] *Singh v Commonwealth* (2004) 222 CLR 322, 331–2 [10] (Gleeson CJ).

of the Australian colonies. The Commonwealth was 'not born into a vacuum' but 'came into existence within a system of law already established'.[43] The Constitution applies and employs those concepts in various ways: it vests certain powers in specified office holders and institutions;[44] it sets out requirements for people who do things such as hold office or vote;[45] it imposes conditions on the passage of certain types of laws.[46] Thus, the Constitution does not simply replicate the constitutional position which existed in Britain or the colonies but adapts those terms and concepts to produce a 'distinctly Australian system of national governance'.[47] As a result, traditional conceptions of responsible government are likely to have suffered modification in their translation to the Australian federal context.[48]

To take some examples, the Constitution establishes the institutions of Parliament, the executive and the judiciary, and vests (or in the case of the executive, recognises the vesting of) legislative, executive and judicial power in those institutions, but without defining legislative, executive or judicial power.[49] Peter Gerangelos has argued that the framers, by not defining the executive power, left 'the scope of the power to inference'.[50] However, at Federation there was a detailed body of constitutional writing which explained and elaborated the concept of executive power;[51] a better view, therefore, is that the framers relied on the pre-existing body of constitutional law to give content to this concept.[52] There is an elaborate constitutional background to provisions such

[43] *Re Richard Foreman & Sons Pty Ltd; Uther v Commissioner of Taxation (Cth)* (1947) 74 CLR 508, 521 (Latham CJ).

[44] Eg, Constitution ss 1, 61, 68, 71.

[45] Eg, ibid ss 8, 30, 42, 44, 46.

[46] Eg, ibid ss 53–56.

[47] *Palmer v Ayres* (2017) 259 CLR 478, 495–6 [42]–[43] (Gageler J). See also *Plaintiff M68/2015 v Minister for Immigration and Border Protection* (2016) 257 CLR 42, 90–1 [115] (Gageler J); *Victoria v Commonwealth* (1975) 134 CLR 338, 354 (Barwick CJ).

[48] *Commissioner of Taxation (Cth) v Munro* (1926) 38 CLR 153, 185 (Isaacs J); Moore, *The Commonwealth of Australia: Four Lectures on the Constitution Bill 1897* (n 9) 81–2. See also *McGinty v Western Australia* (1996) 186 CLR 140, 270 (Gummow J); *Royal Commission on Australian Government Administration* (Canberra, Australian Government Publishing Service, 1976) 11; for a theoretical perspective see Pocock (n 34) 15.

[49] Constitution, ss 1, 61, 71.

[50] Nicholas Aroney et al, *The Constitution of the Commonwealth of Australia: History, Principle and Interpretation* (Port Melbourne, Cambridge University Press, 2015) 385.

[51] This includes Sir William Blackstone, *Commentaries on the Laws of England*, 9th edn (London, 1783) vol 1, ch 7; Joseph Chitty, *A Treatise on the Law of the Prerogatives of the Crown: And the Relative Duties and Rights of the Subject* (London, J Butterworth, 1820); John Allen, *Inquiry into the Rise and Growth of the Royal Prerogative in England*, new edn (London, Longman, Brown, Green, and Longmans, 1849); William Edward Hearn, *The Government of England: Its Structure, and Its Development*, 2nd edn (Melbourne, George Robertson, 1886) chs IV and V; Alpheus Todd, *On Parliamentary Government in England: Its Origin, Development, and Practical Operation*, 2nd edn (London, Longmans, Green and Co, 1887) vol 1, chs V–VII; William Reynell Anson, *The Law and Custom of the Constitution*, 3rd edn (Oxford, Clarendon Press, 1897) vol 1, ch 1.

[52] See *D'Emden v Pedder* (1904) 1 CLR 91, 110 (Griffith CJ). In *Williams v Commonwealth* (2012) 248 CLR 156, 193 [39] French CJ noted that the question of the extent of Commonwealth executive power 'invites consideration of the construction of s 61 by reference to its drafting history and the concept of executive government which informed it'.

as sections 53 to 56, including terms such as 'the ordinary annual services of the Government'. In *Combet v Commonwealth* McHugh J outlined the development of the constitutional rules relating to taxation and expenditure and then noted that '[s]ections 53, 54, 55 and 81 and 83 of our Constitution are the result of these rules of English constitutional law and this convention'.[53] Chapter I of the Constitution provides, among other things, for the election of senators and members of the House of Representatives, but does not explain what their role is; that must be deduced from political practice and convention.

The Constitution contains many such terms that it does not define. The Constitution is not the source of these concepts: they have a long history which pre-dates the enactment of the Constitution and so an understanding of those key terms requires a background understanding of the constitutional law of Britain and the Australian colonies. In *Pape* Gummow, Crennan and Bell JJ held:

> Matters of Imperial and colonial history respecting the raising and expenditure of public moneys support these conclusions respecting the power of appropriation conferred by the Constitution. A knowledge of legal history is indispensable to an appreciation of the essential characteristics of the power of appropriation in the Constitution; it affords an understanding of the setting in which the Constitution was formulated.[54]

Although their authority is now to be sourced in the Constitution rather than the pre-existing common law or constitutional law, the meaning and content of these terms must be elucidated from that pre-existing body of law rather than the Constitution itself:[55] the common law 'is the source of the legal conceptions that govern us in determining the effect of the written instrument'.[56] The content of these concepts is derived from their location within 'referential chains' of meaning, signalled by the employment of specialised terms without defining them.[57]

As noted, the High Court has often emphasised that the text of the Constitution should be the primary or exclusive focus when interpreting the Constitution. Responsible government presents an acute challenge to this approach. This is because the constitutional text, interpreted solely with reference to the language employed, presents an utterly misleading picture of its functioning. The provisions of the Constitution which incorporate, or assume, the system of responsible government are deliberately sparse and rely on

[53] *Combet v Commonwealth* (2005) 224 CLR 494, 536 [45].

[54] *Pape v Federal Commissioner of Taxation* (2009) 238 CLR 1, 75 [187].

[55] *Singh v Commonwealth* (2004) 222 CLR 322, 331–2 [10] (Gleeson CJ). See also *Australian Capital Television Pty Ltd v Commonwealth* (1992) 177 CLR 106, 209 (Gaudron J).

[56] Sir Owen Dixon, *Jesting Pilate and Other Papers and Addresses*, 3rd edn (Annandale, Federation Press, 2019) 205. See also *Convention Debates* (1891) 767 (Wrixon), 769 (Deakin).

[57] Patrick Emerton, 'Political Freedoms and Entitlements in the Australian Constitution – An Example of Referential Intentions Yielding Unintended Legal Consequences' (2010) 38 *Federal Law Review* 169.

unwritten understandings and conventions which must be gleaned from other sources.[58] As Gleeson CJ wrote, '[a] notable feature of our system of representative and responsible government is how little of the detail of that system is to be found in the Constitution, and how much is left to be filled in by Parliament'.[59] Jeffrey Goldsworthy described the provisions of Chapter II of the Constitution as 'so terse and elliptical as to be positively misleading'[60] and Brian Galligan wrote that '[i]t is obvious that the meaning of responsible government cannot be established from the constitutional text'.[61] Those provisions cannot be understood without an understanding of the constitutional and historical context, which includes the constitutional principles of responsible government as understood as at Federation.[62]

Another crucial aspect of a document's historical context is its purpose. All texts are written with a particular purpose or intention, and it is necessary to understand that purpose when construing the text.[63] Justice Edelman has argued that on 'almost any view' there is a need 'to focus upon the purpose of a provision' in legal interpretation.[64] This is also true of a Constitution: a Constitution is intended to achieve particular goals and bears the stamp of its authorship. The purpose of the Australian Constitution, namely to unite the colonies into a federal Commonwealth, pervades the instrument, and the text of the Constitution would make little sense without an understanding of that purpose. When determining the purpose of the Constitution and its various provisions, the intentions of the framers may shed valuable light.

There has often been resistance to the use of the subjective intentions of the framers when interpreting the Constitution.[65] While it has been said that legal construction means interpreting a legal instrument consistently with the

[58] Colin Howard and Cheryl Saunders, 'The Blocking of the Budget and Dismissal of the Government' in Gareth Evans (ed), *Labor and the Constitution, 1972–1975* (Heinemann, 1977) 265.

[59] *Mulholland v Australian Electoral Commission* (2004) 220 CLR 181, 188 [6] (Gleeson CJ); *Re Patterson; Ex parte Taylor* (2001) 207 CLR 391, 415 [63] (Gaudron J).

[60] Jeffrey Goldsworthy, 'Australia: Devotion to Legalism' in Jeffrey Goldsworthy (ed), *Interpreting Constitutions: A Comparative Study* (Oxford, Oxford University Press, 2007) 108. See also George Winterton, 'The Relationship between Commonwealth Legislative and Executive Power' (2004) 25 *Adelaide Law Review* 21, 34–5.

[61] Brian Galligan, 'The Founders' Design and Intentions Regarding Responsible Government' (1980) 15 *Politics* 1, 1.

[62] *Australian Capital Television Pty Ltd v Commonwealth* (1992) 177 CLR 106, 230 (McHugh J); see also 208–9 (Gaudron J).

[63] *Singh v Commonwealth* (2004) 222 CLR 322, 336 [19] (Gleeson CJ).

[64] Justice James Edelman, 'Constitutional Interpretation' (2019) 45 *University of Western Australia Law Review* 1, 27.

[65] *Municipal Council of Sydney v Commonwealth* (1904) 1 CLR 208, 213–4 (Griffith CJ); *Cole v Whitfield* (1988) 165 CLR 360, 385 (Mason CJ, Wilson, Brennan, Deane, Dawson, Toohey and Gaudron JJ); *Singh v Commonwealth* (2004) 222 CLR 322, 337 [21] (Gleeson CJ); *New South Wales v Commonwealth* (2006) 229 CLR 1, 97 [120] (Gleeson CJ, Gummow, Hayne, Heydon and Crennan JJ); Justice Virginia Bell, 'Section 80 – The Great Constitutional Tautology' (2014) 40 *Monash University Law Review* 7, 14.

intentions of those who drafted it,[66] that intention is typically discerned objectively from the text rather than the subjective intentions of the drafters.[67] There may be difficulties in determining the framers' intentions,[68] given that the framers often had conflicting viewpoints, and not all the framers were forthcoming in expressing their opinions. Thus, in *Singh*, Gleeson CJ held:

> A search for the collective, subjective intention of the framers of the Constitution would be impossible, and the individual subjective intention of any one of them, if it could be established, would not be relevant, because it would not advance any legitimate process of reasoning to a conclusion about the meaning of the text.[69]

Two points may be made in response to this. First, as noted in chapter one, respectable scholarly arguments have been made in support of the concepts of group intention such as legislative intention. For the purposes of this book, I adopt a definition of legislative intention as the legislature's reasoned response to a particular matter,[70] although other accounts are plausible.[71] Thus, the intention or intentions of the framers is not an incoherent concept: it is the reasoned conclusion of the framers in relation to a particular matter. The framers debated the terms of the Constitution following an agreed process consistent with standard rules of parliamentary procedure and the *Convention Debates* contain a detailed record of the deliberations of the framers and the conclusions they reached in relation to many provisions of the Constitution. It is true that there was sometimes vigorous disagreement about the provisions of the Constitution and that not all of the clauses were adopted unanimously. For example, as is well known, the Constitution embodies a compromise position struck by the framers over the respective powers of the Senate and the House of Representatives, reflecting rival conceptions of responsible government and federalism, and this is reflected in provisions such as sections 53–57.[72] Despite this disagreement, having accomplished the task of negotiating the terms of the Federation, the framers accepted the resulting Constitution as having been produced according

[66] Michael Coper, 'The Place of History in Constitutional Interpretation' in Gregory Craven (ed), *The Convention Debates 1891–1898: Commentaries, Indices and Guide* (Sydney, Legal Books, 1986) 12; Drakeman (n 24) 19, 21.

[67] *Re Wakim; Ex parte McNally* (1999) 198 CLR 511, 549 [35], 551 [40] (McHugh J); *Eastman v R* (2000) 203 CLR 1, 46 [146] (McHugh J); *Singh v Commonwealth* (2004) 222 CLR 322, 385 [159] (Gummow, Hayne and Heydon JJ); Edelman (n 64) 13.

[68] *Hematite Petroleum Pty Ltd v Victoria* (1983) 151 CLR 599, 616 (Gibbs CJ); *Theophanous v Herald & Weekly Times Ltd* (1994) 182 CLR 104, 168 (Deane J); Gageler, 'Beyond the Text' (n 7) 141–2.

[69] *Singh v Commonwealth* (2004) 222 CLR 322, 337 [21]. See also *Brownlee v R* (2001) 207 CLR 278, 285 [8].

[70] Richard Ekins, *The Nature of Legislative Intent* (Oxford, Oxford University Press, 2012) 224, 243; Christian List and Philip Pettit, *Group Agency: The Possibility, Design and Status of Corporate Agents* (Oxford, Oxford University Press, 2011) 77; Justice Stephen Gageler, 'Legislative Intention' (2015) 41 *Monash University Law Review* 1, 12.

[71] Eg, David Tan, 'Uncommon Legislative Attitudes: Why a Theory of Legislative Intent Needs Nontrivial Aggregation' (2021) 34 *Ratio Juris* 139.

[72] *A-G (Cth) ex rel McKinlay v Commonwealth* (1975) 135 CLR 1, 58 (Stephen J).

to the agreed process and voted as a Convention to approve the Constitution.[73] The intention of the framers is 'the fully negotiated conclusion' rather than their initial preferences.[74]

It is therefore possible to discern the intentions of the framers in relation to many provisions of the Constitution, and to discern how that conclusion is embodied in the text of the Constitution. The intention of the framers in relation to a particular issue is the reasoned determination of the Federation Conventions in relation to that issue, as recorded in the *Convention Debates*. It is not an examination of the subjective wishes of individual framers, nor is it an attempt to guess how the framers would have decided a particular present-day controversy. Further, it is not likely to be possible to ascertain the intention of the framers in relation to every provision of the Constitution given that the *Convention Debates* do not provide sufficient detail to enable the framers' reasoned conclusion to be discerned in relation to every particular provision of the Constitution.

Second, the High Court's actual practice appears to be at variance from its professed resistance to relying on the framers' intentions. Donaghue and Wood have recently argued that when interpreting the Constitution the High Court has in many cases relied on historical materials that reveal the subjective intentions of the framers.[75] The Court has referred to what the framers believed or may be taken to have understood when drafting the Constitution[76] and also to what the framers may be taken to have intended certain provisions to mean.[77] It has long been accepted that it is legitimate to have regard to materials such as the Federal Convention Debates in order to discover the mischief which a constitutional provision was intended to remedy.[78] The Court frequently refers to statements made by delegates to the Federal Conventions and has referred to 'the subjective intentions of the framers of the Constitution as bearing upon the meaning of the constitutional text'.[79] In *Lange v Australian*

[73] *Convention Debates* (1898) 2464–5.

[74] Drakeman (n 24) 53.

[75] Stephen Donaghue and Thomas Wood, 'The Evolving Role of History in Constitutional Interpretation' (2020) 31 *Public Law Review* 248.

[76] *Australian Capital Television Pty Ltd v Commonwealth* (1992) 177 CLR 106, 136 (Mason CJ), 228–9 (McHugh J); *R v Davison* (1954) 90 CLR 353, 382 (Kitto J).

[77] *R v Commonwealth Court of Conciliation & Arbitration; Ex parte Tramways (No 1)* (1914) 18 CLR 54, 61 (Griffith CJ), 66 (Barton J); *Victoria v Commonwealth* (1975) 134 CLR 338, 394 (Mason J); *Re Tracey; Ex parte Ryan* (1989) 166 CLR 518, 584–5 (Deane J); *Cheatle v The Queen* (1993) 177 CLR 541, 556 (Mason CJ, Brennan, Deane, Dawson, Toohey, Gaudron and McHugh JJ); *Gould v Brown as Liquidator of Amann Aviation Pty Ltd (in liq)* (1998) 193 CLR 346, 422 [120], 424 [123], 430 [140] (McHugh J); *Williams v Commonwealth* (2012) 248 CLR 156, 205 [60] (French CJ); *Private R v Cowen* (2020) 271 CLR 316, 364 [126] (Nettle J).

[78] In *Municipal Council of Sydney v Commonwealth* (1904) 1 CLR 208, 213–4 Griffith CJ said that the Federal Convention debates are 'no higher than parliamentary debates, and are not to be referred to except for the purpose of seeing what was the subject-matter of discussion, what was the evil to be remedied, and so forth'; *R v Pearson; Ex parte Sipka* (1983) 152 CLR 254, 262 (Gibbs CJ, Mason and Wilson JJ).

[79] Donaghue and Wood (n 75) 253.

Broadcasting Corporation, what 'the Constitution intended' and what the Second Australasian Convention resolved were treated as synonymous.[80] Carl McCamish has argued that in many cases the High Court has referred to historical materials and that '[m]uch of the reasoning underlying the court's use of these materials relies implicitly on ascertaining the subjective views of the framers'.[81] McCamish also argued that the 'distinction between what the founders 'subjectively intended' on the one hand, and the approved searches for 'contemporary meaning', 'subject to be addressed' and 'objectives of the movement towards federation' on the other is not drawn 'coherently or consistently by High Court judges'.[82] Further, Ekins and Goldsworthy have argued that a sharp contrast between subjective and objective intentions cannot be drawn, and that objective intentions are simply those subjective intentions that can reasonably be known based on publicly available information.[83]

Despite the difficulties in determining the framers' intentions in some cases, it does not seem possible to do away with intention entirely, as many provisions of the Constitution make little sense without an understanding the framers' intentions. For example, the inclusion and wording of section 116 can only be understood by reference to the framers' desire to reserve power to the states to legislate in relation to religion.[84] The tension between responsible government and federalism, and the manner in which this compromise was resolved, explains the drafting of provisions such as sections 53–55.[85] The framers' intentions shed vital light on the meaning of the cryptic words of section 92.[86]

It is important to emphasise that the intentions of the framers as such have no particular weight or relevance and that the framers' intentions have no epistemic superiority or normative value in and of themselves.[87] Whether one or more of the framers would have agreed that a particular law is within the scope of the legislative power conferred by the Constitution, or intended that government would have functioned in a particular way, is irrelevant to the interpretation of the Constitution.[88] The relevance of the framers' intentions stems rather from

[80] *Lange v Australian Broadcasting Corporation* (1997) 189 CLR 520, 557 (Brennan CJ, Dawson, Toohey, Gaudron, McHugh, Gummow and Kirby JJ).

[81] Carl McCamish, 'The Use of Historical Materials in Interpreting the Commonwealth *Constitution*' (1996) 70 *Australian Law Journal* 638, 640.

[82] ibid 638–9.

[83] Ekins and Goldsworthy (n 37) 46–51.

[84] See Benjamin B Saunders and Alex Deagon, 'Religion and the *Constitution*: A Response to Luke Beck's Safeguard against Religious Intolerance Theory of Section 116' (2021) 44 *University of New South Wales Law Journal* 1558.

[85] LJM Cooray, *Conventions, the Australian Constitution and the Future* (Sydney, Legal Books, 1979) 12.

[86] Justice Stephen Gageler, 'The Section 92 Revolution' in James Stellios (ed), *Encounters with Constitutional Interpretation and Legal Education: Essays in Honour of Michael Coper* (Annandale, Federation Press 2018).

[87] *Theophanous v Herald & Weekly Times Ltd* (1994) 182 CLR 104, 128 (Mason CJ, Toohey and Gaudron JJ), 196–7 (McHugh J).

[88] See *Australian Capital Television Pty Ltd v Commonwealth* (1992) 177 CLR 106, 135 (Mason CJ).

the fact that the Constitution is a historical text, and the task of constitutional interpretation is to interpret that text. 'It is only to the extent that the historical intentions of the framers are in some way inscribed into the text of the constitution that they become part of the law', and thus they only have relevance to the extent that they illuminate the meaning of the text.[89]

Responsible government in the Australian constitutional system is a good illustration of this point. It is widely accepted that the Australian Constitution incorporates or assumes responsible government, but there is little in the text of the Constitution that indicates this beyond the establishment of a parliamentary executive: the concept of responsible government 'is not one which is elaborated in the Constitution'.[90] That the Constitution incorporates or assumes responsible government can only be demonstrated historically, from the intentions of the framers, and the constitutional background of parliamentary government. That the framers understood responsible government to be an inherently flexible and unconstrainable system of government designed to ensure the self-government of the Australian people is essential to understand the Australian Constitution, because this explains the drafting of the provisions of the Constitution, especially Chapter II.

I have argued that the Constitution needs to be interpreted historically, and that historical context is a necessary starting point when interpreting the Constitution. It should be noted that this is not an originalist argument, and emphasising history in this way does not preclude changes in the meaning of the constitutional text. There is sometimes unease about being governed by a document written during a time where social and political values were far different from our own.[91] To read the Constitution historically is not to suggest that the meaning of the Constitution must be confined to its historical meaning. Perhaps paradoxically, reading the Constitution in the way I propose points in the opposite direction.[92] This arises from the nature of the common law as well as the tradition of British constitutionalism which the framers incorporated into the Constitution. Chapter two argued that the British Constitution was conceived as a Constitution in being, constantly in flux, and the conception of responsible government incorporated by the framers was an expressly

[89] Nicholas Aroney, 'Originalism and Explanatory Power: Text, Structure and the Interpretation of Constitutions' in Lisa Burton Crawford, Patrick Emerton and Dale Smith (eds), *Law under a Democratic Constitution: Essays in Honour of Jeffrey Goldsworthy* (Oxford, Hart, 2019) 99, 101.

[90] *Re Patterson; Ex parte Taylor* (2001) 207 CLR 391, 415 [63] (Gaudron J); W Harrison Moore, *The Constitution of the Commonwealth of Australia*, 2nd edn (Melbourne, Charles F Maxwell, 1910) 168–9.

[91] Eg, David A Strauss, *The Living Constitution* (Oxford, Oxford University Press, 2010) 18, Samuel Freeman, 'Constitutional Democracy and the Legitimacy of Judicial Review' (1990) 9 *Law and Philosophy* 327; Samuel Freeman, 'Original Meaning, Democratic Interpretation, and the Constitution' (1992) 21 *Philosophy and Public Affairs* 3.

[92] See contra Greg Craven, 'Heresy as Orthodoxy: Were the Founders Progressivists?' (2003) 31 *Federal Law Review* 87.

flexible and evolutionary one. This was also a distinctive feature of the common law: the British common law tradition conceived of the common law as a body of law which contains, 'and should contain, a built-in mechanism for organic change and that it survives, and should survive, by development, by growth'.[93] This suggests that the interpretation of the provisions of the Constitution which relate to responsible government should permit change.

To take an example, section 61 states that the 'executive power of the Commonwealth is vested in the Queen and is exercisable by the Governor-General as the Queen's representative' but does not define the term 'executive power'.[94] This has two consequences. First, as has been argued, the content of the term executive power is to be ascertained from the pre-Federation body of British and colonial constitutional law, which included the common law and any applicable statutes and conventions.[95] One of the distinctive features of British constitutional law was its evolutionary nature: it was not a static body of principles, but constantly changing in response to new developments and circumstances. Thus, second, by not defining 'executive power' the Constitution allows for development in the meaning of that term along the lines of the British Constitution and the common law. Incorporating common law concepts into the Constitution necessarily incorporates the common law methodology of evolutionary change.[96] As such, the executive power of the Commonwealth may expand or contract in response to new circumstances and the changing needs of the times, within the constraints of the Constitution as a whole. However, it should be emphasised that, although some development in the meaning of the provisions of the Constitution is inevitable, when interpreting the Constitution, the Court's role remains that of interpreting the text.

Jeffrey Goldsworthy has argued that the orthodox interpretive methodology employed by the High Court is one which takes relevant evidence of the founders' intentions seriously but does not exclude consideration and application of contemporary concepts and values.[97] Goldsworthy proposes four situations in which departures from original meaning are appropriate.[98] Some changes in

[93] Harold J Berman, 'The Origins of Historical Jurisprudence: Coke, Selden, Hale' (1993) 103 *Yale Law Journal* 1651, 1654.

[94] Constitution, s 61; *Commonwealth v Colonial Combing, Spinning and Weaving Co Ltd* (1922) 31 CLR 421, 437 (Isaacs J); *Davis v Commonwealth* (1988) 166 CLR 79, 92–3(Mason CJ, Deane and Gaudron JJ); *Pape v Commissioner of Taxation* (2009) 238 CLR 1, 62 [131] (French CJ); *Williams v Commonwealth* (2012) 248 CLR 156, 372 [588] (Kiefel J); *Plaintiff M68/2015 v Minister for Immigration and Border Protection* (2016) 257 CLR 42, 96 [129] (Gageler J).

[95] See *CPCF v Minister for Immigration and Border Protection* (2015) 255 CLR 514, 538 [42] (French CJ).

[96] See Winterton, 'The Relationship between Commonwealth Legislative and Executive Power' (n 60) 34.

[97] Jeffrey Goldsworthy, 'Originalism in Constitutional Interpretation' (1997) 25 *Federal Law Review* 1; Jeffrey Goldsworthy, 'Original Meanings and Contemporary Understandings in Constitutional Interpretation' in HP Lee and Peter Gerangelos (eds), *Constitutional Advancement in a Frozen Continent: Essays in Honour of George Winterton* (Annandale, Federation Press, 2009).

[98] Goldsworthy, 'Constitutional Interpretation: Originalism' (n 25) 689–91.

meaning are inescapable to avoid absurd consequences: it would not generally be considered controversial that the reference to 'the naval and military defence of the Commonwealth' in section 51(vi) of the Constitution should be interpreted so as to include air forces and other developments since Federation.[99]

Another source of changes in the meaning of constitutional terms arises from the inherent ambiguity of various provisions: many provisions in the Constitution 'have no fixed or intrinsic meaning and it would be vain to attempt to search for one'.[100] As such, the text is not determinative.[101] This also suggests caution in expecting that a historically-informed reading will be able to solve contested issues of interpretation. The historical evidence relating to a constitutional provision may not yield a clear meaning. Identifying a particular historical meaning may not resolve a particular contemporary controversy. Thus, the approach proposed in this book does not preclude development in the meaning of the constitutional text. As Justice Gageler has argued:

> There is a difference between being informed by history as to the provenance of a constitutional command expressed in grand and emphatic terms and being captured in the application of that command by the historical position as it appears to have existed at a particular point in time.[102]

Interpreting the Constitution in light of its historical context is consistent with orthodox principles of interpretation endorsed by the High Court and does not rule out developments in the meaning of constitutional terms to take account of changed circumstances since Federation. The historical material examined in this book provides essential context for understanding responsible government under the Australian Constitution. This book has examined the constitutional and common law background which the framers drew upon when formulating the terms of the Constitution and the framers' intentions, that is, their reasoned response to the various problems they were forced to resolve. Given that the Constitution is not a self-contained document and that 'the meaning of responsible government cannot be established from the constitutional text',[103] that historical context is essential for interpreting the provisions of the Constitution that relate to responsible government.

III. IMPLICATIONS FOR CONSTITUTIONAL LAW AND INTERPRETATION

Responsible government has played an important role in several key aspects of constitutional jurisprudence in Australia. This section considers the implications

[99] JO Morris, 'Some Aspects of the Commonwealth Parliament's Defence Power Under the *Constitution*' (1941) 2 *Res Judicatae* 221; *Thomas v Mowbray* (2007) 233 CLR 307, 395–6 [252] (Kirby J).

[100] Gageler, 'Beyond the Text' (n 7) 140–1.

[101] See also Cooray (n 85) 15.

[102] Gageler, 'Beyond the Text' (n 7) 143.

[103] Galligan (n 61) 1.

of the account of responsible government developed in this book for the interpretation of the Constitution, arguing that some aspects of existing jurisprudence are consistent with that account, and critiques other aspects of the High Court's approach.

A. A Flexible, Non-prescriptive Approach

This book has argued that responsible government, as adopted or assumed by the Australian Constitution, is an inherently flexible and unconstrainable system of government designed to ensure the self-government of the Australian people. Responsible government is intended to enable the politically sovereign people of Australia to govern themselves in the manner they see fit. Responsible government is fundamentally political, not readily susceptible of judicial enforcement or codification. That understanding is enshrined in the text and structure of the Constitution, and is deliberately non-prescriptive regarding the structure of the executive branch and its relationship to the Parliament.

The first major implication of this understanding of responsible government is interpretive minimalism when construing the provisions of the Constitution which relate to responsible government. That is, the primary means by which the sovereign people are to govern themselves is through the political mechanisms of government, namely Parliament and the executive which is politically accountable to Parliament and the electorate. Decisions as to policy, legislation, and the structure of government are political decisions for the electorate and their representatives to make. Judicially imposed restrictions on the structure of government which are not evident in the text of the Constitution are likely to hinder the freedom of the sovereign people of Australia to govern themselves in the manner they consider best.

There is a tendency to argue for a greater 'constitutionalisation' of responsible government. As discussed below, some scholars have argued that the conventions of responsible government should be judicially enforceable and others have argued that responsible government has implications for the structure of government, limiting the types of executive agencies that may be created. The argument of this book suggests that views such as these are incorrect.[104] The nature of responsible government as inherently evolutionary and flexible suggests caution in drawing implications from the incorporation of responsible government into the Constitution which limit the ability of Parliament and the executive to structure the institutions of government. The framers deliberately resisted entrenching the key features of responsible government on the ground that its working is not fixed, but something to be shaped and moulded by the people of each generation.

[104] See further Benjamin B Saunders, 'Responsible Government, Statutory Authorities and the Australian *Constitution*' (2020) 48 *Federal Law Review* 4.

The High Court has often stated that the Constitution should be interpreted flexibly to enable it to apply in changing circumstances, without reading in limitations not found in the express words of the text.[105] In 1908, O'Connor J said that 'it must always be remembered that we are interpreting a Constitution broad and general in its terms, intended to apply to the varying conditions which the development of our community must involve'.[106] This applies with all the more force in relation to the provisions of the Constitution which concern responsible government. In *Re Patterson; Ex parte Taylor* Gleeson CJ held that the provisions of Chapter II of the Constitution 'are expressed in a form which allows the flexibility that is appropriate to the practical subject of governmental administration', and that '[f]or the framers of the Constitution to have descended into greater specificity would have imposed an unnecessary and inappropriate degree of inflexibility upon constitutional arrangements that need to be capable of development and adaptability'.[107] Gummow and Hayne JJ considered that the Court 'should favour a construction of section 64 which is fairly open and which allows for development in a system of responsible ministerial government'.[108] As the plurality in *Egan v Willis* warned:

> It should not be assumed that the characteristics of a system of responsible government are fixed or that the principles of ministerial responsibility which developed in New South Wales after 1855 necessarily reflected closely those from time to time accepted at Westminster.[109]

The deliberately flexible nature of the Constitution has many benefits. For instance, it has allowed for the transfer of significant power from Britain to Australia without the need for formal constitutional amendment.[110] As such, the courts should be reluctant to imply restrictions on Parliament or government that are not apparent in the Constitution, because these may have the effect of taking power away from the sovereign people of Australia to govern themselves.[111] As discussed further below, such well-intentioned restrictions may be counter-productive, hindering effective solutions to the changing problems of governance.

[105] *Australian National Airways Pty Ltd v Commonwealth* (1945) 71 CLR 29, 81 (Dixon J); *R v Public Vehicles Licensing Appeal Tribunal (Tas); Ex parte Australian National Airways Pty Ltd* (1964) 113 CLR 207, 225–26 (Dixon CJ, Kitto, Taylor, Menzies, Windeyer and Owen JJ); *R v Coldham; Ex parte Australian Social Welfare Union* (1983) 153 CLR 297, 314 (Gibbs CJ, Mason, Murphy, Wilson, Brennan, Deane and Dawson JJ); *Commonwealth v Tasmania* (1983) 158 CLR 1, 127–128 (Mason J).

[106] *Jumbunna Coal Mine NL v Victorian Coal Miners' Association* (1908) 6 CLR 309, 367–8.

[107] *Re Patterson; Ex parte Taylor* (2001) 207 CLR 391, 401 [11], 402 [14].

[108] ibid 459 [211].

[109] *Egan v Willis* (1998) 195 CLR 424, 451 [41] (Gaudron, Gummow and Hayne JJ). See also *Re Patterson; Ex parte Taylor* (2001) 207 CLR 391, 402–3 [13]–[17] (Gleeson CJ), 460–5 [211]–[221] (Gummow and Hayne JJ).

[110] See *Western Australia v Commonwealth* (1975) 134 CLR 201, 278 (Jacobs J).

[111] *Cf McGinty v Western Australia* (1996) 186 CLR 140, 186 (Dawson J).

B. Interpretive Implications

My argument should not be taken as suggesting that responsible government has no implications beyond the specific text of the Constitution. The principles of responsible government, including the requirement in section 64 of the Constitution that ministers of the Crown must be members of Parliament, entails that a strict conception of the separation of powers is inapplicable; as such, the courts have resisted drawing an implication which prevents the Commonwealth legislature from conferring power to make regulations and other subordinate legislation on executive bodies.[112] The important constitutional role played by Parliament in scrutinising the executive implies that the Houses of Parliament must have sufficient powers to undertake that function, including the power to summon ministers to appear and provide information.[113] Members of the High Court have also acknowledged that the effective functioning of the cabinet system requires that cabinet discussions remain confidential, which means that there is a public interest against 'disclosure of cabinet proceedings and of other high level policy deliberations'.[114]

Perhaps the most important implication is that the powers of the executive are subject to regulation by statute. The principle of legislative supremacy over the executive is a fundamental constitutional principle which is not expressly stated in the Constitution.[115] Some commentators have argued that the express conferral of power on the executive by the Constitution means that certain of these powers are not subject to regulation by the legislature. JE Richardson argued that the Constitution confines executive power in relation to the execution and maintenance of the Constitution and laws of the Commonwealth to the Queen and the Governor-General and that section 61 'cannot become a complete sacrificial victim to the legislative powers'.[116] As such, any Act which sought to remove the residual responsibility of the Governor-General in relation to the execution and maintenance of the Constitution and laws of the Commonwealth would be constitutionally invalid.[117]

[112] *Victorian Stevedoring & General Contracting Co Pty Ltd v Dignan* (1931) 46 CLR 73, 101–2 (Dixon J), 114–17, 123 (Evatt J); *R v Trade Practices Tribunal; Ex parte Tasmanian Breweries Pty Ltd* (1970) 123 CLR 361, 389–90 (Windeyer J).

[113] *Egan v Willis* (1998) 195 CLR 424; Colin Turpin, 'Ministerial Responsibility' in Jeffrey Jowell and Dawn Oliver (eds), *The Changing Constitution*, 3rd edn (Oxford, Clarendon Press, 1994) 112.

[114] *Sankey v Whitlam* (1978) 142 CLR 1, 40–1 (Gibbs ACJ), 98 (Mason J).

[115] Nicholas Aroney, 'The High Court on Constitutional Law: The 2012 Term – Explanatory Power and the Modalities of Constitutional Reasoning' (2013) 36 *University of New South Wales Law Journal* 863, 881. But see *Victoria v Commonwealth* (1975) 134 CLR 338, 406 (Jacobs J); *Plaintiff M68/2015 v Minister for Immigration and Border Protection* (2016) 257 CLR 42, 93 [121]–[122] (Gageler J).

[116] JE Richardson, 'The Executive Power of the Commonwealth' in Leslie Zines (ed), *Commentaries on the Australian Constitution* (Sydney, Butterworths, 1977) 82.

[117] ibid 84–5.

The High Court has held that Parliament has the power to modify or displace executive power;[118] in *Brown v West* the Court held that, '[w]hatever the scope of the executive power of the Commonwealth might otherwise be, it is susceptible of control by statute'.[119] Dawson, Toohey and Gaudron JJ noted in *Re Residential Tenancies Tribunal (NSW)* that 'it is of the very nature of executive power in a system of responsible government that it is susceptible to control by the exercise of legislative power by Parliament'.[120] In *Williams v Commonwealth (No 1)* Gummow and Bell JJ noted that the Australian Constitution imports 'the basal assumption of legislative predominance inherited from the United Kingdom'.[121] The Parliament 'is sovereign over the Executive' and its legislative power extends to anything that is 'within the competence of the Executive under s. 61'.[122] This is surely correct. As at Federation, the principles of the British Constitution included legislative supremacy over the executive[123] and it would be surprising if anything in section 61 of the Constitution overturned such a fundamental constitutional principle. Section 51(xxxix) also supports the existence of such a power.[124]

Responsible government is also relevant for the interpretation of statutory provisions. In *Hughes Aircraft Systems International v Airservices Australia* Finn J held that the constitutional context of responsible government means that ministers have a prima facie right to communicate with and obtain information from a statutory corporation within their portfolio, and that the legislation governing the entity (in this case the Civil Aviation Act 1988 (Cth)) was to be interpreted presupposing the existence of such a right.[125]

[118] *Re Richard Foreman & Sons Pty Ltd; Uther v Commissioner of Taxation (Cth)* (1947) 74 CLR 508, 514 (Latham CJ), 523 (Rich J), 531 (Dixon J); *Barton v Commonwealth* (1974) 131 CLR 477, 488 (Barwick CJ), 491 (McTiernan and Menzies JJ), 501 (Mason J); *Victoria v Commonwealth* (1975) 134 CLR 338, 406 (Jacobs J); *Brown v West* (1990) 169 CLR 195, 202 (Mason CJ, Brennan, Deane, Dawson and Toohey JJ); *Ling v Commonwealth* (1994) 51 FCR 88, 92 (Gummow, Lee and Hill JJ); *Re Residential Tenancies Tribunal (NSW); Ex parte Defence Housing Authority* (1997) 190 CLR 410, 459 (McHugh J); *Ruddock v Vadarlis* (2001) 110 FCR 491, 501 [33], 507 [61] (Black CJ), 539 [181] (French J); *Jarratt v Commissioner of Police for New South Wales* (2005) 224 CLR 44, 69–70 [85] (McHugh, Gummow and Hayne JJ); *Northern Territory v Arnhem Land Trust* (2008) 236 CLR 24, 58 [27] (Gleeson CJ, Gummow, Hayne and Crennan JJ); *Cadia Holdings Pty Ltd v New South Wales* (2010) 242 CLR 195, 204 [14] (French CJ), 228 [94] (Gummow, Hayne, Heydon and Crennan JJ); *CPCF v Minister for Immigration and Border Protection* (2015) 255 CLR 514, 600–1 [277], [279], 602 [284] (Kiefel J).

[119] *Brown v West* (1990) 169 CLR 195, 202 (Mason CJ, Brennan, Deane, Dawson and Toohey JJ).

[120] *Re Residential Tenancies Tribunal (NSW) and Henderson; Ex parte Defence Housing Authority* (1997) 190 CLR 410, 441 (footnote omitted).

[121] *Williams v Commonwealth* (2012) 248 CLR 156, 232 [136] (Gummow and Bell JJ).

[122] *Victoria v Commonwealth* (1975) 134 CLR 338, 406 (Jacobs J).

[123] See, eg, AV Dicey, *Introduction to the Study of the Law of the Constitution*, 6th edn (London, MacMillan, 1902) 37–8, 50, 66–7, 368–9; William Reynell Anson, *The Law and Custom of the Constitution*, 3rd edn (Oxford, Clarendon Press, 1897) vol 1, 36; Joseph Chitty, *A Treatise on the Law of the Prerogatives of the Crown* (London, J Butterworth, 1820) 382–3.

[124] *Victoria v Commonwealth* (1975) 134 CLR 338, 406 (Jacobs J); *Plaintiff M68/2015 v Minister for Immigration and Border Protection* (2016) 257 CLR 42, 93 [121]–[122] (Gageler J).

[125] *Hughes Aircraft Systems International v Airservices Australia* (1997) 76 FCR 151, 231, 246.

In *Hocking v Director-General, National Archives of Australia* the High Court by majority held that correspondence between Sir John Kerr, the former Governor-General of Australia, and Buckingham Palace, which was held by the National Archives, was a 'Commonwealth record' under the Archives Act 1983 (Cth), which was relevantly defined as 'a record that is the property of the Commonwealth or of a Commonwealth institution'.[126] Kiefel CJ, Bell, Gageler and Keane JJ held that correspondence between the Queen and the Governor-General were not private communications, but rather 'communications the content and means of which must fall within the purview of the Executive Government of the Commonwealth within the framework of responsible government established by Ch II of the Constitution'[127] and were to be considered Commonwealth records.

In *Loielo v Giles* Ginnane J considered whether it was appropriate for emergency powers that had the effect of shutting down most of Victoria to be exercised by a departmental medical officer who was not accountable to Parliament. Arguably, given the significance of the decision and its impact on the State of Victoria, such decisions should be made by a minister 'who is responsible to Parliament and therefore to the public' rather than an administrative officer who may not even be senior.[128] However, these considerations did not affect the outcome, and his Honour simply prompted Parliament to reconsider 'who should exercise these emergency powers and whether their exercise should be required to take into account matters such as the social and economic consequences of their exercise'.[129]

Finally, the principles of responsible government are relevant to the interpretation of statutory powers conferred on ministers. Under the *Carltona* principle, the courts have held that ministers are able to exercise administrative functions through duly authorised officers.[130] In *Carltona Ltd v Commissioners of Works* Lord Greene MR said:

> It cannot be supposed that this regulation meant that, in each case, the minister in person should direct his mind to the matter. The duties imposed upon ministers and the powers given to ministers are normally exercised under the authority of the ministers by responsible officials of the department. Public business could not be carried on if that were not the case. Constitutionally, the decision of such an official is, of course, the decision of the minister. The minister is responsible.[131]

Underlying this principle is the recognition that the functions of modern government are so voluminous that a minister could not carry them out personally; in

[126] Archives Act 1983 (Cth), s 3(1).
[127] *Hocking v Director-General, National Archives of Australia* (2020) 271 CLR 1, 50 [107].
[128] *Loielo v Giles* (2020) 63 VR 1, 9 [13], 40–1 [131]–[133], 46 [151].
[129] *Loielo v Giles* (2020) 63 VR 1, 41 [133].
[130] *Minister for Aboriginal Affairs v Peko-Wallsend Ltd* (1986) 162 CLR 24, 30–1 (Mason J).
[131] *Carltona Ltd v Commissioners of Works* [1943] 2 All ER 560, 563 (Lord Greene MR).

addition, the principle rests on the 'special position of constitutional responsibility which Ministers occupy'.[132] Several High Court cases appear to have endorsed the reasoning in *Carltona*,[133] although Basten JA considered that 'the scope and status of the principle are uncertain'.[134]

C. Responsible Government and the Structure of the Executive

One significant question is how the structures of modern government fit in relation to the conventions of responsible government. Drafted in an era when government had a much smaller range of functions than today, the Constitution contemplates the business of government being managed by ministers who are responsible to Parliament.[135] The executive has changed enormously since Federation, in ways that could not have been foreseen by the framers. Government today consists of many thousands of public sector officials, politicised ministerial advisers play an increasingly important role, and there are many non-departmental bodies such as ombudsmen, auditors-general, statutory agencies and government corporations upon which are conferred extensive powers.[136] In *Hughes Aircraft Systems* Finn J described the constitutional status of statutory corporations that are subject to ministerial direction as a significant fissure in Australian jurisprudence.[137]

How should a constitutional framework centred on responsible government and ministerial responsibility deal with these changes? Some see the growth of non-departmental agencies as a threat to responsible government by creating agencies that are not subject to the conventions of ministerial responsibility.[138] Some scholars have argued that modern government ought to conform to responsible government, or more accurately a particular model of responsible government. Geoffrey Lindell argued that the British system of responsible government 'does not countenance the existence of government officials for whom no one is accountable or responsible in the Parliament', and so legislation which creates government entities which are not under the control of

[132] *O'Reilly v Commissioners of State Bank of Victoria* (1983) 153 CLR 1, 11 (Gibbs CJ).

[133] ibid 10–11 (Gibbs CJ), 19–20 (Mason J), 30–31 (Wilson J); *Minister for Aboriginal Affairs v Peko-Wallsend Ltd* (1986) 162 CLR 24, 30–1 (Mason J); *Re Patterson; Ex parte Taylor* (2001) 207 CLR 391, 449 [176] (Gummow and Hayne JJ).

[134] *New South Wales Aboriginal Land Council v Minister Administering the Crown Lands Act* (2014) 88 NSWLR 125, 129 [11].

[135] Terence Daintith and Yee-Fui Ng, 'Executives' in Cheryl Saunders and Adrienne Stone (eds), *The Oxford Handbook of the Australian Constitution* (Oxford, Oxford University Press, 2018) 596; *Ansett Transport Industries (Operations) Pty Ltd v Commonwealth* (1977) 139 CLR 54, 87 (Murphy J).

[136] Margit Cohn, *A Theory of the Executive Branch: Tension and Legality* (Oxford, Oxford University Press, 2021) 31.

[137] *Hughes Aircraft Systems International v Airservices Australia* (1997) 76 FCR 151, 179.

[138] Eg, IDF Callinan, 'Responsible Government – in Dilution' (2008) 52:4 *Quadrant* 16; see discussion in *Royal Commission on Australian Government Administration* (n 48) 90.

a minister may be of questionable constitutional validity.[139] Discussing the position of executive agencies exercising statutory functions, JE Richardson argued that section 61 mandates that the Governor-General must retain a residual role to ensure that Commonwealth legislation is administered consistently with the intention of Parliament, and that any act which sought to remove this residual responsibility would be constitutionally invalid.[140] Such views see a 'strong form' version of ministerial responsibility as central to the accountability of public agencies.[141]

In my view, these arguments are misguided. Ministerial responsibility is unlikely to be an effective form of accountability for the entirety of the public sector.[142] The increasing complexity and size of the modern public sector renders it difficult for Parliaments to hold the executive to account. Parliamentary scrutiny of the executive is ad hoc rather than continuous, and judicial scrutiny has similar limitations, which means that the effectiveness of parliamentary (and judicial) mechanisms of scrutiny depends to a large extent on the structure and organisation of the executive branch itself.[143] It has long been recognised that executives are not accountable solely to Parliament, but also to a network of other actors such as courts, tribunals and investigatory bodies.[144]

Further, I have argued that the governance framework relating to statutory authorities and government corporations creates an intractable agency problem centred in the position of the minister. Under the conventions of responsible government, ministers are expected to hold such entities to account, but they also exercise powers analogous to those exercised by boards of directors and shareholders in relation to private sector companies, such as the power to make board appointments, determine strategy and issue directions. Thus, ministers are expected to hold to account entities for whom they bear some political responsibility and so are not able to fulfil their accountability function impartially.[145] One implication of this is that in order for effective accountability to exist in the public sector, it may be necessary to supplement ministerial responsibility by establishing mechanisms which

[139] Geoffrey Lindell, *Responsible Government and the Australian Constitution – Conventions Transformed into Law?* (Leichhardt, Federation Press, 2004) 18 (emphasis in original removed).

[140] Richardson (n 116) 84–5.

[141] A similar approach was adopted in *Hughes Aircraft Systems International v Airservices Australia* (1997) 76 FCR 151, 245–6 (Finn J); for critique see Christos Mantziaris, 'Interpreting Ministerial Directions to Statutory Corporations: What Does a Theory of Responsible Government Deliver?' (1998) 26 *Federal Law Review* 309.

[142] Richard Mulgan, 'Assessing Ministerial Responsibility in Australia' in Keith Dowding and Chris Lewis (eds), *Ministerial Careers and Accountability in the Australian Commonwealth Government* (Acton, ANU E Press, 2012) 191.

[143] Terence Daintith and Alan Page, *The Executive in the Constitution: Structure, Autonomy, and Internal Control* (Oxford, Oxford University Press, 1999) 4.

[144] RAW Rhodes, John Wanna and Patrick Weller, *Comparing Westminster* (Oxford, Oxford University Press, 2011) 126; Mulgan (n 142) 177, 180.

[145] Benjamin B Saunders, 'Ministers, Statutory Authorities and Government Corporations: The Agency Problem in Public Sector Governance' (2022) 45 *Melbourne University Law Review* 695.

lie outside the traditional structures of parliamentary accountability, including mechanisms within the executive itself. Insisting on the primacy of an outdated conception of responsible government would hinder rather than promote effective accountability. Proposals such as those of Lindell rest on a conception of responsible government which correspond to the nature of government in a bygone age.

A better view is that doctrine should adapt to reality rather than vice versa: that is, the changes that have occurred in government since Federation necessitate a change in the nature of responsible government and our conception of what responsible government requires should evolve to take account of those changed realities. Callinan and Heydon JJ noted in *McKinnon v Secretary, Department of Treasury* that the principle of individual ministerial responsibility needs significant qualification given the nature of modern government departments:

> Departments of public service are today so large, so dispersed throughout the nation, and so numerous in staff, as to make harsh any unqualified application in modern times of the convention that a Minister is responsible for everything that happens or should have happened, or every document produced, in the department that he administers.[146]

This points to the need for flexibility in allowing the executive to be structured so as to attain meaningful accountability.[147] While there has been limited judicial consideration of these issues, the High Court has assumed that the Commonwealth has power to create statutory entities that are not subject to ministerial control[148] and the *Royal Commission on Australian Government Administration* considered that section 64 of the Constitution does not prevent Parliament from conferring powers and functions on executive officers which are exercisable independent of ministers.[149]

D. Enforcing the Conventions of Responsible Government

Some scholars have proposed that responsible government should have greater constitutional effect or even be legally enforceable. George Winterton argued that responsible government is clearly implied in the Constitution and that the High Court has shown a willingness to give 'constitutional status' to at least some of the elements of responsible government.[150] He argued further

[146] *McKinnon v Secretary, Department of Treasury* (2006) 228 CLR 423, 464 [114].

[147] See also Mantziaris (n 141).

[148] See James Stellios, *Zines's the High Court and the Constitution*, 6th edn (Annandale, Federation Press, 2015) 408.

[149] *Royal Commission on Australian Government Administration* (n 48) 61.

[150] George Winterton, *Parliament, the Executive and the Governor-General: A Constitutional Analysis* (Melbourne, Melbourne University Press, 1983) 4–5. See also Cooray (n 85) 23.

that 'the implied constitutional requirement that, except when exercising a 'reserve power', the Governor-General must act only on ministerial advice ought to be judicially enforceable'.[151] James Stellios argued that, as a result of the greater recognition of representative and responsible government by the High Court, '[i]t would seem to follow that the rules, derived from constitutional convention, which are designed to ensure that the will of the people's representatives, and ultimately that of the people themselves, is made effective will also be seen as rules of law implied in the Constitution', especially the conventions that require the Governor-General to act on the advice of ministers and to choose ministers that possess the confidence of the lower house.[152]

There has certainly been a long term trend to extend the 'classes of questions open to judicial investigation',[153] and enforcing the conventions of responsible government would be consistent with this trend. However, the argument of this book suggests that it is unlikely that the courts will enforce the constitutional conventions of responsible government, and probably undesirable for them to do so. The intentions of the framers that lie behind the Constitution are hostile to the enforcement of constitutional conventions, and there is little in the Constitution to warrant such an approach. As Aroney has noted, 'arguments over the enforceability of constitutional conventions turn … ultimately upon arguments founded upon the text and structure of the Constitution itself and the objectively ascertainable intentions that lie behind it'.[154] The provisions of the Constitution that relate to the executive are premised on the distinction between law and convention, assuming that the provisions of the Constitution will be applied and interpreted in accordance with the conventions of responsible government.[155]

Although it has been subjected to criticism, the distinction between law and convention remains generally accepted,[156] and a constitutional convention which has become legally enforceable remains 'one of the holy grails of Commonwealth constitutional scholarship'.[157] Courts will not generally enforce conventions but the consequences for their breach are dealt with by means of

[151] Winterton (n 150) 125.

[152] Stellios, *Zines's the High Court and the Constitution* (n 148) 369.

[153] Geoffrey Sawer, *Federation Under Strain: Australia 1972–1975* (Carlton, Melbourne University Press, 1977) 173.

[154] Nicholas Aroney, 'On the Distinction Between Law and Convention' in Brian Galligan and Scott Brenton (eds), *Constitutional Conventions in Westminster Systems* (Cambridge, Cambridge University Press, 2015) 43.

[155] Moore, *The Constitution of the Commonwealth of Australia* (n 90) 168–9.

[156] See, eg, *Egan v Willis* (1998) 195 CLR 424, 443 [20], 449 [36], 454 [50] (Gaudron, Gummow and Hayne JJ), 510 [182] (Callinan J).

[157] NW Barber, 'Laws and Constitutional Conventions' (2009) 125 *Law Quarterly Review* 294, 302; Geoffrey Marshall, *Constitutional Conventions: The Rules and Forms of Political Accountability* (Oxford, Clarendon Press, 1987) 15, 210–11. See contra Farrah Ahmed, Richard Albert and Adam Perry, 'Judging Constitutional Conventions' (2019) 17 *International Journal of Constitutional Law* 787.

the political process.[158] The framers of the Constitution 'plainly believed that there is a sharp distinction to be drawn between law and convention and that the Constitution must reflect this distinction'.[159] Thus, without clear warrant from the text and structure of the Constitution, and given that the Constitution reflects a clear distinction between law and convention, it seems unlikely that the courts would take this step.

Further, while the incorporation of responsible government into the Constitution provides the basis for arguing that its conventions should be enforceable, the conception of responsible government which underlies the Constitution militates against the enforcement of conventions. As chapter six argued, the functioning of responsible government under the Australian constitutional system is inherently political. While it is difficult to draw a hard distinction between the realms of 'law' and 'politics',[160] it remains true that the conduct of politics is for the political realm, with the government accountable to the electorate for the conduct of government. The political process is the primary constitutional means of holding executive officers to account and providing remedies for poor governmental performance.[161] The consistency of governmental actions with constitutional conventions 'occurs in a zone of governmental activity that the Australian constitutional system allocates to branches other than the judiciary, branches that are accountable through the political process to the people'.[162]

Further, if the purpose of seeking to constitutionalise conventions is to ensure the good functioning of government, then those proposals are unlikely to have their desired effect. This book has emphasised that a fundamental aspect of the Australian tradition of responsible government is a strongly political conception of constitutionalism whereby the conduct and practice of government cannot be prescribed by law but depends on the character of the people and their representatives. As James Bryce put it, '[t]o expect any form of words, however weightily conceived, with whatever sanctions enacted, permanently to restrain the passions and interests of men is to expect the impossible'.[163] For instance, rendering the

[158] Amanda Sapienza, *Judicial Review of Non-Statutory Executive Action* (Alexandria, Federation Press, 2020) 85.

[159] Aroney, 'On the Distinction Between Law and Convention' (n 154) 42.

[160] *Melbourne Corporation v Commonwealth* (1947) 74 CLR 31, 82 (Dixon J).

[161] *McCloy v New South Wales* (2015) 257 CLR 178, 226–7 [111]–[113] (Gageler J); *Marks v Commonwealth* (1964) 111 CLR 549, 557–558 (Kitto J); *Amalgamated Society of Engineers v Adelaide Steamship Co Ltd* (1920) 28 CLR 129, 151–2 (Knox CJ, Isaacs, Rich and Starke JJ); *Australian Communist Party v Commonwealth* (1951) 83 CLR 1, 152–4 (Latham CJ), 242 (Webb J); *Theodore v Duncan* [1919] AC 696, 706 (Viscount Haldane); Stephen Gageler, 'Foundations of Australian Federalism and the Role of Judicial Review' (1987) 17 *Federal Law Review* 162.

[162] Sapienza (n 158) 86. See also *R (Miller) v Secretary of State for Exiting the European Union* [2018] AC 61, 164–6 [141]–[146].

[163] James Bryce, *The American* Commonwealth, 2nd edn (London, Macmillan, 1891) vol 1, 270, 291, 396. See also Hearn (n 51) 116, 176, 190.

conventions of responsible government judicially enforceable could have the effect of requiring a Governor-General to follow ministerial advice. However, no mandate from a court could force an opposition – or a government – to act with propriety, however that might be defined.

Finally, another key theme of this book is that responsible government is an inherently flexible system. The Constitution is intended to enable the Australian people to govern themselves politically, and so entrenches few of the features of responsible government. It seems likely that the result of constitutionalising the conventions of responsible government would be to introduce rigidity where flexibility is required. As Anne Twomey put it, '[t]he point of relying on conventions and eschewing rigid rules is to achieve the flexibility that ensures the Constitution is capable of adapting to changed conditions, rather than snapping and breaking under strict rules that have become unworkable'.[164]

E. Implied Freedom of Political Communication

As is well known, the High Court has discerned an implied freedom of political communication in the Constitution, which imposes constraints on the ability of the Commonwealth Parliament (and the state and territory Parliaments) to enact laws which limit the freedom to communicate in relation to government and political matters.[165] This freedom was derived from the system of representative and responsible government established by the Constitution, especially the requirement in sections 7 and 24 that members of Parliament must be 'directly chosen by the people', and also the conventions of responsible government and the provisions of the Constitution that assume the existence of those conventions.[166] In more recent cases this has developed into a constitutionally entrenched guarantee of universal adult suffrage subject to reasonable and proportionate limitations[167] and a guarantee of '[e]quality of opportunity to participate in the exercise of political sovereignty'.[168] The Court has not extended the freedom to encompass freedom of association or movement beyond any protection which is afforded as a corollary of the freedom of communication.[169]

[164] Anne Twomey, *The Veiled Sceptre: Reserve Powers of Heads of State in Westminster Systems* (Cambridge, Cambridge University Press, 2018) 28.

[165] *Lange v Australian Broadcasting Corporation* (1997) 189 CLR 520; *Nationwide News Pty Ltd v Wills* (1992) 177 CLR 1; *Australian Capital Television Pty Ltd v Commonwealth* (1992) 177 CLR 106; *Coleman v Power* (2004) 220 CLR 1; *Unions NSW v New South Wales* (2013) 252 CLR 530.

[166] *McCloy v New South Wales* (2015) 257 CLR 178, 222–3 [101]–[102] (Gageler J).

[167] *Roach v Electoral Commissioner* (2007) 233 CLR 162.

[168] *McCloy v New South Wales* (2015) 257 CLR 178, 207 [45] (French CJ, Kiefel, Bell and Keane JJ).

[169] *Gerner v Victoria* (2020) 270 CLR 412, 426–7 [24] (Kiefel CJ, Gageler, Keane, Gordon and Edelman JJ); *Mulholland v Australian Electoral Commission* (2004) 220 CLR 181, 234 [148] (Gummow and Hayne JJ), 297 [334]–[335] (Callinan J), 306 [364] (Heydon J); *Wainohu v New South Wales* (2011) 243 CLR 181, 230 [112] (Gummow, Hayne, Crennan and Bell JJ); *Tajjour v New South*

The account of responsible government developed in this book might be thought to support the existence of the implied freedom. Chapter six noted that one of the key elements of responsible government as incorporated into the constitutional system was popular sovereignty, namely the self-government of the Australian people acting through the political mechanisms of Parliament. This could be thought to be consistent with the drawing of an implication which restricts the ability of Parliament to limit political communication. Several justices have argued that the implied freedom of political communication is necessary to promote the political sovereignty of the people because it is indispensable to enable the people to 'exercise a free and informed choice as electors'.[170] Keane J and other judges have argued that the implied freedom of communication serves 'to preserve the political sovereignty of the people of the Commonwealth' by ensuring that there is a free flow of political communication among the Australian people.[171] As put by Kiefel CJ, Keane and Gleeson JJ in *LibertyWorks Inc v Commonwealth*, the freedom 'is recognised as necessarily implied because the great underlying principle of the Constitution is that citizens are to share equally in political power and because it is only by a freedom to communicate on these matters that citizens may exercise a free and informed choice as electors'.[172]

I argue that this is misconceived. While it is true that the Constitution assumes the operation of responsible government, the particular nature of responsible government provided for by the Constitution is not conducive to the drawing of judicially-enforceable implications from that fact. The account developed by this book is that responsible government is deliberately flexible, intended to allow the politically sovereign people of Australia to govern themselves in the manner they wish. The framers of the Constitution refused to entrench the key features of responsible government other than the requirement that ministers must be members of Parliament on the ground that responsible government is something to be shaped and moulded by the people of each generation. The nature of responsible government as inherently evolutionary and flexible suggests that the Court ought to be cautious before deriving implications from the Constitution which limit the ability of the people to govern

Wales (2014) 254 CLR 508, 566–7 [95] (Hayne J), 576–8 [136]–[143] (Gageler J), 605–6 [242]–[245] (Keane J).

[170] *Gerner v Victoria* (2020) 270 CLR 412, 426 [24] (Kiefel CJ, Gageler, Keane, Gordon and Edelman JJ); *Coleman v Power* (2004) 220 CLR 1, 48 [89] (McHugh J).

[171] *Unions NSW v New South Wales* (2013) 252 CLR 530, 578 [135] (Keane J); *Tajjour v New South Wales* (2014) 254 CLR 508, 593 [196], 601 [225] (Keane J); *Brown v Tasmania* (2017) 261 CLR 328, 359 [88] (Kiefel CJ, Bell and Keane JJ); *Unions NSW v New South Wales* (2019) 264 CLR 595, 614 [40] (Kiefel CJ, Bell and Keane JJ); *Clubb v Edwards* (2019) 267 CLR 171, 196 [51] (Kiefel CJ, Bell and Keane JJ).

[172] *LibertyWorks Inc v Commonwealth* (2021) 95 ALJR 490, 503–4 [44] (Kiefel CJ, Keane and Gleeson JJ).

themselves. And it is 'a distinctly unsound approach' to adopt an interpretation of the Constitution that the framers were 'united in rejecting'.[173]

The view of some judges that there is a risk of legislative or executive impairment of 'the capacity of, or opportunity for, the Australian people to form the political judgments required for the exercise of their constitutional functions'[174] and which needs to be safeguarded by the courts is somewhat paradoxical. While it is conceivable that the people may need to be protected from legislative or executive overreach, under the system of representative and responsible government established by the Constitution, members of Parliament are elected by and accountable to the people. Parliament is therefore an emanation of the people, and its role is to govern in the public interest, in accordance with the wishes of those people. As Edelman J noted in *Comcare v Banerji*, it is 'fundamentally important, and indeed essential, that in a system of modern representative government a parliament has freedom to make laws that implement the policy decisions it makes for the welfare of the governed'.[175] The imposition by the courts of a constitutional restriction on Parliament's capacity to legislate in the public interest is akin to mandating that the people need to be protected from themselves.

Constitutional restrictions on legislative and executive power imposed by the courts limit the power of the Australian people to govern themselves and implement laws for the public interest. The enormous irony of the implied freedom cases is that, while professing to reject an approach to constitutional interpretation which deprived 'what was intended to be a living instrument of its vitality and its adaptability to serve succeeding generations',[176] that is precisely their effect.

The implied freedom has attracted significant criticism. Nicholas Aroney has argued that the reasoning employed by the High Court to justify the derivation of the implied freedom consists of a series of 'third order' implications and the importation of a concept of representative government which the Constitution does not expressly provide for.[177] As such, although the High Court claimed that the implied freedom was a necessary implication derived from the text and structure of the Constitution,[178] the idea of freedom of political communication employed by the Court has only 'a very tenuous relationship to the text

[173] *Gerner v Victoria* (2020) 270 CLR 412, 429 [34] (Kiefel CJ, Gageler, Keane, Gordon and Edelman JJ), citing *Codelfa Construction Pty Ltd v State Rail Authority (NSW)* (1982) 149 CLR 337, 353.

[174] *Nationwide News Pty Ltd v Wills* (1992) 177 CLR 1, 51 (Brennan J); *McCloy v New South Wales* (2015) 257 CLR 178, 227 [114]–[115] (Gageler J).

[175] *Comcare v Banerji* (2019) 267 CLR 373, 457 [205] (Edelman J).

[176] *Theophanous v Herald & Weekly Times Ltd* (1994) 182 CLR 104, 171 (Deane J).

[177] Nicholas Aroney, *Freedom of Speech in the Constitution* (St Leonards, Centre for Independent Studies, 1998). Aroney defines 'third-order implications' as 'good' or 'desirable' applications of constitutional provisions: 99–100.

[178] *Lange v Australian Broadcasting Corporation* (1997) 189 CLR 520, 566–7 (Brennan CJ, Dawson, Toohey, Gaudron, McHugh, Gummow and Kirby JJ).

or structure of the Constitution'.[179] Jeffrey Goldsworthy has argued that the implied freedom is not a necessary or obvious implication from the Constitution and that the framers deliberately chose not to include a judicially enforceable right to free speech in the Constitution: thus, while free speech is necessary, 'a judicially enforceable right to it is not'.[180] Against these views, Patrick Emerton has argued that the existence of the implied freedom 'follows from a simple consideration of what is required for a political event to be an instance of direct choice, as the Constitution mandates'.[181] The account of responsible government developed by this book adds weight to the critiques of the implied freedom made by scholars such as Aroney and Goldsworthy.

The implied freedom can be seen as reflecting the tension that exists between legal and political constitutionalism in Australia, perhaps due to persistent concern that the judiciary may be straying beyond its legitimate role.[182] There has been substantial deference to legislative judgement and legislation has only rarely been invalidated on the basis that it infringes the implied freedom.[183] This arguably reflects the inherently political nature of constitutionalism in Australia, and the fact that there is little direct textual support in the Constitution for the implied freedom: Edelman J noted that determining the boundaries of free speech is 'generally the province of parliament; the judiciary can constrain the choices of a parliament only at the outer margins for reasons of systemic protection'.[184] A more intrusive standard of review would risk interfering with the political sovereignty that it is the ostensible purpose of the implied freedom to protect.

This tension is also reflected in the nature of the test applied by the High Court.[185] In order to be compatible with the implied freedom, a law which burdens the freedom of communication in relation to government or political matters must serve a legitimate purpose and be reasonably appropriate

[179] Nicholas Aroney, 'A Seductive Plausibility: Freedom of Speech in the Constitution' (1995) 8 *University of Queensland Law Journal* 249, 259.

[180] Jeffrey Goldsworthy, 'Constitutional Implications Revisited' (2011) 30 *University of Queensland Law Journal* 9, 28.

[181] Emerton (n 57) 194.

[182] James Stellios, 'Using Federalism to Protect Political Communication: Implications from Federal Representative Government' (2007) 31 *Melbourne University Law Review* 239, 241.

[183] ibid 245. Cases which have invalidated legislative provisions on the basis they infringe the implied freedom include *Nationwide News Pty Ltd v Wills* (1992) 177 CLR 1; *Australian Capital Television Pty Ltd v Commonwealth* (1992) 177 CLR 106; *Unions NSW v New South Wales* (2013) 252 CLR 530; *Brown v Tasmania* (2017) 261 CLR 328. See also *Clubb v Edwards* (2019) 267 CLR 171, 239 [207] (Gageler J).

[184] *Comcare v Banerji* (2019) 267 CLR 373, 442 [164], see also 457 [205] (Edelman J).

[185] There is an ongoing debate among members of the Court about the proper test to be applied when determining whether the implied freedom has been infringed: *McCloy v New South Wales* (2015) 257 CLR 178, 235–7 [141]–[148] (Gageler J), 288–9 [338]–[339] (Gordon J); *Murphy v Electoral Commissioner* (2016) 261 CLR 28, 72–4 [101]–[110] (Gageler J), 123–4 [299]–[305] (Gordon J); *Brown v Tasmania* (2017) 261 CLR 328, 376–9 [159]–[166] (Gageler J), 461–8 [415]–[438] (Gordon J).

and adapted to advance that legitimate object in a manner that is 'compatible with the maintenance of the constitutionally prescribed system of representative and responsible government'.[186] While it may be true that the freedom to communicate on political matters 'is of such importance to representative government that any effective statutory burden upon it must be justified',[187] it does not follow that the appropriate body in which that justification ought to be carried out is the High Court.[188] As Stephen Gardbaum has argued, 'too great a focus on legal and judicial rights reasoning' may come 'at the expense of more independent political judgment that takes a broader and more direct approach to the moral and policy issues involved'.[189]

Indeed, there exist mechanisms for examining the compatibility of legislation with rights within the executive and legislative branches. Those who develop and scrutinise legislative proposals and draft legislation, namely government departments and Parliament, may be expected to weigh the benefits of legislative proposals in light of any infringements of rights or liberty. The Commonwealth *Legislation Handbook* requires consideration within the executive of the impact of legislation on rights, providing that the Attorney-General's Department should be consulted on legislative proposals that may be inconsistent with international human rights instruments.[190] The Attorney-General's Department has also published guidance for Commonwealth policy makers to assess the human rights compatibility of Bills and legislative instruments.[191]

In the Commonwealth, as well as Victoria, Queensland and the Australian Capital Territory, there exists a parliamentary process for examining the compatibility of legislation with human rights, including the preparation of a statement of compatibility with human rights, although these mechanisms may have limited impact in practice.[192] Statements of compatibility typically consider whether the Bill advances a legitimate objective, the extent to which rights are limited, and whether any limitations on rights 'are reasonable, necessary and

[186] *Lange v Australian Broadcasting Corporation* (1997) 189 CLR 520, 561–2, 567–8 (Brennan CJ, Dawson, Toohey, Gaudron, McHugh, Gummow and Kirby JJ); *Coleman v Power* (2004) 220 CLR 1, 51 [95]–[96] (McHugh J), 78 [196] (Gummow and Hayne JJ), 82 [211] (Kirby J); *McCloy v New South Wales* (2015) 257 CLR 178, 193–5 [1]–[2] (French CJ, Kiefel, Bell and Keane JJ); *Brown v Tasmania* (2017) 261 CLR 328, 363–4 [104] (Kiefel CJ, Bell and Keane JJ).

[187] *LibertyWorks Inc v Commonwealth* (2021) 95 ALJR 490, 504 [45] ((Kiefel CJ, Keane and Gleeson JJ).

[188] See Rosalind Dixon, *Responsive Judicial Review: Democracy and Dysfunction in the Modern Age* (New York, Oxford University Press, 2023) ch 4.

[189] Stephen Gardbaum, *The New Commonwealth Model of Constitutionalism: Theory and Practice* (Cambridge, Cambridge University Press, 2013) 237.

[190] Department of the Prime Minister and Cabinet, *Legislation Handbook* (Canberra, Commonwealth of Australia, 1999) [6.34].

[191] Attorney-General's Department, 'Tools for Assessing Compatibility with Human Rights' www.ag.gov.au/rights-and-protections/human-rights-and-anti-discrimination/human-rights-scrutiny/tools-assessing-compatibility-human-rights.

[192] Human Rights (Parliamentary Scrutiny) Act 2011 (Cth), ss 7–9; Human Rights Act 2004 (ACT), ss 37–38; Charter of Human Rights and Responsibilities Act 2006 (Vic), ss 28–30; Human Rights Act 2019 (Qld), ss 38–41.

proportionate to the legitimate objective of the Bill'.[193] This, of course, is very similar – almost identical – to the test applied by the courts when considering whether a law infringes the implied freedom.

That is, the Court's implied freedom analysis considers whether legislative burdens on the freedom to communicate in relation to political matters are justified, applying largely the same test as that employed within the executive and parliamentary processes, with reference to a much narrower range of rights, and, except in rare cases, typically reaching the same conclusion. It may be queried what further benefit to the Australian political and constitutional system arises from this duplicative judicial scrutiny. The Court is seemingly reluctant to adopt a more intrusive standard of review given that it is primarily Parliament's role to determine the boundaries of free speech,[194] and that more intrusive review would limit the power of the Australian people to govern themselves.

F. Executive Power and Parliamentary Control

The courts have struggled to resolve the question of the extent of non-statutory executive power in a satisfactory fashion.[195] In several recent cases the High Court has employed the principle of responsible government in significantly re-shaping Commonwealth executive power. This issue can be seen to reflect the tension between legal and political approaches to constitutionalism and also competing conceptions of responsible government.

One aspect of executive power that has been accompanied by persistent uncertainty is the extent to which prior statutory authority is required for government action such as entering into contracts.[196] In *Churchward v The Queen*, Shee J referred to the 'notorious inability of the crown to contract unconditionally for such money payments in consideration of such services'.[197] On the one hand, '[i]t is a function of the Executive, not of Parliament, to make contracts on behalf of the Crown', and this is a power exercised by ministers. The duty of Parliament, on the other hand, is '[d]eliberation, and not despatch'.[198] However, a well-accepted constitutional principle is that the expenditure of funds by the executive requires parliamentary appropriation. Should the executive have power to enter into binding contracts which commit it to make payments without parliamentary approval?

[193] Eg, Explanatory Memorandum, Foreign Influence Transparency Scheme Bill 2017 (Cth) [85].

[194] *Comcare v Banerji* (2019) 267 CLR 373, 442 [164], 457 [205] (Edelman J).

[195] Stellios, *Zines's the High Court and the Constitution* (n 148) 380–7.

[196] See Nicholas Seddon, *Government Contracts: Federal State and Local*, 6th edn (Leichhardt, Federation Press, 2018) ch 2.

[197] *Churchward v R* (1865) LR 1 QB 173, 209.

[198] *New South Wales v Bardolph* (1934) 52 CLR 455, 509 (Dixon J), 472 (Evatt J), quoting AJV Durell, *The Principles and Practice of the System of Control over Parliamentary Grants* (Portsmouth, Gieves, 1917) 20.

In answering this question, the principles of responsible government have been employed to reach very different conclusions. It has been argued that contracts with the executive do not possess legal validity unless authorised by Parliament.[199] In some early cases Isaacs J appeared to argue that statutory authorisation is necessary for contracts entered into by the executive to be valid. His Honour held in the *Wool Tops* case that 'the Crown's discretion to make contracts involving the expenditure of public money would not be entrusted to ministers unless Parliament had sanctioned it', on the basis that:

> Parliamentary discretion would be severely fettered if the Executive could make a compact binding the Crown in law to pay away portion of the public funds and leaving to Parliament the alternative of assenting to the payment or disavowing a public obligation. That would be seriously weakening the control by Parliament over the public Treasury.[200]

However, that was not the accepted position. The 'general constitutional principle' was that contracts entered into by the executive for the expenditure of money within power were considered valid, subject to a condition that parliamentary appropriation is necessary before funds are paid under the contract.[201] Thus, the general doctrine was that 'all obligations to pay money undertaken by the Crown are subject to the implied condition that the funds necessary to satisfy the obligation shall be appropriated by Parliament'.[202] Indeed, in 1930, Isaacs J (then Isaacs CJ) himself accepted that this was the position.[203] That is, the courts drew a distinction between the validity of contracts and their enforcement, and parliamentary approval was not a condition precedent to the validity of a contract.[204]

This is not to suggest that the executive's power to enter into contracts was unlimited. Evatt J's well-known statement in *New South Wales v Bardolph* that the Crown 'never seems to have been regarded as being less powerful to enter into contracts than one of his subjects'[205] appears broad, but is narrower when read in its context. Evatt J laid down three criteria for the validity of government contracts, namely that such contracts must be entered into in the ordinary course of government administration, authorised by a responsible minister and referable to a parliamentary appropriation.[206] As such, the case can be understood

[199] *New South Wales v Bardolph* (1934) 52 CLR 455, 501 (Starke J).

[200] *Commonwealth v Colonial Combing, Spinning and Weaving Co Ltd* (1922) 31 CLR 421, 448–51 (Isaacs J) (*'Wool Tops Case'*); *Commonwealth v Colonial Ammunition Co Ltd* (1924) 34 CLR 198, 220 (Isaacs and Rich JJ).

[201] *Churchward v R* (1865) LR 1 QB 173, 209 (Shee J); *New South Wales v Bardolph* (1934) 52 CLR 455, 467 (Evatt J), 498 (Rich J).

[202] *New South Wales v Commonwealth* (1932) 46 CLR 155, 176 (Rich and Dixon JJ).

[203] *Australian Railways Union v Railways Commissioners (Vic)* (1930) 44 CLR 319, 353 (Isaacs CJ).

[204] *New South Wales v Bardolph* (1934) 52 CLR 455, 475 (Evatt J), 498 (Rich J), 510, 514 (Dixon J); *Australian Railways Union v Railways Commissioners (Vic)* (1930) 44 CLR 319, 353 (Isaacs CJ).

[205] *New South Wales v Bardolph* (1934) 52 CLR 455, 475.

[206] ibid 474.

to stand for the proposition that, as put by Rich J, 'the Crown has a power independent of statute to make such contracts for the public service as are incidental to the ordinary and well-recognized functions of Government',[207] which is a concept that has been heavily criticised.[208] Further, while Evatt J's statement may be generally true of the Crown, it would not apply in the Commonwealth; thus, the High Court has held that the Commonwealth does not possess a general power to contract.[209]

In determining the scope of the executive's non-statutory power to enter into contracts, the principle of responsible government has been employed to widely divergent effect. As noted, in the *Wool Tops* case, Isaacs J considered that responsible government requires that the executive's power to contract is limited, otherwise this would make a nullity of parliamentary control of finance.[210] By contrast, Evatt J held in *Bardolph* that a requirement that all expenditure under every contract entered into by the Crown must be expressly authorised in an Act of Parliament would reduce to a nullity the responsibility of ministers for the ordinary course of governmental administration.[211] Dixon J held as follows:

> The principles of responsible government impose upon the administration a responsibility to Parliament, or rather to the House which deals with finance, for what the Administration has done. It is a function of the Executive, not of Parliament, to make contracts on behalf of the Crown. The Crown's advisers are answerable politically to Parliament for their acts in making contracts. ... But the principles of responsible government do not disable the Executive from acting without the prior approval of Parliament, nor from contracting for the expenditure of moneys conditionally upon appropriation by Parliament and doing so before funds to answer the expenditure have actually been made legally available.[212]

That is, Evatt J and Dixon J argued that under the system of responsible government it is sufficient for there to be general parliamentary oversight of the activities undertaken by the executive, and it was not necessary for there to be prior authorisation for every individual contract. This reflects a largely flexible and political model of accountability under which the executive has discretion to act and is accountable politically to Parliament for the exercise of its powers.

Recent cases have employed the concept of responsible government to radically re-shape and restrict the content of Commonwealth executive power. It is not controversial that the constitutional relationship between Parliament and the executive imposes limitations on executive power. Among other things,

[207] ibid 462, 474 (Evatt J), 496 (Rich J), 502–3 (Starke J), 507–8 (Dixon J).
[208] Enid Campbell, 'Federal Contract Law' (1970) 44 *Australian Law Journal* 14; Enid Campbell, 'Commonwealth Contracts' (1970) 44 *Australian Law Journal* 580.
[209] *Commonwealth v Colonial Combing, Spinning and Weaving Co Ltd* (1922) 31 CLR 421.
[210] ibid 448–51 (Isaacs J).
[211] *New South Wales v Bardolph* (1934) 52 CLR 455, 471–2.
[212] *New South Wales v Bardolph* (1934) 52 CLR 455, 509.

executive power cannot change the law, create an offence, impose taxation, authorise detention in a time of peace or dispense with obedience to the law.[213] This relationship also means that the prerogative is not capable of increasing.[214] In recent cases, members of the High Court have gone considerably beyond this to limit the scope of the executive power of the Commonwealth based on the concept of responsible government. In *Pape v Federal Commissioner of Taxation* the Court held that sections 81 and 83 of the Constitution do not confer power on the Commonwealth to spend monies and that such a power must be found in another provision of the Constitution such as section 61 or a valid statute.[215] The constitutional relationship between Parliament and the executive, including the principles of responsible government, was an important aspect of the reasoning of the majority judges.[216] For instance, Hayne and Kiefel JJ wrote:

> determination of the ambit of the Commonwealth Executive's power in matters of raising and expending public moneys must not ignore the carefully delineated intersection between the respective roles of the Executive and the Parliament that not only lies at the centre of a proper understanding of the provisions of Pt V of Ch I and Ch IV of the Constitution but also informs the meaning that is to be given to s 61 in matters of executive power with respect to public moneys.[217]

In *Williams v Commonwealth (No 1)* the Court held that the Commonwealth executive power in section 61 does not include a general power to contract and spend money in relation to matters which fall within the heads of Commonwealth legislative power. French CJ considered that a Commonwealth executive with 'a general power to deal with matters of Commonwealth legislative competence ... would undermine parliamentary control of the executive branch and weaken the role of the Senate'.[218] Gummow and Bell JJ held that a proposition 'that the spending power of the executive branch of government is co-extensive with those activities which could be the subject of legislation supported by any head of power in section 51 of the Constitution' should not be accepted because that

[213] Sapienza (n 158) 16; Peta Stephenson, 'The Relationship between the Royal Prerogative and Statute in Australia' (2021) 44 *Melbourne University Law Review* 1001, 1003.

[214] *British Broadcasting Corporation v Johns* [1965] Ch 32, 79 (Diplock LJ); *R v Secretary of State for the Home Department; Ex parte Northumbria Police Authority* [1989] 1 QB 26; Winterton, *Parliament, the Executive and the Governor-General* (n 150) 120; George Winterton, 'The Prerogative in Novel Situations' (1983) 99 *Law Quarterly Review* 407, 408; Anne Twomey, 'Pushing the Boundaries of Executive Power: Pape, the Prerogative and Nationhood Powers' (2010) 34 *Melbourne University Law Review* 313, 319–20; Peter Gerangelos, 'The Executive Power of the Commonwealth of Australia: Section 61 of the Commonwealth *Constitution*, 'Nationhood' and the Future of the Prerogative' (2012) 12 *Oxford University Commonwealth Law Journal* 97, 121–2, 126–7.

[215] *Pape v Federal Commissioner of Taxation* (2009) 238 CLR 1, 55 [111] (French CJ), 73 [178], 75 [184]–[186] (Gummow, Crennan and Bell JJ), 113 [320] (Hayne and Kiefel JJ), 210 [600], 212–3 [606]–[607] (Heydon J).

[216] *Pape v Federal Commissioner of Taxation* (2009) 238 CLR 1, 36–45 [53]–[80] (French CJ), 72–75 [175]–[186] (Gummow, Crennan and Bell JJ), 103–5 [291]–[296] (Hayne and Kiefel JJ).

[217] ibid 119 [338] (Hayne and Kiefel JJ).

[218] *Williams v Commonwealth* (2012) 248 CLR 156, 205 [60].

would undermine 'the basal assumption of legislative predominance inherited from the United Kingdom and so would distort the relationship between Ch I and Ch II of the Constitution'.[219] Crennan J held that the principles of responsible government and parliamentary control of the executive 'operate inevitably to constrain the Commonwealth's capacities to contract and to spend',[220] but without specifying what those constraints are. Kiefel J cryptically held that '[c]onsiderations as to the supremacy of Parliament which underlie the doctrine of responsible government may provide a basis for limiting executive power to certain of the legislative heads of power'.[221]

The conception of responsible government articulated in this book casts considerable doubt on the reasoning underlying these cases. As enshrined in the Constitution, responsible government provides a means by which the exercise of executive power is held to account by requiring that ministers must be members of Parliament. It has little or nothing to say about the *content* of that power. There is no universal institution called responsible government, but rather 'infinite varieties and infinite degrees of a responsible government'; as Holroyd J wrote in 1888, '[t]here is no cut-and-dried institution called responsible government, identical in all countries where it exists'.[222] The mere fact that the Australian Constitution assumes the principles of responsible government of itself has few implications for the scope of the executive power conferred by section 61.

Further, the Australian Constitution contemplates a fundamentally political system of constitutionalism, under which the functioning of that system depends on the character of the people and their representatives. Parliamentary accountability in relation to the executive may be exercised through legislation, by specifying the content of executive power and imposing conditions on its exercise, or by scrutinising the conduct of the executive through such mechanisms as question time, committee inquiries and estimates hearings. Thus, while it is not in doubt that Parliament has power to regulate the exercise of power through legislation, this is not the only means by which Parliament holds the executive to account. It is simply not true that 'the Parliament can control expenditure only by legislation'.[223] And it is for Parliament, not the courts, to determine the manner in which it exercises this oversight.

The *Williams* litigation and its aftermath also illustrates a key theme of this book, namely that good governance in public institutions cannot be mandated by law. Under the principles of responsible government, the executive is accountable to Parliament, and the effectiveness of that accountability depends on political considerations. As noted by Stellios, '[w]hat seems to be at the heart of

[219] ibid 232 [134]–[136].
[220] ibid 351–2 [516], 358 [544].
[221] ibid 370 [581].
[222] *Chung Teong Toy v Musgrove* (1888) 14 VLR 349, 418–9 (Williams J), 428 (Holroyd J).
[223] *Williams v Commonwealth* (2012) 248 CLR 156, 271 [252] (Hayne J).

the majority judgments in *Williams v Commonwealth (No 1)* is a concern about the perceived failures of representative and responsible government', driven by executive dominance of the House of Representatives and the limited control provided by the appropriation process.[224] Thus, the High Court's decision was based on a view that responsible government demands that the executive must engage with the Parliament in a particular way when spending public money, namely by obtaining prior parliamentary authorisation in legislation.[225] Gummow and Bell JJ in particular were concerned to ensure greater engagement by the executive with the institutions of representative government.[226]

However, it is doubtful that the court's assertion of control over responsible government[227] was successful in achieving this aim, as can be seen by the legislative response to *Williams v Commonwealth (No 1)*. The High Court handed down its decision on 20 June 2012, holding that the impugned expenditure was beyond power. As a result of this ruling, many Commonwealth funding programs were put at risk of invalidity. Parliament therefore passed correcting legislation to ensure the validity of the programs.[228] The relevant Bill was introduced into the House of Representatives on 26 June 2012 – less than one week after the High Court's decision – and passed on the same day. It was introduced into the Senate on the following day and also passed that same day. Amendments were proposed in both Houses of Parliament, including a sunset clause which was intended to ensure that the constitutional validity of the Bill could be considered properly, but none were accepted.[229] In *Williams v Commonwealth (No 2)* the Court held that the correcting legislation was not valid in its operation with respect to the Scripture Union Queensland Funding Agreement and payments made under that agreement, but did not otherwise invalidate the correcting legislation.[230]

Delimiting executive power in legislation can of course bring important benefits.[231] However, it is doubtful that merely collating a list of broadly worded Commonwealth funded programs and appending them in subordinate legislation in order to ensure their validity represents meaningful engagement with the

[224] Stellios, *Zines's the High Court and the Constitution* (n 148) 397.

[225] Sapienza (n 158) 13–14.

[226] *Williams v Commonwealth* (2012) 248 CLR 156, 235 [145].

[227] Stellios, *Zines's the High Court and the Constitution* (n 148) 397.

[228] The Financial Framework Legislation Amendment Act (No 3) (Cth), which introduced a new Division 3B into the Financial Management and Accountability Act 1997 (Cth), providing that the Commonwealth has power to administer arrangements under which public money may be payable by the Commonwealth which are specified in regulations. The Act also inserted a new Schedule 1AA into the Financial Management and Accountability Regulations 1997 (Cth) which listed a broad range of such funding programs.

[229] Commonwealth, *Parliamentary Debates*, Senate, 27 June 2012 (George Brandis) 4653.

[230] *Williams v Commonwealth (No 2)* (2014) 252 CLR 416, 456 [32], 457 [36] (French CJ, Hayne, Kiefel, Bell and Keane JJ).

[231] Margit Cohn has argued that, 'in the absence of a clear authorization to act', executive action, especially non-statutory executive action, 'challenges the legitimacy of modern democratic government and carries a higher potential for unchecked abuse': Cohn (n 136) 257.

institutions of representative government[232] or adds any meaningful accountability in relation to the administration of those programs.[233] The legislation which supported the validity of the impugned spending programs was designed 'by the same executive organs which formulated, introduced and administered appropriation legislation', and is now protected by 'a façade of 'parliamentary control''.[234] If it is true that underlying the Court's decision was a 'concern about the perceived failures of representative and responsible government',[235] and a desire to 'prod' Parliament to perform its supervisory obligations more effectively,[236] then the Court's attempt to prod Parliament foundered on the political realities which caused the deficiencies with representative and responsible government in the first place – assuming they are in fact deficiencies. Given that the executive politically controls Parliament, which is one of the key concerns that drove the majority decision in *Williams*, any control of the executive that results from the decision in *Williams v Commonwealth (No 1)* may amount to little in practice. The *Williams* litigation and its legislative aftermath can be seen as illustrative of the difficulties of attempting legal solutions to political problems.

In addition, the Court's approach reflects an anachronistic conception of the nature of government that was hardly accurate in the 'golden age of parliamentary government', let alone today. As chapter two of this book argued, by the mid-nineteenth century British politics was carried on by means of a two-party system, characterised by relatively high levels of party cohesion, and cabinet dominated the proceedings of the House of Commons.[237] Even during the mythic golden age of parliamentary government the executive had by far the predominant power in relation to public finance. Parliament allocated the initiative in financial matters to the executive, which formulated and originated the majority of public financial legislation.[238] The system of public expenditure during the nineteenth century 'left an enormous degree of flexibility to the executive … and was predominately retrospective'.[239] The consequence of this was to give significant levels of control to Treasury, which 'exercised all significant financial planning authority, leaving Parliament to rubber-stamp expenditure legislation and impotent to create tax laws'.[240] This trend towards

[232] As desired by Gummow and Bell JJ: *Williams v Commonwealth* (2012) 248 CLR 156, 235 [145].
[233] See Seddon (n 196) 71–2.
[234] Will Bateman, *Public Finance and Parliamentary Constitutionalism* (Cambridge, Cambridge University Press, 2020) 187.
[235] Stellios, *Zines's the High Court and the Constitution* (n 148) 397.
[236] Gabrielle Appleby, 'Unwritten Rules' in Cheryl Saunders and Adrienne Stone (eds), *The Oxford Handbook of the Australian Constitution* (Oxford, Oxford University Press, 2018) 219.
[237] Angus Hawkins, *British Party Politics, 1852–1886* (New York, St Martin's Press, 1998); Gary W Cox, *The Efficient Secret: The Cabinet and the Development of Political Parties in Victorian England* (Cambridge, Cambridge University Press, 1987).
[238] Bateman (n 234) 51, 56.
[239] ibid 34.
[240] ibid 61, also 56, 59.

the consolidation of financial authority in executive governments accelerated in the twentieth century.[241] Constitutional doctrine and reality have long been at variance.

It is not only Parliament (and the courts) that has an interest in ensuring effective supervision and accountability in relation to the activities of the government. The executive itself has an incentive to self-regulate and in so doing may exercise much more effective supervision than Parliament (and the courts) could.[242] As this book has emphasised, there have been significant changes in the size and structure of the executive government since Federation. Responsible government under the Constitution is not static but allows for the mechanisms of government to evolve to meet the needs of new generations and for new forms of executive scrutiny to be developed. That of course is what has occurred. There is now a well-developed system of scrutiny of the activities of government, which includes political, legal, financial and professional forms of accountability, and includes parliamentary, executive and judicial forms of scrutiny.[243]

Intra-executive mechanisms for control of the executive are a very important aspect of this framework, especially given that parliamentary and judicial scrutiny of the executive are intermittent. Parliament and the courts 'have no capacity for continuous supervision' and the effectiveness of their controls in relation to the executive depends on the executive's own implementation of those controls.[244] By contrast, executive scrutiny is professional and continuous. The executive, especially the minister and Department of Finance, exercises significant levels of oversight over government expenditure, with detailed budgeting, reporting and audit requirements.[245]

That is, the Court's approach in *Williams* posits an unhelpful solution to an inadequately diagnosed problem. The mere fact that Parliament's role in relation to the exercise of executive power (including public expenditure) is limited does not mean that there are inadequate controls in relation to executive action. And even were the Court's diagnosis correct, its attempt to ensure greater parliamentary oversight of executive spending foundered on the political realities which led to that supposed lack of oversight in the first place. A simplistic requirement that the executive must procure legislation (from a Parliament which it largely controls) authorising its expenditure programs rests on an outdated conception of government and ignores both the detailed system of intra-executive control which exists in relation to expenditure and the significant delegation

[241] ibid ch 5.

[242] Daintith and Page (n 143) 105, 396; Posner and Vermeule (n 25) ch 4.

[243] Diana Nestorovska, 'Assessing the Effectiveness of ASIC's Accountability Framework' (2016) 34 *Company & Securities Law Journal* 193, 201–7 contains a useful description of these forms of accountability in relation to one Commonwealth agency, the Australian Securities and Investments Commission.

[244] Daintith and Page (n 143) 4, 392.

[245] Public Governance, Performance and Accountability Act 2013 (Cth) pts 2-3–2-4.

of authority by Parliament itself onto executive officers and agencies.[246] This system of scrutiny is arguably more effective than any scrutiny that could be provided by Parliament.

G. Public Finance and Appropriation

The Constitution provides that all funds raised by the Commonwealth form part of the Consolidated Revenue Fund and that no money shall be expended except under an appropriation made by law.[247] These provisions are said to ensure parliamentary control of finance and are an important aspect of the constitutional relationship between Parliament and the executive.[248] One question the courts have grappled with is the extent to which these provisions require appropriations to be detailed and specific. There is a tendency for appropriations to adopt broad and general description of the purposes for which the Consolidated Revenue Fund are appropriated,[249] which has led to concern about the effectiveness of parliamentary control of finance. As Professor Lindell noted, 'Parliament is gradually losing control over the expenditure of public funds. Appropriations are increasingly permanent rather than annual and they are also framed in exceedingly broad terms'.[250]

Notwithstanding these legitimate concerns, it has not been considered appropriate for the Court to mandate greater specificity in appropriations to ensure a higher level of parliamentary control. Gummow, Hayne, Callinan and Heydon JJ held in *Combet v Commonwealth* that '[i]t is for the Parliament to identify the degree of specificity with which the purpose of an appropriation is identified'.[251] Gleeson CJ also held:

> The Constitution, consistently with the background of constitutional history and parliamentary practice with which the framers were familiar, reserves to the Parliament, and especially the House of Representatives, the power associated with control of funding through appropriation. It is for Parliament, consistently with the Constitution, to decide how it exercises that control. One factor of practical significance is the degree of specificity with which appropriations are made. Section 81 of

[246] *Royal Commission on Australian Government Administration* (n 48) 60.

[247] Constitution, ss 81 and 83.

[248] *Victoria v Commonwealth* (1975) 134 CLR 338, 384 (Stephen J).

[249] *Williams v Commonwealth* (2012) 248 CLR 156, 261 [222] (Hayne J).

[250] Geoffrey Lindell, submission No 10, quoted in Senate Standing Committee on Finance and Public Administration, Parliament of Australia, *Transparency and Accountability of Commonwealth Public Funding and Expenditure* (Canberra, 2007) 15.

[251] *Combet v Commonwealth* (2005) 224 CLR 494, 577 [160] (Gummow, Hayne, Callinan and Heydon JJ). See also *Wilkie v Commonwealth* (2017) 263 CLR 487, 532 [91] (Kiefel CJ, Bell, Gageler, Keane, Nettle, Gordon and Edelman JJ); *New South Wales v Commonwealth (Surplus Revenue Case)* (1908) 7 CLR 179, 192; *Pape v Federal Commissioner of Taxation* (2009) 238 CLR 1, 78 [197] (Gummow, Crennan and Bell JJ).

> the Constitution provides for the Consolidated Revenue Fund "to be appropriated for the purposes of the Commonwealth". It is for the Parliament, in making appropriations, to determine what purposes are purposes of the Commonwealth. It is also for the Parliament to determine the degree of specificity with which such purposes are expressed.[252]

While there is considerable flexibility, there are some limitations. For instance, the High Court has affirmed that 'there cannot be appropriations in blank, appropriations for no designated purpose, merely authorizing expenditure with no reference to purpose',[253] and '[t]here can be no appropriation in gross, authorizing the withdrawal of whatever sum the Executive Government may decide in the exercise of an unfettered discretion'.[254] An appropriation must be for a 'legislatively determined purpose', which serves to authorise expenditure and restrict it to the particular purpose.[255]

The account of responsible government developed in this book suggests that this approach is correct. Responsible government has been structured so as to enable maximum flexibility, such that there is freedom to shape the governance arrangements to meet the needs of each generation. Further, concerns about the loss of parliamentary control must be seen in the context of the changes in the nature and structure of the executive branch since Federation. Parliament has enacted legislation conferring significant oversight roles on executive bodies in relation to government expenditure,[256] and these executive controls are continuous and professional, in contrast to the intermittent control exercised by Parliament and the courts. Arguably, therefore, Parliament can be seen to have delegated a significant level of responsibility in relation to public finance to the executive branch itself. There is nothing in principle illegitimate or constitutionally improper about this.

And as this book has sought to emphasise, an attempt by the courts to ensure better governance practice is unlikely to be successful. Simply requiring detailed specificity in appropriations may not lead to any greater level of control over the executive by Parliament. As Lawson has argued, 'breaking the link between appropriations and a calculation of the amounts of money actually held by the Commonwealth means that parliamentary scrutiny of appropriations may no longer be a good mechanism for ensuring the accountability and

[252] *Combet v Commonwealth* (2005) 224 CLR 494, 522 [5] (references omitted).

[253] *A-G (Vic) ex rel Dale v Commonwealth* (1945) 71 CLR 237, 253 (Latham CJ); *Brown v West* (1990) 169 CLR 195, 208 (Mason CJ, Brennan, Deane, Dawson and Toohey JJ); *Wilkie v Commonwealth* (2017) 263 CLR 487, 526 [71] (Kiefel CJ, Bell, Gageler, Keane, Nettle, Gordon and Edelman JJ).

[254] *Northern Suburbs General Cemetery Reserve Trust v Commonwealth* (1993) 176 CLR 555, 582 (Brennan J).

[255] *Wilkie v Commonwealth* (2017) 263 CLR 487, 525–6 [69]–[70] (Kiefel CJ, Bell, Gageler, Keane, Nettle, Gordon and Edelman JJ), citing *Brown v West* (1990) 169 CLR 195, 208 and *Victoria v Commonwealth* (1975) 134 CLR 338, 392.

[256] Public Governance, Performance and Accountability Act 2013 (Cth) pts 2-3–2-4.

transparency of expenditure because appropriations exceed the amounts of actual money'.[257] Unless the Parliament has the capacity and the inclination to exert greater levels of control and accountability, and develops 'new skills, processes and procedures to properly scrutinise government's expenditures',[258] mandating further legal or constitutional requirements may yield little benefit. This suggests that any reforms relating to the appropriation and expenditure of public moneys must come from the executive itself rather than being judicially mandated.[259]

IV. CONCLUSION

This chapter has articulated an approach to constitutional interpretation which places emphasis on the text of the Constitution understood in its historical context and has considered the implications of the historical account of responsible government for specific areas of constitutional doctrine. I have sought to demonstrate how the approach articulated in this chapter is consistent with the orthodox principles of interpretation adopted by the High Court. The sparsity of the provisions of the Constitution that deal with the executive means that those provisions cannot be accurately interpreted without understanding their constitutional and historical background.[260] The historical context is therefore crucial to understand the Constitution.

This book has argued that the Australian principle of responsible government is an inherently flexible system of government designed to enable the politically sovereign people of Australia to govern themselves in the manner they see fit. Responsible government is fundamentally political, not readily susceptible of judicial enforcement or even codification and this understanding explains the deliberately non-prescriptive drafting of Chapter II of the Constitution. One major implication of this is that there should be caution in drawing constitutional implications that hinder the freedom of the sovereign people of Australia to govern themselves in the manner they deem best.

[257] Charles Lawson, 'Re-Invigorating the Accountability and Transparency of the Australian Government's Expenditure' (2008) 32 *Melbourne University Law Review* 879, 894.

[258] ibid 916.

[259] Will Bateman has also noted the difficulties of ensuring compliance with appropriation legislation by means of judicial review: Bateman (n 234) 182, 184, 211.

[260] Stellios, *Zines's the High Court and the Constitution* (n 148) 399.

8

Conclusion

> The Constitution of the Commonwealth of Australia bears every mark of confidence in the capacity of the people to undertake every function of government.[1]
>
> W Harrison Moore (1910)

THIS BOOK HAS developed an account of responsible government under the Australian Constitution by drawing on the understanding of responsible government held by the framers, and their intentions in incorporating it into the constitutional structure in their historical and constitutional context, and considered the implications for the interpretation of the Constitution.

The Australian Constitution is sometimes viewed as disappointing. It was not preceded by a revolutionary conflict. It contains no declaration of the sovereignty of the people and no grand statements of rights. The Constitution does not set out fundamental principles or values and plays a limited role in Australian political debate.[2] In 1993 Paul Finn wrote:

> The Australian people seem often enough to be an afterthought in discussion of this country's system of government. That the people are sovereign, that government and its institutions exist for them and to their ends, are ideas that exert only muted influence on the constitutional and political imagination.[3]

This book has sought to show that behind the sparse words of the Constitution lies a rich and multi-faceted set of constitutional and political beliefs. The lack of express recognition of such matters in the text of the Constitution does not mean that the framers were unconcerned with rights, good governance or popular sovereignty. It means rather that the framers trusted in the political mechanisms of responsible government to achieve those goals rather than in judicially enforceable mechanisms.

[1] W Harrison Moore, *The Constitution of the Commonwealth of Australia*, 2nd edn (Melbourne, Charles F Maxwell, 1910) 613.

[2] Dylan Lino, 'The Australian Constitution as Symbol' (2020) 48 *Federal Law Review* 543. See also Hugh Collins, 'Political Ideology in Australia: The Distinctiveness of a Benthamite Society' in Stephen R Graubard (ed), *Australia, the Daedalus Symposium* (North Ryde, Angus & Robertson, 1985) 145–69.

[3] Paul Finn, 'Public Trust and Public Accountability' (1993) 65 *Australian Quarterly* 50, 50.

Contrary to the view of Finn, this book has argued that the framers saw 'the people' as central to Australia's system of government, in aspiration and reality. They conceived of responsible government as a system that was designed to, and did, enable self-government by the people, who would govern indirectly, and actively, through the institution of Parliament. The framers also conceived of responsible government as a relationship that was not fixed but would be moulded by the people, being worked through evolving democratic processes. The framers considered that future generations would govern themselves as they saw fit, and that Constitution-makers could not prescribe or control how they did so. The framers intended to establish a government and a Parliament for a sovereign people and they created a deliberately flexible form of executive so that the sovereign people of Australia could shape their institutions to govern themselves as they saw best.

This book has argued that responsible government in Australia must be understood synchronically and diachronically: it drew from the long tradition of thinking about the British Constitution, and also provided for flexibility suited to changing circumstances and the political temper of the people. Chapter two noted that the core of the doctrine of responsible government was the linking of the government's tenure of office with the requirement to obtain the confidence of the lower house. Parliament's functions included choosing the government, holding it to account by watching over and scrutinising its activities and controlling public finance by granting or withholding supply. Leading constitutional writers also considered a stable two-party system to be essential for the proper working of responsible government, to provide the working majorities necessary for stable government. The practice and the ideal of responsible government incorporated elements of both executive and liberal models.

The British Constitution was not conceived as separate from the rest of the law, but consisted of the mass of precedents, laws and conventions relating to the institutions of government, which had not been deliberately designed but had evolved over centuries. Any modification to the laws or even the customs or political practices which related to the British government meant a modification to the Constitution. Those practices and conventions were constantly changing, and so the British Constitution was conceived as being in constant flux. As an inherently evolutionary system, the British Constitution could be adapted and moulded to the circumstances in which it functioned, while providing an overall framework of stability and continuity.

Chapter three examined the introduction of responsible government into the Australian colonies. Given the long history of self-government in the colonies, a desire to ensure popular self-government occupied a central place in the colonial conception of responsible government. In the 1850s a demand for greater autonomy from Britain was a central part of colonists' demands for constitutional reform; in the 1880s and 1890s increasing attention was being paid to questions of the efficacy of responsible government and the cabinet system, and whether the institutions of government accurately gave effect to the will of the people. Common to both was a belief in self-government by the people of the Australian colonies. The British Constitution was considered the model for responsible government, subject to such variations as were rendered necessary by the peculiar characteristics of the colonies. In each of the colonies responsible government took a path that was distinct both from Britain and the other colonies, highlighting that responsible government was not fixed but subject to local variations.

Chapters two and three also considered the various proposals that were put forward to attempt to fix the problems with cabinet dominance. These received sustained attention by contemporaries, including prominent delegates to the Federation Conventions, to the extent that a royal commission in Victoria examined the issue, but none were accepted. By the time of Federation, the problems with cabinet and party government were well known, but no satisfactory alternative had been devised. A period of unprecedented stability occurred in the 1890s, where the premiers of Victoria, New South Wales, South Australia, Tasmania and Western Australia held office for long periods. Not only did this enable the premiers to develop a long-standing working relationship among themselves, but it may have encouraged an optimism and even complacency about responsible government.

This context is crucial to understanding the political constraints facing the framers, and the political and constitutional ideas which informed their conception of responsible government. As discussed in chapters four and five, several competing views of responsible government vied for acceptance throughout the Convention debates. The first was a strongly normative view argued for by several of the delegates from the more populous colonies, who were concerned to ensure that Federation would not lead to a minority overriding the will of the majority. Those who held to this view considered that responsible government should be closely modelled on the British Constitution, and emphasised lower house predominance as an inherent feature of responsible government. The second view was a more descriptive and evolutionary view, which saw the patterns of politics in Britain at the time of Federation as a particular development of responsible government at a particular time, which would continue to evolve after Federation. For these framers, the normative view was static and rigid, attempting to 'fix the changeable, and to make the unalterable the alterable', which would have ossified a particular historically contingent development of responsible government.[4] Both views drew on strands of British constitutional thought; both views acknowledged that under the British Constitution as it functioned at the time of Federation, the lower house was the superior house; they differed as to whether this was an inherent feature of responsible government.

While elements of lower house supremacy were included in the Constitution, this book has argued that the evolutionary view prevailed. Chapters four and

[4] *Convention Debates* (1891) 279 (Hackett).

five argued that the framers, even those who advocated the normative view, widely accepted that responsible government was a dynamic and constantly evolving set of practices that could not be prescribed or predicted in advance.[5] This view was accepted by the Federal Conventions and underlies the drafting of the Constitution. This conception of responsible government explains how the framers could incorporate both responsible government and a strong Senate into the constitutional framework. Rather than simply incorporating inconsistent principles, if lower house predominance was not an inherent feature of responsible government, but merely the development of that system of government as at the time of Federation, then responsible government could continue to evolve and adapt to the existence of a powerful upper house. The framers did not entrench any particular form of responsible government in the Constitution but built in scope for it to evolve and be developed by future generations.[6]

In addition to constitutional evolution, this book has argued that popular sovereignty was a key principle underlying the framers' approach to responsible government, and that they intended that the Constitution would be democratic and function in accordance with the will of the people. The people should have the right to govern themselves in the manner they see fit, and the framers did not consider it was their role, or even possible, to attempt to limit or prescribe how they would do so. The people would express their will and govern themselves as they see fit, and the manner in which they chose to do so would vary from time to time. As such, it was improper, and even impossible, to attempt to specify the relationship between Parliament and the executive.

Chapters six and seven drew from the history developed in chapters two to five to develop an account of responsible government under the Australian Constitution and consider the implications for its interpretation. Often there is resistance to the use of history in constitutional interpretation, and a desire not to be bound by the 'dead hand of the framers'.[7] The High Court has emphasised that its role in constitutional interpretation is to determine the meaning of the provision in question objectively from the language used, and it has shown a reluctance to employ extrinsic materials.[8] Responsible government presents an acute challenge to an exclusive focus on text. The features of responsible government are not self-contained within the text of the Constitution, and its text contains little express recognition of responsible government. The provisions of the Constitution which incorporate, or assume, the system of responsible

[5] See also Jeffrey Archer and Graham Maddox, 'The 1975 Constitutional Crisis in Australia' (1976) 14 *Journal of Commonwealth and Comparative Politics* 141, 148.

[6] Contra George Winterton, *Parliament, the Executive and the Governor-General: A Constitutional Analysis* (Melbourne, Melbourne University Press, 1983) 5–6.

[7] Eg, David A Strauss, *The Living Constitution* (Oxford, Oxford University Press, 2010) 99–100.

[8] *Amalgamated Society of Engineers v Adelaide Steamship Co Ltd* (1920) 28 CLR 129, 142, 149 (Knox CJ, Isaacs, Rich and Starke JJ); Henry Burmester, 'The Convention Debates and the Interpretation of the Constitution' in Gregory Craven (ed), *The Convention Debates 1891–1898: Commentaries, Indices and Guide* (Sydney, Legal Books, 1986) 25.

government are deliberately spare and rely on unwritten understandings and conventions which must be gleaned from other sources.[9] The Constitution assumes a constitutional background which is necessary to understand to make sense of its text.[10] The sparsity of the provisions of the Constitution that deal with the executive means that those provisions cannot be accurately interpreted without understanding their constitutional and historical background.[11]

The historical context is therefore crucial to understand the Constitution, especially those provisions that relate to the executive and its constitutional relationship with Parliament. I have also sought to demonstrate how the approach articulated in this book is consistent with the orthodox principles of interpretation adopted by the High Court. As discussed in chapter seven, many High Court cases have noted that the Constitution needs to be interpreted according to its text understood in light of the history, and in numerous cases the Court has drawn on historical materials when interpreting the Constitution. Further, reading the Constitution historically does not mean confining it to its historical meaning, but allows for evolution in the meaning of its text. Incorporating concepts into the Constitution which are drawn from the common law and the British tradition of constitutionalism necessarily imports the methodology of evolutionary change inherent in those traditions.

Rosalind Dixon has argued that the courts should engage more expressly with constitutional values when interpreting the Constitution, given that formal legal materials are often insufficient to determine a particular controversy. This 'functionalist' approach insists that the values relied on should be expressly anchored in the text, history and structure of the Constitution rather than a more pragmatic, policy-oriented approach.[12] This book has argued that examining the text of the Constitution in light of its historical and constitutional context demonstrates that the constitutional values of popular sovereignty, a strongly political model of constitutionalism and an evolutionary conception of responsible government had a significant influence on the Australian Constitution. If it is true, as Dixon argues, that the High Court is increasingly likely to engage more openly with constitutional values,[13] then the approach of this book may

[9] Colin Howard and Cheryl Saunders, 'The Blocking of the Budget and Dismissal of the Government' in Gareth Evans (ed), *Labor and the Constitution, 1972–1975: Essays and Commentaries on the Constitutional Controversies of the Whitlam Years in Australian Government* (Richmond, Heinemann Educational Australia, 1977) 265.

[10] See, eg, *Ryder v Foley* (1906) 4 CLR 422, 448 (O'Connor J); *Commissioner of Taxation (Cth) v Munro* (1926) 38 CLR 153, 187–8 (Isaacs J).

[11] *Egan v Willis* (1998) 195 CLR 424, 447 [29] (Gaudron, Gummow and Hayne JJ); *Plaintiff M68/2015 v Minister for Immigration and Border Protection* (2016) 257 CLR 42, 96 [129] (Gageler J); James Stellios, *Zines's the High Court and the Constitution*, 6th edn (Annandale, Federation Press, 2015) 399.

[12] Rosalind Dixon, 'Functional Constitution: Re-reading the 2014 High Court Constitutional Term' (2015) 43 *Federal Law Review* 455.

[13] Rosalind Dixon, 'Functionalism and Australian Constitutional Values' in Rosalind Dixon (ed), *Australian Constitutional Values* (Portland, Hart, 2020) 7.

provide a fruitful methodology for identifying key values which are a part of the Australian constitutional tradition.

Responsible government establishes conventions by which the legal exercise of power is held to account, by ensuring that those who exercise executive power are members of, and must hold the confidence of, Parliament, which provides the primary mechanism by which the executive is held to account. Parliamentary control of the executive is both legal and political. Given that members of Parliament are elected by the people of Australia, the principles of responsible government are intended to make both government and Parliament accountable to the people.[14] Under responsible government the functioning of Parliament, and the mechanisms of accountability, are inherently political, and electoral choice is the principal constraint on the exercise of executive and legislative power, and is the 'ordinary constitutional means' by which that constraint occurs.[15]

I have suggested that one principal implication of this understanding of responsible government is interpretive minimalism, namely caution in drawing implications from the incorporation of responsible government into the Constitution and a resistance of the 'constitutionalisation' of responsible government. The Constitution should be interpreted to enable maximum flexibility for the Australian people and their representatives to govern themselves as they see fit, free from judicially-imposed restrictions which are not contained in the text of the Constitution.

There have been enormous changes in the size and nature of government since Federation.[16] Under the British Constitution, at the time of Federation, the lower house was the more representative house, and members of the House of Lords held their positions by virtue of their social rank, with the result that the upper house was the democratically inferior house. A two-party alignment existed with political parties that were cohesive but lacked the discipline of modern parties. The House of Commons possessed the power to control the ministry, for example by passing a motion of no confidence or withholding supply, and actually exercised that power; independence was a normative ideal for MPs and sometimes a possibility. As at 1909, there were approximately 13,500 employees employed by the Commonwealth government.[17]

Today, the stranglehold of party discipline means that the executive typically controls the lower house rather than the other way around.[18] It is rare for

[14] *Australian Capital Television Pty Ltd v Commonwealth* (1992) 177 CLR 106, 138, 139 (Mason CJ), 230 1 (McHugh J); *Nationwide News Pty Ltd v Wills* (1992) 177 CLR 1, 47 (Brennan J), 70 (Deane and Toohey JJ).

[15] *McCloy v New South Wales* (2015) 257 CLR 178, 226–7 [111]–[113] (Gageler J); *Marks v Commonwealth* (1964) 111 CLR 549, 557–558 (Kitto J).

[16] *Williams v Commonwealth* (2012) 248 CLR 156, 204 [59] (French CJ).

[17] Public Service Commissioner, *List of Permanent Officers of the Commonwealth Public Service as on 1 January 1909* (January 1909).

[18] Jacqueline Lipton, 'Responsible Government, Representative Democracy and the Senate: Options for Reform' (1997) 19 *University of Queensland Law Journal* 194, 195.

a government to lose the confidence of the House of Representatives between elections, and unheard of for the lower house to withhold supply, its other major tool for controlling the executive.[19] The Senate is genuinely a representative house, unlike the nineteenth century House of Lords.[20] There are now over 180 Commonwealth departments and entities, over 240,000 Commonwealth employees and over 1,600,000 people employed by Australian state governments.[21] In many respects the role of Parliament has diminished since Federation, and that of the executive has grown. The executive is vastly superior to Parliament in both number and resources. In theory Parliament controls the executive, but in reality the executive largely controls the Parliament. While it is notionally the role of Parliament to enact legislation, in practice the policy-making process by which legislation is conceived and drafted is firmly within the control of the executive. Parliament is supposed to exercise control over government finance and expenditure but in practice largely ratifies the financial proposals initiated by the executive.

Sometimes changes such as these are seen as evidence of the failure or inadequacy of responsible government.[22] A better view is that the Constitution has been expressly designed to be flexible so as to accommodate such changes. Given the inherently flexible nature of responsible government, claims that certain features of responsible government are necessary or inherent to that system[23] must be viewed with some caution. Changes in the structure of government since Federation are not a departure from the 'true' principles of responsible government, but rather a legitimate evolution in response to circumstances and societal values which the Constitution is deliberately structured to provide for. What was appropriate during the 1890s or 1900s is unlikely to be appropriate for a modern society. Our conception of responsible government needs to permit evolution so as to reflect the reality of modern government.[24]

These developments signal profound changes in the functioning of our parliamentary system and can be viewed through different lenses. On the one

[19] Michael Coper, *Encounters with the Australian Constitution* (North Ryde, CCH Australia, 1987) 254.

[20] Elaine Thompson, 'The Senate and Representative Democracy' (Papers on Parliament No 34, Parliament of Australia, 1999). In recent times the election of candidates on a very small proportion of the primary vote has led some to query whether this genuinely reflects the electorate's will: eg, Joint Standing Committee on Electoral Matters, Parliament of Australia, *Interim Report on the Inquiry into the Conduct of the 2013 Federal Election: Senate Voting Practices* (Canberra, 2014).

[21] Australian Bureau of Statistics, *Employment and Earnings, Public Sector, Australia, 2020–21 Financial Year* www.abs.gov.au/statistics/labour/employment-and-unemployment/employment-and-earnings-public-sector-australia/2020-21.

[22] See, eg, Gabrielle Appleby, 'Unwritten Rules' in Cheryl Saunders and Adrienne Stone (eds), *The Oxford Handbook of the Australian Constitution* (Oxford, Oxford University Press, 2018) 229–30.

[23] *Cf* RAW Rhodes, John Wanna and Patrick Weller, *Comparing Westminster* (Oxford, Oxford University Press, 2011) 1–2, 221–2.

[24] JR Archer, 'The Theory of Responsible Government in Britain and Australia' (1980) 15 *Politics* 23, 30.

hand, criticisms are often levelled at our current political arrangements. The Australian political system is dominated by political parties with high levels of discipline and cohesion, such that MPs rarely vote against their party.[25] It is widely acknowledged that the Australian Parliament has declined in power relative to the executive, which largely dominates and controls its proceedings;[26] as a result the Parliament (especially the lower house) has little ability to control the executive and so cannot fulfil the role ascribed to it under the theory of responsible government.[27] Recent Parliaments have also seen a loss of the stability which is often considered the trade-off for party dominance.[28] The Senate has also been criticised for obstructiveness and interfering with the government's policy proposals. Due to defects such as these, some consider that responsible government no longer prevails in Australia: what exists instead is party government,[29] and some consider that the framers did not intend the Australian political system to function in such a problematic way.[30]

[25] John Warhurst, 'Conscience Voting in the Australian Federal Parliament' (2008) 54 *Australian Journal of Politics and History* 579; Alan J Ward, *Parliamentary Government in Australia*, rev edn (North Melbourne, Australian Scholarly Publishing, 2012) 186.

[26] LF Crisp, *Australian National Government*, 5th edn (Melbourne, Longman Cheshire, 1983) 267; Stanley Bach, *Platypus and Parliament: The Australian Senate in Theory and Practice* (Canberra, Department of the Senate, 2003) 242–3; John Summers, 'Parliament and Responsible Government' in Dennis Woodward, Andrew Parkin and John Summers (eds), *Government, Politics, Power and Policy in Australia*, 9th edn (Frenchs Forest, Pearson Australia, 2009) 76; GS Reid, 'Australia's Commonwealth Parliament and the 'Westminster Model'' (1964) 2 *Journal of Commonwealth Political Studies* 89, 93; Campbell Sharman, 'Reforming Executive Power' in George Winterton (ed), *We the People: Australian Republican Government* (St Leonards, Allen and Unwin, 1994) 113; John Halligan, Robin Miller and John Power, *Parliament in the Twenty-first Century: Institutional Reform and Emerging Roles* (Carlton, Melbourne University Publishing, 2007) 2–4.

[27] John Uhr and John Wanna, 'The Future Roles of Parliament' in Michael Keating, John Wanna and Patrick Weller (eds), *Institutions on the Edge? Capacity for Governance* (St Leonards, Allen & Unwin, 2000) 14; Ward (n 25) 266; Brad Selway, 'The 'Vision Splendid' of Ministerial Responsibility versus the 'Round Eternal' of Government Administration' in Clement Macintyre and John Williams (eds), *Peace, Order and Good Government: State Constitutional and Parliamentary Reform* (Kent Town, Wakefield Press, 2003) 169–70.

[28] See John Wanna, 'Political Chronicles: Commonwealth of Australia' (2015) 61 *Australian Journal of Politics and History* 278; John Wanna, 'Commonwealth of Australia July to December 2015' (2016) 62 *Australian Journal of Politics and History* 282. On stability within the Australian party system see Linda Botterill and Geoff Cockfield, 'From "Unstable" to "Stable" Minority Government: Reflections on the Role of the Nationals in Federal Coalition Governments' (2015) 61 *Australian Journal of Politics & History* 53; Aaron Martin and Juliet Pietsch, 'Future Shock or Future Stability? Generation Change and the Australian Party System' (2013) 59 *Australian Journal of Politics and History* 212; David Charnock and Peter Ellis, 'The Structure of the Australian Party System and its Strategic Consequences' (2003) 38 *Australian Journal of Political Science* 423.

[29] David Hamer, 'Senate Committees – Keeping Parliament Responsible' (Papers on Parliament No 12, Parliament of Australia, 1991) 41; Thomas Penberthy Fry, *Australian Contributions to the Evolution of Parliamentary Government* (Brisbane, University of Queensland, 1947) 5; Chandran Kukathas, 'Democracy, Parliament and Responsible Government' (Papers on Parliament No 8, Parliamentary Library, Parliament of Australia, 1990). For a contrary view, see RS Parker, 'The Meaning of Responsible Government' (1976) 11 *Politics* 178, 183.

[30] Ian Marsh, *Beyond the Two Party System: Political Representation, Economic Competitiveness, and Australian Politics* (Melbourne, Cambridge University Press, 1995); Ward (n 25) 261, 263.

On the other hand, our current arrangements are not without their merits. The dominance of the lower house typically means stable and effective government, and governments are usually able to secure passage of supply and their policy commitments. Executive dominance of Parliament has been a feature of British parliamentary government since the mid nineteenth century. The business of drafting legislation is delegated to experienced parliamentary counsel and its implementation to the public service, who for the most part carry out these tasks competently.[31]

Pessimistic assessments of our governance arrangements may neglect the fact that parliamentary scrutiny is not the only means of holding the executive to account, and that other mechanisms of executive control exist. There are extensive mechanisms of internal control, and it might be that these intra-executive controls, carried out by full time professionals, exercise more effective control and scrutiny over executive expenditure than Parliament, consisting of ad hoc committees of non-specialists. What is lacking in parliamentary scrutiny is, arguably, provided by the executive itself. Parliament and the courts are not the only institutions of government concerned with accountability. Intra-executive constraints may serve to strengthen the executive's powers by increasing its credibility, and so executives have a strong incentive to self-regulate.[32] Arguably, therefore, adequate mechanisms for the scrutiny of the executive have been developed to meet the changed needs of modern government, under which parliamentary control is just one of many constraints on the executive.

Perhaps there is merit in both perspectives. To the extent that current mechanisms for executive constraint are inadequate, this raises the question of how best to address those deficiencies. Regardless of which lens is correct, the argument of this book suggests that judicial attempts to mandate more effective governance will likely not be successful. One theme of this book is the tension and interplay between political and legal constitutionalism, which arises from the incorporation (or assumption) of a fundamentally flexible and political form of government within a written, judicially enforceable Constitution.

There is a tendency in constitutional scholarship to give primacy to the legal and downplay the non-legal. For instance, Gabrielle Appleby has argued that responsible government, 'with its heavy reliance on convention to facilitate political accountability of the government, has largely fallen out of favour as constitutional best practice'.[33] There are persistent calls to constitutionalise responsible government, such as arguments that the conventions relating to

[31] See Sarah Maddison and Richard Denniss, *An Introduction to Australian Public Policy: Theory and Practice*, 2nd edn (New York, Cambridge University Press, 2013) ch 7.

[32] Eric A Posner and Adrian Vermeule, *The Executive Unbound: After the Madisonian Republic* (Oxford, Oxford University Press, 2010) ch 4; Terence Daintith and Alan Page, *The Executive in the Constitution: Structure, Autonomy, and Internal Control* (Oxford, Oxford University Press, 1999) 105, 396.

[33] Appleby (n 22) 229–30.

responsible government should be legally enforceable,[34] and a noticeable trend in this direction in High Court jurisprudence. Underlying this is a particular conception of constitutionalism, which places primacy on the legal and the judicially enforceable over the political.

This book has argued that the framers did not attempt to prescribe the working of responsible government because they did not think this was possible. They considered that the ways of the nineteenth century may not be suitable for future generations, and so each generation would, and should, work out how best to govern itself. During the Convention Debates Western Australian delegate Walter James remarked:

> It amuses me almost to hear some members of this Convention endeavoring to wetnurse responsible government. That institution is of such a vigorous growth that if we in this Convention dared to place undue restriction on it, it would sweep us away like cobwebs. Let us adopt the true principle, being assured that responsible government is so much a part of us, and of the atmosphere we have always breathed in our political life, that no Constitution we can frame can interfere with the essential principles of its growth.[35]

Had he lived to see it, perhaps Mr James would have chuckled at the High Court's recent attempts to 'wetnurse responsible government'. If the practical character of a system of government depends on 'the political habits of the people', and if '[t]o expect any form of words, however weightily conceived, with whatever sanctions enacted, permanently to restrain the passions and interests of men is to expect the impossible',[36] then this is a largely fruitless exercise. Well-meaning judicial attempts to solve political problems through legal means has the result that those attempts are foiled by the political realities that caused the problem in the first place. The concept of responsible government which underlies our constitutional system ultimately depends for its good functioning on an engaged citizenry and a vibrant political culture.

[34] See, eg, Amelia Simpson, 'Parliaments' in Cheryl Saunders and Adrienne Stone (eds), *The Oxford Handbook of the Australian Constitution* (Oxford, Oxford University Press, 2018).
[35] *Convention Debates*, Adelaide (1897) 548, see also *Convention Debates*, Sydney (1897) 522.
[36] Bryce (n 15) vol 1, 270, 291, 396.

Bibliography

FEDERATION DEBATES

Craven, G (ed), The Convention Debates 1891–1898: Commentaries, Indices and Guide (Sydney, Legal Books, 1986).

Official Record of the Proceedings and Debates of the Australasian Federation Conference, Melbourne 1890 (Melbourne, Government Printer, 1890).

Official Report of the National Australasian Convention Debates, Sydney, 2 March to 9 April, 1891 (Sydney, Acting Government Printer, 1891; reprinted Legal Books, 1986).

Official Report of the National Australasian Convention Debates, Adelaide, March 22 to May 5, 1897 (Adelaide, Government Printer, 1897; reprinted Legal Books, 1986).

Official Record of the Debates of the Australasian Federal Convention, Second Session: Sydney, 2nd to 24th September 1897 (Sydney, Government Printer, 1897; reprinted Legal Books, 1986).

Official Record of the Debates of the Australasian Federal Convention, Third Session: Melbourne, 20th January to 17th March, 1898, 2 vols (Melbourne, Government Printer, 1898; reprinted Legal Books, 1986).

Proceedings, People's Federal Convention, Bathurst, November, 1896 (Sydney, Gordon and Gotch, 1897).

NINETEENTH AND EARLY TWENTIETH CENTURY AUSTRALIAN WORKS

Anonymous, 'Australian Federation: The Story of a Great Fight' (1898) 12 *Review of Reviews* 690.

Anonymous, 'Draft of a Bill to Constitute the Commonwealth of Australia, 1898' (1899) 190 *Quarterly Review* 289.

Anonymous, 'More Aspects of Party Government', *The Bulletin* (Sydney), 1 December 1894.

Anonymous, 'Party Government', *The Bulletin* (Sydney), 9 August 1890.

Anonymous, 'Party Government in the Commonwealth', *The Bulletin* (Sydney), 3 April 1897.

Anonymous, 'The Attainment of Federation: What was Lacking in the Convention Bill, Being a Reprint of Eight Articles from the *Sydney Daily Telegraph*' (Sydney, 1898).

Anonymous, 'The Commonwealth of Australia' (Jul 1899) *Review of Reviews* 48.

Anonymous, *The Evils of Party Government: Proposals for the Elective System of Selecting Cabinet Ministers* (Melbourne, David Syme, 1904).

Anonymous, 'The Federal Bill' (1898) 12 *Review of Reviews* 297.

Anonymous, 'The Federation of Australia' (Nov 1891) *Review of Reviews* 494.

Anonymous, 'The Federation of Australia' (1899) 87 *Saturday Review* 516.

Anonymous, 'The Last Resort in Political Warfare', *The Spectator*, 25 September 1897.

A'Beckett, TT, *The Power of the Purse Considered Constitutionally* (Melbourne, Samuel Mullen, 1867).

Baker, RC, *A Manual of Reference to Authorities for the Use of the Members of the National Australasian Convention* (Adelaide, WK Thomas & Co, 1891).

—— *Federation* (Adelaide, 1897).

—— *The Executive in a Federation* (Adelaide, Government Printer, 1897).

—— 'South Australia: Powers and Practice of The Two Houses of Parliament In Reference to Money Bills' in *Proceedings of the Australasian Federal Convention 1898*, Victoria Parliamentary Paper No 18 (1898).

—— *Notes on the Constitution of South Australia* (Adelaide, Hussey & Gillingham, 1899).
Barton, E, *Draft Federation Bill: Speech by the Hon E Barton, QC, MLC Delivered in the Legislative Council on July 14, 1897* (Sydney, Government Printer, 1897).
Barton, GB, *The Draft Bill to Constitute the Commonwealth of Australia* (Sydney, Government Printer, 1891).
—— *Notes on Australian Federation and the Draft Constitution Bills Framed by the Conventions of 1891 and 1897* (Sydney, Government Printer, 1897).
—— 'The Troubles of Australian Federation' (1901) 11 *Imperial and Asiatic Quarterly Review and Oriental and Colonial Record* 303.
Braddon, ENC, 'The Federation Movement in Australasia' (1896) 233 *Nineteenth Century* 156.
Brassey, Lord, 'Australian Federation' (1899) 266 *Nineteenth Century* 548.
Chapman, HS, *Parliamentary Government; or, Responsible Ministries for the Australian Colonies* (Hobart, Pratt and Son, 1854).
Clark, AI, 'Our Australian Constitutions' (1874) 1 *Quadrilateral* 56 (Pt 1), 81 (Pt 2), 107 (Pt 3).
—— *Australasian Federation* (Hobart, 1891).
—— 'The Commonwealth of Australia', *Daily Telegraph*, 24 October 1900, 6 (Pt 1), 31 October 1900, 6 (Pt 2).
—— *Studies in Australian Constitutional Law* (Melbourne, Charles F Maxwell, 1901).
Cockburn, JA, *Election of Ministers, Speech Delivered in the House of Assembly, South Australia, on September 9, 1891* (Adelaide, Burden & Bonython, 1891).
—— 'Should the Cabinet System be Changed?' (1895) 6 *Review of Reviews* 399.
—— *Australian Federation* (London, Horace Marshall & Son, 1901).
—— 'The Commonwealth of Australia' (1901) 49 *Journal of the Society of Arts* 381.
—— 'The Sphere of State Activity in Australia' (1901) 50 *Journal of the Society of Arts* 589.
—— 'The Biology of Federation' (1903) 52 *Journal of the Society of Arts* 272.
Deakin, A, 'The Federation of Australia' (1891) 10 *Scribner's Magazine* 549.
—— 'Federal Council of Australasia' (1895) *Review of Reviews* 154.
—— 'The Present Federal Crisis' in *Proceedings, People's Federal Convention, Bathurst, November, 1896* (Sydney, Gordon and Gotch, 1897).
—— *The Crisis in Victorian Politics, 1879–1881: A Personal Retrospect* (Carlton, Melbourne University Press, 1957).
—— *'And Be One People': Alfred Deakin's Federal Story*, 3rd edn (Carlton South, Melbourne University Press, 1995).
Deakin, A and Lord Brassey (eds), *Speeches on Australian Federation by the Premiers of Victoria, South Australia, Queensland, Tasmania, and Western Australia* (Melbourne, G Robertson & Co, 1899).
FitzGibbon, EG, *Government by Committees: All Members all Ministers* (Melbourne, S Mullen, 1872).
—— *Parliamentary Reform, Permanent Government and Progress Vice Selfishness, Party Wrangling, and Stagnation: Suggestions for an Alteration of the Parliamentary Constitution of Victoria* (Melbourne, Samuel Mullen, 1875).
—— *What Next?* (Melbourne, Fergusson & Moore, 1879).
—— *True Coalition: Permanent Government and Peace Instead of Party Wrangling for Place* (Melbourne, Fergusson & Moore, 1886).
—— *Party Government and Suggestions for Better* (Melbourne, Melville, Mullen & Slade, 1893).
Forrest, J, *Speech by the Right Honourable Sir John Forrest, on the Federation of Australia, on the terms proposed in the Commonwealth Bill passed by the Federal Convention, 1898* (Perth, Government Printer, 1898).
Fysh, Sir PO, 'Why Tasmania Should Accept the Federal Bill' (1898) 12 *Review of Reviews* 299.
Garran, RR, *A Problem of Federation under the Crown: The Representation of the Crown in Commonwealth and States* (Brisbane, 1895).
—— *The Coming Commonwealth: An Australian Handbook of Federal Government* (Sydney, Angus & Robertson, 1897).

—— *Draft Bill to Constitute the Commonwealth of Australia: As Finally Adopted by the Australasian Federal Convention, at Melbourne, on the 16th March, 1898, together with an Explanation of its Provisions* (Melbourne, Government Printer, 1898).
—— 'The Making and Working of the Constitution' (1932) 4(14) *Australian Quarterly* 13.
—— 'The Making and Working if the Constitution (Continued)' (1932) 4(15) *Australian Quarterly* 5.
—— 'The Federation Movement and the Founding of the Commonwealth' in Ernest Scott (ed), *Cambridge History of the British Empire* (London, Cambridge University Press, 1933) vol 7, pt I.
Glynn, PM, *Federation: Speech by P McM Glynn* (Adelaide, WK Thomas & Co, 1897).
Griffith, SW, 'Political Geography of Australia' (1891) 6 *Royal Geographical Society of Australasia Queensland Geographical Journal* 68.
—— *Notes on Australian Federation: Its Nature and Probable Effects: A Paper Presented to the Government of Queensland* (Brisbane, Government Printer, 1896).
—— *Some Conditions of Australian Federation* (Brisbane, Government Printer, 1896).
—— *Notes on the Draft Federal Constitution Framed by the Adelaide Convention of 1897: A Paper Presented to the Government of Queensland* (Brisbane, Government Printer, 1897).
—— 'The Draft Federal Constitution Framed by the Adelaide Convention of 1897: A Criticism' (1897) 11 *Review of Reviews* 56.
—— *Australian Federation and the Draft Commonwealth Bill: A Paper Read before the Members of the Queensland Federation League, on Friday, 26th May, 1899* (Brisbane, Government Printer, 1899).
Henry, J, *Address to the Electors of Tasmania on the Federal Constitution Bill* (Devonport, Printed at 'The North-West Post' Office, 1898).
Higgins, HB, *The Convention Bill of 1898: Address Delivered by HB Higgins to His Constituents in Geelong, April 18th, 1898* (Melbourne, Atlas Press, 1898).
—— The Australian Federation Act' (1900) *Contemporary Review* 480.
—— *Essays and Addresses on the Australian Commonwealth Bill* (Melbourne, Atlas Press, 1900).
—— 'The Rigid Constitution' (1905) 20 *Political Science Quarterly* 203.
Holder, FW, 'The Sydney Convention of 1897' (15 October 1897) *Review of Reviews* 441.
—— 'Why South Australia Should Accept the Bill' (1898) 12 *Review of Reviews* 302.
Isaacs, I, *Speech on Introducing the Commonwealth of Australia Bill 1897 for the Consideration of the Legislative Assembly, 20th July, 1897* (Melbourne, 1897).
Jenks, E, *The Government of Victoria (Australia)* (Melbourne, George Robertson & Co, 1897).
Just, TC, *Leading Facts Connected with Federation: Compiled for the Information of the Tasmanian Delegates to the Australasian Federal Convention* (Hobart, 1891).
Kingston, CC, *The Democratic Element in Australian Federation* (Adelaide, L Bonython & Co, 1897).
McLaren, A, *Federation: The Draft Bill Exposed* (Sydney, Sir Robert Bear, 1891).
McMillan, W, *Speech on the Referendum as a Mode of Settling Disputes Between the Two Houses of Parliament: Delivered in the Legislative Assembly, 29th October 1896* (Sydney, Angus & Robertson, 1896).
Moore, WH, *The Commonwealth of Australia: Four Lectures on the Constitution Bill 1897* (Melbourne, George Robertson and Co, 1897).
—— 'Constitution Making in Australia' (1898) 31 *National Review* 269.
—— *The Constitution of the Commonwealth of Australia*, 2nd edn (Melbourne, Charles F Maxwell, 1910).
—— 'Constitutional Development in Australia' (1931) 3 *Australian Quarterly* 16.1
Nemo, 'Cabinets in Collapse' (1899) 15 *Review of Reviews* 755.
Parkes, H, *Responsible Government: What Is It?* (Sydney, WR Piddington, 1872).
—— *The Union of the Colonies: Speeches Delivered in the Legislative Assembly of New South Wales, May 16th and 23rd, 1895* (Sydney, Turner and Henderson, 1895).
Piddington, AB, *Popular Government and Federation* (Sydney, Angus & Robertson, 1898).

Quick, J, *The Inauguration of the Parliamentary Government in Victoria* (JW Burrows, 1888).
—— *A Digest of Federal Constitutions* (Bendigo, JB Young, 1896).
—— 'The Progress and Present Conditions of Federation' (1896) 8 *Review of Reviews* 248.
—— *The Federation Bill: Complete Official Text; Full Explanation by Dr Quick, Delegate to Convention* (Melbourne, Wilson and MacKinnon, 1898).
—— 'Why Victoria Should Accept the Bill' (1898) 12 *Review of Reviews* 305.
—— *The Legislative Powers of the Commonwealth and the States of Australia with Proposed Amendments* (Melbourne, Charles F Maxwell, 1919).
Quick, J and Garran, RR, *The Annotated Constitution of the Australian Commonwealth* (Sydney, Angus & Robertson, 1901).
Reeves, WP, *State Experiments in Australia & New Zealand* (London, Grant Richards, 1902).
Reid, GH, 'The 'Commonwealth of Australia'' (1891) 173 *Nineteenth Century* 145.
—— 'The Conference of Premiers at Hobart' (February 1895) *Review of Reviews* 149.
—— 'The Outlook of Federation' (January 1897) *Review of Reviews* 33.
Rogers, E N, *Is Federation Our True Policy? The Politician Revealed To Himself* (George Robertson and Company, 1898).
Russell, JW, 'Australian Federation' (1898) 167 *North American Review* 27.
Spence, WG, *Australia's Awakening: Thirty Years in the Life of an Australian Agitator* (Sydney, Worker Trustees, 1909).
Syme, D, *Representative Government in England: Its Faults and Failures* (London, K Paul, Trench & Co, 1881).
Symon, JH, *Speech by JH Symon, QC on the Constitution of the Senate Delivered 10th September, 1897* (William Applegate Gullick, 1897).
—— *The Australian Commonwealth Bill: The Spectator's Criticism: A Reply* (Adelaide, Hussey & Gillingham, Printers, 1900).
Wentworth, WC, *A Statistical, Historical, and Political Description of the Colony of New South Wales* (London, G and WB Whittaker, 1819).
Willoughby, H, *Australian Federation, Its Aims and Its Possibilities* (Melbourne, Sands & McDougall, 1891).
—— *Federation: The Hope and the Danger: A Lecture, 24th March, 1896* (Melbourne, Australasian National League, 1896).
Wise, BR, *An Australian Appeal to the English Democracy* (Sydney, William Dymock, 1885).
—— 'Australian Politics' (1889) 50 *Macmillan's Magazine* 183.
—— 'Why New South Wales Should Answer 'Yes'' (1898) 12 *Review of Reviews* 310.
—— 'The Commonwealth of Australia' (1899) 33 *National Review* 823.
—— *The Commonwealth of Australia* (London, Pitman, 1909).
—— *The Struggle for Union: Episodes in the Movement for Australian Federation* (Sydney, 1912).
—— *The Making of the Australian Commonwealth, 1889–1900: A Stage in the Growth of the Empire* (London, Longmans Green, 1913).
Wrixon, H, *Democracy in Australia: Being a Consideration of the Cause of our Present Political Difficulties and Their True Remedy* (Melbourne, Heath & Cordell, 1868).
—— *Self-Government in Victoria: Its Present Condition and the Questions it has to Deal With* (Melbourne, George Robertson, 1876).
—— *The Constitution of the Commonwealth of Australia: An Address* (Melbourne, Melville, Mullen & Slade, 1901).

NINETEENTH AND EARLY TWENTIETH CENTURY BRITISH WORKS

Anonymous, 'Extracts from the Diary of an MP' (1833) 3 *Tait's Edinburgh Magazine* 409.
Anonymous, ''Her Majesty's Opposition' in 1887' (1887) 141 *Blackwood's Edinburgh Magazine* 719.
Anonymous, 'Party Government' (1858) 69 *Westminster Review* 402.

Anonymous, 'Party Government' (1886) 125 *Westminster Review* 429.
Anonymous, 'Party Politics' (1874) 10 *Fraser's Magazine* 1.
Anonymous, 'Party Politics' (1881) 619 *Fraser's Magazine* 132.
Anonymous, 'Responsible Government' (1856) 2 *Saturday Review* 121.
Anonymous, 'Sir Robert Peel's Address to the Electors of the Borough of Tamworth' (1835) 53 *Quarterly Review* 261.
Anonymous, 'The Crisis of Parliamentary Government' (1882) 53 *Saturday Review* 4.
Anonymous, 'The Decline of Parliamentary Government' (1929) 147 *Saturday Review* 33.
Anonymous, 'The Faction-Fights' (1859) 1 *Bentley's Quarterly Review* 343.
Allen, J, *Inquiry into the Rise and Growth of the Royal Prerogative in England*, new edn (London, Longman, Brown, Green, and Longmans, 1849).
Anson, WR, *The Law and Custom of the Constitution*, 3rd edn (Oxford, Clarendon Press, 1897).
Bagehot, W, *The English Constitution* (London, Chapman and Hall, 1867).
—— *The English Constitution*, 2nd edn (London, Chapman and Hall, 1872).
—— *The English Constitution, and Other Political Essays*, rev edn (Appleton, 1902).
Blackstone, Sir W, *Commentaries on the Laws of England*, 9th edn (London, W Strahan, 1783).
Brougham, Lord H, *The British Constitution: Its History, Structure and Working*, 2nd edn (London, Griffin, Bohn and Co, 1861).
Bryce, J, *The American Commonwealth*, 2nd edn (London, Macmillan, 1891).
Buller, C, *Responsible Government for Colonies* (London, J Ridgway, 1840).
Burke, E, 'Thoughts on the Cause of the Present Discontents' in *The Works and Correspondence of the Right Honourable Edmund Burke*, new edn (London, F & J Rivington, 1852) vol 3.
—— 'Speech to the Electors of Bristol' in *The Works of Edmund Burke* (Boston, Little and Brown, 1839) vol 2.
Cecil, Lord R, 'Parliamentary Opposition' (1855) 101 *Edinburgh Review* 1.
Chitty, J, *A Treatise on the Law of the Prerogatives of the Crown: And the Relative Duties and Rights of the Subject* (London, J Butterworth, 1820).
Courtney, L, 'The Decline of Parliament' (1904) 17 *Monthly Review* 13.
Cox, H, *The British Commonwealth, or, A Commentary on the Institutions and Principles of British Government* (London, Longman, Brown, Green, and Longmans, 1854).
Creasy, ES, *The Rise and Progress of the English Constitution* (London, Richard Bentley, 1853).
Dicey, AV, 'Federal Government' (1885) 1 *Law Quarterly Review* 80.
—— 'Will the Form of Parliamentary Government be Permanent?' (1899) 13 *Harvard Law Review* 67.
—— *Introduction to the Study of the Law of the Constitution*, 6th edn (London, MacMillan, 1902).
Durham, E, *Report on the Affairs of British North America, from the Earl of Durham, Her Majesty's High Commissioner* (London, House of Commons, 1839).
Fischel, E, *The English Constitution* (London, Bosworth and Harrison, 1863).
Fisher, FV, 'Party Government' (1893) 140 *Westminster Review* 425.
Freeman, EA, *The Growth of the English Constitution from the Earliest Times,* 3rd edn (London, Macmillan, 1890).
—— *Historical Essays*, first series (London, Macmillan, 1871).
Gladstone, WE, *Gleanings of Past Years, 1843–1878* (London, John Murray, 1879).
Grey, E, *Parliamentary Government Considered with Reference to Reform*, 2nd edn (London, John Murray, 1864).
Harris, G, *The True Theory of Representation in a State* (London, Longman, Brown, Green, Longmans, and Roberts, 1857).
Harrison, F, 'The Deadlock in the House of Commons' (1881) 10 *Nineteenth Century* 317.
—— 'The Crisis of Parliamentary Government' (1882) 11 *Nineteenth Century* 9.
Hearn, WE, *The Government of England: Its Structure, and Its Development*, 2nd edn (Melbourne, George Robertson, 1886).
Lieber, F, *Manual of Political Ethics* (Boston, CC Little and J Brown, 1838).

de Lolme, JL, *The Constitution of England* (London, 1826).
Low, S, 'If the House of Commons Were Abolished?' (1894) 36 *Nineteenth Century* 846.
—— 'The Decline of the House of Commons' (1895) 37 *Nineteenth Century* 567.
—— 'Current Politics' (1901) 49 *Nineteenth Century* 147.
—— *The Governance of England* (London, Fisher Unwin, 1914).
Maine, HS, *Popular Government: Four Essays*, 3rd edn (London, John Murray, 1886).
Mill, JS, *Utilitarianism, Liberty, and Representative Government* (London, Dent & Sons, 1910.
Millar, J, *An Historical View of the English Government* (Indianapolis, Liberty Fund, 2006 [1803]).
Ostrogorski, M, *Democracy and the Organization of Political Parties* (New York, Macmillan, 1902).
Paley, W, *The Principles of Moral and Political Philosophy* (Indianapolis, Liberty Fund, 2002 [1785]).
Park, JJ, *The Dogmas of the Constitution: Four Lectures* (London, B Fellowes, 1832).
Stephen, JF, 'Parliamentary Government' (1873) 23 *Contemporary Review* 1 (Pt 1), 165 (Pt 2).
Todd, A, *On Parliamentary Government in England: Its Origin, Development, and Practical Operation*, 2nd edn (London, Longmans, Green and Co, 1887).
—— *Parliamentary Government in the British Colonies*, 2nd edn (London, Longmans, Green, 1894).
Wilkinson, K, 'A Plague On Both Your Parties!' (1895) 57 *Fortnightly Review* 757.
Wilson, EDJ, 'The Caucus and its Consequences' (1878) 4 *Nineteenth Century* 695.

AUSTRALIAN POLITICAL AND CONSTITUTIONAL HISTORY

Atkinson, M (ed), *Australia: Economic and Political Studies* (Melbourne, Macmillan, 1920).
Bailey, KH, 'Self-Government in Australia, 1860–1900' in E Scott (ed), *Cambridge History of the British Empire* (Cambridge, Cambridge University Press, 1933) vol 7, pt I.
Bannon, J, *The Crucial Colony: South Australia's Role in Reviving Federation, 1891 to 1897* (Canberra, Federalism Research Centre, 1994).
—— *Supreme Federalist: The Political Life of Sir John Downer* (Kent Town, Wakefield Press, 2009).
Bennett, S, *The Making of the Commonwealth* (Melbourne, Cassell Australia, 1971).
—— *Federation* (North Melbourne, Cassell Australia, 1975).
Birrell, B, *Federation: The Secret Story* (Potts Point, Duffy and Snellgrove, 2001).
Bolton, G, *Edmund Barton: The One Man for the Job* (St Leonard's, Allen & Unwin, 2000).
Bongiorno, F, 'The Origins of Caucus, 1856–1901' in J Faulkner and S Macintyre (eds), *True Believers: The Story of the Federal Parliamentary Labor Party* (Crows Nest, Allen & Unwin, 2001).
Brett, J, *Australian Liberals and the Moral Middle Class: From Alfred Deakin to John Howard* (Port Melbourne, Cambridge University Press, 2003).
Callaghan, PS, *Political Alignments in the Queensland Legislative Assembly, 1878–99* (BA (Hons) Thesis, University of Queensland, 1968).
Castles, AC, 'The Voyage of the "Lucinda" and the Drafting of the Australian Constitution in 1891' (1991) 65 *Australian Law Journal* 277.
Clark, CMH (ed), *Select Documents in Australian History, 1851–1900* (London, Angus and Robertson, 1955).
Clark, D, 'The South Australian Compact of 1857: The Rise, Fall and Influence of a Constitutional Compromise' (2006) 10 *Legal History* 145.
Clarke, DP, 'The Colonial Office and the Constitutional Crises in Victoria, 1865–68' (1952) 18 *Historical Studies* 160.
Clark, M, *A History of Australia, Volume 5: The People Make Laws 1888–1915* (Carlton, Melbourne University Press, 1981).
Clune, D and Griffith, G, *Decision and Deliberation: The Parliament of New South Wales, 1856–2003* (Sydney, Federation Press, 2006).
Cochrane, P, *Colonial Ambition: Foundations of Democratic Australia* (Melbourne, Melbourne University Press, 2006).

Collins, H, 'Political Ideology in Australia: The Distinctiveness of a Benthamite Society' in Stephen R Graubard (ed), *Australia, the Daedalus Symposium* (North Ryde, Angus & Robertson, 1985).

Combe, GD, *Responsible Government in South Australia* (Adelaide, Government Printer, 1957).

Cowen, Z, 'A Historical Survey of the Victorian Constitution, 1856 to 1956' (1957) 1 *Melbourne University Law Review* 9.

Crisp, LF, *Federation Fathers* (Carlton, Melbourne University Press, 1990).

Currey, CH, 'The Centenary of Responsible Government in New South Wales' (1956) 42 *Journal of the Royal Australian Historical Society* 97.

Curthoys, A and Mitchell, J, 'The Advent of Self-Government, 1840s–1890' in A Bashford and S Macintyre (eds), *The Cambridge History of Australia* (Cambridge, Cambridge University Press, 2013).

Davidson, A, *The Invisible State: The Formation of the Australian State 1788–1901* (Cambridge, Cambridge University Press, 1991).

Dickey, B, 'Parliament and the Trade Unions, 1880–1900' (1961) 47 *Journal of the Royal Australian Historical Society* 195.

—— 'Responsible Government in New South Wales: The Transfer of Power in a Colony of Settlement' (1974) 60 *Journal of the Royal Australian Historical Society* 217.

Dyrenfurth, N and Bongiorno, F, *A Little History of the Australian Labor Party* (Sydney, University of New South Wales Press, 2011).

Evans, H, 'Bryce's Bible: Why Did it Impress the Australian Founders?' (2001) 8 *New Federalist* 89.

Finn, PD, *Law and Government in Colonial Australia* (Melbourne, Oxford University Press, 1987).

Fitzgerald, R, *From the Dreaming to 1915: A History of Queensland* (St Lucia, University of Queensland Press, 1982).

Galligan, B and Roberts, W, 'The People's Constitution? Exploring Australia's Popular Democracy 1885–1901: A Research Study' (2000) 5 *New Federalist* 87.

De Garis, 'How Popular was the Popular Federation Movement?' (Papers on Parliament No 21, Parliament of Australia, 1993).

Green, FC (ed), *Tasmania: A Century of Responsible Government 1856–1956* (Hobart, Government Printer, 1956).

Greene, JP (ed), *Exclusionary Empire: English Liberty Overseas, 1600–1900* (Cambridge, Cambridge University Press, 2010).

Greenwood, G (ed), *Australia: A Social and Political History* (Sydney, Angus & Robertson, 1974).

Hawker, GN, *The Parliament of New South Wales, 1856–1965* (Ultimo, Government Printer, 1971).

Headon, D and Williams, J (eds), *Makers of Miracles: The Cast of the Federation Story* (Carlton, Melbourne University Press, 1999).

Hirst, JB, *The Strange Birth of Colonial Democracy: New South Wales 1848–1884* (Sydney, Allen & Unwin, 1988).

Hirst, J, 'Federation and the People: a Response to Stuart Macintyre' (Papers on Parliament No 32, Parliament of Australia, 1998).

—— *The Sentimental Nation: The Making of the Australian Commonwealth* (Melbourne, Oxford University Press, 2000).

—— *Freedom on the Fatal Shore: Australia's First Colony* (Melbourne, Black Inc, 2008).

Hunt, EM, *American Precedents in Australian Federation* (New York, AMS Press, 1968).

Ingham, SM, 'Political Parties in the Victorian Legislative Assembly, 1880–1900' (1950) 4 *Historical Studies* 241.

Irving, H, *To Constitute a Nation: A Cultural History of Australia's Constitution* (Cambridge, Cambridge University Press, 1997).

—— (ed), *The Centenary Companion to Australian Federation* (Melbourne, Cambridge University Press, 1999).

—— 'The Commonwealth Constitution 1900–2000' (2001) 7 *New Federalist* 3.

—— 'Making the Federal Commonwealth, 1890–1901' in Alison Bashford and Stuart Macintyre (eds), *The Cambridge History of Australia* (Melbourne, Cambridge University Press, 2013).

Irving, TH, 'The Idea of Responsible Government in New South Wales before 1856' (1964) 11 *Historical Studies* 192.

Jaensch, D, *Political Representation in Colonial South Australia 1857–1901* (PhD Thesis, University of Adelaide, 1973).

La Nauze, JA, *The Making of the Australian Constitution* (Carlton, Melbourne University Press, 1972).

—— 'Federal Conventions – The 1890s and Now' (1973) 45 *Australian Quarterly* 52.

Loveday, P, 'The Federal Convention, An Analysis of the Voting' (1972) 18 *Australian Journal of Politics and History* 169.

—— 'The Legislative Council in New South Wales, 1856–1870' (1965) 11 *Historical Studies* 481.

Loveday, P and Martin, AW, *Parliament Factions and Parties: The First Thirty Years of Responsible Government in New South Wales, 1856–1889* (Melbourne, Melbourne University Press, 1966).

Loveday, P, Martin, AW and Parker, RS (eds), *The Emergence of the Australian Party System* (Sydney, Hale & Iremonger, 1977).

Loveday, P and Martin AW, 'Colonial Politics Before 1890', in P Loveday, AW Martin and RS Parker (eds), *The Emergence of the Australian Party System* (Sydney, Hale & Iremonger, 1977).

Macintyre, S, *A Colonial Liberalism: The Lost World of Three Victorian Visionaries* (South Melbourne, Oxford University Press, 1991).

—— 'Corowa and the Voice of the People' (Papers on Parliament No 32, Parliament of Australia, 1998).

—— 'Some Absentees from Adelaide' (1998) 1 *New Federalist* 16.

—— 'The Idea of the People' (Papers on Parliament No 32, Parliament of Australia, 1998).

Mansfield, B, *Australian Democrat: The Career of Edward William O'Sullivan, 1846–1910* (Sydney, Sydney University Press, 1965).

Magarey, S, *Unbridling the Tongues of Women: A Biography of Catherine Helen Spence*, new edn (Adelaide, University of Adelaide Press, 2010).

Markey, R, 'Trade Union Democracy and the Labor Party in New South Wales, 1880–1914' (1986) 22 *Historical Studies* 71.

Martin, AW, 'Economic Influences in the 'New Federation Movement'' (1953) 6 *Historical Studies* 64.

—— (ed), *Essays in Australian Federation* (Carlton, Melbourne University Press, 1969).

—— *Henry Parkes: A Biography* (Carlton, Melbourne University Press, 1980).

—— 'Parkes and the 1890 Conference' (Papers on Parliament No 9, Parliament of Australia, 1990).

Martin, G and Sir Robert Menzies Centre for Australian Studies, *Australia, New Zealand and Federation, 1883–1901* (London, Menzies Centre for Australian Studies, 2001).

Matthews, M, 'A Forgotten 'Father of Federation': Sir John Quick' (1998) 2 *New Federalist* 55.

McConnel, K, *'Our Wayward and Backward Sister Colony': Queensland and the Australian Federation Movement, 1859–1901* (PhD Thesis, University of Queensland, 2006).

McCormack, PM, *The Popular Movement to Federation in New South Wales 1897–1899* (PhD Thesis, Australian National University, 2009).

McDonald, GW, 'The Eighty Founding Fathers' (1968) 1 *Queensland Historical Review* 38.

McLaren, IF and Victoria, Parliamentary Library Committee, *Representative Government in Victoria, 1851–1993: A Bibliography* (Melbourne, Library Committee, Parliament of Victoria, 1993).

McMinn, WG, *A Constitutional History of Australia* (Melbourne, Oxford University Press, 1979).

McMullin, R, *The Light on the Hill: The Australian Labor Party, 1891–1991* (Melbourne, Oxford University Press, 1991).

Melbourne, ACV, 'The Establishment of Responsible Government' in Ernest Scott (ed), *Cambridge History of the British Empire* (Cambridge, Cambridge University Press, 1933), vol 7, pt I.

—— *Early Constitutional Development in Australia*, 2nd edn (St Lucia, University of Queensland Press, 1963).

Melleuish, G, 'Personal Politics and Being British: Political Rhetoric, Democracy and their Consequences in Colonial New South Wales' (2013) 39 *Australian Journal of Politics and History* 1.

Miller, JDB, 'David Syme and Elective Ministries' (1953) 6 *Historical Studies* 1.

—— 'An Historical Survey: Party Discipline in Australia (I)' (1953) 5 *Political Science* 3.

—— 'Party Discipline in Australia' in CA Hughes (ed), *Readings in Australian Government* (St Lucia, University of Queensland Press, 1968).

Mills, JE, 'The Composition of the Victorian Parliament, 1856–1881' (1942) 2 *Historical Studies* 25.

Murphy, DJ and RB Joyce (eds), *Queensland Political Portraits, 1859–1952* (St Lucia, University of Queensland Press, 1978).

Murphy, DJ, Joyce, RB and Hughes, CA (eds), *Prelude to Power: The Rise of the Labour Party in Queensland 1885–1915* (Milton, Jacaranda Press, 1970).

Nairn, NB, 'The Political Mastery of Sir Henry Parkes: New South Wales, 1871–1891' (1967) 53 *Journal of the Royal Australian Historical Society* 1.

Norris, R, *The Emergent Commonwealth: Australian Federation, Expectations and Fulfilment 1889–1910* (Carlton, Melbourne University Press, 1975).

O'Collins, G, *Patrick McMahon Glynn: A Founder of Australian Federation* (Carlton, Melbourne University Press, 1965).

Parker, RS, 'Australian Federation: The Influence of Economic Interests and Political Pressures' (1949) 4 *Historical Studies* 1.

—— 'Some Comments on the Role of Economic Interests in Australian Federation' (1950) 4 *Historical Studies* 238.

Parkinson, C, 'George Higinbotham and Responsible Government in Colonial Victoria' (2001) 25 *Melbourne University Law Review* 181.

Pickering, PA, '"The Oak of English Liberty": Popular Constitutionalism in New South Wales, 1848–1856' (2001) 3 *Journal of Australian Colonial History* 1.

Preece, AA, 'The British Influence on the Australian Constitution' in MA Stephenson, CF Turner and AA Preece (eds), *Australia, Republic or Monarchy? Legal and Constitutional Issues* (St Lucia, University of Queensland Press, 1994) 132.

Pringle, R, 'The Federation Issue in New South Wales Politics 1891–99' (2008) 21 *Australian Journal of Politics & History* 1.

Puig, GV, 'Intercolonial Free Trade: The Drafting History of Section 92 of the Australian Constitution' (2011) 30 *University of Tasmania Law Review* 1.

Rawson, DW, 'Victoria' in P Loveday, AW Martin and RS Parker (eds), *The Emergence of the Australian Party System* (Sydney, Hale & Iremonger, 1977).

Reid, RL, 'South Australian Politicians and the Proposals for Federation' (1960) 4 *Melbourne Studies in Education* 204.

Reynolds, J, 'A I Clark's American Sympathies and his Influence on Australian Federation' (1958) 32 *Australian Law Journal* 62.

—— *Edmund Barton* (Melbourne, Bookman Press, 1999).

Rhodes, G, *Votes for Australia: How Colonials Voted at the 1899–1900 Federation Referendums* (Nathan, Centre for Australian Public Sector Management, 2002).

Rickard, J, *Class and Politics: New South Wales, Victoria and the Early Commonwealth, 1890–1910* (Canberra, ANU Press, 1976).

Serle, G, *The Golden Age: A History of the Colony of Victoria, 1851–1861* (Parkville, Melbourne University Press, 1963).

—— *The Rush to be Rich: A History of the Colony of Victoria, 1883–1889* (Carlton, Melbourne University Press, 1971).

Strangio, P and Costar, B (eds), *The Victorian Premiers 1856–2006* (Annandale, Federation Press, 2006).

Sweetman, E, *Australian Constitutional Development* (Melbourne, Macmillan, 1925).

Tanner, L, 'A Protracted Evolution: Labor in Victorian Politics 1889–1903' (1982) 42 *Labour History* 40.
Thomson, JA, 'Drafting the Australian Constitution: The Neglected Documents' (1985) 15 *Melbourne University Law Review* 533.
Turner, G et al, *Resolutions of Conference of Premiers on the Bill Drafted by the Australasian National Convention, 1897–8* (Melbourne, Government Printer, 1899).
Twomey, A, 'The Constitution – 19th Century Colonial Office Document or a People's Constitution?' (Background Paper No 15, Parliamentary Library, Parliamentary of Australia, 1994).
Victoria Parliament, *One Hundred Years of Responsible Government in Victoria, 1856–1956* (Melbourne, Government Printer, 1958).
Ward, JM, *Colonial Self-Government: The British Experience, 1759–1856* (London, Macmillan, 1976).
—— 'The Responsible Government Question in Victoria, South Australia and Tasmania, 1851–1856' (1978) 63 *Journal of the Royal Australian Historical Society* 221.
—— *The State and the People: A History of Australian Federation and Nation-Making, 1870–1901* (Leichhardt, Federation Press, 2001).
Waterson, D, 'The Absentees From North of the Tweed' (1998) 1 *New Federalist* 29.
Watson, TG, *The First Fifty Years of Responsible Government in Victoria: The Role of Parliament and Some Statistics of Progress from 1856 to 1906* (Melbourne, J Kemp, 1906).
Waugh, J, 'Chung Teong Toy v Musgrove and the Commonwealth Executive' (1991) 2 *Public Law Review* 160.
—— 'Evading Parliamentary Control of Government Spending: Some Early Case Studies' (1998) 9 *Public Law Review* 28.
—— 'New Federation History' (2000) 24 *Melbourne University Law Review* 1028.
—— 'Blocking Supply in Victoria' (2002) 13 *Public Law Review* 241.
Weller, P, 'Groups, Parliament and Elections: Tasmanian Politics in the 1890s' (1974) 21 *Tasmanian Historical Research Association, Papers and Proceedings* 89.
Williams, JM, 'A Toast to Absent Friends' (1998) 1 *New Federalist* 23.
—— 'The Tenterfield Oration of Henry Parkes' (1998) 1 *New Federalist* 71.
—— *The Australian Constitution: A Documentary History* (Carlton, Melbourne University Press, 2005).
Wilson, MM, *The Development of Party Politics in Queensland, 1859–1900* (MA Thesis, University of Queensland, 1938).
Windeyer, WJV, 'Responsible Government – Highlights, Sidelights and Reflections' (1957) 42 *Journal of the Royal Australian Historical Society* 257.
Wood, FLW, *The Constitutional Development of Australia* (London, George G Harrap, 1933).
Wright, DI, 'The Australasian Federation League in the Federal Movement in New South Wales, 1893–1899' (1971) 57 *Journal of the Royal Australian Historical Society* 58.
Wright, R, *A People's Counsel: A History of the Parliament of Victoria, 1856–1990* (Melbourne, Oxford University Press, 1992).

BRITISH POLITICAL AND CONSTITUTIONAL HISTORY

Aspinall, A, 'English Party Organization in the Early Nineteenth Century' (1926) 41 *English Historical Review* 389.
Beales, DED, 'Parliamentary Parties and the 'Independent' Member, 1810–1860' in Robert Robson (ed), *Ideas and Institutions of Victorian Britain* (London, Bell, 1967).
Berrington, H, 'Partisanship and Dissidence in the Nineteenth-Century House of Commons' (1968) 21 *Parliamentary Affairs* 338.
Birch, AH, *Representative and Responsible Government: An Essay on the British Constitution* (London, Allen & Unwin, 1964).

Briggs, Asa, *The Age of Improvement, 1783–1867* (London, Longman, 1959).

Cox, GW, 'The Development of a Party-Orientated Electorate in England, 1832–1918' (1986) 16 *British Journal of Political Science* 187.

—— *The Efficient Secret: The Cabinet and the Development of Political Parties in Victorian England* (Cambridge, Cambridge University Press, 1987).

—— 'The Development of Collective Responsibility in the United Kingdom' (1994) 13 *Parliamentary History* 32.

Cromwell, V, 'The Losing of the Initiative by the House of Commons, 1780–1914' (1968) 18 *Transactions of the Royal Historical Society* 1.

Dodd, AH, *The Growth of Responsible Government: From James the First to Victoria* (London, Routledge & Kegan Paul, 1956).

Fair, JD, 'Party Voting Behaviour in the British House of Commons 1886–1918' (1986) 5 *Parliamentary History* 65.

Foley, M, *The Politics of the British Constitution* (Manchester, Manchester University Press, 1999).

Fraser, P, 'The Growth of Ministerial Control in the Nineteenth-Century House of Commons' (1960) 76 *English Historical Review* 444.

Gneist, R, *The History of the English Constitution* (Philip A Ashworrth tr, London, W Clowes, 1891).

Hanham, HJ, *The Nineteenth-Century Constitution 1815–1914: Documents and Commentary* (Cambridge, Cambridge University Press, 1969).

Hawkins, A, ''Parliamentary Government' and Victorian Political Parties, c 1830–c 1880' (1989) 104 *English Historical Review* 638.

—— *British Party Politics, 1852–1886* (New York, St Martin's Press, 1998).

—— *Victorian Political Culture: 'Habits of Heart and Mind'* (Oxford, Oxford University Press, 2015).

Horn, DB and Ransome, M (eds), *English Historical Documents, 1714–1783* (London, Eyre & Spottiswoode, 1957).

Hughes, E, 'Sir Erskine May's Views on Parliamentary Procedure in 1882' (1956) 34 *Public Administration* 419.

Jenkins, TA, 'The Whips in the Early Victorian House of Commons' (2000) 19 *Parliamentary History* 259.

—— *Parliament, Party, and Politics in Victorian Britain* (Manchester, Manchester University Press, 1996).

Keir, DL, *The Constitutional History of Modern Britain Since 1485*, 7th edn (London, Black, 1964).

Macaulay, Lord, *History of England: To the Death of William III* (London, Heron Books, 1967).

Maitland, FW, *The Constitutional History of England* (Cambridge, Cambridge University Press, 1911).

Matthew, HCG, 'Disraeli, Gladstone, and the Politics of Mid-Victorian Budgets' (1979) 22 *Historical Journal* 615.

May, TE, *The Constitutional History of England Since the Accession of George the Third, 1760–1860*, 10th edn (London, Longmans, 1891).

McGowen, R and Arnstein, WL, 'The Mid-Victorians and the Two Party System' (1979) 11 *Albion* 242.

Medley, DJ, *A Student's Manual of English Constitutional History*, 4th edn (Oxford, Blackwell, 1907).

Redlich, J, *The Procedure of the House of Commons: A Study of its History and Present Form*, 3 vols (London, Constable, 1908).

Saunders, R, 'Parliament and People: The British Constitution in the Long Nineteenth Century' (2008) 6 *Journal of Modern European History* 72.

Taylor, M, 'Introduction' in W Bagehot, *The English Constitution* (Oxford, Oxford University Press, 2001).

Trollope, A, *Barchester Towers* (London, Dent, 1966 [1857]).

Watson, JS, *The Reign of George III, 1760–1815* (Oxford, Clarendon Press, 1960).
Williams, EN, *The Eighteenth Century Constitution, 1688–1815: Documents and Commentary* (Cambridge, Cambridge University Press, 1960).

OTHER SCHOLARSHIP

Ahmed, F, Albert, R and Perry, A, 'Judging Constitutional Conventions' (2019) 17 *International Journal of Constitutional Law* 787.
Aldons, M, 'The 'Elective Dictatorship' – Fact or Fiction?' (2002) 17 *Australasian Political Review* 69.
Allan, TRS, 'Legislative Supremacy and the Rule of Law: Democracy and Constitutionalism' (1985) 44 *Cambridge Law Journal* 111.
—— 'Common Law Constitutionalism and Freedom of Speech' in J Beatson and Y Cripps (eds), *Freedom of Expression and Freedom of Information: Essays in Honour of Sir David Williams* (Oxford, Oxford University Press, 2000).
—— *Constitutional Justice: A Liberal Theory of the Rule of Law* (Oxford, Oxford University Press, 2001).
—— *The Sovereignty of Law: Freedom, Constitution, and Common Law* (Oxford, Oxford University Press, 2013).
Archer, JR, 'The Theory of Responsible Government in Britain and Australia' (1980) 15 *Politics* 23.
Archer, J and Maddox, G, 'The 1975 Constitutional Crisis in Australia' (1976) 14 *Journal of Commonwealth and Comparative Politics* 141.
Arcioni, E, *'The People' in the Australian Constitution: More than a Vague and Emotionally Powerful Abstraction* (PhD Thesis, University of Sydney, 2015).
—— 'The Core of the Australian Constitutional People – 'The People' as 'The Electors'' (2016) 39 *University of New South Wales Law Journal* 421.
Aroney, N, 'A Seductive Plausibility: Freedom of Speech in the Constitution' (1995) 8 *University of Queensland Law Journal* 249.
—— *Freedom of Speech in the Constitution* (St Leonards, Centre for Independent Studies, 1998).
—— 'Four Reasons for an Upper House: Representative Democracy, Public Debate, Legislative Outputs and Executive Accountability' (2008) 29 *Adelaide Law Review* 205.
—— *The Constitution of a Federal Commonwealth: The Making and Meaning of the Australian Constitution* (Cambridge, Cambridge University Press, 2009).
—— 'The High Court on Constitutional Law: The 2012 Term – Explanatory Power and the Modalities of Constitutional Reasoning' (2013) 36 *University of New South Wales Law Journal* 863.
—— 'On the Distinction Between Law and Convention' in B Galligan and S Brenton (eds), *Constitutional Conventions in Westminster Systems* (Cambridge, Cambridge University Press, 2015).
—— 'Originalism and Explanatory Power: Text, Structure and the Interpretation of Constitutions' in Lisa Burton Crawford, Patrick Emerton and Dale Smith (eds), *Law under a Democratic Constitution: Essays in Honour of Jeffrey Goldsworthy* (Oxford, Hart, 2019).
Aroney, N, Gerangelos, P, Murray, S and Stellios, J, *The Constitution of the Commonwealth of Australia: History, Principle and Interpretation* (Port Melbourne, Cambridge University Press, 2015).
Aroney, N and Saunders, BB, 'On Judicial Rascals and Self-Appointed Monarchs: The Rise of Judicial Power in Australia' (2017) 35 *University of Queensland Law Journal* 221.
Aroney, N, Prasser, S and Nethercote, JR (eds), *Restraining Elective Dictatorship: The Upper House Solution?* (Crawley, University of Western Australia Press, 2008).
Bach, S, *Platypus and Parliament: The Australian Senate in Theory and Practice* (Canberra, Department of the Senate, 2003).

—— 'Crisp, the Senate, and the Constitution' (2008) 54 *Australian Journal of Politics and History* 545.

Barber, NW, 'Laws and Constitutional Conventions' (2009) 125 *Law Quarterly Review* 294.

Bateman, W, *Public Finance and Parliamentary Constitutionalism* (Cambridge, Cambridge University Press, 2020).

Beck, L, *Religious Freedom and the Australian Constitution: Origins and Future* (London, Routledge, 2018).

Beetham, D and Weir, S, *Political Power and Democratic Control in Britain: The Democratic Audit of the United Kingdon* (London, Routledge, 1999).

Bell, JV, 'Section 80 – The Great Constitutional Tautology' (2014) 40 *Monash University Law Review* 7.

Bellamy, R, *Political Constitutionalism: A Republican Defence of the Constitutionality of Democracy* (Cambridge, Cambridge University Press, 2007).

Berman, HJ, 'The Origins of Historical Jurisprudence: Coke, Selden, Hale' (1993) 103 *Yale Law Journal* 1651.

Bevir, M (ed), *Encyclopedia of Political Theory* (Thousand Oaks, Sage, 2010).

Blackshield, AR, 'The Implied Freedom of Communication' in G Lindell (ed), *Future Directions in Australian Constitutional Law: Essays in Honour of Professor Leslie Zines* (Sydney, Federation Press, 1994).

Blewett, N, 'Parliamentary Reform: Challenges for the House of Representatives (1993) 65 *Australian Quarterly* 1.

Bogdanor, V, *The Monarchy and the Constitution* (Oxford, Clarendon Press, 1995).

—— *The Coalition and the Constitution* (Oxford, Hart, 2011).

Botterill, L and Cockfield, G, 'From "Unstable" to "Stable" Minority Government: Reflections on the Role of the Nationals in Federal Coalition Governments' (2015) 61 *Australian Journal of Politics & History* 53.

Boutmy, É, *Studies in Constitutional Law* (EM Dicey tr, London, Macmillan, 1891).

Bowden, JWJ and MacDonald, NA, 'Cabinet Manuals and the Crown' in DM Jackson and P Lagassé (eds), *Canada and the Crown: Essays on Constitutional Monarchy* (Montreal, McGill-Queen's University Press, 2013).

Brennan, G, 'Australian Parliamentary Democracy: One Cheer for the Status Quo' (Papers on Parliament No 22, Parliament of Australia, 1994).

Bryce, J, *Modern Democracies* (London, Macmillan, 1921).

Burmester, H, 'Limitations on Federal Adjudication' in B Opeskin and F Wheeler (eds), *The Australian Federal Judicial System* (Carlton South, Melbourne University Press, 2000).

Butler, D, 'Australia's Contribution to Political Institutions' (2001) 7 *New Federalist* 47.

Byers, M, 'The Australian Constitution and Responsible Government' (1985) 1 *Australian Bar Review* 233.

Callinan, IDF, 'Responsible Government – in Dilution' (April 2008) 52:4 *Quadrant* 16.

Campbell, E, 'Federal Contract Law' (1970) 44 *Australian Law Journal* 14.

—— 'Commonwealth Contracts' (1970) 44 *Australian Law Journal* 580.

Campbell, I, 'Groups, Parties and Federation' in P Loveday and I Campbell, *Groups in Theory and Practice* (Melbourne, Cheshire, 1962).

Castles, AC, *An Australian Legal History* (Sydney, Law Book Co, 1982).

Cecil, Lord H, *Conservatism* (London, Williams & Norgate, 1912).

Chalmers, J and Davis, G, 'Power: Relations Between the Parliament and the Executive' (Research Paper No 14, Parliamentary Library, Parliament of Australia, 2000).

Charnock, D and Ellis, P, 'The Structure of the Australian Party System and its Strategic Consequences' (2003) 38 *Australian Journal of Political Science* 423.

Clinton, RN, 'Original Understanding, Legal Realism and the Interpretation of "This Constitution"' (1987) 72 *Iowa Law Review* 1177.

Cohn, M, *A Theory of the Executive Branch: Tension and Legality* (Oxford, Oxford University Press, 2021).
Cole, RW, 'Responsible Government and the Public Service' (1980) 15 *Politics* 168.
Collins, HN, 'What Shall we do with the Westminster Model?' in RFI Smith and P Weller (eds), *Public Service Inquiries in Australia* (St Lucia, University of Queensland Press, 1978).
Cooray, LJM, *Conventions, the Australian Constitution and the Future* (Sydney, Legal Books, 1979).
Coper, M, *Encounters with the Australian Constitution* (North Ryde, CCH Australia, 1987).
Coper, M and Williams, G (eds), *Power, Parliament and the People* (Leichhardt, Federation Press, 1997).
Costar, B (ed), *Deadlock or Democracy? The Future of the Senate* (Sydney, University of New South Wales Press, 1999).
Craven, G, 'The Convention Debates: Still More Sinned Against than Sinning' (1998) 1 *New Federalist* 67.
—— 'Heresy as Orthodoxy: Were the Founders Progressivists?' (2003) 31 *Federal Law Review* 87.
Crisp, LF, *Australian National Government*, 5th edn (Melbourne, Longman Cheshire, 1983).
Crommelin, M, 'The Executive' in Gregory Craven (ed), *The Convention Debates 1891–1898: Commentaries, Indices and Guide* (Sydney, Legal Books, 1986).
Crossman, RHS, 'Introduction' in W Bagehot, *The English Constitution* (Glasgow, Fontana Collins, 1963).
Dahl, RA, *Democracy and its Critics* (New Haven, Yale University Press, 1989).
Daintith, T and Page, A, *The Executive in the Constitution. Structure, Autonomy, and Internal Control* (Oxford, Oxford University Press, 1999).
Daley, J, *The Bases for the Authority of the Australian Constitution* (DPhil Thesis, Oxford University, 1999).
Davis, G, 'Executive Government: Cabinet and the Prime Minister' in J Summers, D Woodward and A Parkin (eds), *Government, Politics, Power and Policy in Australia*, 7th edn (Frenchs Forest, Longman, 2002).
Dawson, Sir D, 'Intention and the Constitution – Whose Intent?' (1990) 6 *Australian Bar Review* 93.
Deagon, A and Saunders, BB, 'Principles, Pragmatism and Power: Another Look at the Historical Context of Section 116' (2020) 43 *Melbourne University Law Review* 1033.
Dillon, A, 'A Turtle by Any Other Name: The Legal Basis of the Australian Constitution' (2001) 29 *Federal Law Review* 241.
Dixon, Sir O, *Jesting Pilate and Other Papers and Addresses*, 3rd edn (Annandale, Federation Press, 2019).
Dixon, R, 'Functional Constitution: Re-reading the 2014 High Court Constitutional Term' (2015) 43 *Federal Law Review* 455.
—— (ed), *Australian Constitutional Values* (Oxford, Hart, 2020).
—— *Responsive Judicial Review* (Oxford, Oxford University Press, 2023).
Dixon, R and Appleby, G, 'Constitutional Implications in Australia: Explaining the Structure – Rights Dualism' in R Dixon and A Stone (eds), *The Invisible Constitution in Comparative Perspective* (Cambridge, Cambridge University Press, 2018).
Donaghue, S and Wood, T, 'The Evolving Role of History in Constitutional Interpretation' (2020) 31 *Public Law Review* 248.
Dowding, K and Lewis, C (eds), *Ministerial Careers and Accountability in the Australian Commonwealth Government* (Acton, ANU E Press, 2012).
Drakeman, DL, *The Hollow Core of Constitutional Theory: Why We Need the Framers* (Cambridge, Cambridge University Press, 2020).
Duxbury, N, *Elements of Legislation* (Cambridge, Cambridge University Press, 2013).
Edelman, Justice J, 'Constitutional Interpretation' (2019) 45 *University of Western Australia Law Review* 1.
Edwards, M et al, *Public Sector Governance in Australia* (Acton, ANU Press, 2012).
Ekins, R, *The Nature of Legislative Intent* (Oxford, Oxford University Press, 2012).

Ekins, R and Goldsworthy, J, 'The Reality and Indispensability of Legislative Intentions' (2014) 36 *Sydney Law Review* 39.

Emerton, P, 'Political Freedoms and Entitlements in the *Australian Constitution* – An Example of Referential Intentions Yielding Unintended Legal Consequences' (2010) 38 *Federal Law Review* 169.

Emy, H, 'The Mandate, the Senate and Responsible Government' (1996) 30 *Australia and World Affairs* 5.

Epps, D and Sitaraman, G, 'How to Save the Supreme Court' (2019) 129 *Yale Law Journal* 148.

Evans, G, 'Labor and the Constitution' (1976) 35 *Meanjin* 3.

—— (ed), *Labor and the Constitution, 1972–1975: Essays and Commentaries on the Constitutional Controversies of the Whitlam Years in Austrlaian Government* (Richmond, Heinemann Educational Australia, 1977).

Evans, H, 'Reflections on the Founders', *The House Magazine*, 1 March 1995.

Evans, S, 'Why Is the Constitution Binding? Authority, Obligation and the Role of the People' (2004) 25 *Adelaide Law Review* 107.

Faulkner, J, 'A Labor Perspective on Senate Reform' (Papers on Parliament No 34, Parliament of Australia, 1999).

Finn, C, 'The Concept of 'Justiciability' in Administrative Law' in M Groves and HP Lee (eds), *Australian Administrative Law: Fundamentals, Principles and Doctrines* (Port Melbourne, Cambridge University Press, 2007) 154.

Finn, P, 'Public Trust and Public Accountability' (1993) 65 *Australian Quarterly* 50.

Freeman, S, 'Constitutional Democracy and the Legitimacy of Judicial Review' (1990) 9 *Law and Philosophy* 327.

—— 'Original Meaning, Democratic Interpretation, and the Constitution' (1992) 21 *Philosophy and Public Affairs* 3.

Fry, TP, *Australian Contributions to the Evolution of Parliamentary Government* (Brisbane, University of Queensland, 1947).

Gageler, JS, 'Foundations of Australian Federalism and the Role of Judicial Review' (1987) 17 *Federal Law Review* 162.

—— 'Beyond the Text: A Vision of the Structure and Function of the Constitution' (2009) 32 *Australian Bar Review* 138.

—— 'James Bryce and the Australian Constitution' (2015) 43 *Federal Law Review* 177.

—— 'Legislative Intention' (2015) 41 *Monash University Law Review* 1.

—— 'The Section 92 Revolution' in J Stellios (ed), *Encounters with Constitutional Interpretation and Legal Education: Essays in Honour of Michael Coper* (Annandale, Federation Press 2018).

Galligan, B, 'The Founders' Design and Intentions Regarding Responsible Government' (1980) 15 *Politics* 1.

—— 'The Kerr-Whitlam Debate and the Principles of the Australian Constitution' (1980) 18 *Journal of Commonwealth and Comparative Politics* 247.

—— *Politics of the High Court* (St Lucia, University of Queensland Press, 1987).

—— *A Federal Republic: Australia's Constitutional System of Government* (Melbourne, Cambridge University Press, 1995).

Galligan, B and Warden, J, 'The Design of the Senate' in G Craven (ed), *The Convention Debates 1891–1898: Commentaries, Indices and Guide* (Sydney, Legal Books, 1986).

Galligan, B and Brenton, S (eds), *Constitutional Conventions in Westminster Systems: Controversies, Changes and Challenges* (Cambridge, Cambridge University Press, 2015).

Gardbaum, S, *The New Commonwealth Model of Constitutionalism: Theory and Practice* (Cambridge, Cambridge University Press, 2013).

Gardner, J, 'Can There Be a Written Constitution?' in L Green and B Leiter (eds), *Oxford Studies in Philosophy of Law* (Oxford, Oxford University Press, 2011) vol 1.

Gearty, C, *Principles of Human Rights Adjudication* (Oxford, Oxford University Press, 2004).

Gee, G and CN Webber, GCN, 'What Is a Political Constitution?' (2010) 30 *Oxford Journal of Legal Studies* 273.

Gerangelos, P, 'The Executive Power of the Commonwealth of Australia: Section 61 of the Commonwealth Constitution, 'Nationhood' and the Future of the Prerogative' (2012) 12 *Oxford University Commonwealth Law Journal* 97.

Ginsburg, T and Huq, AZ, *How to Save a Constitutional Democracy* (Chicago, University of Chicago Press, 2018).

Goldring, J, 'Accountability of Commonwealth Statutory Authorities and "Responsible Government"' (1980) 11 *Federal Law Review* 353.

Godbout, J-F and Smaz, M, 'Party Development in the Early Decades of the Australian Parliament: A New Perspective' (2016) 51 *Australian Journal of Political Science* 478.

Goldsworthy, J, 'Originalism in Constitutional Interpretation' (1997) 25 *Federal Law Review* 1.

—— *The Sovereignty of Parliament: History and Philosophy* (Oxford, Clarendon Press, 1999).

—— 'Australia: Devotion to Legalism' in J Goldsworthy (ed), *Interpreting Constitutions: A Comparative Study* (Oxford, Oxford University Press, 2007).

—— 'Constitutional Interpretation: Originalism' (2009) 4 *Philosophy Compass* 682.

—— 'Constitutional Implications Revisited' (2011) 30 *University of Queensland Law Journal* 9.

Goodlad, Sir A, 'Political Structure and Constitutional Reform in the United Kingdom' (Papers on Parliament No 38, Parliament of Australia, 2001).

Greenwood, G, *The Future of Australian Federalism: A Commentary on the Working of the Constitution*, 2nd edn (St Lucia, University of Queensland Press, 1976).

Griffith, JAG, 'The Political Constitution' (1979) 42 *Modern Law Review* 1.

Halligan, J, Miller, R and Power, J, *Parliament in the Twenty-first Century: Institutional Reform and Emerging Roles* (Carlton, Melbourne University Publishing, 2007).

Hamer, D, 'Senate Committees – Keeping Parliament Responsible' (Papers on Parliament No 12, Parliament of Australia, 1991).

—— *Can Responsible Government Survive In Australia?* (Canberra, Department of the Senate, 2004).

Hamilton, A, Madison, J and Jay, J, *The Federalist Papers*, Clinton Rossiter (ed) (New York, Mentor, 1961).

Harvey, M NC, 'James Bryce, 'The American Commonwealth', and the Australian Constitution' (2002) 76 *Australian Law Journal* 362.

Heydon, JD, 'Theories of Constitutional Interpretation: A Taxonomy' (2007) *Bar News* 12.

Holland, I, 'Senate Committees and the Legislative Process' (Research Paper No 7, Parliamentary Studies Centre, Australian National University).

Horwitz, MJ, 'A Historiography of the People Themselves and Popular Constitutionalism' (2006) 81 *Chicago-Kent Law Review* 813.

Howard, C and Saunders, C, 'The Blocking of the Budget and Dismissal of the Government' in G Evans (ed), *Labor and the Constitution, 1972–1975: Essays and Commentaries on the Constitutional Controversies of the Whitlam Years* (Richmond, Heinemann Educational Australia, 1977).

Hughes, CA, *The Government of Queensland* (St Lucia, University of Queensland Press, 1980).

Hume, D and Williams, G, *People Power: The History and Future of the Referendum in Australia* (Sydney, University of New South Wales Press, 2010).

Huhn, WR, 'Constantly Approximating Popular Sovereignty: Seven Fundamental Principles of Constitutional Law' (2010) 19 *William & Mary Bill of Rights Journal* 291.

Indyk, M, 'Making Government Responsible: The Role of Parliamentary Committees' (1980) 15 *Politics* 93.

Irving, H, *Five Things to Know about the Australian Constitution* (Cambridge, Cambridge University Press, 2004).

—— 'Constitutional Interpretation, the High Court, and the Discipline of History' (2013) 41 *Federal Law Review* 95.

Jaensch, D, *The Government of South Australia* (St Lucia, University of Queensland Press, 1977).
Jennings, I, *Cabinet Government*, 3rd edn (Cambridge, Cambridge University Press, 1969).
Jones, BT, *Republicanism and Responsible Government: The Shaping of Democracy in Australia and Canada* (Montreal, McGill–Queen's University Press, 2014).
Jupp, J, *Party Politics: Australia 1966–1981* (Sydney, Allen & Unwin, 1982).
Keating, M, Wanna, J and Weller, P (eds), *Institutions on the Edge? Capacity for Governance* (St Leonards, Allen & Unwin, 2000).
Keith, AB, *Responsible Government in the Dominions* (Oxford, Clarendon Press, 1912).
Kelly, P, *November 1975* (St Leonards, Allen & Unwin, 1995).
Kerr, D, 'The High Court and the Executive: Emerging Challenges to the Underlying Doctrines of Responsible Government and the Rule of Law' (2009) 28 *University Of Tasmania Law Review* 145.
Killey, I, *Constitutional Conventions in Australia: An Introduction to the Unwritten Rules of Australia's Constitutions* (Melbourne, Australian Scholarly Publishing, 2009).
Kinley, D, 'Governmental Accountability in Australia and the United Kingdom: A Conceptual Analysis of the Role of Non-Parliamentary Institutions and Devices' (1995) 18 *University of New South Wales Law Journal* 409.
Kirby, M, 'Constitutional Interpretation and Original Intent: A Form of Ancestor Worship?' (2000) 24 *Melbourne University Law Review* 1.
Kirk, J, 'Constitutional Interpretation and a Theory of Evolutionary Originalism' (1999) 27 *Federal Law Review* 323.
Kukathas, C, 'Democracy, Parliament and Responsible Government' (Papers on Parliament No 8, Parliament of Australia, 1990).
Larkin, P, 'Ministerial Accountability to Parliament' in K Dowding and C Lewis (eds), *Ministerial Careers and Accountability in the Australian Commonwealth Government* (Acton, ANU E-Press, 2012).
Law, DS, 'Generic Constitutional Law' (2005) 89 *Minnesota Law Review* 652.
Law, DS and Versteeg, M, 'The Declining Influence of the United States Constitution' (2012) 87 *New York University Law Review* 762.
Laws, Sir J, 'Law and Democracy' [1995] *Public Law* 72.
Lawson, Cs, 'Re-Invigorating the Accountability and Transparency of the Australian Government's Expenditure' (2008) 32 *Melbourne University Law Review* 879.
—— *Regulating Executive Power under the Australian Commonwealth Framework* (Black Jettie, 2011).
—— 'The Legal Structures of Responsible Government and Ministerial Responsibility' (2011) 35 *Melbourne University Law Review* 1005.
Lecky, WEH, *Democracy and Liberty*, new edn (New York, Longmans, Green and Co, 1903).
Lee, HP and Winterton, G (eds), *Australian Constitutional Landmarks* (Port Melbourne, Cambridge University Press, 2003).
Lee, HP and Gerangelos, P (eds), *Constitutional Advancement in a Frozen Continent: Essays in Honour of George Winterton* (Annandale, Federation Press, 2009).
Levy, R and Orr, G, *The Law of Deliberative Democracy* (London, Routledge, 2016).
Levy, R, Silva, N and Saunders, BB, 'Deliberation at the Founding: Deliberative Democracy as an Original Constitutional Value' (2017) 28 *Public Law Review* 41.
Lim, B, *Australia's Constitution After Whitlam* (Cambridge, Cambridge University Press, 2017).
Lindell, GJ, 'Why Is Australia's Constitution Binding? – The Reason in 1900 and Now, and the Effect of Independence' (1986) 16 *Federal Law Review* 29.
Lindell, G, 'Responsible Government' in P D Finn (ed), *Essays on Law and Government, Volume 1: Principles and Values* (North Ryde, Law Book Co, 1995).
—— *Responsible Government and the Australian Constitution – Conventions Transformed into Law?* (Leichhardt, Federation Press, 2004).
—— 'The Role of a State Governor in relation to Illegality' (2012) 23 *Public Law Review* 268.

—— 'Judicial Review and the Dismissal of an Elected Government in 1975: Then and Now?' (2014) 38 *Australian Bar Review* 118.

Lino, D, 'The Australian Constitution as Symbol' (2020) 48 *Federal Law Review* 543.

Lipton, J, 'Responsible Government, Representative Democracy and the Senate: Options for Reform' (1997) 19 *University of Queensland Law Journal* 194.

List, C and Pettit, P, *Group Agency: The Possibility, Design and Status of Corporate Agents* (Oxford, Oxford University Press, 2011).

Lumb, RD, *Australian Constitutionalism* (Sydney, Butterworths, 1983).

Macintyre, C and Williams, J (eds), *Peace, Order and Good Government: State Constitutional and Parliamentary Reform* (Kent Town, Wakefield Press, 2003).

Maddigan, J, 'Ministerial Responsibility: Reality or Myth?' (2011) 26 *Australasian Parliamentary Review* 158.

Maddison, S and Denniss, R, *An Introduction to Australian Public Policy: Theory and Practice*, 2nd edn (New York, Cambridge University Press, 2013).

Mantziaris, C, 'Interpreting Ministerial Directions to Statutory Corporations: What Does a Theory of Responsible Government Deliver?' (1998) 26 *Federal Law Review* 309.

Marchant, S, *The Historical Traditions of the Australian Senate: The Upper House We Had to Have* (PhD Thesis, Australian National University, 2009).

Marsh, I, *Beyond the Two Party System: Political Representation, Economic Competitiveness, and Australian Politics* (Melbourne, Cambridge University Press, 1995).

Marshall, G, *Constitutional Conventions: The Rules and Forms of Political Accountability* (Oxford, Clarendon Press, 1984).

—— 'What are Constitutional Conventions?' (1985) 38 *Parliamentary Affairs* 33.

Martin, Aaron and Juliet Pietsch, 'Future Shock or Future Stability? Generation Change and the Australian Party System' (2013) 59 *Australian Journal of Politics and History* 212.

McCamish, C, 'The Use of Historical Materials in Interpreting the Commonwealth Constitution' (1996) 70 *Australian Law Journal* 638.

McDonald, L, 'The Denizens of Democracy: The High Court and the Free Speech Cases' (1994) 5 *Public Law Review* 160.

McGrath, FR, *The Intentions of the Framers of the Commonwealth of Australia Constitution* (PhD Thesis, University of Sydney, 2006).

Michels, R, *Political Parties: A Sociological Study of the Oligarchical Tendencies of Modern Democracy* (New York, Collier, 1915).

Miragliotta, N, Errington, W and Barry, N, *The Australian Political System in Action*, 2nd edn (Melbourne, Oxford University Press, 2013).

Moore, T, Bourke, S and Maddox, G, 'Australia and the Emergence of the Modern Two-Party System' (1998) 44 *Australian Journal of Politics and History* 17.

Morris, JO, 'Some Aspects of the Commonwealth Parliament's Defence Power Under the Constitution' (1941) 2 *Res Judicatae* 221.

Mulgan, R, 'Assessing Ministerial Responsibility in Australia' in K Dowling and C Lewis (eds), *Ministerial Careers and Accountability in the Australian Commonwealth Government* (Acton, ANU Press, 2012).

Nestorovska, D, 'Assessing the Effectiveness of ASIC's Accountability Framework' (2016) 34 *Company & Securities Law Journal* 193.

Nethercote, JR, 'Professor LF Crisp and the Australian Senate: A Comment on Stanley Bach's Analysis' (2009) 55 *Australian Journal of Politics and History* 557.

Ng, Y-F, *Ministerial Advisers in Australia: The Modern Legal Context* (Annandale, Federation Press, 2016).

—— 'Political Constitutionalism: Individual Responsibility and Collective Restraint' (2020) 48 *Federal Law Review* 455.

Orr, G, 'Suppressing Vote-Buying: the 'War' on Electoral Bribery from 1868' (2006) 27 *Journal of Legal History* 289.

—— 'Party Primaries for Candidate Preselection? Right Question, Wrong Answer' (2011) 34 *University of New South Wales Law Journal* 964.
Page, B, 'Ministerial Resignation and Individual Ministerial Responsibility in Australia 1976–1989' (1990) 28 *Journal of Commonwealth & Comparative Politics* 141.
Parker, RS, 'The Meaning of Responsible Government' (1976) 11 *Politics* 178.
—— 'Responsible Government in Australia' (1980) 15 *Politics* 11.
Parkin, A, 'Pluralism and Australian Political Science' (1980) 15 *Politics* 50.
Pierce, J, *Inside the Mason Court Revolution: The High Court of Australia Transformed* (Durham, Carolina Academic Press, 2006).
Pocock, JGA, *Virtue, Commerce and History: Essays on Political Thought and History, Chiefly in the Eighteenth Century* (Cambridge, Cambridge University Press, 1985).
Poole, T, 'Back to the Future – Unearthing the Theory of Common Law Constitutionalism' (2003) 23 *Oxford Journal of Legal Studies* 435.
Posner, EA and Vermeule, A, *The Executive Unbound: After the Madisonian Republic* (Oxford, Oxford University Press, 2010).
Power, J (ed), *Public Administration in Australia: A Watershed* (Sydney, Hale & Iremonger, 1990).
Prosser, B and Denniss, R, 'Lobbying and Minority Government in Australia: The Concept of the Marginal Member' (2015) 50 *Australian Journal of Political Science* 496.
Radin, M, 'Statutory Interpretation' (1930) 43 *Harvard Law Review* 863.
Raffin, L, 'Individual Ministerial Responsibility During the Howard Years: 1996–2007' (2008) 54 *Australian Journal of Politics and History* 225.
Reid, GS, 'Australia's Commonwealth Parliament and the 'Westminster Model'' (1964) 2 *Journal of Commonwealth Political Studies* 89.
—— 'Parliamentary-Executive Relations: The Suppression of Politics' in Henry Mayer, (ed), *Australian Politics: A Second Reader* (Melbourne, Cheshire, 1970).
—— 'Responsible Government and Ministerial Responsibility' (1980) 39 *Australian Journal of Public Administration* 301.
Reid, GS and Forrest, M, *Australia's Commonwealth Parliament 1901–1988: Ten Perspectives* (Carlton, Melbourne University Press, 1989).
Rhodes, RAW, Wanna, J and Weller, P, *Comparing Westminster* (Oxford, Oxford University Press, 2011).
Richardson, JE, 'The Executive Power of the Commonwealth' in L Zines (ed), *Commentaries on the Australian Constitution: A Tribute to Geoffrey Sawer* (Sydney, Butterworths, 1977).
Richardson, J, 'Resolving Deadlocks in the Australian Parliament' (Research Paper 9, Parliament of Australia, 2000).
Rydon, J, 'Some Problems of Combining the British and American Elements in the Australian Constitution' (1985) 23 *Journal of Commonwealth & Comparative Politics* 67.
Sampford, CJG, 'Reconciling Responsible Government and Federalism' in MP Ellinghaus, AJ Bradbrook and AJ Duggan (eds), *The Emergence of Australian Law* (Sydney, Butterworths, 1989).
—— 'Responsible Government and the Logic of Federalism: An Australian Paradox?' [1990] *Public Law* 90.
Sapienza, A, *Judicial Review of Non-Statutory Executive Action* (Alexandria, Federation Press, 2020).
Saunders, BB, 'Democracy, Liberty and the Prerogative: The Displacement of Inherent Executive Power by Statute' (2013) 41 *Federal Law Review* 363.
—— 'The Public Sector Duty of Care and Diligence' (2019) 42 *University of New South Wales Law Journal* 652.
—— 'Responsible Government, Statutory Authorities and the Australian Constitution' (2020) 48 *Federal Law Review* 4.
—— 'Ministers, Statutory Authorities and Government Corporations: The Agency Problem in Public Sector Governance' (2022) 45 *Melbourne University Law Review* 695.

Saunders, BB and Deagon, A, 'Religion and the Constitution: A Response to Luke Beck's Safeguard against Religious Intolerance Theory of Section 116' (2021) 44 *University of New South Wales Law Journal* 1558.

Saunders, BB and Kennedy, SP, 'Popular Sovereignty, 'the People', and the Australian Constitution: A Historical Reassessment' (2019) 30 *Public Law Review* 36.

—— 'History and Constitutional Interpretation: Applying the 'Cambridge School' Approach to Interpreting Constitutions' (2020) 40 *Oxford Journal of Legal Studies* 591.

Saunders, C, 'Future Prospects of the Australian Constitution' in R French, G Lindell and C Saunders (eds), *Reflections on the Australian Constitution* (Annandale, Federation Press, 2003).

—— 'Interpreting the *Constitution*' (2004) 15 *Public Law Review* 289.

Saunders, C and Stone, A (eds), *The Oxford Handbook of the Australian Constitution* (Oxford, Oxford University Press, 2018).

Sawer, G, *Federation Under Strain: Australia 1972–1975* (Carlton, Melbourne University Press, 1977).

Seddon, N, *Government Contracts: Federal State and Local*, 6th edn (Leichhardt, Federation Press, 2018).

Shepsle, KA, 'Congress is a 'They', Not an 'I': Legislative Intent as Oxymoron' (1992) 12 *International Review of Law and Economics* 239.

Schumpeter, JA, *Capitalism, Socialism and Democracy* (London, Routledge, 2010).

Sharman, C, 'The Australian Senate as a States House' (1977) 12 *Politics* 64.

—— 'Australia as a Compound Republic,' (1990) 25 *Politics* 1.

—— 'Reforming Executive Power' in G Winterton (ed), *We the People: Australian Republican Government* (St Leonards, Allen and Unwin, 1994).

Shergold, P et al, 'Reforming Our Democracy: Options for Renewing Democracy in Australia' (University of Melbourne, The New Democracy Foundation and the Susan McKinnon Foundation, 2019).

Skinner, Q, 'Meaning and Understanding in the History of Ideas' (1969) 8 *History and Theory* 3.

—— *The Foundations of Modern Political Thought* (Cambridge, Cambridge University Press, 1978).

Stellios, J, 'Using Federalism to Protect Political Communication: Implications from Federal Representative Government' (2007) 31 *Melbourne University Law Review* 239.

—— *Zines's The High Court and the Constitution*, 6th edn (Annandale, Federation Press, 2015).

—— *The Federal Judicature: Chapter III of the Constitution*, 2nd edn (Sydney, LexisNexis, 2020).

Stephenson, P, 'Statutory Displacement of the Prerogative in Australia' in J Boughey and LB Crawford (eds), *Interpreting Executive Power* (Alexandria, Federation Press, 2020).

Stephenson, P, 'The Relationship between the Royal Prerogative and Statute in Australia' (2021) 44 *Melbourne University Law Review* 1001.

Strangio, P, 'The Ancestry of the Australian Prime Ministership: "The Blue Ribbon of the Highest Possible Ambition"' (2015) 61 *Australian Journal of Politics and History* 19.

Strangio, P, Hart, P and Walter, J, *Settling the Office: The Australian Prime Ministership from Federation to Reconstruction* (Carlton, Miegunyah Press, 2016).

Strauss, DA, *The Living Constitution* (Oxford, Oxford University Press, 2010).

Summers, J, 'Parliament and Responsible Government' in D Woodward, A Parkin and J Summers (eds), *Government, Politics, Power and in Australia*, 9th edn (South Melbourne, Addison Wesley Longman, 2010).

Tan, D, 'Uncommon Legislative Attitudes: Why a Theory of Legislative Intent Needs Nontrivial Aggregation' (2021) 34 *Ratio Juris* 139.

Taylor, G, *The Constitution of Victoria* (Annandale, Federation Press, 2006).

Taylor, RB, 'The Contested Constitution: An Analysis of the Competing Models of British Constitutionalism' [2018] *Public Law* 500.

Thomson, JA, 'Constitutional Interpretation: History and the High Court: A Bibliographical Survey' (1982) 5 *University of New South Wales Law Journal* 309.

Thompson, E, 'The 'Washminster' Mutation' (1980) 15 *Politics* 32.

—— 'The Senate and Representative Democracy' (Papers on Parliament No 34, Parliament of Australia, 1999).
—— 'The Constitution and the Australian System of Limited Government, Responsible Government and Representative Democracy: Revisiting the Washminster Mutation' (2001) 24 *University of New South Wales Law Journal* 657.
Thynne, I and Goldring, J, 'Government 'Responsibility' and Responsible Government' (1981) 16 *Politics* 197.
Tomkins, A, *Our Republican Constitution* (Portland, Hart, 2005).
—— 'The Role of the Courts in the Political Constitution' (2010) 60 *University of Toronto Law Journal* 1.
Turpin, C, 'Ministerial Responsibility' in J Jowell and D Oliver (eds), *The Changing Constitution*, 3rd edn (Oxford, Clarendon Press, 1994).
Twomey, A, 'Pushing the Boundaries of Executive Power: Pape, the Prerogative and Nationhood Powers' (2010) 34 *Melbourne University Law Review* 313.
Twomey, A, *The Veiled Sceptre: Reserve Powers of Heads of State in Westminster Systems* (Cambridge, Cambridge University Press, 2018).
Uhr, J, *Deliberative Democracy in Australia: The Changing Place of Parliament* (Melbourne, Cambridge University Press, 1998).
—— 'Explicating the Australian Senate' (2002) 8 *Journal of Legislative Studies* 3.
—— 'Reforming the Parliament' in Clement Macintyre and John Williams (eds), *Peace, Order and Good Government: State Constitutional and Parliamentary Reform* (Kent Town, Wakefield Press, 2003).
Waldron, J, 'The Dignity of Legislation' (1995) 54 *Maryland Law Review* 633.
—— *Law and Disagreement* (Oxford, Oxford University Press, 1999).
—— 'The Core of the Case Against Judicial Review' (2006) 115 *Yale Law Journal* 1346.
Wanna, J, 'Political Chronicles: Commonwealth of Australia July to December 2014' (2015) 61 *Australian Journal of Politics and History* 278.
—— 'Political Chronicles: Commonwealth of Australia July to December 2015' (2016) 62 *Australian Journal of Politics and History* 282.
Ward, AJ, 'Exporting the British Constitution: Responsible Government in New Zealand, Canada, Australia and Ireland' (1987) 25 *Journal of Commonwealth and Comparative Politics* 3.
—— *Parliamentary Government in Australia*, rev edn (North Melbourne, Australian Scholarly Publishing, 2012).
Warhurst, J, 'Conscience Voting in the Australian Federal Parliament' (2008) 54 *Australian Journal of Politics and History* 579.
Weller, P and Jaensch, D (eds), *Responsible Government in Australia* (Richmond, Australasian Political Studies Association, 1980).
Whitlam, EG, *On Australia's Constitution* (Camberwell, Widescope, 1977).
Whittington, KE, 'Originalism: A Critical Introduction' (2013) 82 *Fordham Law Review* 375.
Wilks-Heeg, S, Blick, A and Crone, S, *How Democratic is the UK? The 2012 Audit* (Liverpool, Democratic Audit, 2012).
Williams, G and Hume, D, *Human Rights under the Australian Constitution*, 2nd edn (South Melbourne, Oxford University Press, 2013).
Winterton, G, *Parliament, the Executive and the Governor-General: A Constitutional Analysis* (Melbourne, Melbourne University Press, 1983).
—— 'The Prerogative in Novel Situations' (1983) 99 *Law Quarterly Review* 407.
—— 'The Relationship between Commonwealth Legislative and Executive Power' (2004) 25 *Adelaide Law Review* 21.
Wood, D, 'The Senate, Federalism and Democracy' (1989) 17 *Melbourne University Law Review* 292.
Wright, JSF, 'Anglicizing the United States Constitution: James Bryce's Contribution to Australian Federalism' (2001) 31 *Publius* 107.

Young, L, 'Parliament and the Executive' in P Boreham, G Stokes and R Hall (eds), *The Politics of Australian Society: Political Issues for the New Century*, 2nd edn (Frenchs Forest, Pearson Education, 2004).

GOVERNMENT AND PARLIAMENTARY DOCUMENTS

Commonwealth of Australia, *Final Report of the Constitutional Commission 1988* (Canberra, Australian Government Publishing Service, 1988).

Department of Finance, *Commonwealth Grants Rules and Guidelines* (Canberra, Commonwealth of Australia, 2017).

Department of Finance, *Commonwealth Procurement Rules 1 July 2022: Achieving Value for Money* (Commonwealth of Australia, 1 July 2022).

Department of the Prime Minister and Cabinet, *Legislation Handbook* (Canberra, Commonwealth of Australia, 1999).

Department of the Prime Minister and Cabinet, *Resolving Deadlocks: A Discussion Paper on Section 57 of the Australian Constitution* (Canberra, Commonwealth of Australia, 2003).

House of Representatives Standing Committee on Procedure, Parliament of Australia, *Building a Modern Committee System: An Inquiry into the Effectiveness of the House Committee System* (Canberra, 2010).

Joint Standing Committee on Electoral Matters, Parliament of Australia, *Interim Report on the Inquiry into the Conduct of the 2013 Federal Election: Senate Voting Practices* (Canberra, 2014).

Report of the Royal Commission on Constitutional Reform (Melbourne, Victorian Government Printer, 1894).

Royal Commission on Australian Government Administration (Canberra, Australian Government Publishing Service, 1976).

Senate Finance and Public Administration References Committee, Parliament of Australia, *Compliance by Former Ministers of State with the requirements of the Prime Minister's Statement of Ministerial Standards* (Canberra, 2019).

Silvester, E (ed), *New South Wales Constitution Bill: The Speeches in the Legislative Council of New South Wales on the Second Reading of the Bill for Framing a New Constitution for the Colony* (Sydney, 1853).

Senate Legal and Constitutional References Committee, Parliament of Australia, *Administration and Operation of the Migration Act 1958* (Canberra, 2006).

Senate Standing Committee on Finance and Public Administration, Parliament of Australia, *Transparency and Accountability of Commonwealth Public Funding and Expenditure* (Canberra, 2007).

Victoria, Parliament, *Papers on Federation, Circulated on Consideration of Draft Federal Constitution, 1897* (Melbourne, Government Printer, 1897).

Index

www.ingramcontent.com/pod-product-compliance
Ingram Content Group UK Ltd.
Pitfield, Milton Keynes, MK11 3LW, UK
UKHW020801290926
15470UKWH00003B/886

9 781509 955794